School of American Research
Advanced Seminar Series

JONATHAN HAAS AND DOUGLAS W. SCHWARTZ
GENERAL EDITORS

SCHOOL OF AMERICAN RESEARCH
ADVANCED SEMINAR SERIES

Published by Cambridge University Press

Dreaming: Anthropological and
Psychological Interpretations
BARBARA TEDLOCK

The Anasazi in a Changing Environment
GEORGE J. GUMERMAN

Regional Perspectives on the Olmec
ROBERT J. SHARER and DAVID C. GROVE

The Chemistry of Prehistoric Human Bone
T. DOUGLAS PRICE

Published by the University of New Mexico Press

Reconstructing Prehistoric Pueblo
Societies
WILLIAM A. LONGACRE

New Perspectives on the Pueblos
ALFONSO ORTIZ

Structure and Process in Latin America
ARNOLD STRICKON and SIDNEY M.
GREENFIELD

The Classic Maya Collapse
T. PATRICK CULBERT

Methods and Theories of
Anthropological Genetics
M. H. CRAWFORD and P. L.
WORKMAN

Sixteenth-Century Mexico: The Work
of Sahagun
MUNRO S. EDMONSON

Ancient Civilization and Trade
JEREMY A. SABLOFF and C. C.
LAMBERG-KARLOVSKY

Photography in Archaeological Research
ELMER HARP, JR

Meaning in Anthropology
KEITH H. BASSO and HENRY A.
SELBY

The Valley of Mexico: Studies in Pre-
Hispanic Ecology and Society
ERIC R. WOLF

Demographic Anthropology:
Quantitative Approaches
EZRA B. W. ZUBROW

The Origins of Maya Civilization
RICHARD E. W. ADAMS

Explanation of Prehistoric Change
JAMES N. HILL

Explorations in Ethnoarchaeology
RICHARD A. GOULD

Entrepreneurs in Cultural Context
SIDNEY M. GREENFIELD, ARNOLD
STRICKON and ROBERT T. AUBEY

The Dying Community
ART GALLAHER, JR and HARLAND
PADFIELD

Southwestern Indian Ritual Drama
CHARLOTTE J. FRISBIE

Lowland Maya Settlement Patterns
WENDY ASHMORE

Simulations in Archaeology
JEREMY A. SABLOFF

Chan Chan: Andean Desert City
MICHAEL E. MOSELEY and KENT C.
DAY

Shipwreck Anthropology
RICHARD A. GOULD

Elites: Ethnographic Issues
GEORGE E. MARCUS

The Archaeology of Lower Central
America
FREDERICK W. LANGE and DORIS Z.
STONE

Late Lowland Maya Civilization:
Classic to Postclassic
JEREMY A. SABLOFF and E. WYLLYS
ANDREWS V

The emergence of modern humans

THE EMERGENCE OF
MODERN HUMANS

Biocultural adaptations in the later Pleistocene

EDITED BY
ERIK TRINKAUS
Department of Anthropology
University of New Mexico

A SCHOOL OF AMERICAN RESEARCH BOOK

The right of the
University of Cambridge
to print and sell
all manner of books
was granted by
Henry VIII in 1534.
The University has printed
and published continuously
since 1584.

CAMBRIDGE UNIVERSITY PRESS
Cambridge
New York · Port Chester · Melbourne · Sydney

Published by the Press Syndicate of the University of Cambridge
The Pitt Building, Trumpington Street, Cambridge CB2 1RP
40 West 20th Street, New York, NY 10011, USA
10 Stamford Road, Oakleigh, Melbourne 3166, Australia

Cambridge University Press 1989

First published 1989

Printed in Great Britian by Redwood Burn Limited, Trowbridge, Wiltshire

British Library cataloguing in publication data

The emergence of modern humans: biocultural adaptations in the later Pleistocene.
1. Man. Evolution
I. Trinkaus, Erik, 1948– II. Series
573.2

Library of Congress cataloguing in publication data

The Emergence of modern humans: biocultural adaptations in the later Pleistocene/edited by
Erik Trinkaus.
    p.   cm. – (School of American Research advanced seminar series)
Bibliography.
Includes index.
ISBN 0–521–37241–0
1. Human evolution. 2. Neanderthals. I. Trinkaus, Erik,
II. Series.
GN281.E475 1989
573.2–dc20   89–1039 CIP
ISBN 0 521 37241 0

WV

Contents

List of contributors   page ix

Foreword   xi

Preface   xiii

1 Issues concerning human emergence in the later Pleistocene
  ERIK TRINKAUS   1

2 Isolating the transition to cultural adaptations: an organizational
  approach
  LEWIS R. BINFORD   18

3 The Upper Pleistocene transition
  ERIK TRINKAUS   42

4 Documenting the origin of modern humans
  C. B. STRINGER   67

5 The place of the Neandertals in human evolution
  MILFORD H. WOLPOFF   97

6 From the Middle to the Upper Paleolithic: transition or
  convergence?
  JEAN-PHILIPPE RIGAUD   142

vii

7 Upper Pleistocene cultural stratigraphy in southwest Asia
OFER BAR-YOSEF   154

8 The adaptive basis of Neandertal facial form, with some thoughts
on the nature of modern human origins
FRED H. SMITH and STEVEN P. PAQUETTE   181

9 Toward a contextual understanding of the earliest body ornaments
RANDALL WHITE   211

References   232

Index   277

Contributors

ERIK TRINKAUS
Department of Anthropology
University of New Mexico
Albuquerque, NM 87131, USA

and

U.A. 376 du C.N.R.S.
Laboratoire d'Anthropologie
Université de Bordeaux I
33405 Talence, France

OFER BAR-YOSEF
Department of Geo-Isotopes
Weitzmann Institute of Sciences
Rehovot 76100, Israel

and

Department of Anthropology
Harvard University
Cambridge, MA 02138, USA

LEWIS R. BINFORD
Department of Anthropology
University of New Mexico
Albuquerque, NM 87131, USA

STEVEN P. PAQUETTE
U.S. Army Natick Research and Development Center
Natick, MA 01760–5019, USA

ix

JEAN-PHILIPPE RIGAUD

Direction des Antiquités Préhistoriques
26–28 place Gambetta
33074 Bordeaux, France

FRED H. SMITH

Department of Anthropology
University of Tennessee
Knoxville, TN 37996-0720, USA

C. B. STRINGER

Department of Palaeontology
British Museum (Natural History)
Cromwell Road
London SW7 5BD, England

RANDALL K. WHITE

Department of Anthropology
New York University
25 Waverly Place
New York, NY 10003, USA

MILFORD H. WOLPOFF

Department of Anthropology
University of Michigan
Ann Arbor, MI 48109, USA

Foreword

When I first approached Erik Trinkaus about the possibility of a seminar on Neanderthals, it was with the specific hope that such a seminar could resolve outstanding questions about the relationship between Neanderthals and modern humans. As a non-specialist in the topic, I was aware of an ongoing debate over whether Neanderthals were the direct ancestors of modern *Homo sapiens sapiens* (at least in western Europe) or an evolutionary side track in the human family tree. It seemed that the Advanced Seminar program would offer an optimal forum for proponents of the different positions to reexamine the problem in light of the rich bodies of new archaeological and paleontological data collected in recent years. The seminar did prove to be an excellent forum for reviewing the debate, but – to my naive disappointment – a resolution was not forthcoming.

Instead, both the physical anthropologists and the archaeologists working in the later Pleistocene and Middle to Upper Paleolithic had the opportunity to proceed through intense and fruitful discussion to a common understanding of the bases of disagreement and the key areas for future empirical research. The interaction between the two subfields itself proved to be highly productive in working toward an integrated, interdisciplinary approach to understanding the emergence of modern humans.

Although the evolutionary relationship between Neanderthals and modern humans remains a key historical question for those working in western Europe, it is but one small part of a much broader problem of how and why modern humans evolved from their archaic ancestors. No longer wed to the question of whether Neanderthals were direct ancestors or a side track in human evolution, physical anthropologists and archaeologists have now turned to much more interesting issues. Their concern is now with process, adaptation, and evolution rather than with historical sequences.

The key point of agreement in the course of the seminar was that sometime during the later Pleistocene, in a relatively brief period of transition, there was a transformation from archaic to modern humans – a transformation manifested in both culture and biology. There were certainly local variations in the timing of the transformation, but all across the Old World, in Africa, Asia, and Europe, anatomically modern humans, *Homo sapiens sapiens*, emerged in the later Pleistocene, and with them came a florescence of culture. It is through the fossils and artifacts of this time, tens of thousands of years ago, that anthropology reveals the birth of humanity.

As I sat through the seminar and read the papers in this volume, I became increasingly convinced that understanding the emergence of modern humans is absolutely vital to the broader understanding of basic human nature. The transformation from archaic to modern human witnessed not only the reorganization of the brain and body and a shift in stone working from a simple, expedient technology to a complex and elegant craft, but also the first appearance of true art and symbolism and the blossoming of formal systems of language. Binford even goes so far as to say that "culture" in its strict sense makes its first appearance in this period. Thus, if we are seeking to understand the underlying biocultural foundations of the human species, we must look to the causal factors behind the evolution of modern humans from their archaic ancestors.

JONATHAN HAAS
School of American Research

Preface

During the late nineteenth century and the first half of the twentieth century, paleoanthropological interest and research was focused primarily on the human paleontological and archaeological remains of the later Pleistocene. It was primarily for this period that sufficient prehistoric material existed in a sufficiently secure chronological framework to allow the consideration of questions about past human biological and behavioral evolution. Especially after the discovery of a series of rich Middle and Upper Paleolithic sites, several of which contained Neandertal partial skeletons, in western and central Europe in the first two decades of the twentieth century, it became possible to provide syntheses of the later Pleistocene (late Middle and Upper Pleistocene) archaeological and human fossil records. Such syntheses, engaged in by most paleoanthropologists during the second and third decades of our century, set the stage for a general consensus on our knowledge of recent human evolution. Despite some disagreement during this time period on the actual phylogenetic relationships, both biological and cultural, between various prehistoric human groups, there was general agreement that we were dealing with an archaic group, characterized by a combination of ancestral ("simian") and derived ("specialized") features, which was replaced during the last ("Würm") glacial by noble creatures who were biologically, culturally, and morally similar to ourselves. Into this predominant view were incorporated most new discoveries of later Pleistocene human fossil and archaeological remains.

After World War II, the evolutionary synthesis, the recognition of the hominid status of members of *Homo erectus* ("Pithecanthropus" and "Sinanthropus," among others) and *Australopithecus*, and the uncovering of the modern and/or fraudulent origins of so-called "Pre-Sapiens" specimens (such as Piltdown and Galley Hill) led to the recognition of the apparently rather modern nature of the Neandertals and other late archaic humans. As a result, all of these later Pleistocene humans were included within *Homo sapiens*, and contrasts between their anatomies and archaeological remains and those of recent humans were ascribed to their greater antiquity and hence less elaborated cultural systems. Orthogenesis retreated with the emergence of the evolutionary synthesis, but the concept of an orderly and natural progression (with the emphasis on "progress") of human biological and cultural evolution continued.

With this reappraisal of later Pleistocene paleoanthropology and the emergence of a new consensus during the 1950s, emphasis in paleoanthropology shifted increasingly to the period of hominid origins, the Pliocene and Lower Pleistocene. New discoveries and analyses of later Pleistocene material were seen largely to fill in those (supposedly) few gaps in our paleoanthropological knowledge. Into this atmosphere, a few researchers, realizing the potential of the later Pleistocene prehistoric record for answering interesting human evolutionary questions, began to go back to this time period, question old assumptions, collect new data, and attempt to provide new, more realistic syntheses of the period that led up to and saw the emergence of modern humans. This work began during the 1960s, but it has grown, primarily during the 1970s and into the 1980s.

As a result of this renewed interest in the later Pleistocene, the late 1980s has seen a considerable resurgence of interest in and discussion about the nature of the events and processes that led to the emergence of biological and cultural systems similar to those known ethnographically for human hunter-gatherers. It is in the context of this interest in the later Pleistocene that I organized, through the School of American Research, the Advanced Seminar entitled "The Origins of Modern Human Adaptations." This conference was intended to provide discussion on many of the interpretive issues that have arisen during the past couple of decades. It was fully recognized that few specific problems would be resolved; however, it was felt that the state of our knowledge and understanding of the later Pleistocene paleoanthropological record was such that increased focus on general issues was warranted.

The Advanced Seminar included Ofer Bar-Yosef (Weitzmann Institute of Science, Israel), Lewis R. Binford (University of New Mexico, USA), Jean-Philippe Rigaud (Direction des Antiquités Préhistoriques de l'Aquitaine, France), Fred H. Smith (University of Tennessee, USA), Chris Stringer (British Museum [Natural History], England), Randall White (New York University, USA) and Milford H. Wolpoff (University of Michigan, USA) as primary participants, Jane Buikstra (University of Chicago, USA) as a discussant, and myself as organizer, chair, and general participant. It was held at the School of American Research facilities in Santa Fe, New Mexico, from April 21 to 25, 1986. The Advanced Seminar was supported by the L.S.B. Leakey Foundation, Jean M. Auel, and the School of American Research; to all of them we are very grateful.

The following introduction and papers are part of the fruits of this Advanced Seminar. They represent much of the variety of views current in the study of later Pleistocene human paleontology and archaeology. At the same time, they furnish an overview of the current issues associated with late archaic humans and the origins of modern humans. The introduction is largely a compilation, through the eyes of the organizer, of the issues that were discussed during the Advanced Seminar and brought into focus in the resultant papers. The papers fill out the discussion of many of the issues, furnishing both state-of-the-art statements on specific problems and pointing toward future directions for later Pleistocene paleoanthropological research.

The Advanced Seminar and the resultant papers have been possible through the cooperation and assistance of many individuals. These include especially Dr. Douglas Schwartz, president of the School of American Research, and Dr. Jonathan Haas, director of programs and research. Mrs. Jean M. Auel, through her financial support and attendance at the conference, provided invaluable assistance. The participants, although feisty at times, have all contributed in their ways. Jane Kepp, director of publications at the School of American Research, and Lynn T. Baca, Mary Kay Day and Steven E. Churchill at the University of New Mexico all assisted with the editing of this volume. To all of them I am thankful.

1
Issues concerning human emergence in the later Pleistocene

ERIK TRINKAUS

The study of human origins, whether addressed by archaeologists or by human paleontologists, has been concerned primarily with understanding the evolutionary roots of modern humans. This has been true since its inception during the late nineteenth century, and it continues very much today. In the past century and a half, research has progressed significantly, from the need to document a remote human antiquity in the nineteenth century, to the establishment of the basic patterns and sequence of past human biological and behavioral evolution during the first half of the twentieth century, to the beginnings of an understanding of the potential processes involved in human biobehavioral evolution since the mid-twentieth century. Yet, we are still far from a consensus on the nature of the biobehavioral patterns and processes that led, during the later Pleistocene, to the emergence of humans who were behaviorally and biologically very similar to modern human hunters and gatherers. Since the paleoanthropological (archaeological, human paleontological and paleoenvironmental) record for the later Pleistocene (later Middle and Upper Pleistocene) far exceeds in preservation and size that which is known for any previous period of pre-agricultural human prehistory, it should be possible for us to achieve, if not a consensus about, at least a synthesis of, the events and processes that were involved.

With these thoughts in mind, I organized, at the invitation of the School of American Research, an Advanced Seminar entitled "The Origins of Modern Human Adaptations." The purpose of the Advanced Seminar was not to present a survey of the state of our knowledge of the paleoanthropological record relevant to the biobehavioral origins of modern humans. Such a task is best performed by a team of specialists writing contributions under the direction of a strong-minded editor. The purpose was, in contrast, to generate discussion concerning what we know about this period of human evolution, emphasizing the patterns and processes that were involved and approaches that can be taken toward understanding those patterns and processes. The Advanced Seminar consisted of the discussion of pre-conference papers, revised versions of which are included in this volume, and an attempt to draw together diverse approaches sufficiently to allow us to focus on the essential aspects of the process which we refer to as the origins of modern humans.

In these introductory remarks, I have summarized the major, and some minor, issues that arose during discussion at the Advanced Seminar. They are intended to provide a focus for ongoing investigations into the evolutionary origins of the biobehavioral complex which we associate with modern human hunter-gatherers. Most of them are addressed by individual authors in the following papers, and all of them were discussed, some at great length, during the Advanced Seminar. Their presentation here, however, represents my interpretation of and additions to the results of the seminar discussion, especially with respect to emphasis and organization.

The eight papers which follow these introductory remarks represent, more than anything else, the diversity of approaches that are currently being taken to the analysis of the biobehavioral foundations of modern people. No one paper summarizes the overall issues, since each, in the manner of its author(s), addresses what are perceived to be some of the more relevant current issues. These introductory comments and the eight papers thus provide a statement as to our position with regard to the origins of modern humans, biologically and behaviorally, in the late 1980s. From here, we can only build on what is already a substantial foundation.

In the following discussion, I have indicated which issues are

2

considered by the individual papers which follow, in each case by placing the authors' names parenthetically at the end of the presentation of each issue. Yet, since most of the papers deal, directly or indirectly, with most of these issues, this should be considered as only a general guide to the papers, rather than as a detailed index of their contents.

REGARDING DEFICIENCIES IN OUR KNOWLEDGE

It is fully recognized that, despite its relative richness, the currently known paleoanthropological record of the later Pleistocene contains numerous gaps and possesses temporal and geographical biases. It was not the intention of the Advanced Seminar to remedy this situation; all of the participants and many other researchers are actively working to fill in gaps in our knowledge, but that takes time, luck, imagination, and resources. In the meantime, it was deemed most important to recognize these deficiencies in our knowledge, and then to proceed from that point to more general issues, recognizing that some agreement on those issues will be necessary before we would be able to fill appropriately all of the perceived and as yet unrecognized gaps and biases in our understanding. These deficiencies need, nonetheless, to be highlighted.

First, our knowledge is heavily biased toward four geographical areas, which are, in order of descending weight, western Europe, the Levant, central Europe and southern Africa. For each of these areas, we now have extensive archaeological data from both natural shelters (caves and rockshelters) and open-air sites, reasonable (although by no means sufficient) chronological control, adequate paleoenvironmental information, and variable amounts of human paleontological remains (southern Africa being weakest in the last). For the remainder of the Old World, we have geographically and chronologically widely scattered data points (both archaeologically and paleontologically) that permit us to do little more than assess, more or less adequately, whether our four best-known regions are representative of worldwide human evolutionary processes during the later Pleistocene. They appear to be representative for the western Old World; they may very well not be for the eastern Old World.

Secondly, our control of fine chronology (even at the level of 5–10 kyr [5,000–10,000 yr] intervals) is inadequate for periods prior to the finite limits of radiocarbon dating (*c.* 35 kyr B.P.) and from there back through

3

most of the Middle Pleistocene. Thirdly, certain kinds of data, especially those that derive from the associations of remains in the ground, are poorly known in the archaeological record, due more to reigning archaeological paradigms than to the vagaries of post-depositional destructive processes. Fourthly, much of the archaeological and human paleontological record remains incompletely analyzed according to those state-of-the-art techniques which will provide us with data relevant to understanding the biobehavioral process involved in the origins of modern human adaptations. And fifthly, interregional comparisons of paleoanthropological remains are frequently inadequate.

Despite these apparent deficiencies and biases in our knowledge, it was possible to address the more general issues presented at the Advanced Seminar. We in fact know a considerable amount about later Pleistocene human behavioral and biological evolution, far more than the frequent emphasis on gaps in our knowledge and disagreements over interpretations would indicate.

A PERCEIVED DICHOTOMY

The primary issue concerning the origins of modern humans, biologically and behaviorally during the later Pleistocene, derives from a generally recognized contrast between what I will refer to as *late archaic humans* and *early modern humans*. In this, the terms "archaic" and "modern" are used in both behavioral ("cultural") and biological senses.

First, during the late Middle Pleistocene and extending into the early Upper Pleistocene (to a geographically variable extent as yet to be determined), there were anatomically archaic humans across the Old World with total behavioral patterns, and hence adaptive systems, that were significantly different from those known ethnographically and ethnohistorically for recent human hunter-gatherers in terms of technology, subsistence, organization, and probably communication. Secondly, during the last glacial period, certainly by the middle of the late glacial (approximately oxygen isotope stage 2), across the Old World there were human hunter-gatherers who were anatomically very similar to recent regional populations of living humans and were engaged in fully cultural behavioral patterns similar to those of recent human hunter-gatherers. Clearly, between these two periods, there were a number of significant changes in human skeletal anatomy and in the archaeological record left behind by these prehistoric humans. Each of

4

these spheres of data indicates that a series of significant behavioral changes took place during this time period. Since modern humans are both biological and cultural organisms, it is only logical to expect that these paleontologically and archaeologically documented changes are but different reflections of the same evolving behavioral/adaptive system.

GENERAL ISSUES

From this observation and the implied dichotomy between late archaic and early modern humans, several general and a series of more specific questions emerge. The more general issues are central to any eventual understanding of the emergence of the hunter-gatherer biobehavioral pattern we identify with recent humans. They can be divided into six major questions:

I. To what extent were the changes in human behavior, as reflected in the archaeological record, causally interrelated with the changes in human biology, as reflected in the human paleontological record? In other words, can we understand the evolutionary changes evident in either the human paleontological sphere or the archaeological sphere without direct reference to the contemporaneous changes in the other? Some researchers, reacting negatively to any form of "biological determinism," would see the behavioral processes as enabled but in no way directly influenced by human biology, whereas others would see a changing biological basis for the "cultural" capabilities of later Pleistocene humans as of primary significance to our understanding of modern human emergence. Neither of these extreme positions is likely. I would argue that the archaeological and human paleontological spheres are inseparable, and that we will understand changes in each only by reference to the total paleoanthropological context of the change in question. This holds even if we are unlikely to be able to describe precisely the actual natures of any causal (or, more accurately, feedback) relationships between changing aspects of human behavior and human biology during the Upper Pleistocene. Yet, rarely do researchers explicitly lay out their views on this issue, even though all are influenced by their positions with respect to it when they attempt to synthesize the events and processes of this time period. (Rigaud, Stringer, Trinkaus)

II. To what extent was the emergence of modern humans a transition, as opposed to a continuation of previously existing tempos of evolution-

5

ary change? (In this a "transition" is taken to indicate a relatively rapid shift from one state to another.) In other words, can the perceived rate of human biobehavioral change during the later Pleistocene be best characterized by one continuous curve, even if that curve is exponential, or was there a significant change in the tempo of human evolutionary change around a definable and short transition? And if the latter, can that change in tempo around a transition be best characterized by a change in the slope of the curve, a step in the curve indicating a short period of exceptionally rapid change, or a combination of the two? Since there is little question that there were significant biobehavioral changes throughout this period (from the late Middle Pleistocene to the mid late-last-glacial), this question relates to whether one can define a brief, transitional time segment during the larger time period. If so, does that "transitional" period correspond to any degree to the traditional divisions between late archaic humans and early "anatomically modern" humans in the human paleontological sphere and between the Middle Paleolithic (*sensu lato*) and the Upper Paleolithic (*sensu lato*) in the archaeological sphere (given that those two do not correspond precisely in time)? (Rigaud, Trinkaus, Wolpoff)

III. To what extent was there geographical diversity in the nature of biobehavioral changes during the later Pleistocene, diversity that cannot be accounted for simply in terms of environmental differences or probable variations in important subsistence and raw material resource availability? If one assumes that there was some geographical diversity, was that diversity due to relatively minor regional variants in elements that can be reliably attributed to "style," or did it exist in more fundamental aspects of subsistence, organization, and related adaptive behaviors? Furthermore, can the documentable geographical diversity be explained, at least in part, in terms of the chronological relationships between associated changes in neighboring regions? In other words, can we understand the diachronic changes in one region solely in terms of that region's human biological and "cultural" sequence, or is it necessary to comprehend the contemporaneous evolutionary changes in neighboring geographical areas? Clearly, the human evolutionary trajectories during the later Pleistocene in neighboring geographical areas must have been related; what remains at issue is the extent to which local change should be understood primarily in terms of itself or seen as only one relatively small part of the greater whole. The current biases in the prehistoric record, and especially the large geographical gaps in our knowledge and difficulties in determining the relative chronologies of neighboring areas, tend to emphasize the autonomous natures of regional sequences, whereas interregional influences, particularly over time periods that encompassed many human generations and major shifts in ecozonal distribution, must have been important. (Binford, Rigaud, Smith and Paquette, Stringer, Trinkaus, White, Wolpoff)

IV. To what extent was the emergence of a modern human biobehavioral pattern, one similar to that of recent hunter-gatherers, a geographically variable cumulative process in which elements now identified as part of the modern human biobehavioral complex gradually coalesced to produce recent human cultural behavior? In this, what we might identify paleoanthropologically as a "transition" during the later Pleistocene could be seen as a threshold, in which the sum of the parts came to equal more than merely an accumulation of "cultural" elements. Alternatively, could there have been a major structural reorganization of human biobehavioral patterns (at least ones that are paleoanthropologically identifiable, analyzable, and presumably of primary adaptive significance) at some point during this transitional period that produced, for the first time in human evolution, a novel and fully cultural (in the modern ethnographic sense) human adaptive system?

If such a structural reorganization took place, two issues are raised. First, can we justify interpreting human "cultural" elements prior to this "reorganization" strictly by analogy with their meaning(s) in recent ethnographic contexts? Secondly, do we identify this "reorganization" in the prehistoric record only when many elements of it are archaeologically and paleontologically evident, or on the basis of the appearance of a few, presumably critical, indications of reorganization at one time period, perhaps well before most of the hallmarks of such a "reorganization" appear in the paleoanthropological record? (Binford, Rigaud, Smith and Paquette)

V. Closely related to the preceding point is the issue of whether human behavioral systems, which existed prior to the existence of hunter-gatherers deemed to have been behaviorally similar to those known ethnographically, can be considered to have been "cultural" systems. Clearly, there are many and varied definitions of "culture." However, nearly all that purport to be universal for modern humans and serve to distinguish us from (at least) living non-human primates see "culture" as a basic human, non-biologically based (even though the capacity for it is biologically based), technologically aided adaptive system, that is transmitted through learned behavior in social contexts using arbitrary, symbolically based communication systems. Given this description of "culture" (or one of many other closely related ones that do indeed distinguish us from living non-human primates), can we justify its application to the archaic human biobehavioral pattern that apparently existed prior to this later Pleistocene "transition" (whether we talk about a true transition or a long transitional period)? Did late archaic humans possess a total adaptive system that was structurally the same as that of recent human hunter-gatherers, although perhaps technologically and organizationally simpler than the more recent ones? Or was their adaptive system structurally significantly different, although possessing many of the traits included within modern human cultural systems? Again, as with the preceding issue of whether a "threshold" or a "reorganization" characterized this later Pleistocene "transition," assumptions as to whether late archaic humans were fully "cultural" predetermine the appropriateness of using relatively direct analogy from the ethnographic present to interpret prehistoric data. (Binford)

VI. To what extent is it necessary for us to sort out historical issues before we can address questions concerning the evolution of past human adaptations? To what extent do we have to resolve phylogenetic and culture-history arguments about the origins of various human biological and/or behavioral traits or complexes (e.g., local emergence versus diffusion [demic and cultural] versus migration) prior to posing and answering questions about shifting human adaptive patterns during the later Pleistocene? Some would argue that we can understand the adaptive, or evolutionary, significance of a paleoanthropologically identifiable complex only if we know where it came from and the steps by which it appeared in the region and at the time in question. These researchers tend to place most of their emphasis on tracing (and arguing about) origins (whether local or distant) of various paleontologically and archaeologically delimited groups and/or traits, frequently using "functional" interpretations to justify or refute different points of view. Others would argue that, while one needs a certain minimum of geographical and chronological control as to the sequence of paleontologically and archaeologically defined complexes, fine resolution is unnecessary and, in many cases, unobtainable. However, when there is a clear sequence whereby one adaptive system replaces another, whether rapidly or gradually through frequency shifts in identifiable traits, one can argue that the succeeding adaptive system (as a whole) was selectively superior to the preceding one. Thus one can pose, without direct reference to historical questions, hypotheses regarding the adaptive significance(s) of the succeeding complex. This approach need not degenerate into a hyperfunctionalism, so long as the traits or complexes under analysis are seen as parts of evolving adaptive systems and not merely as adaptive units by themselves. The orientations of different researchers with regard to this issue are seldom explicitly stated, but they are usually readily apparent from the manners in which the researchers present their arguments. (Rigaud, Stringer, Trinkaus, Wolpoff)

Needless to say, there is considerable disagreement as to the resolutions to these general issues. Different emphases remain, and contrasting preferences continue regarding which biobehavioral processes were primarily involved in the origins of modern humans. This diversity of opinion arises in large part from the contrasting intellectual traditions of various paleoanthropologists, including the slightly different trajectories that Paleolithic archaeology and human paleontology have taken. Many of these differences, which are manifest in the papers in this volume, are fundamental to the approaches of the researchers involved, and they are thus unlikely to change significantly in a short period of time. However, they are real factors that must be recognized in any attempt to reach an eventual understanding (and consensus?) concerning this human evolutionary period.

MORE SPECIFIC ISSUES

In addition to these general concerns that derive from the perceived dichotomy between late archaic humans and early modern humans, there are a number of more specific issues that relate to the study of modern human emergence. Some of these issues are treated in the following papers; others remain to be considered at length elsewhere.

1. To what extent have the paleozoogeographical settings of the regions providing the best later Pleistocene paleoanthropological data influenced our interpretations? The Near East, and especially the Levant, has long been recognized as a faunal corridor between Africa and Eurasia, whereas western Europe and southern Africa are culs-de-sac. Since Pleistocene human populations may well have been

influenced by such zoogeographical parameters, much as other mammals were, should we not take this into account in evaluating the data from these particularly rich regions? (Bar-Yosef, Rigaud, Stringer, Trinkaus)

2. Was the period which we perceive as the transitional one in a specific region best seen in terms of local evolution combined with some level of interregional diffusion (demic and cultural) or in terms of major populational and/or cultural replacement? This issue again may be one of emphasis, and, it must be remembered, the particular level of local evolution/diffusion/replacement in one region need not indicate the dominant process that took place in another, even neighboring, region. Furthermore, the level of resolution of the issue deemed necessary depends to a large extent on one's historical versus adaptive emphasis (see number VI above). (Bar-Yosef, Rigaud, Smith and Paquette, Stringer, Trinkaus, Wolpoff)

3. A related issue concerns the extent to which our reconstructions of the behavioral patterns of regional late archaic humans have any bearing on the potential roles in the ancestry of subsequent early modern humans in the same region. In other words, does an interpretation of certain late archaic humans as adaptively significantly different from their regional early modern human successors exclude them from the ancestry of those successors? Some researchers apparently feel that it might (and use such considerations to argue for either population replacement or non-significant adaptive differences), whereas others recognize that modern humans are descended from behaviorally archaic predecessors and see such adaptive contrasts as expected and consequently unimportant in assessing phylogenetic and/or cultural historical questions. (Smith and Paquette, Stringer, Trinkaus, Wolpoff)

4. An additional related issue concerns whether late archaic humans and modern humans should be distinguished at the species level. Since the 1950s, most paleoanthropologists have included both within *Homo sapiens*, usually distinguishing them at the subspecies level. Recently, several paleontologists have suggested that *H. sapiens* be restricted to "anatomically modern humans" (including early modern humans and recent humans), assuming that clear criteria distinguishing "anatomically modern humans" from late archaic humans can be identified. If so, then *Homo neanderthalensis* would be the species name with priority which would be used for late archaic humans (*H. erectus*, if then considered conspecific with late archaic humans, would become a

junior synonym of *H. neanderthalensis*). Whether one refers to late archaic humans as *H. neanderthalensis* or as a set of extinct geographical subspecies of *H. sapiens*, it needs to be kept in mind that such taxonomic distinctions have no direct bearing on the phylogenetic relationships of the two groups. The Linnean taxonomic system is non-evolutionary, and at the intrageneric level it is best used only to describe perceived degrees of difference. Questions of ancestry (involving clado-genesis and/or anagenesis) should be based on other criteria, not on whether one's perceptions of the morphological differences between two groups appear to warrant a species-level distinction. (White, Wolpoff)

5. To what extent might the available time scale (usually dictated by the level of radiometric chronological resolution) predetermine the perceived rate of change during this later Pleistocene "transition" (see number II above)? (Bar-Yosef, Binford)

6. In archaeological considerations of change during this later Pleistocene "transition" (see number II above), emphasis is frequently placed upon the archaeologically perceived Middle-to-Upper Paleolithic transition, especially with respect to Europe. If there was indeed a short period during the later Pleistocene which can be defined as transitional, one during which major behavioral changes occurred, is it best defined archaeologically by that Middle-to-Upper Paleolithic transition? Did most of the significant behavioral change take place then, or had it already occurred within the Middle Paleolithic (*senso lato*)? This question, although recognized for some time, has been brought in focus recently by the realization that, in most of the western Old World (all except western Europe), the biological shift to early modern humans apparently occurred within Middle Paleolithic contexts. (Bar-Yosef, Binford, Rigaud, Smith and Paquette, Stringer, Wolpoff)

7. It is necessary to distinguish between the actual behaviors of prehistoric human groups (as inferred from the paleoanthropological record) and possibly implied behavioral capacities. Descriptions of behavioral patterns that were substantially different from those of recent hunter-gatherers for late archaic humans or even the earliest modern humans have been taken to imply significantly different behavioral capabilities in those prehistoric humans. In fact, no such implication can be justified; we simply cannot determine the behavioral potentials of prehistoric humans. We can, however, assess the extent to which their behavioral patterns differed from those of ethnographically known

11

recent humans. Since evolution acts through actual behavior, and not potential behavior, it is their paleoanthropologically documented behavior which is of concern and not their potentials. (Binford, Smith and Paquette, White, Wolpoff)

8. One of the primary characteristics of modern human hunter-gatherer adaptive systems is their high level of planning depth (especially in higher-latitude and marginal environments). Did such planning depth exist among late archaic humans in similar environments, and how might it have changed with the emergence of early modern humans? How do we identify it in the paleoanthropological record? Approaches to it have tended to emphasize past patterns of abundant resource utilization, since such materials provide large archaeological data sets. However, such emphasis on abundant materials, such as lithics (especially in regions such as western Europe and the Levant where high-quality raw material is plentiful), may hide significant changes in planning depth, given the absence of a need to ration or plan the acquisition of such easily obtained resources. Analysis of less abundant raw materials, or of lithics in areas of relative scarcity, combined with indications of locomotor behavioral patterns from human anatomy, may provide better indications of past levels of planning depth, despite the difficulties of analysis and smaller available data sets. (Binford, Rigaud, Trinkaus)

9. A related question concerns the evolution of the organization of space and the patterning of site structures during the later Pleistocene. Assuming that site modification and patterning reflect the level of spatial organization of activities among these later Pleistocene groups, do we see significant changes in sites through time and, if so, in what contexts? Such a question need not presume that we can identify relatively short-term occupations of sites and the distribution of features, artifacts, and debris within those "living floor" accumulations. It need only assume that we can achieve sufficient taphonomic control to be able to observe shifts in the patterns of feature, artifact, and debris accumulation on prehistoric land surfaces. (Bar-Yosef, Binford, Rigaud, Trinkaus)

10. Changes in human planning depth and site organization would imply shifts in the utilization of the landscape, including the exploitation of geographically dispersed resources and possible periodic movements of social groups on that landscape. How might we document, from the archaeological and human paleontological records, such alterations in habitual use of the landscape? Many of the same con-

siderations mentioned in numbers 8 and 9 above apply here. (Bar-Yosef, Binford, Rigaud, Trinkaus, White, Wolpoff)

11. What might have been the roles of climatic (especially stadial/interstadial) fluctuations during the later Pleistocene in determining the geographical movements of prehistoric human groups? Obviously, extreme cold and/or aridity would lead to regional population decrease, or even extinction, whereas more productive environments would have permitted human population expansion. With gradual shifts in ecozones, especially latitudinally, it is possible that human populations technologically adapted to those ecozones would have moved with them. Yet, can we assume that geographical shifts in ecozones would have led to significant geographical movement of human populations, movements that would appear as migrations in the paleoanthropological record? In other words, were later Pleistocene human populations, both late archaic and early modern, moving with ecozones much as the rest of the mammalian fauna did? Alternatively, could they have had patterns of geographical movement that cross-cut multiple ecozones and were thus semi-independent of these climatic fluctuations? (Bar-Yosef, Trinkaus)

12. Human evolution has resulted in a number of shifts in life-cycle parameters, including gestation length, developmental rates, and longevity. Were there major changes in any or all of these across this later Pleistocene "transition"? If so, how might they have been interrelated with aspects of demography, group size, distribution on the landscape, and levels of organizational complexity? Many aspects of recent human life-cycle parameters permit the elaboration of cultural systems, but at certain demographic and energetic costs. This issue, which relates back to general issues IV and V, is therefore concerned with determining whether the full life-cycle underpinnings of modern human cultural behavior existed prior to the later Pleistocene "transition" or emerged into their recent form only at that time. (Stringer, Trinkaus, White)

13. What was the nature of human symbolic behavior during the later Pleistocene, and how is it reflected in the prehistoric record? There was clearly a major increase in the frequency of decorative objects and the introduction of representational and notational forms with the advent of the Upper Paleolithic (at least in Europe). Does this emergence of "art" represent an evolving information system (with the objects and notations acting as mnemonic devices) or merely some aspects of personal ornamentation in a social context? Since complex symbolic behavior is a hallmark of recent human cultural behavior, the emergence or significant expansion of a symbolic communication system, however indirectly indicated in the paleoanthropological record, should be highly significant to our understanding of this transitional period in human evolution. (Bar-Yosef, Binford, Rigaud, Smith and Paquette, Stringer, Trinkaus, White)

14. Many of the "art" objects that appear in the Upper Paleolithic, as well as those present in the Middle Paleolithic, are best seen as items of personal ornamentation. Does their appearance in the Middle Paleolithic and their marked expansion in the early Upper Paleolithic (again, at least in Europe) imply a significant reorganization of social roles and the complexity of those social interactions? If so, how might we interrelate the evolution of personal ornamentation with that of the contemporaneous intentional human burials so as to provide a more complete picture of the changing levels of human social interactions during this time period? (Bar-Yosef, Rigaud, Smith and Paquette, Trinkaus, White)

15. Intentional burials first appeared among late archaic humans and continued throughout the emergence of early modern humans. Does their presence among late archaic humans imply that the same complex of behaviors associated with the ritual disposal of the dead as is known ethnographically, was present among these archaic humans? The answer to this question is closely related to the resolution of the issues (numbers IV and V above) concerning the nature of the later Pleistocene "transition" and the time-depth of truly "cultural" behavior. (Bar-Yosef, Rigaud, Trinkaus, White)

16. The previous three issues, and especially number 13, relate closely to the evolution of human language. Did it emerge in its fully modern structural form only at the time of this later Pleistocene "transition," or was it present in a similar but less complex form previously? The human paleontological data, to the extent that they shed light upon this issue, are compatible with a fully modern human capacity for articulate language among late archaic humans (the real basis being neurological, which is paleontologically invisible at the level of concern here). A presumed modern human biological capacity for language does not, however, indicate whether the form of communication among those late archaic humans was structurally the same as that of recent humans. That must be determined, indirectly, from analyses

14

of archaeological and human paleontological data relevant to assessments of their levels of organizational and symbolic communication complexity. (Binford, Smith and Paquette, White)

17. To what extent were there significant changes in subsistence patterns at the time of this later Pleistocene "transition"? Since the vast majority of the available relevant data concerns the exploitation of medium-sized to large mammals, and since there is little intraregional change in species representation in faunal assemblages (independent of climatic shifts) through this transitional period, this issue concerns primarily possible changes in the organization of and technology used for predation on these mammals. With the exception of southern Africa, little of the appropriate taphonomic analysis has yet been done, and the available data are rather equivocal as to the rapidity of a shift in human subsistence patterns around any later Pleistocene "transition." (Bar-Yosef, Binford, Rigaud, Stringer, Trinkaus)

18. A related issue concerns the relative abilities of later Pleistocene human groups to compete with large and social carnivores for carcasses and space. At what point were humans able to obtain and maintain primary access to animal carcasses? And at what point were humans able to maintain exclusive use of natural shelters? This issue is highly relevant to many of the preceding issues, since most of the above-mentioned behavioral patterns assocated with recent human hunter-gatherers assume or are greatly facilitated by the ability to compete effectively for space and food with other mammals.

19. To what extent was the appearance of early modern humans associated with significant changes in human manipulative behaviors? Technologically aided task solving is one of the hallmarks of modern human cultural behavior; it assumes a biological basis for fine manipulation (both musculo-skeletal and neurological) and the ability to develop flexible and effective implements. The level of neurological fine-tuning of later Pleistocene human manipulative anatomy remains invisible to us, but there were significant shifts in human upper limb skeletal morphology around this later Pleistocene "transition" and associated changes in lithic and bone/antler technology. What remain at issue are the behavioral implications of the anatomical changes and the extent to which changes in the technology resulted in significant alterations in its task specificity and mechanical effectiveness. The resolution of this issue is related to aspects of organization (see numbers

15

IV, 8 and 9) and to the subsistence and competitive effectiveness of the humans involved (see numbers 17 and 18). (Bar-Yosef, Rigaud, Smith and Paquette, Stringer, Trinkaus)

20. Were there significant changes in human abilities to deal with environmental stress, especially thermal stress, both behaviorally and physiologically, at this time period? This concerns primarily the ability to resist cold stress, since humans are physiologically tropical mammals. Late archaic humans were the first to survive, by the end of the Middle Pleistocene, in mid-latitude glacial climates, but it was not until toward the end of this transitional time period (certainly during the late last glacial) that humans were able to survive in high-latitude regions. To what extent can changes in human body size and proportions be related to the spread of humans into cold latitudes, keeping in mind that some eco-geographical patterning is to be expected in all widely dispersed homeothermic species? And to what extent was the increasing human ability to exploit extremely cold environments due to increased thermal protection (through improved insulation and pyrotechnology) and/or greater organizational capabilities (such as are necessary in such marginal environments)? This issue is related, again, back to a number of the preceding ones that concern the evolving structural complexity of human behavior during the later Pleistocene. (Bar-Yosef, Rigaud, Stringer, Trinkaus, Wolpoff)

These are some of the more specific issues concerning the patterns and processes that were involved in the emergence of early modern humans from late archaic ones. The list represents only a sample of the more salient issues raised by the participants in the Advanced Seminar and related research. Many of these minor issues are potentially resolvable through the appropriate analysis of available paleoanthropological data. All would be made easier to investigate if some of the data deficiencies mentioned above were reduced, but we should be able to arrive at reasonable solutions to many of them through analysis of current collections and data. More importantly, many of them are not as dependent upon intellectual preconceptions as are the more general issues discussed above, even though all are likely to be influenced by the general theoretical positions of individual investigators.

16

CONCLUDING REMARKS

A thorough understanding of the events and processes that were involved in the emergence of the biobehavioral pattern we associate with recent human hunter-gatherers is still rather distant. This is due in part to the deficiencies and biases of the available data. It is produced in part by the limitations in time and resources of the individuals involved in related research. Yet, it must be kept in mind that it is also related in large part to the diversity of theoretical points of view and approaches of those individuals. However, research related to this question is sufficiently advanced to enable us to become aware of the more general issues involved and to focus on some of the more specific problems that face us. It is hoped that these introductory remarks and the papers that follow will go a long way toward helping us reach an eventual comprehension of the evolutionary processes that led to ourselves.

2
Isolating the transition to cultural adaptations: an organizational approach

Lewis R. Binford

Writing in the early 1920s, A. L. Kroeber commented on the "transition" to fully modern humankind[1] as follows:

The lower paleolithic culture, at least in its latest form, was carried by Neanderthal man; Upper Paleolithic culture is in great part associated with Cro-Magnon man, whose anatomy was nearer our own. Did not this relatively modern structure involve also a relatively modern set of mental faculties, and these in turn, by their own sheer worth, produce the richer culture? (Kroeber 1923:396)

Early textbooks in American anthropology almost without exception noted the marked contrast between the Upper Paleolithic and what preceded it. The Old Paleolithic, as it was sometimes called, was appreciated as having been produced by creatures different from us in perhaps fundamental ways. Since early anthropological thought was essentially an idealist's view both of modern man's distinctiveness and of his predecessors' "deficiencies," it is not surprising that Kroeber chose to contrast early man with modern man in terms of mental faculties:

Patience and forethought of a rather high order are thus involved in the making of implements of the Neolithic type... By comparison, the earliest man lacked these traits. They would not sit down to-day to commence something that

18

would not be available for use until a month later. What they wanted they wanted quickly. To think ahead, to sacrifice present convenience to future advantage, must have been foreign to their way of life. (Kroeber 1923:144)

There may be some advantage to a return, at least in part, to this point of view. Focusing on the behavioral consequences of planning and on the organization of early hominid use of tools may be among the most productive avenues of research on the transition between the archaeological remains deposited before and after the appearance of *Homo sapiens sapiens*.

PLANNING, DEPTH, TACTICAL DEPTH, AND CURATION

Modern populations commonly take actions that will make possible further action at a much later time, indeed often initiating the sequence long before the anticipated conditions are observable in the environment. A move to a fish camp along a salmon stream, for example, is generally made before salmon appear in the stream (O'Leary 1985), on the basis of stored and analyzed knowledge of the environment and of the behavior of fish. The group may well engage in the manufacture and repair of fishing gear long before any direct indication that salmon are present, will be present, or might be exploited. When the salmon arrive, heavy labor investments are made in obtaining fish, which are then processed for stores that may serve as food for the group over a six- to eight-month period. In this example we clearly have an instance of planning. The potentially variable length of time between anticipatory actions and the actions they facilitate, amount of investment in anticipatory actions, and proportion of activities so facilitated may be conceived as *planning depth*, and the technologies of modern populations exhibit this depth to a high degree.

A second characteristic of technological systems designed and maintained by *H. sapiens sapiens* is a high degree of what I shall call *tactical depth* – the variable capacity, based on stored knowledge of mechanical principles, environmental characteristics, and hence opportunities, to find more than one way to skin a cat. While people may plan the manufacture, maintenance, and replacement of technological elements, their ability to anticipate future conditions is not always perfect. A hunting party equipped with well-designed weapons may be unsuccessful and shift its food-procurement endeavors to fishing. Under these

19

conditions it may find its hunting gear inappropriate and use it as a source of raw materials for manufacturing fishing gear on the spot. Again, the members of the party may lose their gear, for example, while crossing a swollen river, and look around in their immediate environment (which they generally know quite well) for raw materials with which to manufacture replacements. This equipment is designed to play a very different role from that of the lost gear – a short-term, expedient role – and may be formally unlike it.

For the archaeologist, this capacity for technological adjustment to the immediate circumstances results in interesting and complicated patterns. The archaeological remains of fully modern humankind exhibit great variation arising from the frequent combination of tactical options conditioned by immediate circumstances. When this flexibility is combined with considerable planning depth, the variation may be bewildering. Assemblages are reticulated compounds of differentiated components, and rarely is any strong set of "categorical" differences recognizable among "types" of places occupied by a single system. Likewise, when independent measures of the conditions being coped with at the time of archaeological deposition (e.g., environmental indicators and faunal remains) can be monitored at different places and different times, there is rarely any categorical patterning of association between particular tools and given species or activities. The ability to shift tactics to accommodate unanticipated conditions precludes such robust and simple patterning (see, for example, Straus 1987b).

Another aspect of modern mankind's behavior that is variable and interesting is the degree to which technology is *maintained* – the amount of labor investment in the design and production of tools so as to ensure them a long use-life. I have called this maintenance behavior *curation* (Binford 1979). While planning depth may be present without curation, it is difficult to imagine curation without planning depth.

Curation may be signaled in the archaeological record by the differential selection of raw materials. Again, items playing long-term roles may be transported many times to many places and therefore they may be expected to co-occur only rarely with the debris from their manufacture. Such items may also have major investments made in their maintenance along the way. Curation may be most obvious in complicated tool designs yielding both great durability and easy maintenance, such as modular ones; parts that are more subject to breakage

20

(such as projectile points) may be designed for ease of manufacture and replacement.

As planning depth increases, so do the number of manufacturing steps and the variety of tools used to produce the final product, i.e., a tool designed for use in directly coping with the environment. The larger the inventory of tools performing interjacent roles relative to these instrumental end products, the more reticulate and "non-categorical" the patterning among tool forms when different sites are compared. For instance, where an instrumental technology is primarily manufactured from non-lithic raw materials, with lithics being used interjacently, the lithics may in comparison appear impoverished and "crude." We may be further led astray by comparing the interjacent tools of one system with the crude and poorly designed instrumental tools of an earlier system.[2] Very different planning depths will underlie these two situations. To avoid these kinds of errors we need an organizational understanding of the contexts of the tools. Tools designed to facilitate repair or maintenance of other tools are direct clues to planning depth, as also is independence between the disposition of tools used to make tools and that of the tools designed to be used in directly coping with the environment.

The techno-adaptive strategies of modern hunter-gatherers are extremely variable in planning depth, tactical depth, and curation. Technological features reflecting differences in the components of these strategies scale remarkably well with environmental variables in the near-modern world (Binford 1980; Kelly 1983). In addition, this patterning has been strongly linked to regularly varying patterns of mobility (also responsive to environmental variables) and has been elaborated and explicated by further research (Torrence 1983) regarding time scheduling of labor inputs for both production and maintenance of technologies. The work done to date clearly supports the view that planning depth, tactical depth, and curation differentially contribute to adaptive success in different environments.

The relatively fine-tuned relationships between technological characteristics, viewed in these terms, and environmental variables document the fact that culturally organized technologies are modern humans' extrasomatic means of adaptation. Woodburn (1980) recognized an analogous distinction in speaking of immediate- and delayed-return strategies with regard to labor investments, but he fails to take the next step in seeking to understand the contrasts he recognizes. Marshack (1972a:14) has pointed to some of these same properties in identifying "time-factored" processes and behavior. He notes correctly that "sciences ... are themselves 'time-factored,' since the processes of cognition and recognition, of planning, research, analysis, comparison, and interpretation are also sequential, interrelated, developmental and cumulative."

Despite the geographic (Binford 1983d) and sequential (Binford 1980) patterning in their adaptations, it is primarily the scheduling variations in both space and time in the accessibility of resources, coupled with the incongruent patterns of availability for needed suites of resources, that condition the degree of planning depth, tactical depth, and curation among modern hunter-gatherers (Binford 1980). There is a global pattern of variation that is understandable largely in ecological terms.

First, "technological areas" or "culture areas" correspond nicely to environments of differing forms and dynamics. Studies of the material products of modern preindustrial peoples (e.g., Wissler 1914; Kroeber 1939) have long since demonstrated this, but the causal implications have not been pursued. Secondly, more planning depth, tactical depth, and curation seem to characterize technologies in relatively inhospitable environments, those that are most variable in terms of seasonal productivity. This pattern betrays a very consistent evolutionary set of responses to the earth's environments, presumably the consequence of the interactions between the structure of the environments and the "capacity" of modern human populations to solve problems in nearly identical ways.

Consideration of the transition from earlier forms to fully modern man often takes the form of citing the earliest evidence for certain categorical forms of behavior recognized as characteristic of the latter – the earliest evidence for symbolism, for an esthetic sense, for a "human" form of social organization, etc. There is, I think, a kind of chauvinism, ethnocentrism, or even racism associated with this approach. It is not uncommon to hear that the properties that we consider most admirable in our behavior are those to be differentially investigated. This tends to place many researchers on the defensive with reference, for example, to the seeming lack of technological achievement of even relatively modern peoples living in equatorial and subequatorial settings (e.g., Watanabe 1969, 1985; Hutterer 1977a, 1977b). The criteria for identifying fully modern human behaviors must be developed in the context of a firm understanding of what conditions variation among modern populations in the way our "human nature" is expressed in different environments. The global patterning just mentioned is only now being recognized. Much of the variation among modern hunter-gatherer societies is not yet understood. Nevertheless, I do not consider it premature to seek an understanding of the transition in terms of our budding appreciation for such patterning. [3]

The earliest evidence for technologically aided adaptations is largely restricted to the subequatorial zones. Thus, any assessment of the role of technology and the organizational basis for adaptations among the early hominids must be made in the context of our understanding of the adaptations of mobile hunter-gatherers in such settings. A striking difference between modern hunter-gatherer adaptations in sub-equatorial zones and in equatorial forests has to do with mobility. In the forest, residential mobility is high and "logistical" mobility low, as is the extent of foraging coverage relative to a "base camp" (Kelly 1983). Technology may be curated, and much of the instrumental technology is manufactured of light materials, such as bamboo and wood and combinations thereof. While the inventory of tools may be small, their designs tend to be ingenious, facilitating a wide range of specific activities. The deeper in the forest, generally the smaller the package size of the foods exploited. Scavenging is rarely reported, consumption of animal products seems to be immediate, and no storage of such products is indicated.

Table 2.1 summarizes the contemporary ethnographic data on productivity of habitat and types of weapons used in obtaining animal foods in equatorial settings. These patterns seem to put to rest the notion of a "Garden of Eden," the claim that humans should respond only to the quantity of potential food available (e.g., Foley 1982). It is very clear that the technology varies with the character of the environment. In high-biomass tropical settings, blowguns and relatively small poisoned arrows permit the hunter to gain access to the generally small animals of the canopy and may be used in conjunction with nets for taking the very small animals of the forest floor. As productivity goes down (in this setting an indication of drier conditions), larger shock weapons (bow and arrow, lance, spear) become more important. In the relatively dry tropical forests and forest savannah margins, a wide variety of relatively small terrestrial animals can be effectively hunted with strong shock

Table 2.1. *Productivity of the environment, diet, and hunting equipment of modern equatorial and subequatorial hunter-gatherers*

Group	NAAP (per sq m)	Dependence on plants (%)	Hunting equipment	Reference
Walbiri	174	60	Spear thrower and spear	Meggitt (1962)
G/wi	252	87	Bow and poisoned arrow	Silberbauer (1972:288–90)
!Kung	329	80	Bow and poisoned arrow	Lee (1979:116–57)
Hadza	666	65	Bow and poisoned arrow	Woodburn (1968:52)
Dorobo	1144	40	Bow and poisoned arrow, poisoned spear or lance	Huntingford (1955:620)
Aweikomo	1623	40	Bow and arrow, lance	Henry (1964:166–8)
Guyakie	1715	40	Bow and arrow	Clastres (1972:145–7)
Aeta	2073	35	Bow and arrow, dogs, net (drives)	Griffin (1984:47)
Siriono	2115	70	Bow and arrow	Holmberg (1969:14–16)
Mbuti	2200	60	Bow and arrow, net (drives), poisoned arrow for monkeys	Putnam (1963:330)
Semang	2814	65–70	Bow and poisoned arrow, blowgun with poisoned darts	Murdock (1934:89)
Punam	3535	80	Blowgun with poisoned darts, dogs	Urquhart (1951:256)

NAAP = Net above-ground productivity, or the amount of new (non-root) plant cell production each year, calculated by this author. This estimate is derived from rainfall and temperature data available in contemporary world weather records. The estimate is the result of a three-step inferential sequence using Bailey (1960), Rosenzweig (1974), and additional information from Chang (1963) on the natural history of runoff. The procedure will be explained in detail in a forthcoming publication by this author on hunting and gathering adaptations. Dependence on plants as a percentage of total diet calculated by Murdock and Morrow (1970).

weapons. Groups living in environments with both small and large animals (for instance, the Hadza) use poison when taking larger prey. The body sizes of the animals regularly taken with shock weapons commonly range from about 15 kg up to 65 kg, with the latter size being rather rare. Animals in the larger body-size range are almost invariably taken with poisoned projectiles. It is in these settings that groups are most commonly described as regularly scavenging meat from natural animal deaths as well as kills by nonhuman predators. In still less productive environments, poison is incorporated into weapons designed for use against the larger animals of the forest margins and the savannah, and shock weapons drop out of the primary technology.

The technologies of these modern hunter-gatherers vary in design and principle with variations in the environments in which the technologies are employed. Quite literally, the technology is basic to the subsistence adaptations worked out relative to each environment.

In high-biomass equatorial forests, residential mobility is quite high and duration of occupancy of any one place short (Kelly 1983). In addition, there is less spatial differentiation in the organization of the technology. Mobility and flexibility in group size are the means by which hunter-gatherers adjust to the varying availability of subsistence resources in their habitats.

Finally, although modern hunter-gatherer technologies vary in planning and tactical depth and in the role of curation, they all have planning-based adaptations. We therefore find patterned contrasts between the places occupied by groups, where artifacts are discarded during the course of the production, repair, and maintenance of the technology, and the places in which instrumental tools are lost or abandoned while they are being used to obtain subsistence or other products from the environment.

In the light of all this, what can be said about the organization of technology in the pre-*sapiens sapiens* adaptations?

THE ORGANIZATION OF ADAPTATIONS IN THE LOWER PALEOLITHIC

The periods prior to the Mousterian of the Rissian era are characterized by a lack of evidence for planned occupation of locations. While modern humans occupying a given place produce a structured set of spatial relationships among the components of the occupied surface that indicates planning (see Yellen 1972, 1977; Binford 1978a, 1983a; Hayden 1979; Kent and Vierich in press), early hominid sites exhibit differential patterns of tool or debris density (Isaac 1981b), but the organization of space relative to events anticipated to occur in it is not clearly indicated. Identifications of base camps and other organized aspects of a settlement system in the Lower Paleolithic (Isaac 1971; Harris 1978) are an artifact of the researchers' views of the archaeological record (Binford 1987a). For instance, the criterion for a "living floor" in the Lower and Middle Paleolithic is usually the vertical and horizontal concentration of artifacts and fauna, but the contents of so-called living floors do not differ from clear aggregates of tools derived from so-called diffuse deposits (Binford 1987a). This seems to me to indicate that adaptation was not achieved technologically; rather, technology was an aid to adaptations organized in other terms.

Early tool-assisted systems of behavior show a robust pattern of division into expediently produced and used and transported components.[4] This pattern is now demonstrable in the Oldowan (Binford 1985b) and continues throughout the Acheulean (Clark and Kurashina 1976; Isaac 1977). In Oldowan assemblages there is a component of minimally modified small tools accompanied by lithic debris of the same raw material, with tool production (pebble smashing) and use occurring in the same place. The other side of the technological coin is the modification of pebble "cores" to produce choppers, chopping tools, and polyhedrons. The raw materials used are different from those found in the expedient, "small-tool" component, and manufacture does not normally appear to have taken place where the tools are found. When this does occur, a very different type of lithic reduction procedure – hammerstone or anvil flaking of hand-held items as opposed to impacting of pebbles resting on a surface – seems to be indicated. Finally, items that appear to have been recycled or used for a long time and "miscellaneous" or unique tool forms regularly covary with this transported component.

Although the forms of the tools are somewhat different, the same basic pattern is demonstrable in the Acheulean; there is a transported aspect to the technology (here in the form of handaxes and sometimes cleavers) that is not commonly associated with the debris from their manufacture or with many (or many varieties of) small tools and an expedient small-tool aspect that is commonly associated with lithic debris.[5]

These two aspects of the technology vary inversely with one another in interassemblage comparisons and are associated with different kinds of faunal assemblages. The expedient component covaries with faunas composed primarily of lower limbs and head parts, primarily mandibles; the transported component is associated with faunas composed of more axial skeletal parts and indicators of carcasses or carcass parts. The total amount of bone is generally less with the transported component, and indicators of naturally accumulated "background" faunas occur with these assemblages, with fewer artifacts being deposited per episode of "occupation." All of the early sites dominated by the transported component appear to be palimpsests of episodic events.

The early time ranges present a picture of tool-assisted behavior that is episodic and "individual" in focus. Among modern hunter-gatherers, as we have seen, technologies tend to include curation that normally takes place in a camp. Many (if not most) of the places in which tools are used to procure food are thought by some researchers to be largely below the visibility threshold of the archaeologist (see, e.g., Yellen 1977). The patterning seen in the early time ranges seems to represent a nearly opposite type of organization and role for technology. The highly visible archaeological "sites" seem to be the places where the technology is used in coping with the environment. For instance, the battered "hammers" known particularly from the early levels at Olduvai Gorge seem to relate to the immediate lakeside setting, and phytoliths derived from aquatic tuberous plants, "cattails" in American terms, have been recovered from these tools (Isaac pers. comm., 1985). The frequencies of these tools seem to vary with the presence in the environment of this type of plant, and they are found in the spots where the plants occurred. Hammers of the Olduvai Gorge type are rare or absent at Koobi Fora (Bunn et al. 1980; Bunn 1982), and the microenvironment there has not been described as supporting large numbers of such plants; the same applies to the essentially streamside locations known from Bed II at Olduvai Gorge. On the other hand, lakeside sites from Ethiopia are more analogous to the situations of Bed I at Olduvai, and the hammers reappear in them even though they are considered later than the Bed II deposits at Olduvai (Clark and Kurashina 1976). This same situation seems to apply to other aspects of the Oldowan technology. Tools are concentrated where they were used, not where persons employing a planned technological exploitation of the environment resided and returned with both products of their technology and the means to maintain it.

Another contrast with modern technology is the fact that, whereas modern tools that are regularly transported are also frequently among the most curated, the early transported tools commonly do not show much evidence of use and may accumulate in large numbers in certain places. It is hard to imagine a planned strategy in which large tools are considered essential that might produce either of these conditions. If transport of tools was backed by much planning depth, one would expect a tool to be used until its functioning was impaired by damage. Again, if someone was anticipating work in a place in which he had performed it many times before, it is hard to imagine that he would not know that there were many appropriate tools already there. It is therefore unlikely that the concentrations of transported tools represent base camps. The depositional contexts are consistent with an episodic accumulative process rather than a planned, integrated strategy of land use. Once again one can argue that the artifacts accumulated on the landscape where the hominids were engaging nature, not where they were living and planning subsistence activities.

In one of the few intensive regional studies of the Acheulean as well as later remains, the distribution of Acheulean handaxes is strongly "tethered" to the raw materials from which they were made (G. Sampson pers. comm., 1987). There is a very steep fall-off curve in handaxe frequency as one moves away from the raw material sources. This small-scale spatial distribution does not support a view of substantial planning depth or curation; rather, it reflects only very small-scale mobility relative to very short periods during which the tool was functioning in the technological system. This same pattern seems to characterize the distributions of handaxes in the Hunsgai Valley of India (K. Paddayya pers. comm., 1987).

The Acheulean provides us with another important and puzzling contrast to the technologically based adaptations of modern non-agricultural humans; we have Acheulean materials from many different environments in Africa, western Europe, the Near East, and India, and except for possible minor variations that can be understood in terms of the types of raw materials available for artifact production and distribution (Villa 1978), no patterned differentiations convincingly covary with grossly different environments. Given what we know of the modern situation, and leaving aside the question of ethnicity and the sociology of a culture-based human world, this lack of correspondence between technology and environment is surprising. Once again, it suggests that technology is not the means of adaptation but an aid to adaptation, with very little variation in the social organization or the contexts of tool use standing behind the archaeological record over this vast span of space and time.

The remarkable similarity in early hominid technology over vast areas calls to mind what we see in other species of animals, namely, a generic organizational basis of behavior that is common to the species. There is nothing in the data of the Oldowan or the Acheulean to suggest in any way a "cultural" or extrasomatic mechanism of inheritance serving to make possible the occupation of varying niches by subpopulations of a single species. We are not looking at rudimentary or nascent cultural systems (Binford 1973; Binford and Ho 1985); instead we have a

28

technologically aided, biologically based, panspecific form of adaptation.[6]

Because early stone tools were frequently found in association with animal bones, for years it was assumed that the makers of the tools had been hunters. Around 1980 some researchers began to question this simple interpretation (see Binford 1985a). Isaac and his team, working at Koobi Fora, noted that, while most of the sites referable to the Plio-Pleistocene boundary were characterized by clear associations of bones and stone tools, the composition of the fauna was hard to reconcile with a hunting model. Because species and individual animals were often represented by a single bone, scavenging seemed a reasonable alternative to consider (Bunn et al. 1980).

Working at about the same time on tabulations of the bones recovered from Olduvai Gorge, I found many of the patterned associations among skeletal parts strikingly similar to those among bones either abandoned by or transported by nonhominid scavenger–predator animals, such as lions or hyenas. I also found a different pattern of skeletal-part association at natural death and kill sites, where the bones were largely lower leg and head parts of ungulates, than sites left by hominid hunters (Binford 1981). Since these are both the parts that generally yield the least food (Binford 1978b) and the ones commonly abandoned by predator–scavenger animals at the sites of their kills, I suggested that the pattern in the Olduvai data was more consistent with scavenging than with hunting. In the same year, another research team (Potts and Shipman 1981) reported animal tooth marks, sometimes overprinted by tool-inflicted cut marks, on some of the bones recovered by the Leakeys from Olduvai Gorge – exactly what one would expect if the hominids accumulated bones scavenged from carcasses previously ravaged by animals. A striking new view of early hominid diet and the context for site formation was emerging (see Shipman 1983, 1984a, 1984b; Binford 1985a, 1986c; Bunn and Kroll 1986; Binford et al. 1988). If we had been wrong about the occurrence of hunting at the time of the earliest visible archaeological sites, then finding out when hunting did begin became a fascinating challenge.

At Klasies River Mouth, a site on the southern coast of Africa that spans the important time period just preceding and including the appearance of forms of fully modern humans, I attempted to distinguish between hunting and scavenging primarily on the basis of data on skeletal-part frequencies and patterned frequencies of animal gnawing on bones (Binford 1984a). The occupants of the cave at Klasies River Mouth appear to have regularly scavenged marginal parts of medium-sized to large animals, and there was a foreshadowing increase in the hunting of small animals and the young of large species.[7]

To see whether this pattern was unique or represented a first glimpse of a previously unsuspected late shift to hunting, I examined data from Swanscombe and Hoxne in England, dating between 200,000 and 350,000 years ago, and Abri Vaufrey, spanning the period from 300,000 to 90,000 years ago (Binford 1987b). All three sites yielded evidence indicative of scavenging, with Abri Vaufrey and to some extent Hoxne showing a bias toward meat-yielding parts. Study of Zhoukoudian, which dates from about 450,000 to 220,000 years ago, further supported the view that hunting, although assumed, was not demonstrable, and that early man may have been a scavenger (Binford and Ho 1985; Binford and Stone 1986). Restudy of data collected earlier from the French site of Combe Grenal suggested that during very cold periods some 30,000 years before the appearance of fully modern man there may have been some systematic hunting of medium-sized animals, particularly young individuals, but as at Klasies River Mouth, larger animals (horses and cattle) were most likely scavenged throughout the sequence. The surprising pattern seemed to be consistently telling us that our ancestors turned to hunting just prior to the appearance of modern humankind. Like the other characteristics that first appeared in this time period (see Mellars 1973; Straus 1977; Binford 1982a; Pfeiffer 1982; White 1982, 1985; Gilman 1984), hunting may simply have been part of the transition.

While these studies were provocative, there remained the impressive claims for the organized hunting of big game at Torralba, a site at least 250,000 and perhaps as much as 450,000 years old, by men of *H. erectus* grade (see Howell 1965; Freeman 1978). A restudy of the Torralba data (Binford 1987c) revealed some fascinating patterning. The majority of the stone tools at Torralba covary positively with the faunal remains of bovids, equids, and cervids, while this entire group varies inversely with remains of elephants. Denticulates, notches, perforators, bifaces, cores, and retouched flakes covary with the heads and lower limbs of all species, while sidescrapers, endscrapers, utilized flakes, and choppers covary with carcass parts of all species. At the same time, the carcass parts and heads and lower limbs vary independently of

30

each other. Such patterning could only have arisen as independent episodes of hominid activity at the site (Binford 1987c:52). There were no mass kills at Torralba, no game drives, no activity areas in which large quantities of meat were processed by socially differentiated "labor" units. Perhaps equally surprising, the tool suite associated with bones from lower limbs and heads, an association recognized from earlier sites as a tentative indication of scavenging, is the dominant one. It seems likely that, as elsewhere, these bones were accumulated by the hominids rather than representing animals killed there. Finally, although there is a distinctive suite of tools that covaries with carcass indicators, there is no indication that hominids hunted or caused the deaths of the animals. In fact, the pattern of raw material use characteristic of this suite suggests that the hominids encountered carcasses unexpectedly and were forced to produce the tools needed to deal with them using local sources and lithic remains that were already present. This behavior too is consistent with scavenging, and little planning depth stands behind it.

Two major conclusions may be drawn from the recent studies. First, given our current understanding of faunal remains as recognizably referable to scavenging versus hunting, all the arguments that presuppose hunting appear to be unwarranted.[8] Secondly, as discussed in the beginning of this section, the identification of home bases in the archaeological record is a product of the researchers' assumptions about the past, not a result of rigorous analysis.

PATTERNING IN THE MIDDLE PALEOLITHIC

The independent variation noted at Torralba between tool suites dominated by denticulates and notches and scraper-dominated assemblages is perhaps the most robust and repetitive pattern in the assemblages roughly dated to the early Riss in western Europe and synchronous climatic events around the world.[9] In addition, the Middle Paleolithic is characterized by an increase in the complexity of patterning within assemblages (Bordes 1953, 1961a). As Bosinski (1982:165) has recently summarized the situation,

The spectrums of stone artifacts are more differentiated and the assemblages can be grouped to different industries . . ., which represent space–time units. An important role is played by the appearance of Levallois technique . . . resulting in a greater variability of flake types, as well as of retouched tools.

Rather than seeing the beginnings of macroregional patterning as the emergence of "culture" in the sense of self-conscious "ethnic" groups, I view it as heralding a shift in the role technology played in hominid adaptations. In the earlier part of this period hominids appear to radiate into northern latitudes during phases of relative warmth and then are regularly wiped out or retreat south with shifting floral zones in some areas as warm climate is replaced by colder conditions (see Bosinski 1982; Freund 1982; Roe 1982; Tuffreau 1982). Roughly coincident with these radical shifts in range is the "regionalization" just mentioned.

This shift is not unique to the margins of the hominid range; regional patterning also occurs within the African continent (Clark 1982), beginning around 200,000 years ago. While the situation in the Near East is similar, the picture there is clouded by the attempts of Jelinek (1982a) to force this variation into the period after 130,000 years ago.[10] I feel quite confident that the Near East will be found to fall more in line with the trends seen in the Middle Paleolithic elsewhere as more work is done, particularly at the important site of Kebara (Bar-Yosef et al. 1986). The situation is also clouded in Central Europe by a conservative adherence to culture-historical approaches (see Lyubin 1977; Valoch 1982) and a consequent failure to seek an understanding of the patterning documented in the archaeological record.

Very little can be said about India and China, although progress is being made in unraveling the temporal and typological jumble that the archaeological record there presents (see Paddayya 1982; Misra and Bellwood 1985). The patterns of assemblage variability seen elsewhere for the Middle Paleolithic are, however, not yet documented there (Ghosh 1982). In China I found it difficult to distinguish stone tools said to date to the very early time ranges from tools recovered from sites said to date as recently as 120,000 years ago or even from sites geologically dated to as recently as 30,000 years ago. While the summary articles treating the area speak of a Middle Paleolithic (Qui 1985), this period is not defined or described in a manner that would permit comparison between the Chinese materials and materials from the West.[11] Since quantitative summaries are not generally reported from the Chinese sites, discussion of assemblage variability in this important time period is impossible. Nevertheless, there is a clear regional distinctiveness to the material, and there are indications of considerable variation among the sites of this time period.

Middle Paleolithic regionalism is coupled with some increase in the hominid range, and one can see these two as the first glimmerings of evidence for a new role for technology. Technology may be increasingly serving as the basis for hominid adaptations in diverse environments.

In the Middle Paleolithic of Western Europe, there is a fascinating pattern of "alternation of industries" at sites yielding long temporal sequences (see Bordes 1961a; Laville et al. 1980) that is unlike anything known from the archaeological record of modern man. There are also repetitive patterns over time regardless of assemblage form. Long ago Bordes noted a correlation between denticulate-dominated assemblages and inflated frequencies of horse bones at Combe Grenal. This pattern has recently been measured, and Bordes's general impressions have been confirmed (Chase 1986). At Torralba a similar denticulate-dominated suite of tools was strongly associated with equids as well as bovids and cervids, and the bones, like those linked with denticulates at Combe Grenal, were predominantly parts yielding marginal food returns. This long-term association between a suite of tools and a very particular faunal context would be difficult if not impossible to duplicate in the archaeological remains of fully modern groups.

Even more striking is the discovery in the French Mousterian (Geneste 1985) of a strong dichotomy between assemblages manufactured on high-quality raw material using the Levallois technique, representing movement of raw material away from its sources, and rich in Mousterian points, scrapers, and bifaces, and assemblages made of local raw material using non-Levallois methods of reduction and characterized by high frequencies of notches and denticulates as well as abruptly retouched pieces and pieces with irregular retouch. These two types of assemblages clearly imply a technology that is certainly transported and perhaps minimally planned and an expedient tool kit largely produced on the spot – the old pattern seen initially in the Oldowan.

In addition, many researchers conclude that mobility was high, group size was small, and planning depth, even with regard to the transported material, was limited. There is a general fall-off in the size and degree of utilization of material with distance from known sources that suggests that the technology was being carried along rather than made and repaired in a central place. Middle Paleolithic sites are palimpsests of many episodes of use and not planned occupations of any substantial duration. In further contrast to sites produced under modern human conditions, they do not display the variation in sequentially accumulated remains that results from tactical exploitation of their

33

environments in terms of planned strategies. In thick deposits that are similar overall from bottom to top, arbitrary levels separating the deposits into subunits do not exhibit statistically meaningful variation (Binford 1982b). I view this as evidence that there is no organized integration between the social domain and its "needs" and the tactical flexibility in the technology.

Another clue to organizational differences between fully modern humans and hominids of the Middle Paleolithic relates to the relationship between bones and artifacts. Although variable with site function, among modern groups the "turnover rate" in the technology is commonly much slower than the consumer rate for foods. Among groups heavily dependent upon hunting, this generally results in there being many more bones in sites than there are tools. In the archaeological remains dating prior to 40,000 years ago, this pattern seems to be reversed. For instance, at the Mousterian site of Combe Grenal, which spans approximately 80,000 years, there are 17,389 tools and only 6,932 bone fragments. There is little evidence that this ratio is affected by preservation. What seems to be suggested is that animal foods played less of a role in the diet, at least in places selected for use as shelters, and tools did not stay in the system very long – another clue to a lack of planning depth.

Some researchers, including myself, suspect that the western Mousterian includes tools for makng tools, which may mean that there were several planning steps in the technology. Thus far, however, planning steps are not easy to relate to a spatial organization of technologically integrated behaviors. Tool manufacture seems to be subordinated to the movements of the hominids. Interjacent tools appear incidental rather than regularly differentiated and planned as such. The planning alternatives that seem to stand behind the major axes of technological differentiation, at least as far as lithics are concerned, continue to be limited to whether or not to carry tools.

Early tool assemblages, including those of the Middle Paleolithic, appear very "wasteful." What appears to be "recycling" has been suggested for some of the Torralba tools and is strongly suspected for many forms of Mousterian ones – limaces, some Quina scrapers, cores, etc.[12] Rather than being an indicator of greater planning depth and even curation, this may simply be the result of palimpsest accumulations at "magnet" locations in the habitat that were regularly used as lithic sources by poorly equipped groups or by groups arriving without tools.

Such an interpretation is consistent with the strong indication that the mobile groups commonly manufactured tools from local materials on the spot. This interpretation is well illustrated by one of the few sites in the world where the extensive exploitation of an elephant carcass during the Middle Paleolithic time range seems clearly indicated, Mwanganda's Village (Clark and Haynes 1970). Here the tools were manufactured of local material on the spot and then used and discarded in direct association with the body parts exploited. This suggests that the hominids were not equipped with tools when they discovered the elephant carcass and had not planned to hunt elephants. Similarly, the limited exploitation of the elephant carcass at Lehringen (Adam 1951), carried out with what appear to be transported tools, suggests that the carcass was a chance encounter rather than a result of planned hunting. We simply do not yet understand the organizational contexts in which tools were transported versus those in which groups were not tool-equipped during the Middle or the Lower Paleolithic. One thing is certain, however; these dichotomous patterns are unlike anything thus far known from the archaeology of fully cultural systems of the last 25–35,000 years.

Perhaps the greatest contrast between the Mousterian and the culturally organized systems of modern hunter-gatherers is in the relationships among mobility, environment, and technological organization. Modern hunter-gatherer adaptations achieve their stability and security by highly flexible patterns of movement within their environments and flexible group size and composition. In turn, mobility and flexibility in social unit composition are strongly correlated with the manner in which the technology is organized. In the Middle Paleolithic, all indications are that groups were uniformly small and mobility very high whatever the environmental form or dynamics (Clark 1985; Geneste 1985). Related to this lack of mobility and group-size flexibility is the minimal organization of the technology, its quick turnover rate, and the lack of planning depth.

THE TRANSITION

Among the remarkable changes in the content of the archaeological record across the threshold represented by the appearance of fully modern groups in many regions are the elaboration of burial; art; personal ornaments; new materials, such as bone, antler, and soft stone;

long-distance movement and/or circulation of goods; and increased variation in site size, duration, and content (Binford 1968a; Marshack 1972a; Mellars 1973; Conkey 1978; Harrold 1980; Pfeiffer 1982; White 1982, 1985; Binford 1982a; Isaac 1983; Gilman 1984; Orquera 1984, to mention only a few). Many of these new archaeological features directly inform us about something organizationally quite new: the presence of language (see White 1985 for an excellent review and Pfeiffer 1982). In short, they signal the appearance of culture.

How are we to understand the process of transition? It is well documented that we have examples of anatomically modern humans with what appear to be full Mousterian assemblages (Jelinek 1982b); similarly, we have Neanderthals with what had previously been judged to be distinctively "Upper Paleolithic" assemblages (Vandermeersch 1984). To further complicate the picture, there appear to be areas of the world where the transition closely coincides chronologically with the appearance of *H. sapiens sapiens* and areas, such as northern Asia, in which the appearance of fully modern humankind seems to be roughly coincident with its occurrence in other areas, but the transition in terms of symbolic indicators appears delayed until around 22,000 years ago. In marked contrast have been the claims for very early fully modern humans in southern Africa (Beaumont et al. 1978) and equally early claims for stone-tool industries that have properties suggestive of exceptional planning depth by Middle Paleolithic standards (Beaumont et al. 1978; Singer and Wymer 1982).

While I suspect that language is the basis of culture as we know it, I am quite sure that culture develops in response to evolutionary processes. It does not simply "bloom" in response to somatically based behavioral potentials or realities. Indicators of language need not signal fully culturally organized systems of adaptation as we know them among modern populations. Many researchers have seen the transition as a "punctuated" event or a kind of Rubicon, and in one way of thinking this view has some merit. The long, tedious, and relatively unchanging patterns of the Middle and particularly the Lower Paleolithic contrast so dramatically with more recent remains that a disjunction is indicated when one looks ahead from the past. Looking back from the present, however, we have generally failed to seek a processual understanding of this transitional event. If culture is subject to evolutionary conditioning, then surely the early days of populations possessing a cultural capacity must have been importantly different from later times. For example, while the early Aurignacian remains from Germany have a very "modern" feel (Hahn and Owen 1985), the contemporary and even more recent "Aurignacian" of central France, which sometimes alternates in a "Mousterian" fashion with the Châtelperronian (Roc de Combe [Bordes 1967]), does not. Perhaps it is our concepts of what "feels" more modern as opposed to what "feels" older that are at fault. Time may well have little to do directly with the process, since other sources of variability, some probably functionally based, might be more important.

Archaeologists are making great strides in unraveling the picture of the Upper Paleolithic in western Europe (see Bailey 1983; Price and Brown 1985), but a nagging problem remains: the conditions and selective contexts that favor the origin of culturally organized systems as such are apt to be different from those that favor diversification and increase in complexity of those systems. Once evidence for symbolic behavior is apparent, the general approach has been one that seeks to understand variation and change as if selection were operating on systems fully organized culturally; the interesting era of the restructuring of hominid adaptations into human adaptations is ignored. Evolution is lost to view.

Only in cultural evolution can an easy transition occur in the character of the behaviors subjected to selection. We need to see this latter transition as distinct from the evolutionary events that occurred when the populations being modified were not fully cultural in their organization. Addressing this problem demands an understanding of the organizational basis for the hominid adaptations pre-dating the transition. Models and projections from the present to the ancient past have misguided interpretation for far too many years. Gamble has aptly commented that "it is during this period that a change occurred in the dominant relations between social and ecological systems" (1986:382). As archaeologists we will not grasp the transition unless we begin to worry about how to measure variables such as planning depth, mobility, group size, and compositional variability and then proceed to see how these properties vary with environmental conditions as a clue to the ecology of ancient populations. A shift from describing the consequences of dynamics, the artifacts, to seeking methods that permit us to use the artifacts to illuminate those dynamics, is crucial for productive work.

One of our greatest challenges as archaeologists is to explore the limits of relevance of our theories and our knowledge of "mankind" and "culture." The transition probably represents a major boundary of relevance for both. Only recently have archaeologists suspected this; hence, most interpretation of the ancient past is made by analogy with what we think we know about modern humans and modern hunter-gatherers. Such an approach ensures that we will never understand either the transition or the ancient past. In conference discussion, for example, Wolpoff maintained that language and "culture" must have been present in the Lower/Middle Paleolithic, arguing first that only selection operating on a cultural capacity could explain the demonstrable increase in brain size during the period between roughly 2,000,000 and 40,000 years ago and second that the stability in tool assemblages can be understood only in terms of learning rooted in language and culture. I agree that we can accommodate our data from the past to such a model; this has clearly been done by most archaeologists. I disagree that such accommodative argument demonstrates the accuracy of the model. The best approach is to adopt the null hypothesis, thus putting the burden on the archaeologist to demonstrate that other possibilities are untenable and/or that the preferred method is unambiguously the best. Only with this strategy will we be in a learning posture relative to the ideas and beliefs we use in interpreting the archaeological record. Only with such a skeptical attitude toward the traditional "wisdom" that has guided our interpretations will we ever learn about the actual conditions characteristic of the past.

The conference discussion among the physical anthropologists was largely a debate between those who saw the biological changes at the transition as continuous relative to earlier populations in the same region and those who saw discontinuity, implying population replacements or changes in patterns of gene flow. Waiting in the wings was discussion of perhaps a far more important set of issues, namely, what the changes and the various regional morphological patterns implied in terms of *behavior* and its ecological context. While I find the historical questions interesting, I return to the question, "How do we explain history?" There was little discussion of *how* and *why* a hominid population should have radiated, the type of discussion that is crucial for guiding good research by archaeologists. This seems to me to be the contemporary situation in all treatments of the transition, and therefore the central issue is how we are to gain the knowledge we need. I have suggested that we need different approaches; we need to use our knowledge of modern humankind in different ways from those that have characterized most previous work, and we need to rethink some of the properties commonly ascribed to the past.

Notes

1 Throughout this paper I will refer to *Homo sapiens* as fully modern man, humans, humankind, etc. The terms "hominid" or "early man" indicate *H. sapiens neanderthalensis* and earlier groups.

2 This is the error that was made by Hayden (1979) in his study of Australian lithic tools.

3 There is a very vocal group of contemporary researchers who endlessly seek to justify the position that we cannot generalize from near-modern hunter-gatherers. It is claimed that they are not "pristine" because they exist in the complicated modern world. History is frequently cited as the cause of both their presence and their ethnographic characteristics; therefore, it is claimed, comparative study and generalization are unwarranted and misguided endeavors. We are asked instead to return to the sterility of historical particularism and cultural relativism (Schrire 1984). These postures are central to those who adhere to such archaic views as "free will" and human choice as the causes of cultural variability (e.g., Sackett 1982). These idealists decry comparative study and demand that both comparative and scientific approaches are "wrong" and inappropriate by virtue of the "uniqueness" of the human condition, suggesting that all we can do is essentially become moral philosophers (e.g., Hodder 1982; Saitta 1983). I consider such postures misguided and embarrassing to our science and, while acknowledging their existence, I do not consider them worthy of serious discussion.

4 It is the latter characteristic that has led some (e.g., Toth 1985) to infer curation for these systems.

5 During the Acheulean, certain areas yield artifact suites that are, strictly speaking, not Acheulean in form, apparently lacking the major diagnostic, handaxes. In many places these assemblages are called by different names: the Clactonian (Collins 1969; Ohel 1979), the Sohan in India (Sankalia 1974), and variants of the "chopper–chopping tool tradition" in China and northern Asia (Movius 1944). In the former two cases it is unclear whether these are "non-handaxe variants" of the dichotomous "Acheulean" as known in the west or are "true" regional variants differing from the Acheulean. Most researchers have been persuaded, however, that the "chopper–

chopping tool tradition" of Asia is non-Acheulean in the handaxe sense of the term, although what I consider to be unconvincing challenges to this view appear from time to time (Kim and Chung 1978; Bae 1980).

The types of analysis that led to the recognition of a dichotomy in Acheulean assemblages have generally not been employed in the analysis of the Asian material, but my analysis of the stone tool assemblages from Zhoukoudian (Pei and Chang 1985) reveals a very similar dichotomous pattern. What are generally called choppers and chopping tools covary with whole flakes and flakes struck off the choppers, although these latter artifacts occur only in small numbers. This set of tools is positively associated with "bolas" (spheroids, in African terms) and reflects a hand-held lithic reduction technique. Retouched tools (small tools, in an Africanist's sense) are not generally associated. The raw materials are very diverse, and most were brought to the site from elsewhere. This is unmistakably the transported component recognizable in the Oldowan and the Acheulean. Varying independently of and inversely with this component is a component consisting of small retouched tools, mostly of local materials and almost exclusively produced by a bipolar technique, and much lithic debitage.

6 When researchers first began to recognize the surprising patterning of the Lower and Middle Paleolithic, it was originally interpreted in cultural historical terms. This interpretation was challenged as unrealistic during the 1960s (see Binford and Binford 1966; Binford 1972, 1973). As was the general procedure at the time, this challenge was offered in terms of expectations derived from comparative considerations of modern hunter-gatherer behavior. It was suggested that the emerging patterning of the Middle and Lower Paleolithic reflected organized activity variants, such as were then becoming demonstrable for the archaeological remains of modern hunter-gatherers. Subsequently I learned more about the types of patterning seen among modern hunter-gatherers (Binford 1975, 1976, 1978a, 1978b, 1979, 1980, 1981, 1982b, 1983a, 1983c, 1984a, 1984b, 1985a, 1986a; Binford and O'Connell 1984), and instead of clarifying our understanding of Middle and Lower Paleolithic patterns of assemblage variability, the Middle and Lower Paleolithic began to appear more and more distinct from anything we could see or understand about the culturally based adaptations of fully modern populations. This apparent contrast led me to be more and more skeptical of interpretative techniques used on early materials: that is, interpretation by simple reference to seeming analogies between the archaeological remains of early man and

piecemeal knowledge of modern man. One of the more controversial areas of research that my skepticism led me to consider was diet.

7 This conclusion has been controversial (e.g., Deacon 1985; Scott 1986; Singer and Wymer 1986), but see Binford 1986b for a response to most of these objections.

8 The supposed sexual division of labor between (male) hunting and (female) gathering, regarded as the structural or evolutionary context for our long period of juvenile dependence, food sharing, and parenting support during the postweaning, prepubescent period, and the patterns of sexual dimorphism seen among fully modern humans are not historically sustained at this point. This does not mean that food sharing, particularly between adult females and their juvenile offspring, did not occur, only that hunting does not appear to be its basis.

9 The "fit" between the Torralba lithic patterning and that known from other Riss and more recent European sites makes me skeptical of the earlier dating for this site that has been suggested in many publications.

10 Jelinek (1982a) has argued that there is a normative directional temporal trend in flake size throughout the Near Eastern Middle Paleolithic. Since one can expect lithic reduction strategy to be responsive to technological needs in differing resource environments, I strongly doubt that this pattern will be confirmed by future research.

11 "Parallel traditions" have been suggested for the Chinese material (see Jia et al. 1972). While I certainly agree that forms of assemblage differ widely, I do not think that "cultural tradition" is the way to interpret this variation.

12 Some researchers have noted differences in ratios of flakes to cores and have inferred "economizing" behavior on the part of Middle Paleolithic hominids (e.g., Munday 1977b, 1979).

3
The Upper Pleistocene transition

ERIK TRINKAUS

It has long been recognized that there were important human evolution-ary changes during the Upper Pleistocene, both biological and cultural. Over the years, in part developing out of the nineteenth-century perceived dichotomy between the Middle and Upper Paleolithic and the early-twentieth-century distinction between the Neandertals of the northwestern Old World and early "anatomically modern" humans, research has been focused on this "Upper Pleistocene transition." This transition, between late archaic humans and early robust versions of people anatomically similar to ourselves, and between Middle Paleolithic (*sensu lato*) side-scraper-dominated industries and Upper Paleolithic (*sensu lato*) end-scraper- and worked-bone-dominated industries, has usually been seen as either a major watershed in human evolutionary history or an artifact of our typological approaches to the prehistoric record, which obscure gradual continuities in human anatomy and behavior. Recent research involving both new discoveries and reanalyses of previous existing remains, is painting a picture of this transitional period that is both more complex and more realistic.

This Upper Pleistocene transition is increasingly being shown to be real, in the sense of being a period of accelerated change relative to rates of change prior to and after the transitional period. However, there were

42

also both considerable regional diversity in the nature of this transitional period and a lack of direct chronological concordance during the transitional period between various human biological changes, between archaeologically documented shifts, and between aspects of the biological and behavioral spheres. What emerges is an image of a period during which many aspects of human biology and culture changed and established new relationships with each other to produce adaptive systems similar to those known ethnographically for recent human hunter-gatherers. The actual natures of the populational changes involved in this process are becoming clearer but remain controversial. And the forms and extents of the associated behavioral shifts are still disputed. Yet the paleoanthropological data and interpretations are coming together to provide an understanding of this Upper Pleistocene transition and its evolutionarily profound, yet frequently subtle, changes in human adaptive behavior.

A FEW PHYLOGENETIC ISSUES

Recent research on the phylogenetic roles of the Neandertals and other late archaic humans in the origins of modern humans has revealed a complex picture (Smith and Spencer 1984; Smith 1985; Trinkaus 1986; Smith and Paquette this volume; Stringer this volume; Wolpoff this volume). In this, it has become evident that current descriptions of population dynamics during this time period grossly underestimate their interregional variability. This is reflected in particular in the ongoing inability of the simplistic and polarized views expressed in some of these discussions to resolve current phylogenetic controversies. Nonetheless, some general phylogenetic patterns are evident, as are the regions of insufficient data to resolve current controversies.

It appears that in Africa, east Asia, and Australasia there was considerable morphological continuity across the archaic to early modern human transition (at least in the skull), indicating predominantly local genetic continuity of populations. However, the paucity of well-dated, diagnostic Upper Pleistocene specimens in these regions means that the rates of morphological change and the extent of possible increases in interregional gene flow remain unknown.

In central and western Asia and Europe (the Neandertal range), there was marked morphological change in all regions of the skeleton at this time period, change that occurred in less than 10,000 years (10 kyr) in

43

the Near East and central Europe and in considerably less time in western Europe. Furthermore, since the appearance of early modern humans was progressively later in time from east to west across western Asia and Europe, and since there were early modern humans in Africa at least as early as they appeared in the Levant (Singer and Wymer 1982), it is likely that this transition across the Neandertal range involved considerable elevation in the level of interregional gene flow.

The best evidence for morphological (and hence some genetic) continuity across this transition in the Neandertal range is in central Europe (Smith 1984), but even there the evidence for continuity is primarily in the facial skeleton, with other aspects (postcranial and basicranial) indicating more pronounced changes. It now appears possible that in western Europe there was some contemporaneity of Neandertals and early modern humans, if there was indeed a direct association of Neandertals with the Châtelperronian (Castelperronian) and early modern humans with the Aurignacian (given the interstratification of those industries in that region [Lévèque and Miskovsky 1983]). This should not be surprising, given the cul-de-sac nature of western Europe and relative lateness of the appearance of early modern humans in that region. It is thus likely that the western European Neandertals contributed little to the gene pools of subsequent modern human gene pools.

It is also possible, although currently still debated (compare Bar-Yosef and Vandermeersch 1981; Bar-Yosef 1988, this volume; Valladas et al. 1988, with Trinkaus 1983a, 1984a, 1988), that there was con-temporaneity in the Levant between these two human groups, or alternating use of that region by them, over a period of several tens of thousands of years. If so (and it depends entirely upon the resolution of the dating of hominid-yielding levels at Qafzeh to either the last interglacial or the middle of the last glacial), it would imply sufficiently different patterns of behavior and/or land use, and hence different ecological niches, to maintain the two groups genetically separate and not in ecological competition for thousands of generations. This supposed contemporaneity or alternation of Neandertals and early modern humans in the Levant is difficult to imagine, given the ability of all post-habiline members of the genus *Homo* to exploit diverse ecozones through technologically aided flexible learned behavior. Furthermore, given the morphological contrasts between these two human groups (despite the facial robustness and large teeth of some of the Skhul and Qafzeh individuals, their skeletons contrast strongly with those of the Neandertals in many aspects of cranial, dental, and especially postcranial morphology and proportions and in those features strongly resemble each other [McCown and Keith 1939; Suzuki and Takai 1970; Trinkaus 1983a, 1984a; Vandermeersch 1981a]) and the resultant behavioral implications (suggesting differences in resource exploitation efficiency, but not in the resources exploited; see below), it is difficult to postulate that the Neandertals were able to compete effectively with those early modern humans for resources and space in an area as small as the Levant.

Related to this question is the determination of whether the Near Eastern Neandertals were intrusive into the area during the early Middle Pleistocene (from the north and/or northwest) (Vandermeersch 1981b; Bar-Yosef 1988, this volume) or represent the descendants of preceding regional archaic humans (nonetheless in genetic contact with European Neandertal populations during the early Upper Pleistocene) (Trinkaus 1983a, 1984a, 1988). Since there is evidence of the emergence of the "classic" Neandertal morphology within the Near East during the early Upper Pleistocene (Trinkaus 1983a, 1987a), and since the only preceding Near Eastern human fossils (Zuttiyeh, Tabun Layer E, and Gesher Benot Ya'acov) preserve *no* uniquely derived (autapomorphous) features of either modern humans or Neandertals, one would have to accept some Near Eastern origin for the Neandertals (perhaps in part influenced by gene flow from European Neandertal populations). The origin of early modern humans in that region, especially if they were contemporaries of the Near Eastern Neandertals, could be seen as well in those preceding generally ancestral (plesiomorphous) forms or, more likely, in African populations of early modern humans. The geographical centrality and faunal corridor configuration of the Near East would certainly make a complex pattern of human population movement and interaction during the Upper Pleistocene likely, much more so than in the peripheries of the Old World.

Regardless of the actual population dynamics associated with the Upper Pleistocene transition, it remains difficult, if not impossible, to assess the probable genetic contributions of regional late archaic human populations to subsequent local early modern human gene pools. The genetic and developmental bases of the observable morphological shifts are potentially too variable (Trinkaus and Smith 1985) to allow such conclusions. Only in cases of clear and long-term overlap of morphological groups does some resolution appear feasible, but even in those cases difficulties in dating and incompleteness of the fossil record preclude a consensus at this time. Yet temporal overlap of two human groups only indicates some external influence; it does not exclude the possibility of extensive gene flow between the two groups.

The cultural historical nature of the changes in the archaeological record through the early and middle Upper Pleistocene is even more difficult to decipher, given the compounding effects of local technological evolution, diffusion between populations, probable population movements through time (if only in response to shifting ecological zones), and the flexible and opportunistic nature of human adaptive behavior. Major diffusion with or without population displacement may well have been important in the introduction of "Upper Paleolithic" cultural elements into some regions, as has been frequently proposed since the work of Breuil (1912), or even in the spread of Mousterian technology. Yet, "transitional" industries are known from many regions of the Old World (Ferring 1975; Singer and Wymer 1982; Harrold 1983; Volkman 1983; Bordes 1984a,b), making the resolution of regional cultural historical sequences dependent upon fine chronological control, detailed comparisons between neighboring areas, and a presumed ability to separate "stylistic" elements from more purely technological responses to similar behavioral situations.

BEHAVIORAL SHIFTS ASSOCIATED WITH MODERN HUMAN EMERGENCE

Independent of one's preferred interpretation of Upper Pleistocene human phylogeny and culture history, it is apparent that there were major shifts in human morphology and behavior during this time period. During the early Upper Pleistocene, approximately between 125 and 90 kyr (and perhaps as late as 50 to 60 kyr, depending upon one's preferred dates for sub-Saharan early modern humans and the Qafzeh sample), only archaic humans with Middle Paleolithic (used here to include the European, western Asian and north African Middle Paleolithic, the sub-Saharan African Middle Stone Age [MSA] and technologically similar Asian industries) cultural systems were present. By 30 kyr, there were only robust anatomically modern humans with Upper Paleolithic (used here to include the European, western Asian and north African Upper Paleolithic, African earlier Later Stone Age

[LSA] and similar Asian industries) cultural systems across an expanded geographical range. One can therefore pose the question: What were the selective advantages of the early modern human biocultural system that allowed it to become the sole human pattern after a relatively short period of evolutionary time?

The answer to this question should be the same regardless of the level of regional biological or cultural continuity or the rapidity of the changes. Selection (whether natural selection operating on human biology or cultural selection influencing the cultural sphere) promoting the changes will operate similarly on variations existing within populations and new variants introduced from neighboring populations through gene flow or diffusion. It will also have similar effects in those instances (however rare or common) in which archaic and early modern human populations were sympatrically competing for common resources.

This issue will be considered here in terms of four behavioral complexes: (1) manipulation, (2) locomotion, (3) information and social systems, and (4) environmental buffering. Since this transition was one in which both human biology and culture were involved, the above question must be answered in terms of human biological changes, behavioral alterations and the interactions between them. This is important since it is seldom possible to determine which system, if either, can be considered as a prime mover (Trinkaus 1983b).

It is nonetheless becoming evident that (at least in the western Old World) the emergence of early modern humans took place largely in Middle Paleolithic contexts. The earliest known "anatomically modern humans" in sub-Saharan Africa (e.g., Klasies River Mouth and perhaps Border Cave [Beaumont et al. 1978; Singer and Wymer 1982]), north Africa (e.g. Dar-es-Soltane [Ferembach 1976]), the Near East (Qafzeh and Skhul [Trinkaus 1984a]), eastern Europe (e.g., Starolsel's [Alexeyev 1976]) and central Europe (Krapina A) are associated with Middle Paleolithic (*sensu lato*) industries. Only in the cul-de-sac of western Europe do we find the reverse, in which the latest Neandertal (Saint-Césaire [Vandermeersch 1984]) and the earliest modern humans are associated with early Upper Paleolithic industries. Does this mean that significant human biological changes preceded cultural ones (everywhere but in western Europe), or that there were important behavioral shifts within the Middle Paleolithic that our lithic-dominated perspective on it is not perceiving?

Human paleontological data and, to a lesser extent, archaeological data relevant to these behavioral complexes are known primarily from the Neandertal range. Sufficiently complete postcrania are rare for Upper Pleistocene archaic humans from elsewhere, and faces with teeth from those regions are scarce. Nonetheless, there was a homogeneous postcranial morphology among Middle Pleistocene humans across the Old World (Pycraft 1928; Weidenreich 1941; Day 1971, 1982; Lovejoy 1982; Geraads and Tchernov 1983; Stringer 1986a; Trinkaus unpub. data), one that evolved gradually into that of the Neandertals in the northwestern Old World (Trinkaus 1982a, 1984b), at a period when regional craniofacial contrasts were present. The postcranial morphology of the Neandertals can thus be considered representative of late archaic humans in general. It is likely that some features, such as overall body or limb segment proportions, which correlate with climate, may have been more variable than current non-Neandertal data indicate.

Despite these limitations in the prehistoric record and the temporal separation of the transitions from archaic to early modern humans and from Middle to Upper Paleolithic, one can still use the available data to discuss the question posed: What were the selective advantages of the modern human adaptive pattern that led to its universality after this period of evolutionary transition? Those regional and temporal qualifiers become important in answering the next question: What were the detailed processes that led to the emergence of that modern human adaptive pattern?

Manipulation

The origins of modern humans saw major shifts in human manipulative behaviors, as has long been recognized from the associated Middle to Upper Paleolithic technological shift. Evidence for these changes in manipulation is also found in upper limb morphology and facial anatomy.

Upper limb functional morphology. The transition from archaic to early modern humans saw a marked decrease in the muscularity of the upper limb (Trinkaus 1983a,b, unpub. data). This is evident in reductions in the size of the muscular insertions on the arm and hand skeleton, especially those for the pectoralis major, latissimus dorsi and teres major muscles on the proximal humerus, the pronator quadratus muscle on

48

the distal ulna, the opponens muscles on the first and fifth metacarpals and the extrinsic flexor muscles on the distal phalanges. In contrast, there does not appear to have been a marked change in forearm and hand shaft robusticity (Trinkaus 1983a, unpub. data), as reflected in external shaft dimensions or cortical thicknesses relative to length, even though some reduction in humeral shaft robustness is implied by current data (Smith et al. 1983; Trinkaus 1983a, unpub. data; Hublin et al. 1987).

These muscular changes were combined with several other shifts in upper limb anatomy (Trinkaus 1983a,b, 1986; Trinkaus and Churchill 1988; Churchill and Trinkaus 1988). There was a reduction in scapular breadth, reflecting smaller rotator cuff muscles and reduced rotary lever arms for the muscles between the scapula and the axial skeleton (in particular the trapezius muscle). A decrease in the frequency of a dorsal sulcus (or, more accurately, a dorsal bar) on the scapular axillary border occurred, indicating less dorsally directed bending stress on the inferolateral scapula. There were reductions in the height of the glenoid fossa of the scapula and in the associated diameter of the humeral head associated with lesser ones in glenoid breadth, implying lower joint reaction forces and more emphasis on use of the arm in an externally rotated position. Lateral radial bowing decreased, reducing the muscular tension on the interosseus membrane from the extrinsic hand muscles. Brachial (radius/humerus length) indices increased, reducing forearm flexion power. Radial tuberosities became more anteriorly oriented, reducing the sustained power of the biceps brachii muscle in supination. Palmar carpal tuberosities became smaller, reducing the power of the carpal flexor, thenar, and hypothenar muscles.

In addition, there was a shift in thumb phalangeal length proportions, from subequal lengths among the Neandertals to the distal phalangeal length being about two-thirds of the proximal phalangeal length among modern humans (in the context of no summed thumb phalangeal to metacarpal or thumb to ulnar digit length changes) (Trinkaus 1983a); this indicates a change from greater muscular effectiveness when gripping across the proximal phalanx (as in the power grip) to one emphasizing strength across the distal phalanx (as in the precision grip). However, since these phalangeal length changes took place in concert with the above muscular strength reductions, they merely maintained strength levels at the finger tip at the compounded expense of strength in a power grip.

There was also a marked reduction in the breadths of distal phalangeal apical tufts (Trinkaus 1983a, unpub. data), indicating smaller distal palmar pads among early modern humans. This implies a decrease in resistance through friction to shear stresses on the terminal fingers (Marzke pers. comm.), indicating less transversely oriented impact loading of objects held between the finger tips.

These alterations were associated with an articular orientation change at the elbow (Trinkaus 1983a). The ulnar trochlear notch changed from a more directly anterior orientation to the anteroproximal orientation of modern humans. This shift in articular orientation implies a change in the average habitual peak-loaded position from a more flexed one to a more extended one; it does not indicate any difference in ranges of movement.

And finally, there were alterations in the average configurations of several of the carpometacarpal articulations. The first and fifth carpometacarpal articulations shifted from more condyloid configurations to saddle-shaped ones (Heim 1982a; Trinkaus 1983a, unpub. data), and the second metacarpal to capitate facet became universally large and obliquely oriented. The functional significance of the first and fifth carpometacarpal changes are not understood, but it appears likely that they are related to changes in habitual peak stress directions, and hence habitual grip positions, rather than to any alteration of articular mobility. The second metacarpal to capitate facet change indicates a shift to a more oblique (proximoulnar) habitual loading of the second digit from a more axial one.

These anatomical changes imply that the origins of modern humans saw a marked decrease in the habitual level of strength exerted by the human upper limb, a shift toward more precision use of the hand, more extended positions of the elbow, and changes in habitual grip positions.

Technological shifts. What were the roughly contemporaneous patterns of change in human tool assemblages? If one takes the contrasts between Middle Paleolithic and early Upper Paleolithic assemblages as representative of the associated technological changes, several alterations appear evident. The classic flake to blade and associated side-scraper to end-scraper shifts (in frequency only) (Otte 1979; Bordes 1981, 1984a,b; Delporte 1984) suggest more emphasis on elongated tools with greater mechanical advantages. The development at this time of a polished bone technology (Klima 1963; Delporte 1968, 1984; Klein 1973; Leroy-

Prost 1974; Otte 1979) would have further enhanced this shift by providing less brittle elongated tools. Bone tools existed in the Middle Paleolithic (Martin 1907-10; Tode 1953; Gábori-Csánk 1968; Debenath and Duport 1971; Rigaud 1982), but they were expedient tools with little resemblance to those produced by Upper Paleolithic bone-working technology. Furthermore, there appears to have been a marked increase in the frequency of hafting of lithic working edges across this cultural transition (Clark 1983), probably using many of the polished bone pieces as hafts.

In this context the southern African MSA industries become interesting, since they exhibit a number of "Upper Paleolithic" features, mainly with respect to the use of blades and bone tools (Sampson 1974; Singer and Wymer 1982). Do these represent occasional insignificant occurrences of "Upper Paleolithic elements" in an otherwise Middle Paleolithic technological complex, or an indication of a significant shift in tool kits? This is particularly provocative, given the association of early modern human facial remains with MSA assemblages, at least at Klasies River Mouth (Singer and Wymer 1982).

All of the changes associated with the emergence of the Upper Paleolithic would have reduced the amount of muscular strength needed, on an habitual basis, for tool utilization. In addition, they would have influenced the habitual upper limb positions during tool use, since lithic tools for precision work, such as burins, and hafted implements require different manual positions than do hand-held side-scraper dominated assemblages. Those tools would also reduce the need for the powerful gripping with the finger tips required by large, hand-held lithic chopping and cutting tools, shifting stresses to more oblique trajectories through the carpometacarpal region (Marzke and Shackley 1986). Such precision and hafted tools would also change the habitual peak-loaded positions of both the thumb and little finger (Marzke and Shackley 1986), possibly accounting for the shifts in their carpometacarpal morphologies. Furthermore, effective throwing projectiles, such as could be made with the haftable bone and stone points associated with the early Upper Paleolithic, would emphasize a more extended position of the arm than would the thrusting spears, wooden (Jacob-Friesen 1956; Oakley et al. 1977) or with relatively thick and wide stone points, associated with the Middle Paleolithic.

Most of these contrasts become readily apparent only when the Middle Paleolithic is compared with the later Upper Paleolithic (White

1982; Straus 1983). However, there were sufficient changes in technology between the Middle Paleolithic and the earlier Upper Paleolithic, those that are commonly used to distinguish between them archaeologically, to indicate that a major change did take place around the time of the human anatomical shift of concern here. It remains to be determined what, if any, changes in technology took place within the Middle Paleolithic in regions (especially the Near East) where human upper limb changes are known to have taken place prior to Upper Paleolithic. Were there significant changes in the mechanics of utilization of those Middle Paleolithic tool assemblages which traditional techno-typological analyses (e.g., Singer and Wymer 1982; Jelinek 1982b; Marks and Kaufman 1983; Volkman 1983, Bordes 1984a,b) miss or only hint at?

Non-dietary use of the dentition. Among the Neandertals, there was also extensive use of the anterior dentition as an aid to manipulation. In the transition from Middle Pleistocene archaic humans to the Neandertals across Europe and western Asia, human populations maintained pronounced total facial projection and large anterior teeth, while their posterior teeth reduced in size and their masticatory muscle attachments (zygomatic bones and anterior mandibular ramus margins) migrated posteriorly (Trinkaus 1983a). This produced the characteristic midfacial prognathism of the Neandertals and associated distinctive facial morphology (Smith 1983a; Trinkaus 1983a, 1987a; Rak 1986).

The retention of a Middle Pleistocene level of total facial prognathism (or dental projection) was correlated with their elevated use of the anterior teeth as a vise (Smith and Paquette this volume), especially since biomechanical considerations of Neandertal facial morphology (Smith 1983a; Rak 1986; Trinkaus 1987a) show that they were habitually loading their anterior teeth. Furthermore, those large anterior teeth, containing shovel-shaped incisors, would wear down slowly, sustain high levels of bite force, especially labially directed force, and were thus adapted for extensive use. That they were so used is evident in their accelerated rate of wear relative to that on associated posterior teeth (Trinkaus 1983a), the pronounced labial rounding evident on the incisors of older Neandertals (Heim 1976; Trinkaus 1983a), and the high frequency of labiolingually oriented striae and marginal microchipping on their anterior teeth (Ryan 1980).

The large juxtamastoid eminences of the Neandertals and their predecessors reflect this non-dietary (paramasticatory) dental use, since they provide the posterior insertion for the digastric muscle, a retractor of the mandible. In addition, their lower cervical vertebral spines were large, straight and non-bifurcated (Heim 1976; Trinkaus 1983a, 1985b), indicating large neck muscles. Both of these sets of muscles would resist anteriorly directed forces on the dentition.

With the advent of modern humans across the Neandertal range, there was a loss of midfacial prognathism produced by a posterior retreat of the dentition (Stringer 1978; Trinkaus 1983a), a decrease in anterior tooth size (Frayer 1978; Trinkaus 1983a), a loss of the greater rate of wear on the anterior dentition (Matiegka 1934; McCown and Keith 1939; Jelínek 1959; Vlček 1961; Vandermeersch 1981a; Trinkaus unpub. data), the reduction of the juxtamastoid eminence (Hublin 1978; Santa Luca 1978; Trinkaus unpub. data), and a reduction in the dimensions of cervical vertebral spines (Matiegka 1938; Stewart 1962; Vandermeersch 1981a; Trinkaus unpub. data). Extensive non-dietary use of the teeth was apparently no longer required for successful adaptation.

In contrast, in Africa and eastern Asia total facial prognathism decreased during the late Middle and early Upper Pleistocene as facial robusticity reduced. There was not, evidently, sufficient selective pressure in those regions to maintain a long face. Unfortunately, anterior teeth are rarely preserved for these archaic humans, so that we cannot evaluate the degree to which they might have been used for non-dietary purposes. The only sufficiently intact specimen, Broken Hill 1, exhibits pronounced anterior dental wear and rounding similar to that of older Neandertals, but its position at the beginning of this period means that it can provide only an indication that the Middle Pleistocene African pattern was similar to that of the Neandertals.

Interestingly, the one diagnostic upper limb fossil known for these non-Neandertal archaic humans, Irhoud 4, exhibits marked shaft robustness (Hublin et al. 1987). This suggests that the manipulative behaviors of at least some of these non-Neandertal late archaic humans were similar to those of the Neandertals. The available cranial data, however, suggest that there were nonetheless levels of non-dietary use of the teeth approaching those of early modern humans among these non-Neandertal late archaic humans.

Locomotion

An an essential component of subsistence, patterns of locomotion should be closely correlated with overall adaptive patterns. Given the static nature and site orientation bias of the prehistoric record, it is difficult to infer the nature of landscape exploitation of exinct human groups. However, by combining changes in human locomotor anatomy with interpretations of the archaeological record, it may be possible to obtain a gauge of changes through time.

Locomotor functional morphology. The locomotor anatomy of the Neandertals is very similar to, although slightly less robust than, that of Middle Pleistocene humans. While having articular morphologies and orientations well within modern human ranges of variation, it exhibits features that contrast with those of early modern humans. These include more dorsally rotated ilia, large femoral heads, large and cortically thick femoral shafts that lack pilasters and have pro-ximomedial shaft swellings, large gluteal tuberosities, large and thick patellae, posteriorly displaced tibial condyles, amygdaloid and cortically thick tibial shafts, tali with large trochlea, foot proximal phalangeal shafts that are mediolaterally expanded, and low crural (tibia/femur length) indices (Endo and Kimura 1970; Trinkaus 1976a, 1980, 1981, 1983a,b, 1984a,b,c, unpub. data; Lovejoy and Trinkaus 1980; Rak and Arensburg 1987).

The morphology of their femoral and tibial shafts, and especially their cross-sectional expansion, places them at the limits of or outside of recent human ranges of variation. This robusticity is a reflexion of both strength and endurance. Their tibial shaft amygdaloid cross-sections were a means of maximizing anteroposterior bending and torsional strength, and their essentially round, non-pilastric femoral shafts were probably adapted for considerable torsional and mid-shaft mediolateral bending stress, as well as for axial compressive stress from the quadriceps femoris muscle. The Neandertal patellar and proximal tibial configura-tions increased the mechanical advantage of the quadriceps femoris muscle (through power arm enlargement), as did their low crural indices (through load arm shortening). The femoral head and talar trochlear enlargements were responses to habitually high levels of joint reaction force, and the gluteal tuberosity dimensions are one indication of the overall muscularity of their lower limbs. The pedal phalangeal shaft dimensions suggest an elevation in mediolaterally directed stress across the anterior foot.

Early modern humans across the Old World (although adequately documented primarily in Europe and western Asia) were robust but show none of this extreme postcranial muscular and cortical bone hypertrophy (Matiegka 1938; McCown and Keith 1939; Vallois and Billy 1965; Endo and Kimura 1970; Trinkaus 1976a, 1983a,b, unpub. data; Vandermeersch 1981a; Kennedy 1984a,b). In fact, the oldest known reasonably complete early modern human postcrania, those from Qafzeh and Skhul, are remarkably gracile, more so than those of European early modern humans.

Neandertal locomotor anatomy thus exhibits great strength. However, the shaft hypertrophy of their femora and tibiae also indicates an adaptation for endurance in prolonged locomotion over irregular terrain. Thick shaft cortical bone provides additional strength against both peak biomechanical loads and persistent repetitive stress, given the low resistance of bone to fatigue (Carter and Spengler 1982; Trinkaus 1987b). The level of shaft robusticity of their femora and tibiae thus suggests that they spent a significant portion of their waking hours moving continuously and/or vigorously across the landscape, far more than did early modern humans.

The wide pedal phalanges of the Neandertals indicate, along with the cross-sectional shapes of their femoral and tibial shafts, that this locomotion included considerable irregular movement, rather than the more straight-line striding usually employed by recent humans. Their endurance- and strength-related locomotion was thus also poorly directed towards points in the landscape. These shaft configurations, which were characteristic of all archaic members of the genus *Homo* (Trinkaus 1987b), disappeared with the emergence of modern humans (McCown and Keith 1939; Trinkaus 1976a, 1983a, unpub. data; Lovejoy and Trinkaus 1980; Vandermeersch 1981a; Ruff 1987), indicating a shift to predominantly unidirectional striding gaits among early modern humans.

Given the energetic expense of developing these limbs during growth (and they show up early in Neandertal development [Vlček 1973; Trinkaus 1976a, unpub. data; Heim 1982b; Tompkins and Trinkaus 1987]) and maintaining them as adults, in addition to the development and maintenance of their muscular upper limb and axial anatomies, this strength and endurance must have been a necessary component of

55

the Neandertal (and other archaic human) adaptation. Otherwise selection for more energy-efficient locomotor anatomies, combined with less developmental hypertrophy, would have led to significant reductions in this musculoskeletal robusticity prior to the emergence of early modern humans. This interpretation thus implies that the subsistence-related locomotion of these archaic humans was markedly less organized than that of more recent humans, and hence less efficient.

Three additional changes in the lower limb took place (at least in western Asia and Europe) across the transition to early modern humans. Mean limb length increased about 7% (Trinkaus 1983a), and crural indices increased about 10% (Trinkaus 1981). Both of these increase stride length and efficiency (Kuhn 1984). Pelvic morphology changed to produce a more lateral orientation of the iliac blades (Rak and Arensburg 1987), presumably making the role of the small gluteal muscles more strictly one of abduction. These combined with the loss of the lower limb hypertrophy to provide a more efficient locomotor pattern among early modern humans.

Respiration and endurance locomotion. The Neandertals possess, on the average, the largest and most projecting human skeletal nasal apertures known (Howells 1973; Stringer 1978; Trinkaus 1983a; Franciscus and Trinkaus 1988b). Even though the position and orientation of the medial maxilla along the nasal aperture was probably influenced to some extent by midfacial prognathism and associated non-dietary use of the dentition among the Neandertals (Trinkaus 1983a, 1987a; Rak 1986), the configuration of this region is primarily determined by the demands of the respiratory system and only secondarily by palatal dimensions and masticatory stresses (Chierici et al. 1973; Franciscus and Trinkaus 1988a,b).

It has long been maintained (e.g., Howell 1951; Coon 1962; Wolpoff 1980a) that this nasal configuration reflects an adaptation to Upper Pleistocene glacial climates on the part of the Neandertals. However, the large breadths of Neandertal noses are the opposite of what would be expected in a cold-adapted respiratory system, since the resultant large nares would promote body heat loss during exhalation. Their projecting nasal margins do fit the pattern of cold adaptation among modern humans. Yet that nasal projection is primarily correlated not with cold but with aridity, since the anterior projection of the external nose with its inferiorly directed nares creates turbulence in a structure below body-core temperature during exhalation, which promotes precipitation of moisture from the exhaled breath and hence conserves body moisture (Carey and Steegman 1981). The Neandertal nose, therefore, is best seen as a system for dissipating excess body heat, while retaining body moisture.

In terms of strict climatic adaptation, such a system appears to make little sense for the Neandertals, who inhabited mid-latitude temperate to cold climates. However, when combined with the evidence from the locomotor anatomy for strength plus fatigue resistance and irregular movement across the landscape, it makes more sense. In that context, it becomes a means for them to dissipate the resultant body heat, and hence prevent dangerous overheating, while minimizing moisture loss in cold, and hence arid, climates. As such it is best seen, not as an indication merely of cold adaptation, but as a physiological response to high activity levels in regions of moderate to low humidity. Neandertal noses thus support their locomotor anatomies in indicating endurance-related foraging patterns.

Late archaic crania from elsewhere with preserved nasal regions are scarce. The east Asian Mapa 1 nasal bones suggest considerable nasal projection, even though nasal breadth is unknown (Woo and Peng 1959). The north African Irhoud 1 and earlier (late Middle Pleistocene) east African Laetoli 18 and Broken Hill 1 crania show less nasal projection than the Neandertals (associated with less facial prognathism in the first two), but their lateral nasal margins are clearly everted and their nasal aperture breadths are moderate to large compared to those of most recent humans (Morant 1928; Ennouchi 1962; Howells 1973; Magori and Day 1983). Interestingly, the Broken Hill and Irhoud crania are associated with postcrania indicating the same hypertrophy evident in Neandertal limb remains and those of other Middle Pleistocene hominids (Stringer 1986a; Hublin et al. 1987; Trinkaus unpub. data).

The nasal regions of early modern humans all approach those of modern regional aboriginal populations (Matiegka 1934; McCown and Keith 1939; Vandermeersch 1981a; Singer and Wymer 1982; Stringer et al. 1984; Wolpoff et al. 1984), with regional differences in facial shape (probably influenced by climate, as are those of recent humans [Carey and Steegman 1981]). They lack the extreme breadths and projection seen in Neandertal noses, the Mapa nose and, to a lesser extent, those of African late archaic humans. This implies a shift in respiratory adaptations from one emphasizing heat loss and moisture retention during prolonged (but not necessarily very elevated) periods of locomotion to more intermittent bouts of movement across the landscape.

Land use and subsistence behavior. Attempts to deal with the question of land use by Middle Paleolithic humans have been consistent in indicating a less mobile, less organized utilization of dispersed resources than appears to have been the case in the Upper Paleolithic (Marks and Friedel 1977; Hietala and Marks 1981; Binford 1982a,b, 1984a; White 1982, 1983).

Analayses of Middle Paleolithic associated faunal remains and comparisons to those from Upper Paleolithic assemblages (e.g., Klein 1976, 1978, 1987; Spiess 1979; Binford 1982a, 1984a; Straus 1982, 1983, 1987a; Delpech 1983) imply limited predatory abilities for these archaic humans, suggesting that they were largely opportunistic hunters, taking small to medium-sized or weak game, scavenging larger game and avoiding dangerous prey. Given the apparent limitations of their technology and implications from their upper limb morphology, this should not be surprising. But, just as importantly, it suggests an absence of the planned subsistence patterns characteristic of recent hunter-gatherers and hence a high degree of minimally directed movement during the food quest. This would fit well with the accompanying strength and fatigue resistance evident in their locomotor anatomy and prolonged activity bouts implied by their upper respiratory tracts.

It remains uncertain, given the limited knowledge we have of their hunting-related technologies (wooden thrusting spears plus possibly hafted thick lithic spear points), how they might have obtained the carcasses to which they seem to have had primary access. It is possible that persistence predation, such as is known among recent hunter-gatherers (Carrier 1984), may have been their primary means of predation. The combination of endurance-related anatomies and a dearth in the archeological record of effective projectiles supports such an interpretation (Trinkaus 1987b).

It is still not clear from the archaeological record to what extent subsistence patterns, and the general organization of mobility, changed with the advent of early modern humans. The alterations in their locomotor and respiratory anatomies certainly imply a major increase in the efficiency of subsistence-related mobility patterns.

Information and social complexity

These inferences are echoed by other paleoanthropological data in indicating a significant increase in the organizational complexity of subsistence patterns with the advent of early modern humans.

Organizational complexity. Among the Neandertals or in Middle Paleolithic contexts there are examples of personal adornment (Bordes 1969; Marshack 1976; White this volume), a probable case of artificial cranial deformation (Trinkaus 1983a), and some simple scratches on bone that may or may not be intentional designs (Davis 1974; Marshack 1972b; Rigaud 1982). However, evidence of an esthetic among these archaic humans is rare and in no known case does it approach the art of the Upper Paleolithic. The art is best seen as a form of information processing (Marshack 1972b; Conkey 1978; Pfeiffer 1982; White this volume). The representational nature of much of it and the presence of notations on bone indicate that the associated humans were recording information for transferral through time and space. Its appearance and rapid elaboration at this time imply a major increase in the amount of information being communicated. Since shared information about the distribution of resources in the environment is an essential part of hunter-gatherer adaptations (Gould 1980; Binford 1982b), this suggests the appearance, for the first time in human evolution, of socially oriented, information-based adaptive systems, ones that rely far less on the energetically expensive opportunistic foraging that characterized preceding human adaptive patterns.

This shift in organizational complexity is reflected as well in the relative rates of change in technology on either side of the Upper Pleistocene transition. The technological evolutionary tempo of the Eurasian and north African Middle Paleolithic (excluding late manifestations such as the Aterian) appears to be so low as to be largely imperceptible during most of its duration from the end of the Middle Pleistocene to the middle of the last glacial. This is reflected in, among other things, the applicability of a Middle Paleolithic typology (Bordes 1961b) to geographically dispersed assemblages from throughout that time period. Sub-Saharan African MSA assemblages do not appear to show much more temporally ordered change (Sampson 1974; Singer and Wymer 1982). In contrast, Upper Paleolithic industries (de Sonneville-Bordes and Perrot 1954–6; Sampson 1974) exhibit marked typological and technological evolution during a time period of less than half the duration of the Middle Paleolithic. Clearly the rates of cultural evolution were markedly different on either side of the transition of concern.

At the same time, there are suggestions that prehistoric living floors (to the extent that we can identify them) became more internally differentiated during the transition (Klima 1963; Banesz 1968; Delporte 1968; Klein 1969; Movius 1969; Sampson 1974; Hietala and Stevens 1977; Hietala 1983; Silva et al. 1983), implying greater organization of personal space and activities. This appears to have been accompanied by greater variation in site form, size and location (Marks and Friedel 1977; Binford 1982b; White 1982; Straus 1983), which suggests more organization of activities across the landscape. And burials, one of the few reflections (along with personal ornamentation [White this volume]) we have of the complexity of social roles (Binford 1971; Saxe 1971), became more elaborate and varied (Quechon 1976; Vandermeersch 1976, 1981a; Harrold 1980). Burials of early modern humans contained, for the first time, unquestionable grave goods, and there are suggestions of differential treatment of individuals. This can only mean that the social context of behavior continued the elaborations already started among later archaic humans but experienced a major increase in complexity.

Longevity, trauma, and brains. Human biological reflections of these changes are few but suggestive. There are indications of a shift in maximum longevity. Macroscopic and osteon (histomorphometric) aging of the oldest known Neandertals (Trinkaus and Thompson 1987) provide age estimates in the high 30s to mid 40s. In contrast, the oldest early modern humans exhibit greater dental wear despite an apparently slower rate of attrition, suggesting increased longevity at least into the sixth decade (Smith 1977; Skinner 1981). If this interpretation of an increase in maximum age at death can be substantiated, it would indicate the appearance among early modern humans, for the first time in human evolution, of significant post-reproductive survival. That would indicate an increase in the trans-generational communication of information about variability of resources in the environment. It would also imply increased grandparenting and associated reductions in orphaning and of the subsistence work load per adult (Howell 1982).

There appears to have been a decrease in the level of risk of trauma, since all older, reasonably complete Neandertals exhibit evidence of antemortem trauma (Schaefer 1957; Trinkaus 1983a, 1985b, unpub. data). Similar trauma is less frequent among comparably aged early modern humans. Both groups could keep injured individuals alive for major portions of their lives, but early modern humans apparently developed means of reducing risk.

There was also a shift in neurocranial shape with the emergence of modern humans (Stringer 1978; Trinkaus 1983a), a change from predominantly long and low neurocrania usually with large occipital buns to predominantly higher and rounded ones lacking or having small occipital buns. This indicates an acceleration of early postnatal brain growth relative to cranial vault growth (Trinkaus and LeMay 1982). If ossification rates remained the same, this would imply an increased rate of early brain growth among modern humans, possibly as a product of greater environmental, including social, stimulation during early development.

Although mostly indirect, the above biological and cultural changes imply a major shift in social complexity and information processing levels across this biocultural transition. They can only have been linked in feedback relationships with the contemporaneous changes in manipulative and locomotor behaviour.

Environmental buffering

For physiologically tropical primates living in cold-temperate as well as tropical regions, any increased cultural protection from thermal stress would reduce the energetic cost of survival. Since any mammalian species as widely dispersed as Upper Pleistocene humans would be expected to exhibit eco-geographical patterning of features sensitive to thermal stress, what becomes important is not whether there is evidence of "cold adaptation" in higher-latitude groups, but whether any pattern evident in late archaic humans is more pronounced than among modern humans and hence indicates less cultural buffering.

There have been many attempts to find evidence of anatomical responses to thermal stress in the Neandertals (e.g., Howell 1951; Coon 1962; Badoux 1965; Musgrave 1971; Wolpoff 1980a; Beals et al. 1984). Only their tendency to have short distal limb segments (low brachial and crural indices, similar to those of modern arctic peoples) in both Europe and the Near East indicates a form of biological cold adaptation

(Trinkaus 1981). Given the glacial climate of Europe during the time period sampled by Neandertal partial skeletons, this is not surprising. It is primarily the low brachial and crural indices of the Near Eastern Neandertals, living in slightly more temperate zones, that indicates a minor deviation from expected eco-geographical patterning. Does it represent less thermal protection among these archaic humans or evidence of significant gene flow from Neandertal populations to the north and west? Interestingly, early modern humans from the same region show high brachial and crural indices (Trinkaus 1983a), suggesting both some equatorial ancestry and an increase in their abilities to protect themselves behaviorally from cold stress, presumably through improved pyrotechnology, shelters and clothing. However, as mentioned above, these limb segment proportion changes also had biomechanical consequences for manipulation and locomotion, and the relative contributions of biomechanical versus thermal considerations cannot be easily determined.

The limb segment proportions of equatorial late archaic and early modern humans are not known, even though the very long tibia from Broken Hill suggests that that individual either had a high crural index or was extremely tall, similar to European and Near Eastern early modern human males (Stringer this volume). Either would indicate an adaptation primarily to heat stress, not surprising for an individual from a tropical region. It thus appears probable that geographical patterns in limb segment proportions generally similar to those of modern humans existed among late archaic humans. It was only with the advent of early modern humans into the northwestern Old World that there was a significant disruption of this eco-geographical pattern, suggesting more of an elevation in levels of gene flow than a shift in cold adaptation patterns. Yet, the persistence of equatorial limb segment proportions through the European Upper Paleolithic (Trinkaus 1981) indicates that thermal stresses on those early modern human populations were not very intense.

The large and projecting noses of the Neandertals may indicate some influence of cold stress, through the associated aridity, relative to more equatorial late archaic humans (see above). However, the primary adaptive significance of those prominent noses is related to activity levels and the associated requirements for excess heat loss and moisture retention, and not to adaptation to cold. And, more importantly, the geographical patterning in nasal dimensions and projection among late archaic humans appears to be no more pronounced than among recent humans.

Interestingly, human pyrotechnology increased, at least in Europe and possibly in southern Africa (Singer and Wymer 1982), around the time of this evolutionary transition. Primarily, hearths, on the average, shifted from being thermally inefficient shallow depressions or flat surfaces that would radiate little heat (Gábori-Csánk 1968; Bordes 1971; Debenath 1973; Klein 1973; Perlès 1976) to variable forms of hearths including thermally more effective structures such as stone-lined pits that would conserve heat for extended periods of time (Movius 1966; Bánesz 1968; Delporte 1968; Perlès 1976, 1977) (the latter would also cook food more effectively, which may be related to the associated changes in facial morphology and manipulation). These more elaborate hearths are frequently associated with larger and more complex structures (Klíma 1963; Bánesz 1968; Klein 1969), which would also provide increased thermal protection. In addition, it is at this time in human evolution that people first inhabited the rich but harsh arctic regions of Eurasia (Klein 1973, 1985), implying that it was only then that they had sufficient thermal protection to survive there.

DISCUSSION

This review of paleontological and archaeological changes associated with the Upper Pleistocene transition emphasizes the behavioral shifts that took place. As with any evolutionary transition, there was indeed stasis and continuity in portions of human biology and behavior. Yet, the overall picture is one in which all of the major human behavioral complexes for which we have evidence experienced significant change. Furthermore, it is likely that the observed changes were closely interwoven adaptively and that many of them were due to the combined selective pressures of multiple behavioral complexes.

It is thus increasingly apparent that there was a major shift in human biology and behavior during the Upper Pleistocene. It was geographically variable in its nature and tempo, even though the extent of that variation is poorly known. Furthermore, it was apparently only during this time period that many of the components of the biobehavioral complex that we associate with modern human hunter-gatherers emerged. Their selective value seems to have been, not surprisingly, to enable humans to exploit available resources more efficiently with greater reliance on technology and organization, and less on human biology, than was possible for their archaic human predecessors. The consequences of this were multiple and led, directly and indirectly, to a rapidly accelerating rate of cultural evolution and further reductions in human reliance on direct anatomical adaptations for survival.

Despite the overwhelming evidence that it was only during, or at the end of, this Upper Pleistocene transition that an adaptive pattern similar to those of recent human hunter-gatherers emerged, the nature of the processes involved remains unclear. Most of the human paleontological and archaeological evidence is still derived from western Asian and European sites, with only hints (some very suggestive) as to what was happening in Africa and eastern Asia. This is important, not because the Neandertals are unrepresentative of late archaic humans (except for some aspects of facial morphology and basicranial morphology, plus limb segment proportions, they *are* representative of those late archaic humans), but because the Upper Pleistocene transition in Europe and, to a lesser extent, in western Asia, appears to have occurred relatively late and rapidly compared to other regions of the Old World. The changes there may therefore appear more dramatic and synchronous than elsewhere. This is not important if we are primarily comparing human adaptive patterns before and after the Upper Pleistocene transition, but it becomes crucial if we are to understand the processes of interaction between various components of the human adaptive system, both within and between the biological and cultural spheres, during this time period.

Yet, despite these limitations, a general pattern emerges from the above discussion of Upper Pleistocene human evolution, at least for the western Old World. The transition appears to have begun in sub-Saharan Africa during the earlier Upper Pleistocene, perhaps during the last interglacial but more likely toward the end of that interglacial or the beginning of the last glacial. It involved, to the extent determinable, a gradual and continuous emergence of early modern humans and "Upper Paleolithic" archaeological elements. However, the faunal evidence and the essentially "Middle Paleolithic" nature of the technology suggests that different elements of what we identify as "Upper Paleolithic" emerged at different times over much of the early last glacial. Aspects of this behavioral complex, both biological and cultural, appear to have spread throughout much of sub-Saharan Africa and subsequently beyond.

64

The transition across north Africa exhibits considerable local continuity, both biological and cultural, suggesting that external influence was minor but not necessarily insignificant. In western Asia it appears considerably more complex, with probable influences from both Africa to the southwest and Europe to the north and west creating at least a human biological mixture through the corridors of that region. Did the biological shift there involve an oscillating boundary between early modern humans and Neandertals (whether those Neandertals were of local or European origin) throughout much of the early last glacial, or was there merely a relatively late (post 50 kyr) genetic absorption of the Neandertals by early modern humans of north African origin? Only better chronological control will resolve that issue. Yet, it appears curious that the archaeological record (primarily lithic remains) of that region shows little of the behavioral shift indicated by the anatomies of the associated hominids (Bar-Yosef this volume), even less than is implied by the sub-Saharan African MSA. It is very possible that the abundance of high-quality lithic raw material in the Levant removed the need for a significant shift in lithic exploitation strategies at the time of the human biologically documented behavioral shift, whereas in areas with lower-quality and/or less abundant lithic raw material, such as sub-Saharan Africa and central Europe, the implied behavioral shift appears to have been more immediately reflected in our one abundantly preserved reflection of human behavior, stone tools.

In Europe and Asia from the Alps to Soviet Central Asia, there were major, relatively short-term changes in behavior. Despite the apparent slight chronological precedence of the human biological changes over (at least some of) the cultural changes, the changes across that region seem to be best characterized as a complex mixture of gene flow/diffusion from the south and east with considerable local continuity of populations. Western Europe, as a geographical cul-de-sac, stands out relative to the rest of the western Old World, in the lateness of the transition, its rapidity, and the essentially fully developed modern human nature of the emerging hunter-gatherer adaptation. It may well be that by the time the transition took place in that region, most of the primary elements of the transition had taken place elsewhere, the different core aspects of a modern human hunter-gatherer adaptation had coalesced, and the contrasts between the human populations spreading westward from central Europe and the resident Neandertals were sufficient to lead primarily to replacement through competition rather than the gradual blending and reorganization of elements apparent elsewhere.

CONCLUSION

Regardless of the actual phylogenetic and cultural historical processes involved in this transition, it remains evident that this Upper Pleistocene transition was a major one in the human evolution. Many of the elements of modern human behavior and biology had evolved from more archaic forms previously. But it was only during this period, whether gradually or abruptly, whether synchronously or at different times during the Upper Pleistocene, whether in corridors or in cul-de-sacs, that the essential elements of a modern human hunter-gatherer system emerged. By the end of the transitional period all of these elements had coalesced, in representation and organization, into a human adaptive system that was qualitatively, as well as quantitatively, different from that which preceded the Upper Pleistocene transition.

Acknowledgements

I would like to thank the many paleoanthropological colleagues who have helped me, directly or indirectly, to formulate the ideas expressed in this paper. My gratitude also goes to the many curators of Pleistocene paleontological and archaeological remains who have kindly permitted me to examine materials in their care. This research has been supported, in part, by the Wenner-Gren Foundation, the National Science Foundation, the L.S.B. Leakey Foundation, the University of Pennsylvania, Harvard University, the University of New Mexico, and the Centre National de la Recherche Scientifique.

4

Documenting the origin of modern humans

C. B. STRINGER.

In the last few years there has been a revival of interest in studying the later stages of human evolution, concentrating on the origin of modern *Homo sapiens* (e.g. Smith and Spencer 1984). However, we are not yet close to a consensus concerning the processes which led to the emergence of modern *H. sapiens* (this term used hereafter in the sense of Stringer et al. 1984), and the division of opinion which Howells (1976) distinguished as the "Noah's Ark" and "Neanderthal phase" models still persists. Adherents of the former model believe there was a single, relatively recent origin for all present-day human variation, and that the founder population gave rise to all living humans by a phased dispersal, replacing indigenous archaic (used here to mean non-modern) populations. No continuity with archaic populations would be expected except in the area of evolutionary origin of modern humans, provided there was little or no gene flow between archaic and modern groups. This model would retrodict evolutionary (and behavioural?) discontinuities in many parts of the Old World where an interface existed between endemic archaics and dispersing early moderns. The idea of a single time and place of origin also carries with it the implication that the origin was a unique event which occurred only once under one set of circumstances.

At its most extreme the Neanderthal phase model retrodicts the independent, parallel evolution of modern humans from distinct archaic populations (Weidenreich 1947a; Coon 1962). Thus while the Noah's Ark model explains "racial" features as local and fairly recent superimpositions on an already existing modern anatomy, the Neanderthal phase model would retrodict that "racial" features could have evolved in concert with, or earlier than, the features which characterise all living humans. The former model gives modern human variation a Late Pleistocene origin, while the latter model inevitably takes such variation well back into the Middle Pleistocene. However, both models can be modified to allow for the effects of gene flow between distinct populations. In the Noah's Ark model this can be evoked to explain features of local continuity (Stringer et al. 1984; Bräuer 1984a, b), while in the Neanderthal phase model it may be invoked to explain features of discontinuity, as well as the lack of evolutionary divergence between local lineages (Wolpoff et al. 1984; Trinkaus 1986 and this volume). In models involving both local evolution and gene flow, there must be a balancing effect between local evolutionary changes (leading to increased diversity) and gene flow (leading to increased uniformity).

There are various research strategies which can be adopted to provide data relevant to the origin of modern humans. These include studies of present-day human variation, such as genetic data, which can be used to attempt to reconstruct past events such as dispersals. The physical remains of early humans themselves can provide direct data on the timing of evolutionary events, providing the material can be interpreted unambiguously (a rarer event than we might hope) and dated accurately (although likely to be disputed in more cases than we might like). Ideally such material can be assessed for the presence or absence of features characterising archaic and modern inhabitants of particular areas, to see whether it is consistent with a model of continuity or discontinuity. Gradual local evolutionary establishment of "modern" characters would be consistent with the Neanderthal phase model, as would the presence of actual mosaic fossils which straddle the morphological divide between archaic and modern humans. However, such features would also characterise a model involving gene flow from a neighbouring more modern population, and it would be difficult to distinguish these from the fossil record alone. But in this case the presence of such a neighbouring population, if it existed, should be demonstrable from fossil remains (Smith 1985). Finally, the archaeological record is of vital importance for documenting continuity or change in behavioural patterns associated with the emergence of modern humans, and for providing evidence of possible interactions or decoupling between biological and behavioural changes.

Documenting the presence of modern characteristics in fossil hominids and the way in which they may have been established (i.e. by local evolution, gene flow and/or replacement) does not, of course, explain the mode of origin of those characteristics, which has traditionally been examined in terms of their functional or selective value. However, as with other living organisms, processes of founder effect, bottlenecking, drift, sexual selection, exaptation (Gould and Vrba 1982) and the non-adaptive (or neutral) consequences of changes in patterns of growth or behaviour may also have been involved. Behavioural factors could well have been of critical importance, but it remains difficult to account for the origin of modern humans in a universal way when the evidence for biological and behavioural change has to be drawn primarily from the western Eurasian Neanderthal/"Cro-Magnon" and Mousterian/Upper Palaeolithic interfaces, with a further inevitable concentration on western European events. Even where useful data from other areas exist, they do not always get the attention they deserve, and therefore there is much room for speculation about the singularity or generality of Eurasian biological and behavioural patterns.

Therefore I first intend to review the fossil data from each area, beginning with the European material, and then examine critically some of the models proposed to account for observed patterns of difference and change, including behavioural ones. Chronological considerations inevitably loom large in any discussion of possible evolutionary patterns, so it will be necessary to discuss the dating of certain critical sites in some detail, as well as reporting on cultural associations. I shall not attempt to interpret the archaeological record, since this is being discussed elsewhere in this volume by those more competent to do so. However, I will attempt to highlight areas where those working on the fossil record would welcome informed archaeological comment. Finally, I will summarise what I believe the fossil record indicates about the evolution of modern *H. sapiens*, and attempt to integrate this with genetic and behavioural data.

THE FOSSIL RECORD

Europe

Between about 300 and 35 kyr ago, this area appears to record the relatively gradual development and establishment of the Neanderthal anatomical pattern (Wolpoff 1980a; Hublin 1982; Cook et al. 1982; Stringer et al. 1984; Stringer 1985; Vandermeersch 1985). The area can be conveniently divided into a western component, which has a reasonable Neanderthal but a poor early modern sample, and a central and eastern component, which has (or had, until the destruction of a number of specimens during World War II) a good sample of early moderns, but a relatively poor sample of Neanderthals (compare Stringer et al. 1984 and Smith 1984). The vagaries of preservation, study, and publication have therefore conspired to produce a rather unbalanced view of Neanderthal–modern relationships in Europe. While the western record appears to show little evidence of continuity (e.g. comparing the Neanderthals of La Chapelle-aux-Saints, La Ferrassie and Saint-Césaire with the contrasting Cro-Magnon 1-2, Engis and Grotte des Enfants specimens), that of central and eastern Europe does show evidence of possible continuity (e.g. comparing the Šala and Vindija Neanderthal with the robust Mladeč, Pavlov and Předmostí specimens). The timing of the transition (to use a fairly neutral term for the present) between Neanderthals and modern *H. sapiens* lies on present evidence before 34 kyr in eastern Europe (based on the radiocarbon date of *c.* 34 kyr for an Aurignacian level above that of the modern Velika Pećina frontal bone–Smith 1984). However, the timing of the transition in western Europe is uncertain from the fossil evidence alone, since the best-preserved and associated modern hominids may date from the later Aurignacian (*c.* 28–30 kyr?) rather than from the earliest manifestations of that industry (*c.* 35 kyr?). Furthermore, the Saint-Césaire Neanderthal probably also comes within the time range of the Aurignacian, given its Châtelperronian association and the reported contemporaneity of these industries (Lévèque and Vandermeersch 1981; Leroyer and Leroi-Gourhan 1983; Leroi-Gourhan 1984; Stringer et al. 1984).

The assumption that all Aurignacian-associated hominids represent modern *H. sapiens* seems reasonable from present evidence, although clarification of a possible Neanderthal–Aurignacian association at Vindija (Smith 1984) is needed. However, if this assumption is correct, it is then possible to envisage a diffusion of Aurignacian-associated modern humans from east to wᶒst over a relatively short period, although the origin of the Aurignacian is not as clear as that of the Châtelperronian, which is believed to have derived locally from the Mousterian of Acheulian tradition or the typical Mousterian (Harrold 1983; Rigaud this volume). The roots of the Aurignacian may lie in an industry like that known from layer 11 of the Bacho Kiro cave, and dated at more than 43 kyr by radiocarbon (Kozłowski 1982). But for all its Upper Palaeolithic aspects, this industry seems to lack evidence of the bone-working technology which characterises later Aurignacian levels at the site and throughout Europe (White this volume), although it is interesting to note that an incised bone of Upper Palaeolithic type was reported from an underlying Mousterian level at Bacho Kiro (Marshack 1982).

For me, the European record is ambivalent and even contradictory if we compare the eastern and western records. The fragmentary Vindija Neanderthals from Yugoslavia do display a reduced robusticity and midfacial prognathism (as judged from the mandibles), while the more complete French Saint-Césaire Neanderthal seems little different from earlier specimens and can only indicate stasis rather than progressive change in some Neanderthal populations, even in ones which had developed or adopted some aspects of Upper Palaeolithic technologies. My preference is to emphasise the discontinuity of the western European record and to note the contrast between the establishment of Neanderthal characters over a period of more than 200 kyr, and their disappearance in about 5 percent of that time span. I do not recognise the existence of morphological intermediates during this period and believe that the Hahnöfersand frontal bone is more likely to represent a robust modern than a hybrid or transitional form. Additionally, its dating must be considered dubious until details of determinations are made public or further samples can be obtained for accelerator dating. Similarly, specimens such as the Šala frontal and the Vindija G3 fossils are best considered as gracile Neanderthals rather than as transitional forms, while those from Vindija G1 remain of uncertain status (Smith 1984; Stringer et al. 1984).

While I prefer to generalise from the western European evidence of discontinuity, others prefer to generalise from the signs of cranial continuity present in the eastern European or western Asian records (Smith 1984, this volume; Trinkaus 1984a; Wolpoff this volume).

However, such features of continuity may not extend into postcranial morphology, where a consistent Neanderthal/modern dichotomy exists (Trinkaus 1983a, b; but compare Wolpoff this volume) and where an equatorial ancestry for Eurasian early modern *H. sapiens* may be indicated by limb proportions (Trinkaus 1981). Additionally, some of the evidence for cranial or dental continuity can be questioned, although I have certainly been too strident in dismissing it (Stringer 1982). Apparent evolutionary trends in some features can be demonstrated, but they do not prove continuity. It remains true that on the best data yet assembled (Frayer 1984) only a weak case can be made for unilinear evolutionary trends in dental size reduction in Europe. Whereas 68 percent of changes for Early–Middle–Late Upper Palaeolithic dental dimensions fit a consistent trend, only 35 percent of late Mousterian–EUP–MUP do so, and this poor performance of the Neanderthals as potential ancestors can readily be bettered by using data for Qafzeh (Vandermeersch 1981a; Tillier 1984) instead, giving 58 percent of dental changes in sequence for Qafzeh–EUP–MUP (but compare Wolpoff this volume). This certainly does not identify the Qafzeh specimens as the real ancestors, but it does show up the fragility of such studies of evolutionary change, which are further compromised by the lack of clear dental trends in western Asian Neanderthal and early modern samples (Trinkaus 1983a). Finally, it is important to note that where the early modern specimens *do* differ from living humans (e.g. in general cranial robusticity and in facial shape and proportions), these differences appear to reflect primitive retentions, some of which had been retained by Neanderthals, while others had certainly been lost by them.

I believe that population replacement was the norm in Europe, rather than the exception, and that if Neanderthal genes did enter the modern gene pool, their effect on morphology was brief and localised. If this were not so, we would expect even recent Europeans to show an enhanced frequency of local Neanderthal-specific characters such as midfacial prognathism, retromolar space development, H-O mandibular foramen pattern and the presence of occipitomastoid traits (curvature of occipital plane, presence of suprainiac fossa, relatively large occipitomastoid crest), all of which were presumably under some degree of genetic control. However, in my opinion, based on numerous unpublished observations, this does not appear to be the case, since such features can be found at only low frequencies, distributed in various recent populations throughout the world rather than concentrated in Europe. Another factor which is difficult to explain if recent Europeans are even partly descended from Neanderthals, who apparently had a long-term adaptation to temperate/boreal environments (Trinkaus 1986 and this volume; Wolpoff this volume), is why Europeans show poor physiological adaptations to cold conditions. The physiological adaptations of Europeans are no better than those of aboriginal populations elsewhere in the world (e.g. Australia and the Americas), who probably arrived in their present temperate environments within the last 40 kyr (e.g. Mount 1979).

Western Asia

Since this area is discussed in detail elsewhere (Bar-Yosef this volume), I will merely focus on a few of what I consider to be the outstanding issues. First, what was the nature of the late Middle Pleistocene human population? Was it merely primitive or was it already early Neanderthal (Trinkaus 1984a) or early modern *H. sapiens* (Vandermeersch 1981b)? Secondly, what was the date of the earliest interface or transition between Neanderthal and modern humans in the area? Centering on the dating of the Qafzeh sample (Bar-Yosef and Vandermeersch 1981; Bar-Yosef this volume; Valladas et al. 1988), did this interface occur at more than 65 kyr, making the Qafzeh sample of comparable age to claimed early occurrences of modern *H. sapiens* in Africa, or does the Qafzeh sample perhaps date closer to the Skhūl sample at around 40–45 kyr? This would produce a parallel with the European situation, but the Neanderthal/modern *H. sapiens* interface or transition would be earlier than that of Europe and would have occurred against a Middle Palaeolithic background (Stringer et al. 1984; Trinkaus 1984a). Thirdly, does the fossil record indicate at least some degree of *in situ* evolution of modern humans from Neanderthal ancestors (Trinkaus 1984a), or was replacement more important (Vandermeersch 1981a; Stringer et al. 1984)? Fourthly, both for those who believe in replacement and for those who believe that behavioural changes were instrumental in the evolution of modern *H. sapiens*, where is there evidence for significant behavioural changes within the Middle Palaeolithic record of the area? Fifthly, is there evidence here for the origin of other Eurasian and Australasian modern peoples, as would be expected given an original North African dispersal via this area?

73

The Far East

Interpretations of the Far Eastern hominid record have tended to be framed in terms of local continuity (e.g. Weidenreich 1947a; Coon 1962; Wolpoff 1980a), and this view has been especially favoured by Chinese workers (Wu and Olsen 1985). The Indonesian fossil record can be seen as leading from Early–Middle Pleistocene *H. erectus* through the (probably) late Middle Pleistocene Ngandong specimens to the late Pleistocene Wadjak and Australian modern *H. sapiens* material. Similarly, the predominantly Middle Pleistocene Chinese *H. erectus* fossils can be seen as evolving through forms like the late Middle–early Late Pleistocene Dali and Maba crania into Late Pleistocene modern *H. sapiens* groups as represented by the Zhoukoudian Upper Cave and Liujiang fossils. However, there is an essential similarity between the *H. erectus* fossils of China and Indonesia which allows them to be distinguished from approximately contemporaneous material from Europe and Africa, and in terms of conventional classification, it is likely that some "archaic *H. sapiens*" fossils existed in Africa and Europe during at least part of the time period covered by the Zhoukoudian Lower Cave, Hexian and Ngandong fossils (Santa Luca 1980; Cook et al. 1982; Stringer 1984c, 1985). Furthermore, it is by no means certain that the fossils do indeed form a continuous morphological sequence from local *H. erectus* to modern *H. sapiens* forms. The Dali cranium can be related to "archaic *H. sapiens*" fossils from Europe and Africa as easily as to preceding Chinese *H. erectus* fossils and, if it is correctly dated, the Yinkou partial skeleton is likely to undermine further the concept of gradual *in situ* evolutionary change in China (Wu Rukang 1986). This specimen has a provisional absolute date of 280 kyr, supported by faunal correlations, yet the reconstructed cranium bears more resemblance to African and European Middle Pleistocene specimens generally assigned to "archaic *H. sapiens*" than it does to the late Zhoukoudian *H. erectus* fossils which it apparently approximates in age.

The recognition of great variation in the Pleistocene *H. sapiens* fossils of Australia has also created difficulties for a simple unilinear evolutionary scheme, and this has led to the suggestion that the continent was populated by two groups with distinct evolutionary origins, which coexisted for a long period in the late Pleistocene (Wolpoff et al. 1984). One, represented by the robust Talgai, Cohuna and Kow Swamp specimens, was derived from Indonesian *H.erectus* by way of population such as Ngandong, while the other, represented by the gracile Mungo and Keilor fossils, is seen as of mainland Asian origin, traceable ultimately to the lineage of Chinese *H.erectus*. However, the Noah's Ark model can still be invoked for the Far East (Howells 1983; Stringer et al. 1984), and the Asian and Australian records can be seen as recording the appearance of modern *H. sapiens* of a fundamentally similar type to that found in Europe at about the same age (*c*. 30 kyr for the Cro-Magnon and Mungo specimens).

Although the Zhoukoudian Upper Cave specimens have recently been considered to be related to modern Chinese populations (Wolpoff et al. 1984), Weidenreich himself was unsure of this, and it is possible that they relate instead to the early Mongoloid radiation which produced the Amerindians. Although Amerindians are undoubtedly physically and genetically closely related to Asian populations, Amerindian crania can be considered as less differentiated and superficially more similar to those of Europeans. It is therefore of interest that discriminant functions, which can successfully assign recent crania to their correct population in over 90 percent of cases, classify the only Zhoukoudian skull which could be tested (101) as an "Amerindian" or "Northern European" specimen rather than as Asian (Howells 1983). Perhaps these crania form part of a modern *H. sapiens* radiation into the area similar to that which occurred in Europe. Thus it can still be argued (as in Wolpoff 1980a) that populations of Asian Mongoloid type (such as Liujiang) did not evolve until after this time, which matches the retrodiction of the Noah's Ark model, and can be further supported from the preliminary results of dental analyses conducted by C.G. Turner (1984). However, a much better resolution of chronology for the available specimens is required, which might now be possible with the advent of accelerator dating.

The origin of Australian populations could also readily be viewed as part of a radiation of modern forms into the area by 30 kyr ago, were it not for the great variability of late Pleistocene specimens already mentioned. This view of great variability was challenged by Macintosh and Larnach (1976) before many of the specimens had been studied in detail, but more recently Kennedy (1984a) has demonstrated from femoral morphology that the robust Kow Swamp cranial form is not reflected in their postcrania, which appear to be of modern, even somewhat gracile type. Habgood (1986) has also challenged the dual origin model for Australia, since he finds from multivariate analyses that the Australian robust and gracile groups cluster together before uniting with Asian Pleistocene crania. However, he does accept an ultimate Indonesian origin for all the Australian material from a founding population which arrived prior to 40 kyr, and which may be represented by the Willandra Lakes 50 calvarium. This undated specimen, more than any other yet found, appears to support the model of independent local evolution of *H. sapiens* from an archaic Ngandong-like ancestor. In terms of evolutionary grade it appears similar to African specimens like Irhoud 2 or Ngaloba (Delson 1985), which lie at the furthest fringes of, or even outside of, the modern human range. If the specimen is ancient (>30 kyr?), it would conclusively demonstrate that high variability has been a part of the Australian fossil record virtually from the beginning, rather than something which developed after the arrival of a gracile Mungo-like ancestral population (Stringer et al. 1984). If it is younger, this latter scenario might still be possible, although the redevelopment of "archaic" cranial characters would need to be explained. As it stands, the specimen gives us hints that Indonesian hominids evolved "modern" characters locally or acquired them through gene flow, in line with the model of Wolpoff et al. (1984), or at least that founding populations in the area were more archaic than other early modern humans so far known from Eurasia.

However, there are still other questions to be answered concerning Australasian human evolution. One concerns the mechanism by which two distinct populations were able to remain separate for long periods of time in Australia. Are there archaeological data to support such a scheme? Secondly, does the morphology of the (presumed) late Pleistocene Wadjak material show continuity with preceding Indonesian fossils? I doubt this very much. Thirdly, to what extent are supposed features of local continuity between early Australians and more ancient Indonesians genuine evidence of continuity or evidence of a morphology retained in the Australians from robust non-local *sapiens* ancestors? Large and prognathic faces with large teeth are to be found in the Skhūl–Qafzeh sample as well, although it must be admitted that the frontal morphologies of the groups are quite different. The view that early Australian crania might merely represent morphologically primitive examples of modern *H. sapiens* was espoused by Larnach and Macintosh in 1976. One of these workers had previously spoken of aboriginal Australians showing the "mark of Java" but by 1976 they had reversed their opinions, and considered it "extremely unlikely" that the Ngandong specimens 'could be ancestral to Australians. Furthermore, they considered that there was no special relationship between Indonesian *H. erectus* and Australians. Instead they suggested that the Australians were perhaps "the earliest examples of an evolving generalised modern *H. sapiens sapiens* to arrive in their ultimate area of migration. This hypothesis would also explain why [they] have retained a moderately higher frequency of *Homo erectus* traits than other modern *sapiens* groups" (Macintosh and Larnach 1976:124).

Africa

The African later Pleistocene fossil and archaeological records have tended to be overshadowed by those of Europe, which have seemed superior in their relative completeness, better chronological control, and easier access for study. However, work conducted during the past 20 years has dramatically changed this picture, and a number of African sites now assume global importance in discussions about the origin of modern humans and their behaviour, and I will review some of the evidence from these sites below.

The southern African Klasies River Mouth complex of caves and rock shelters was first excavated systematically during two field seasons conducted between 1966 and 1968, but only recently published in detail (Singer and Wymer 1982). Further research on these sites is in progress (Deacon 1985 and pers. comm.; Deacon et al. 1986; Hendey and Volman 1986). The sites contain sediments deposited during the Late Pleistocene, with an associated faunal and archaeological record covering periods of Middle Stone Age (MSA) and Later Stone Age (LSA) occupation. Klein (references summarised in Klein 1983b) has published detailed analyses of the large mammal faunas from the sites, which lead him to regard the hunting and exploitative abilities of the MSA inhabitants as distinctly inferior to those of the LSA peoples who succeeded them. For example, while they were probably able to obtain eland of prime age by driving them, they were poor at obtaining other ungulates of prime age by hunting. However, Binford (1984a) has proposed a different taphonomic interpretation of the Klasies ungulate material which is even less flattering for the hunting abilities of the MSA inhabitants. He has suggested that in general they were able to hunt only smaller game and mainly had to scavenge the remains of larger animals, including eland. Faunal seriation indicates a trend towards increased hunting up the sequence. This interpretation has in turn been questioned by Scott (1986) and Klein (1986). For an understanding of MSA hunting and foraging patterns and how these can be reconstructed from site data, this discussion is an important one, but for the purposes of this chapter it is more important to note that Klein (1983b) and Binford (1984a) are agreed about the inferiority of MSA hunting abilities compared to those of the LSA.

Considering the above conclusions regarding MSA exploitative abilities, it is, of course, interesting to note that fragmentary fossil remains attributed to modern *H. sapiens* have been recovered from MSA levels at Klasies (Singer and Wymer 1982; Rightmire 1984; Bräuer 1984a). However, Binford (1984a) has also questioned the stratigraphic interpretations of Singer and Wymer, and this is relevant to the dating of the human remains, which are otherwise believed to date between 60 and 120 kyr. He has suggested that the finds which derive from layer 14 of cave 1 are not of relatively early MSA antiquity, but instead are of approximately the same age as the Howieson's Poort (HP) material of shelter 1A, which in his view approximates in age the Upper Palaeolithic of Europe. In addition, he has proposed that layer 10 of shelter 1B (which contains a "modern" mandible) has been wrongly correlated with early MSA deposits, and instead probably falls in age between the HP and late MSA deposits of shelter 1A. From Binford's arguments, many of the supposedly early but modern-looking specimens in fact date from a time close to the Middle/Upper Palaeolithic transition in the area, which would make them approximately contemporaneous with the appearance of modern people in many other areas. However, the rather robust mandible 21776 and the modern-looking frontal fragment 16425, which derive respectively from layers 17 and 16 of the MSA of cave 1, appear unaffected by his arguments.

Not surprisingly, Binford's views on the stratigraphy and correlation of deposits at Klasies have been challenged by the original excavators (Singer and Wymer 1986), as well as by those currently conducting further excavations at the sites in order to clarify problems relating to the previous work (Deacon 1985, pers.comm.; Deacon et al. 1986). Singer and Wymer (1986) reiterated the bases for their conclusions, but in a detailed reply Binford (1986b) has maintained his position regarding the dating of the Klasies sequences.

Recent excavations at Klasies have been designed specifically to check on a number of aspects of the previous work (Deacon pers.comm.), and so far much of the basic stratigraphic and dating frameworks of Singer and Wymer (1982) appear to be holding up under this investigation. A beach of probable oxygen isotope stage 5e age (*c.* 116–127 kyr [CLIMAP 1984]) is preserved in cave 1, but underlies the main MSA sequence and associated hominids (Hendey and Volman 1986; Deacon et al. 1986). Uranium series ages of 98 and 110 kyr date a layer between layers 38 and 14 of Singer and Wymer's sequence, and provide a minimum age for the early MSA sequence and a maximum age for most of the hominid sample. Current estimates for the top of the 1B MSA sequence (and "modern" mandible) centre around 90 kyr, while the major regression recorded in the upper part of the 15-metre thick shelter 1A sequence probably relates to either isotope stage 4 (*c.* 50–70 kyr) or 5b (*c.* 85 kyr). This regression had marked environmental effects and may be reflected in the appearance of the HP substage of the MSA, with a switch from exploitation of coastal resources (including shellfish) to a terrestrial economy, indicated by carbonised plant food residues. While recent excavations have so far supported the basic stratigraphic conclusions of previous work, only one further significant hominid fragment has been recovered. However, it is the oldest yet recorded from the site, since it derives from an equivalent of Singer and Wymer's layer 38, and is therefore likely to be *c.* 110 ky in age. It is an edentulous robust maxilla which appears to have been burnt. Deacon (pers.comm.) suggests that there was either a very variable human population, or there was rapid modernisation, in the period 110–90 kyr at Klasies.

In my opinion the hominid material from Klasies is both *in situ* in MSA levels, as far as can be determined at present, and likely to be older than 70 kyr. There are enough specimens recovered from different areas of the sites and from different beds to discount the possibility of their all being intrusive. Moreover, the stratigraphy appears better established than in many Eurasian sites of comparable age. If this is the case, what do the hominid fossils demonstrate in evolutionary terms? Given their fragmentary nature, this is a difficult question, but the likelihood is that they represent a population at least bordering on the modern anatomical pattern in a manner not demonstrable from the Eurasian fossil record of this time (assuming that the Qafzeh fossils are younger than 70 kyr). However, caution is necessary, as we cannot discern the overall cranial morphology beyond indications of a gracile supraorbital region, a fairly large but flat face, a relatively short and sometimes robust mandible with variable development of a chin, and a cranial vault that was probably rounded, but may still have been quite low and narrow. There is no indication of occipital morphology or endocranial proportions, and only minimal evidence of a gracile postcranial morphology (assuming the clavicle and radius fragments represent adults). In sum, then, the Klasies material suggests that evolution of a gracile and modern anatomical pattern was underway in the MSA inhabitants of southern Africa, at least 30 kyr before manifestations of an Upper Palaeolithic lifestyle appeared locally with the Later Stone Age, and more generally with the Upper Palaeolithic of Eurasia.

Four fossil hominid specimens have been recovered from MSA levels at Border Cave in South Africa (Natal). A frontal bone and other skull fragments (BCI), a mandible (BC2), and various other skeletal fragments were recovered between 1940 and 1942 as a result of uncontrolled excavations for fertiliser and subsequent rescue work. During controlled excavations at this time (1941), an intact burial of an infant (BC3) was recovered from an MSA level. The last MSA-associated hominid, a mandible (BC5), was excavated in 1974 from an "Epi-Pietersburg" (= HP? Volman 1984) level, stratigraphically some 75 cm below charcoal sample dated by radiocarbon at ›49 kyr (details of these discoveries are given in Beaumont et al. 1978 and Beaumont 1980). The hominid material is certainly all assignable to modern *H. sapiens* (Bräuer 1984a; Rightmire 1984) but, even in the case of BC3 and BC5, doubts persist about the possibility of intrusive burials having introduced the material into MSA levels (a grave, and an adjacent "stratigraphic anomaly" were recognised at the time of excavation of BC3 and 5). Relative and absolute dates have been used to support the association of the hominids with MSA levels, although BC1 and BC2 are essentially unprovenanced. However, they must derive from a level higher than the "Fourth White Ash", and matrix on BC1 has been matched with the succeeding stratigraphic level. Beaumont (1980) gives an age of at least 30 kyr for BC1 and 2, and more probably *c.* 110 kyr, while BC3 and 5 are assigned an age of ›49 kyr, and a probable antiquity of *c.* 105 and 90 kyr, respectively. An impressive series of radiocarbon dates has established the antiquity of the MSA levels of Border Cave beyond reasonable doubt, and all appear to lie beyond 40 kyr.

However, doubts remain about the great antiquity assigned to the Border Cave hominids. First, there is the uncertainty concerning the provenance of BC1 and 2, and the likelihood that BC3 and 5 were burials. Secondly, there is the remarkable modernity of this material, estimated to date from 90 to 110 kyr. Overall, the fossils are more modern than the Klasies specimens, with little hint of robusticity (although Bräuer notes the strong supraorbital region of BC1). Thirdly, there is the lack of other evidence of burials from the MSA of southern Africa, unless graves elsewhere were shallow and were subject to disturbance and weathering (Klein 1983b). Finally, associated with the last point, there is the claim that the hominids, including an infant's burial, are so much better preserved than some of the corresponding MSA faunal material (Klein 1983b). If the hominid specimens are of genuine MSA antiquity, this would only be explicable by assuming that they were somehow protected from the postdepositional leaching and profile compaction which seems to have affected some other faunal materials. In conclusion, while no doubt attaches to the modern *H. sapiens* status of BC1, 2, 3 and 5, doubt must still be expressed about their claimed antiquity of 90–110 kyr. Perhaps direct accelerator radiocarbon dating can be applied to these remains in order to exclude the possibility that they are post-MSA burials. In the meantime, given the evidence from Klasies, we should keep an open mind about their age and significance.

The area of Omo (Kibish) in Ethiopia produced two important fossil hominid specimens in 1967 (Leakey et al. 1969). Omo 1 consists of cranial and postcranial fragments, while Omo 2 (found about 2.5 km distant) is a calvaria. A third fragmentary and less well provenanced specimen (Omo 3) consists of only frontal and parietal fragments. Five radiocarbon dates on molluscs from Member III (which contained Omo 3) gave ages of from *c.*27 to >37 kyr, while a uranium series determination gave *c.* 30 kyr. An *Etheria* bank stratigraphically just above the position of the Omo 1 find gave a uranium series age of *c.* 130 kyr and two radiocarbon dates of >39.9 kyr but there must be doubt about the accuracy of such dates on molluscs, particularly those obtained by uranium series (Butzer et al. 1969; Butzer 1980). The Omo 1 partial skeleton was partly *in situ*, with an associated fauna, while Omo 2 was a surface find. Some "undiagnostic" artefacts were found near Omo 1, and these and others from the same levels have been attributed to the MSA (Klein 1983b), although the grounds for this are unclear. The ages of Omo 1 and 2 have been variously assessed as late Middle or early Late Pleistocene, and provided the specimens actually do belong in Member I it is likely that they are well over 40 kyr in age, as some 60 metres of deposit and a number of cycles of deposition separate the dated

Etheria beds which both overlie the stratigraphic position of Omo 1 (Butzer et al. 1969). However, given the uncertainties over the exact stratigraphic position of Omo 2 and the absolute dates obtained, it would be unwise to assume that Omo 1 and 2 must be contemporaneous and are both accurately dated by the determination of 130 kyr.

While Omo 2 displays a mixture of archaic and more modern features, and cannot be assigned to modern *H. sapiens*, Omo 1 falls within the morphological range of modern *H. sapiens* in both cranial and postcranial features, despite its robusticity (Leakey et al. 1969; Day and Stringer 1982; Bräuer 1984a; Kennedy 1984b; Rightmire 1984). This is true regardless of the accuracy of attempted reconstructions of the whole skull (which I would prefer to term "placements of the bones in their approximate anatomical context"). The more recent Omo 3 specimen can only be said to possess a modern-looking glabella region. If the Omo 1 and 2 crania are of comparable (early Late Pleistocene?) age, either one extremely variable, or two distinct, populations are being sampled. My preference has been to separate the specimens and to suggest that Omo 2 represents a more archaic, and perhaps ancestral, population compared to Omo 1 (Stringer 1978; Day and Stringer 1982). However, whatever significance is attached to the variation shown by the specimens, neither shows significant Eurasian Neanderthal features, and all three Omo frontal bones appear to show an approximation to the modern human supraorbital structure. The overall morphological pattern of Omo 1 is that of modern *H. sapiens*, despite an apparent age considerably in excess of 40 kyr, and a possible MSA archaeological context. However, it would be desirable to have much more information about the Omo Kibish Formation and its age in order to assess the significance of these fossils properly.

A fossil which may represent the early MSA population of southern Africa, or its immediate precursor, was recovered from the site of Florisbad (Orange Free State, South Africa). While certainly more modern-looking than the presumedly more ancient crania from Saldanha and Broken Hill, this partial cranium is low and broad, with a newly reconstructed face which emphasises its robusticity (Clarke 1985). New excavations by Clarke lead him to assign an age of 100–200 kyr to the skull and associate it with the level of Peat 1, which underlies an MSA occupation floor (Clarke 1985). Wolpoff (1980a) appropriately noted resemblances between the Florisbad and Djebel Irhoud 1 (Morocco) crania, and I believe the Eliye Springs (Bräuer and Leakey

1986) and Singa skulls may also sample a comparable and widespread pre-modern African population of late Middle/early Late Pleistocene antiquity. The Ngaloba (Laetoli 18) and Omo 2 crania, although more distinct in certain respects, may also be grouped in this sample (Bräuer 1984a; Rightmire 1984; Stringer et al. 1984). This population lacks what I consider to be derived (specialised) characters found in the Eurasian Neanderthals, and it is most unfortunate that we are unable to compare the African and Eurasian groups in postcranial characters where, to extrapolate from the (probably) earlier Broken Hill material, it is possible that the African group might also lack certain Neanderthal characters and be closer to the morphology found in modern *H. sapiens*. This African group represents a plausible ancestral form for the transitional or early modern hominids known from the Klasies, Irhoud 2, Omo 1, Dar-es-Soltane 5 and, perhaps, Border Cave fossils, most or all of which can be dated between 50 and 120 kyr and belong in a Middle Palaeolithic/MSA context.

The date of the morphological transition in Africa can be placed in relation to the youngest archaic and oldest modern fossils if (and this must be a very large "if" in a continent as large and diverse as Africa) the transition was relatively rapid and synchronous across the continent. This would provide a transition period between 90 and 120 kyr, assuming the younger date is appropriate for the more modern Klasies fossils, and perhaps also for Border Cave and Omo 1, and the older date is an appropriate minimum age for Ngaloba, Florisbad and possibly Omo 2. The evolutionary and chronological positions of the Irhoud fossils are important, especially as I would identify Irhoud 2 as the closest approximation, in a fairly complete fossil, to a transitional morphology between archaic and modern humans that I have yet studied (I am excluding here the Willandra Lakes WL 50 fossil which I have already discussed). Using a simple (but by no means perfect–Wolpoff 1986) method of identifying hominids of modern aspect (Day and Stringer 1982; Stringer et al. 1984), the Irhoud 2 cranium displays 50 percent (three out of six) of the derived characters of modern *H. sapiens* which can be tested. Indeed the combination of features in Irhoud 2 appeared so peculiar that some French workers initially believed that the anterior and posterior parts of two different crania had been wrongly reconstructed into a single specimen. Recent assessments of the age of the Irhoud specimens suggest a range between 50 and 120 kyr (Hublin and Tillier 1981; Debenath et al. 1982; Hublin pers.

comm.), and therefore they may also fall within the transitional time period already inferred. They provide further evidence that the morphological transition to modern *H. sapiens* was being accomplished within the time span of the MSA/Middle Palaeolithic from fossils of Neanderthal grade but not character. This can be confirmed independently from the robust but modern morphology already present in the Dar-es-Soltane material, found in early Aterian levels which may date from more than 45 kyr (Clark 1983).

BIOLOGY AND BEHAVIOUR

Trinkaus (1986 and this volume) has provided comprehensive reviews of much data concerning the potential interaction between biology and behavior at the Late Pleistocene interface between archaic and modern humans, and many of the issues he has raised are central to discussions in this volume. In spending a little time reviewing his conclusions, I will be able to cover many points of importance already raised by him and other workers concerning the origin of modern humans (Wolpoff 1980a; Smith 1983a, 1984, 1985; Trinkaus 1983a, b, 1984a, d; Trinkaus and Smith 1985). He points out that there was both major biological and cultural change in the Late Pleistocene, as illustrated by the fact that, between approximately 125 and 75 kyr, only archaic humans associated with Middle Palaeolithic industries existed, while by 30 ky, only modern humans with Upper Palaeolithic industries existed. Then Trinkaus poses for us the essential question of this conference—what were the selective advantages of the early modern human biocultural system that allowed it to become the sole human pattern after a relatively short period of evolutionary time? Trinkaus discusses current knowledge relevant to this issue in terms of five behavioural complexes: manipulation, locomotion, information and social systems, environmental buffering, and (in Trinkaus 1986) reproduction and development. As several aspects are discussed fully elsewhere in this volume, the reader should refer to Trinkaus's papers for relevant details.

Regarding manipulative abilities, it is difficult to generalise from the Neanderthals to other archaic groups because of the lack of equivalent data from other parts of the world, but I certainly feel that the absence of most aspects of the Neanderthal facial or occipitomastoid morphology in the Middle Palaeolithic (or probably Middle Palaeolithic) associated hominids from Qafzeh, Skhūl, Irhoud, Ngaloba, Eliye Springs,

Florisbad, Omo-Kibish, Singa, Dar-es-Soltane, Klasies and perhaps Border Cave, indicates that manipulative behaviours of these hominids may have been distinctive in certain ways from that of the Eurasian Neanderthals. The probable Middle Pleistocene Broken Hill material is somewhat ambivalent on this point since the cranium shows little sign of most Neanderthal-derived traits, but does display midfacial projection approximating that of some Neanderthals, and the anterior dentition shows pronounced rounding wear (Stringer 1978; Trinkaus 1986 and this volume). However, the marked dental pathologies of the cranium may have led to abnormal use of the front teeth, while the separate maxilla is very like the non-Neanderthal Ngaloba maxillae.

I agree with Trinkaus that the slender data base indicates that African Middle Palaeolithic hominids may have been more similar to modern humans in their manipulative behaviours, and it would be instructive to have more information on the extent of geographical variation in the Middle Palaeolithic with regard to the presence of hafting, preponderance of blades, etc. Blades are reported to occur in elevated frequencies in otherwise typical Middle Palaeolithic industries such as the Howieson's Poort substage of the African Middle Stone Age (Singer and Wymer 1982; Clark 1983; Volman 1984), and the "Pre-Aurignacian" of Haua Fteah (McBurney 1967; Clark 1983), while hafting may have been present in the southern African Middle Stone Age and the Aterian (Inskeep 1978; Clark 1983; Volman 1984). Blade production in the Middle Palaeolithic may merely have been the result of an extension of techniques used to regulate flake production, but the discovery or perfection of techniques of hafting may well have revolutionised hunting strategies, if this allowed "killing at a distance" (Binford 1984a).

Trinkaus (1986 and this volume) links changes in the locomotor apparatus at the advent of modern humans to the possible first appearance of planned subsistence activities characteristic of modern hunter-gatherers, but the difficulty here again is that the Middle Palaeolithic-associated hominids from Qafzeh and Skhūl possess a "modern" locomotor anatomy, and the limited data from the Broken Hill tibia (well associated with the cranium) and some of the femora suggest that earlier African hominids were already divergent from Neanderthals in their somewhat differently shaped and proportioned locomotor apparatus. The single Broken Hill tibia is longer than any known Neanderthal specimen (maximum length = 416 mm compared with an estimated value for the largest of nine Neanderthal tibiae measured by Trinkaus [1981] of 386 mm). The tibial data suggest that the limb proportions of the Broken Hill individual concerned were different from those of the Neanderthals, indicating adaptation to warm conditions and/or a more "modern" locomotor pattern, and that the individual was relatively tall, another non-Neanderthal characteristic also present in early modern humans. While the Broken Hill long bones retain an archaic diaphyseal thickening, and one innominate has a strong vertical iliac pillar, nevertheless there are similarities to modern humans in shaft shape and proportions which are not present in Neanderthals (Trinkaus 1983a; Kennedy 1984b; Stringer 1986a).

Regarding information systems and social complexity (Trinkaus 1986 and this volume), there appears to have been a clear decoupling between anatomical and social change, since evidence for a greater degree of social complexity through the use of symbols, art, elaborate burial practices etc. seems to be barely more evident for the Middle Palaeolithic early modern humans of western Asia and Africa than among the Neanderthals (Harrold 1980; Conkey 1983). However, Trinkaus's suggestion that enhanced postreproductive survival was also an important factor should provide a fertile area for further research. Changes in the patterns of growth and morphology of the brain also seem to occur with the advent of modern humans but, as Trinkaus (1986) notes, it is unclear whether there was cerebral reorganisation which can be related to behavioural change at this time. Despite the need for caution (Holloway 1985), I regard it as at least probable that such changes occurred, along with the documented changes in endocranial and cranial shape, and in ontogeny (see below). However, it is difficult to envisage how such differences could be demonstrated from the study of endocranial surfaces and casts when our knowledge of brain function based on whole living brains is still so limited.

Regarding environmental buffering, Trinkaus (1986 and this volume) reiterates that while Neanderthal limb proportions are suggestive of cold adaptation, no such indications are shown by Eurasian early modern humans. Their distinct limb proportions are instead indicative of an equatorial ancestry and better culturally based thermal protection, and/or biomechanical factors related to more effective manipulative or locomotor behaviours. Although comparative data for the earlier Pleistocene are very limited, I believe that the limb proportions of the Eurasian early modern samples are retentions of the African ancestral morphology of long limbs with long distal segments, as exemplified by

86

the WT 15000 skeleton of *H. cf. erectus* (Walker 1987; Stringer, unpublished observations) and by the Broken Hill tibia (see above). Trinkaus (this volume) also considers that geographical variation in limb proportions probably existed among late archaic humans.

Finally, Trinkaus (1986) discusses possible changes in reproduction and development at the advent of modern humans. New data have recently become available which are relevant to this question (Trinkaus 1984d; Bromage and Dean 1985; Bunney 1986; Dean et al. 1986; Rak and Arensburg 1987; Stringer et al. in press; Trinkaus and Tomkins in press). Trinkaus had argued (1984d) that the apparently larger pelvic dimensions of Neanderthal females allowed them to achieve a gestation length of 11–12 months, which he believes is also the gestation length expected for modern humans on the basis of various developmental and comparative data. The change to the shorter gestation length character-istic of modern humans was supposedly reflected in changes in pubic anatomy accomplished by the time of the Middle Palaeolithic associ-ated Skhūl–Qafzeh hominids, and this might only have been possible with the advent of the modern human behavioural pattern. An alterna-tive explanation of Neanderthal pubic morphology did not require a longer gestation period for Neanderthals, but rather saw them as following a pattern believed to be discernible in large-headed but short-bodied modern humans (Rosenberg 1986). Yet another explanation centered on the possibility of faster brain growth during development in Neanderthals, based on the inferred young age and large brain size of the Devil's Tower child (Dean et al. 1986; Bunney 1986).

However, description of the Kebara 2 Neanderthal pelvis (Rak and Arensburg 1987) shows that the previous assessments of both Neander-thal pelvic volume and shape were probably erroneous, and that locomotor functional differences may well account for the contrasts between Neanderthal and modern human pelves. Faster Neanderthal brain and body growth *after birth* still has limited support from recent studies (Stringer et al. in press). However, previous explanations for Neanderthal pubic morphology involving a larger Neanderthal brain size at birth (linked to longer gestation or faster growth *in utero*) or allometric considerations must now be considered dubious (Stringer et al. in press; Trinkaus and Tompkins in press).

Trinkaus (1986) believes that possible reproductive changes at the advent of modern humans may also be related to changes in endocrine levels during growth, with modern humans showing a slowing of growth relative to archaic humans. The consequent longer period for acculturation might then also be reflected in some of the changes in skeletal anatomy which typify modern humans. I think this is a most important observation, since the slowing of growth characteristic of modern humans could have progressively delayed the appearance of robust characteristics which, in archaic humans, may have become accentuated at adolescence. Eventually, such characteristics may either never have developed or would have been only slightly expressed at the attainment of reproductive age and the completion of growth. Such slowing of growth would have been highly advantageous in a society where much information needed to be transferred from one generation to the next via the medium of language, and where many details of brain structure were being finalised in the first few years after birth. What needs further investigation is the timing of the establishment of the prolonged developmental pattern characteristic of modern humans. On the assumption that all anatomically modern humans share such a pattern, it was probably present before 50 kyr ago in Africa and before 40 kyr ago in western Asia, but this does need to be confirmed by further research.

GENETIC DATA ON THE ORIGIN OF *HOMO SAPIENS*

Many workers now emphasise the importance of gene flow in the emergence of modern humans, based on assessments of data from fossils (e.g. Wolpoff et al. 1984; Smith 1985; Trinkaus and Smith 1985). However, attention is rarely paid to actual data concerning genetic variation in living humans, which, if nothing else, should inform us about geographical patterns in the only widely dispersed hominoid species available to us for study (but see also Wolpoff et al. 1984 and this volume). Moreover, extensive data are now becoming available, which, despite the difficulties involved in their analysis and interpretation, we can no longer afford to ignore. I will now attempt to review the results of some of this work.

Mitochondrial DNA (mtDNA) has a clonal mode of inheritance, unlike nuclear DNA, and is inherited through females only. It also appears to evolve about ten times faster than nuclear DNA. It is therefore particularly useful in examining molecular evolution over a relatively short time span and tracing lineages without the complexity

88

caused by recombination during sexual reproduction. Work on mtDNA centered at Berkeley has concerned sequencing geographically diverse samples of living humans from Europe, Asia, Australasia, and Africa. Early indications of a low diversity for human mtDNA variation compared with other primate species were considered indicative of an origin for *H. sapiens* within the recent past (100–200 kyr) (Brown 1980; Ferris et al. 1981). Larger samples have amplified but not changed this picture, and a transient bottleneck (a brief but dramatic event which leads to only a few individuals providing the basis for later population variation) may therefore have occurred quite recently in the formation of our species (Wilson et al. 1985).

Current work at Berkeley (Cann et al. 1987) has extended knowledge of human mtDNA variation and its genealogical history. A sample of 147 humans from four major groups ("African-origin Blacks", "Asians", "Australasians" and "Caucasians") has been analysed using restriction mapping to produce a genealogical tree, with dates of divergence based on an assumed constant rate of nucleotide substitution in line with rates calculated from various other organisms, and testable on historically or archaeologically controlled divergences in vertebrates, including humans (Stoneking, work in progress). The variation is consistent with an origin for all present human variation in the period between 140 and 290 kyr, and an origin for non-African types at perhaps 90–180 kyr ago. Region-specific clusters (and inferred mean ages) can be identified for Africa (90–180 kyr), Asia (53–105 kyr), Australasia (33–65 kyr), New Guinea (23–45 kyr), and Europe (28–55 kyr). Cann et al. (1987) argue that their results support an African origin for recent human mtDNA variation, and little indication of any hybridisation or gene flow from distinct lineages of hominids with an antiquity greater than that indicated for all living *H. sapiens*. While such use of mtDNA for the study of human evolution is not without its critics (Nei 1982; Jorde 1985) and potentially conflicting results have been published by other workers (Johnson et al. 1983), there are many data accumulating from recent research on the differently structured and inherited nuclear DNA or its derivatives to support the model of recent human evolution proposed by Cann et al. (1987), even if calibration varies (usually in proposing an even younger divergence date for present human "races").

Nei (1982) discussed the divergence of "Caucasoid", "Negroid" and "Mongoloid" groups from 85 protein and blood group systems, and concluded from distance measures that European and Asian populations were more closely related to each other than either was related to Africans. When aboriginal Americans and Australasians were added, they clustered with the Eurasian groups, and calibration provided a suggested African/Eurasian split at 110 ±34 kyr, and a subsequent European/Asian split at 41±15 kyr. An analysis of a small number of mtDNA variants in humans produced comparable results (Nei 1982). More recently, Wainscoat et al. (1986a) analysed DNA coding polymorphisms in the beta-globin genes of 601 human chromosomes from eight Eurasian, African, Australasian, and Polynesian populations. A strong geographical patterning separated sub-Saharan samples from those of the rest of the world, and this was interpreted as indicating a more recent divergence for European, Asian, and Australasian populations compared with those of southern Africa. It was possible that bottlenecking had occurred in the founder population of the non-African groups when they left their supposed ancestral African homeland, which restricted their variation and caused the loss of some African genetic characters. Using these and other results, including fossil data, Jones and Rouhani (1986a) reviewed evidence for a recent African origin for *H. sapiens*, and speculated about the extent of bottlenecks in human evolution. In turn this has led to further discussion of the data and difficulties in their interpretation (Van Valen 1986; Giles and Ambrose 1986; Wainscoat et al. 1986b; Jones and Rouhani 1986b; Wainscoat 1987).

Summarising the genetic data, it is apparent that various nuclear and mtDNA studies point to the greater similarity of European, Asian, and Australasian populations, compared to the more divergent and variable genetic make-up of sub-Saharan African samples. For allele frequencies, this might be explicable by a greater degree of gene flow within the rest of the world, compared to gene flow with Africa, or to a more recent divergence of the populations of the rest of the world subsequent to their divergence from African groups (these two explanations are not mutually exclusive and could both be true). For mtDNA sequence differences, the effect of the former factor can be monitored, and it is the latter explanation which is favoured. Estimated divergence times for the hypothetical African/Eurasian split range from up to 180 kyr (Cann et al. 1987) to about 100 kyr ago (Nei 1982; Johnson et al. 1983), and all these dates fall after the time of *H. erectus* and probably also after the origin of the Eurasian Neanderthals (Stringer 1985; Vandermeersch 1985). Of course each of the suggested divergence times must be treated with caution, whether they are based on calibration from an assumed ape/human split at 5–7 my (Johnson et al. 1983) or on inferred rates of change in many other organisms (Nei 1982; Cann et al. 1987). However, it remains true that human genetic diversity is low for such a widely dispersed species. The mtDNA divergence value for 147 geographically and racially diverse humans is less than 10 percent of the value calculated for five orangs and for two crab-eating macaques, only about 33 percent of the value calculated for ten common and for two pygmy chimpanzees, and is only about 65 percent of the value calculated for four lowland gorillas sampled from one small area of Africa (Wilson et al. 1985; Cann et al. 1987).

Unless some special constraint on human mtDNA variation can be posited (which seems improbable, given our close physiological and genetic similarity to our hominid relatives), the most reasonable interpretation of these results appears to be that the low mtDNA variation must be a reflection of its recent origin compared to that found in the other primate species so far tested. Additionally, both nuclear and mtDNA studies show that variation between human populations (even between those of Eurasia and Africa) is low compared with that within populations (Nei 1982; Cann et al. 1987). If human populations have had a long and dispersed evolutionary history, this should not be the case unless there have been large amounts of gene flow between the various populations, which does not match with the observed geographical patterning of genetic variation between Eurasia and Africa. It seems much more likely that the low geographic diversity of human populations is a result of a relatively recent divergence from a presumed African ancestral group, a conclusion which also explains the relatively greater diversity within Africa, since this area would have the longest record of *in situ* evolution of *H. sapiens*.

CONCLUDING REMARKS

The fossil record does seem to demonstrate that modern morphological characters appeared earliest in Africa (Bräuer 1984a; Rightmire 1984; Smith 1985) and this probably remains true even if we discount some of the more disputed cases and just use evidence from sites such as Klasies, Irhoud, and Dar-es-Soltane. However, this statement is also dependent on a relatively late date (*c.*40–50 kyr) for the Qafzeh sample. If the Qafzeh specimens are earlier than this (as proposed by Bar-Yosef [this volume] and reinforced by thermoluminescence determinations from burnt Mousterian flints at Qafzeh [Valladas et al. 1988]), the picture would dramatically change, and the Asian corridor linking the three continents of the Old World would become a critical area for the *origin* of modern humans, rather than for their dispersal.

The evidence from African sites and from Qafzeh and Skhūl shows that the modern anatomical pattern was established before (perhaps well before) the terminal Middle Stone Age/Middle Palaeolithic of Africa and western Asia, and therefore behavioural models which rely on demonstrable differences between Middle and Upper Palaeolithic (especially on Mousterian–later Upper Palaeolithic) behaviour are unlikely to be able to explain the *origin* of modern anatomical features, although they can certainly help to explain the establishment of such features on a global scale (Trinkaus 1986 and this volume).

The European pattern was predominantly or wholly one of replacement of local Neanderthal morphologies, which had a very long history, by new allochthonous characters. Furthermore, I believe that the establishment of modern genes in Eurasia occurred because they were transported inside the bodies of an expanding early modern population, rather than by their gametes mixing with those of local archaic populations. The development of Upper Palaeolithic technologies by 35 kyr was probably instrumental in establishing new peoples in both old and new areas of human occupation, and indeed it may only have been with such cultural developments that the Neanderthals could have been displaced from what was perhaps their optimum environment. Furthermore, the Saint-Césaire skeleton shows that some suggested models of human evolution involving morphological and behavioural feedback mechanisms are inadequate. The specimen has typical Neanderthal features in the face, jaws, teeth, and postcranium, and this is inexplicable if behavioural changes at the Middle–Upper Palaeolithic transition were inevitably leading to the evolution of modern humans. Such models could be saved only by a demonstration that these last Neanderthals were not yet displaying even the terminal Middle Palaeolithic behaviours which elsewhere had supposedly produced modern humans. However, I cannot deny that there are many unsolved problems regarding the pattern of establishment of modern humans and Upper Palaeolithic industries in the area, including the significance of the gracile Vindija sample and the Hahnöfersand specimen. The widespread application of accelerator dating to fossils and sites in the time range of 30–50 kyr is likely to improve chronological resolution considerably, although from our experiences so far, we are likely to receive a number of shocks (three out of four supposed Pleistocene hominids from Britain so far tested have been assigned Holocene ages– Stringer 1986b).

In the Far East we have definite evidence of modern humans in Asia and Australasia by about 30 kyr (perhaps 40 kyr if the age of the Niah skeleton can be confirmed by accelerator dating). I would interpret the appearance of these specimens by a Noah's Ark model rather than by local evolution from archaic predecessors, but the enigmatic Willandra Lakes 50 fossil suggests the possibility of more than one evolutionary source for the origin of modern *H. sapiens* in the area. It would be valuable to have more archaeological data to help resolve some of the outstanding problems of this region, in particular whether the appearance of modern humans in Asia was associated with marked behavioural changes, and whether archaeological data can help to explain the morphological diversity found in Pleistocene Australians.

Regarding proposed models to explain the evolution of modern humans, it is important to distinguish those which involve generalising from specific Neanderthal/modern comparisons and those which are more general in nature. Thus models which attempt to explain a change from what I consider to be the unique facial, gnathic, cranial, and possibly (in respects such as pelvic form and body proportions) post-cranial morphology of Neanderthals to that of modern humans are unlikely to be generally appropriate, and the importance of changes in anterior dental use are likely to fall into this category, regardless of how appealing such models are when considering possible interactions with technological changes. However, less specific biomechanical models, such as ones which provide possible explanations for brow-ridge reduction in concert with changes in the relation of face and vault (Russell 1985), are likely to be widely appropriate and might explain observed parallel evolutionary changes in Africa and Europe, for example the apparent brow-ridge reduction found in the Vindija Neanderthals.

I believe that we are only beginning to appreciate the special nature of the Neanderthals, not as the caricatures of ape-men prevalent earlier in this century, but as specialised high-latitude descendants of archaic hominids, the first people to adapt effectively to the rigours of life through a period dominated by conditions colder than those of Europe today (in fact covering 90 percent of the last 500,000 years). The reproductive strategy hinted at by suggestions of rapid growth in Neanderthal children (Trinkaus 1986; Dean et al. 1986; Stringer et al. in press; Trinkaus and Tompkins in press) was for greater physical maturity in childhood, and its potential value cannot be doubted by those of us who have endured the severity of winters even in "interglacial" Europe. Thus I believe that the Neanderthals were by no means typical of early Late Pleistocene humans, but we will only be able to confirm this by the discovery and study of more complete material from other populations. In the meantime, we should be very cautious about assuming that they can substitute for our actual ancestors.

Furthermore, without knowing the full extent of possible behavioural differences between Neanderthals and modern humans, we should be cautious about the way in which modern characteristics became established. We could waste a lot of time and energy in trying to explain the supposed superiority of the "European" anatomical pattern which recently led to its replacing the aboriginal one over large areas of America or Australia, if we were not aware of the exploitative behavioural system which accompanied those European skeletal characters. That is a very extreme example, but we should be aware of the possibility that some early modern skeletal features may have been of neutral or even negative selective value in Europe, yet they became established because they were an incidental part of a more effective behavioural system (possible examples are the "equatorial" limb proportions of the early modern peoples of Eurasia.

So, what can be concluded about the origin of modern humans and the factors involved? First, that the ultimate origin of modern characters was probably in Africa, from both the fossil and the genetic data. Environmental or behavioural factors which might be associated should be looked for in the late Middle and early Late Pleistocene records of that continent, and in cultural material of Middle Stone Age or Middle Palaeolithic affinities. This means that many of the useful data assembled concerning late Pleistocene environments and cultures are of dubious relevance for explaining the *origin* of modern humans and their behaviour, but are important in documenting the radiation and establishment of the modern human pattern globally. This is unfortunate, because comparable data for the early Late Pleistocene of Africa are poor by comparison, and open to different interpretations (Klein 1983b, 1984, 1986; Binford 1984a, 1986b; Volman 1984; Deacon et al. 1986). Although interglacial–glacial cycles undoubtedly affected the African continent, the most marked environmental effects are known for the glacial maximum of the late Pleistocene, and although the same major increases in aridity can be inferred for each preceding glacial maximum, it is uncertain how African environments of the early Late Pleistocene were affected by the transition from interglacial to (predominantly) glacial conditions in the period 70–116 kyr ago. While many workers believe that important changes in environments can be reconstructed from their effect on faunas and human occupation patterns at this time, Binford (1984a) has instead suggested that environmental–faunal equations for the MSA are strongly suspect, and that it is changes in human ecology and behaviour which are primarily being recorded in the faunal record of sites like Klasies.

Nevertheless, the variety of environments in Africa, and the rapidity with which they are known to have changed during the last 30 kyr, suggest that environmental changes and possible isolation of populations may have been a factor in what seems to have been a very rapid (geologically speaking) emergence of modern humans. Such a punctuational origin is consistent with the available genetic evidence, particularly that of mtDNA. Although the mtDNA bottlenecking event is calibrated at around twice the age assessed for the earliest fossil evidence of modern *H. sapiens*, there is, of course, no necessity that the *genetic* origin of modern humans and particularly that of non-nuclear mtDNA should coincide with the origin of the whole suite of anatomically modern characteristics. Archaeological evidence for behavioural changes at this time in Africa is rather speculative, although there is the possibility that MSA peoples had a greater range of food resources than ESA peoples, and were the first to exploit marine resources systematically. They may have been able to process plant foods more efficiently, and had perhaps discovered the advantages of drying meat. Food surpluses may have allowed a greater degree of self-sufficiency and sedentariness, and an ability to extend the use of Middle Stone Age tools by blade production, hafting, and perhaps by the production of composite tools is indicated from the archaeological evidence (Clark 1983; Volman 1984). However, the extent to which African Middle Stone Age behaviour was quantitatively or qualitatively different from that of the Eurasian Middle Palaeolithic remains to be demonstrated, or is only in the process of being demonstrated. In contrast to the uncertainty about behavioural differences between Eurasian and African early Late Pleistocene humans, I do not believe there is any doubt about morphological differences, which indicate a probable first appearance of modern humans in Africa, consistent with recent genetic evidence, and in the adjacent Levant. On this basis, if behavioural and morphological evolution *are* closely linked, it is in the late Middle or early Late Pleistocene archaeological record of Africa, and perhaps also of western Asia, that the behavioural changes associated with the origin of modern humans remain to be discerned.

The place of the Neandertals in human evolution

MILFORD H. WOLPOFF

The "Neandertal Question" – the place of the Neandertals in human evolution – is paleoanthropology's oldest problem (Spencer 1984), since the first archaic fossil to be discovered was a Neandertal. While it is also the material of the most recent headlines, the issues surrounding the place of the Neandertals in human evolution are better focused than ever before. The "Neandertal problem" is no longer perceived to be a worldwide one, although at least one solution proposed for it involves total population replacements on a worldwide scale. The Neandertals themselves, however, are recognized to be a geographic variant limited to Europe and western Asia, and it is widely accepted that the *term* "Neandertal" should not be used to describe the worldwide *grade* of hominids immediately preceding modern populations, if there was a definable grade (Wolpoff 1986). In particular then, the problem has become one of the relationship of Neandertals to the European populations of today.

Given the resurgence of interest in the behavioral changes associated with events surrounding the Middle to Upper Paleolithic transition in Europe, I believe that we must arrive at a solution to this problem, however tentative. Without a rather specific idea about the relation of the Neandertals to the populations that followed them, nothing else can be determined of the biological processes underway at the time of this archaeological transition. Adaptive models are only relevant if there was adaptive change. Models of physiological or reproductive advantages enhancing gene flow are only relevant if there was gene flow. The effects of behavioral changes cannot be analyzed if it was the compositions of the populations and not the evolutionary importance of their behaviors that changed. Without this basic knowledge, the causes of the transition, if there was a transition and not a simple replacement, cannot be understood. Thus, the phylogenetic relationships of these European populations are fundamental (Wiley 1981).

The bases for the phylogenetic disagreements of today span only the last several decades. Theoretical perspectives have brought into focus the roles of population invasion, gene flow, and selection changes in producing the morphology of the post-Neandertal Europeans. These theoretical perspectives can be traced to the first influences of the synthetic theory of evolution on paleoanthropology, as specifically applied to the Neandertal problem. This influence was clearly evident in a seminal paper on the evolution of Neandertals in Europe and western Asia, published in 1951 by F. C. Howell, examining evolutionary trends within the Neandertals. Because the direction of their evolution seemed to be away from the modern European condition, especially with the (then thought to be earlier) Skhūl remains at their base, Howell concluded that the classic Neandertals of western Europe were peripheral to the mainstream of human evolution. Reasoning that the presence of numerous autapomorphic characters precluded a classic Neandertal ancestry for later European populations, he argued that while the classic Neandertals evolved in western Europe, "at the same time modern man was developing further to the east" (1951:412). It was Howell's position that the evolutionary direction leading to so unique a set of features could only develop with genetic isolation, and he sought to show (1952) that the Neandertal populations of western Europe were indeed isolated by the pattern of glaciation during Würm II.

In a more general restatement of these arguments, Howell (1957) used a larger Neandertal sample to buttress his conclusion that modern populations evolved only from the earlier Neandertals. His discussion of the more fragmentary eastern and central European remains concluded (1957:337) that

east-central and eastern Europe were not particularly isolated during the Early

Last Glacial. . . . there was broad racial continuity at least as far east as the Crimea and southward into the Levant.

The Levant specimen reflecting this continuity was the female from Tabūn. It was this group that, in his view, provided the ancestry for the later Europeans of the Upper Paleolithic.

. . . important structural changes were taking place in the human populations of the Levant during the Early Last Pluvial . . . these were of primary significance for the evolutionary origin of subsequent anatomically modern peoples of the European Upper Paleolithic. (1957:339)

Howell advocated a generalized Neandertal ancestry for the modern Europeans in these publications, for instance in his phyletic summary diagram (1951:Figure 4) showing specimens such as Ehringsdorf and Saccopastore as immediately ancestral to (what he called) the Mount Carmel population, which in turn he regarded as ancestral to modern Europeans. However, he was opposed to the interpretation of a "Neandertal Phase" in the evolution of all modern populations, because of "the marked variability from one [archaic] group to another" (1957:343). In fact, he stated (1957:331), "This point of view has yet to be meaningfully expressed in terms of modern evolutionary theory."

In papers following, both C. S. Coon (1962) and C. L. Brace (1962a, 1964) attempted exactly such an expression. Just as Howell did in his emphasis on regional variation, Coon's thinking reflected the later interpretations of F. Weidenreich (1947a). Weidenreich (1943b) had first regarded the western European classic Neandertals as ancestors of modern Europeans. But by four years later (1947a) he had dropped all mention of the western sample from his discussion of the problem and derived modern Europeans from the classic Neandertals of the Levant (meaning Tabūn) via the Skhūl group. While Coon followed Weidenreich in emphasizing the distinctly geographic, or regional, pattern of human evolution (see Wolpoff et al. 1984), his explanation for temporal patterning differed from Weidenreich's orthogenic one (Weidenreich 1947b; Wolpoff 1985). Coon applied the synthetic theory of evolution, as he understood it, to this problem and approached the explanation of common phases in human evolution by regarding each of the phases as temporal species, separated by distinct boundaries ("thresholds of speciation"). In this context, Coon (1962, 1982) regarded the Neandertals as an evolutionary static, cold-adapted branch of the Caucasoids, absorbed and extinguished by the invasion of more modern Caucasoid populations from the Levant.

Brace (1962b, 1964, 1966, 1979) also reflected Weidenreich's earlier (1943b) views, and brought into a more modern context an explanatory interpretation of the Late Pleistocene fossil record first expressed in detail in publications from central Europe by Schliz (1909), Gorjanović-Kramberger (1918, and see Radovčić 1985), and Hrdlička (1929, 1930). Specifically following Hrdlička (1930), he proposed a worldwide Neandertal stage to human evolution (Brace 1967). Brace was not alone in this; many authors of the time regarded archaic hominids outside of Europe as Neandertal variants; for instance, von Koenigswald (1958) considered the Solo hominids as "tropical Neandertals." In Brace's view the western European Neandertals differed from the more modern Europeans that followed them in time mainly because of their greater skeletal robustness and larger anterior tooth size with supporting facial architecture. This set the stage for his hypothesis of how the Neandertals evolved into these succeeding populations. He regarded the reductions in masticatory robustness and in the size of the anterior teeth as the result of replacing tooth use with a more efficient technology (an idea proposed earlier by both Gorjanović-Kramberger [1904] and Hrdlička [1911, 1914]). Brace believes that the consequent suspension of selection maintaining these features allowed mutations to accumulate which resulted in structural reduction. This explanatory mechanism is not widely regarded as valid, and to some extent its rejection has influenced acceptance of Brace's model.

A rather different theory was set forth by Brose and Wolpoff (1971). We realized that what we regarded as transitional populations, such as Skhūl and Qafzeh, seemed to follow the Neandertals in the Levant but were associated with the same local Mousterian industry, the Levallois-Mousterian. Therefore, we argued that the changes in selection resulting in these transitional Levantine populations must be based on adaptations that were part of the Mousterian culture, and we sought evidence for the direction of biological change in the Mousterian of central and western Europe, as Howell had. However, in contrast we believed that this direction was toward Upper Paleolithic European populations.

There is an alternative viewpoint about the origin of modern Europeans, perhaps most easily characterized by its extreme expression. This is the interpretation that Howells (1976) describes as the "Noah's

Ark" hypothesis and in a more recent expression has been dubbed the "Garden of Eden" theory (for instance as used in Stringer and Andrews 1988) – the proposal that modern groups have a single recent origin from a population that was already modern. Applied to the European situation this hypothesis means that modern Europeans did not originate in Europe. One of the main issues raised by this hypothesis is exactly where outside of Europe the place of origin was. A good deal of effort has been spent in seeking the earliest remains of the modern human form because it is reasoned that the earliest appearance of any modern population in the fossil record will be at the place of origin of all modern populations, a presumption which *assumes* the hypothesis to be tested, namely that modern populations have a single migrational origin. Over the years, the candidate for the earliest modern human has changed considerably, and therefore so has the place of origin. Cautiously, Howells has never been clear in his publications as to where this source area for the modern Europeans (and all other modern populations) might have been, but others have specifically suggested sub-Saharan Africa (Protsch 1975, 1978; Bräuer 1984a, 1984b; Stringer 1984a, 1984b, 1985, 1986b, 1988; Stringer and Andrews 1988; Wainscoat et al. 1986a, Cann et al. 1987), the Levant (Vandermeersch 1970, 1972, 1981a) or more generally western Asia (Howell 1951; Bodmer and Cavalli-Sforza 1976), China (Weckler 1957; Chang 1963; Macintosh and Larnach 1976; Denaro et al. 1981), Australia (Gribbin and Cherfas 1982), or even more unexpected places (Hogan 1977). While sub-Saharan Africa has recently seemed to be the most favored prospective human homeland, if the early dates for western Asia prove to be correct (Valladas et al. 1988) Israel may turn out to play an important role in both the biblical and the scientific "Garden of Eden" interpretations of modern populational origins.

In this paper I address the place of the Neandertals in human evolution by examining the current status of ideas regarding the relations of the Neandertals to the post-Neandertal populations of Europe. I propose to do this by first discussing the total replacement hypothesis in terms of the genetic and morphological bases for invasion leading to replacement without significant hybridization. I will then examine the evidence relating to the less extreme competing hypotheses of demic diffusion, invasion, and/or gene flow with significant admixture, as the source of the post-Neandertal Europeans. The intent is to provide a reasonable and defensible interpretation of the roles of gene flow, selection, and drift in the appearance of the post-Neandertal Europeans. Ultimately, if the hypothesis of complete replacement (i.e. without significant admixture between aboriginal and invading populations) can be rejected, the relation of the Neandertals and the post-Neandertal Europeans must be described in terms of a transition, and this opens the door for an examination of the adaptive, demographic, and reproductive changes that accompanied it and oriented its rate and direction.

THE HOMINID SAMPLE

The European Neandertal sample is divided into pre-Würm and Würm segments. Further subdivision of this sample into Würm I and II segments is problematic at this time, and will remain so until the current disagreements about whether the facies of the European Mousterian seriate and about the stratigraphic and absolute dating of the Neandertal burials (Mellars 1986a, b; Valladas et al. 1986; Ashton and Cook 1986; Binford 1986) are satisfactorily resolved. Given the recent indications of an expanded Würm, the pre-Würm sample is conservatively defined as including Krapina (level 5 and below), Fontéchevade, and Ehringsdorf. The remaining specimens are regarded as belonging to the Würm sample. However, I believe it likely that there also remains a distinguishable late Neandertal sample composed of specimens from Krapina level 7, Vindija level g3, Hortus, Saint-Césaire, the Châtelperronian at Arcy sur Cure, Kůlna, and Šipka.

For the sample representing the putative descendants of the Neandertals, I will use a number of so-called "early modern" humans (but see Wolpoff 1986) from central Europe. Simply put, these are the earliest non-Neandertal people of the region. The earliest specimens are Aurignacian associated. No osteological material is clearly associated with the Szeletian. For the composition of this sample I have relied primarily on Smith's (1982, 1984) discussion (and the references cited therein), except that I have not included Kelsterbach (Smith also expressed reservations about this specimen), Paderborn (even if it is as old as claimed, the cranium is too young for this earliest Aurignacian sample). Hahnöfersand (there are enough geological and stratigraphic uncertainties about this specimen to keep it in the suspense account until its radiometric date can be independently verified), or Podbaba (there are simply too many problems with the provenience of this specimen [Matiegka 1924], and it certainly is *not* a Neandertal as Boaz [1982] thought). In my opinion the circumstances of discovery and the various attempts at dating provide sufficient grounds for doubt that these individuals properly belong to this earliest Upper Paleolithic-associated group from the region (Henke and Xirotiris 1982).

To the west, the temporal and adaptive equivalent of eastern Aurignacian appears to be the earlier portion of the Aurignacian sequence (Valoch 1976; Frayer 1978; Svoboda 1984). Although similarities in tool types relate the various Aurignacian facies (Bordes 1968; Valoch 1976), published radiocarbon dates suggest that the evolved Aurignacian of the west *postdates* the eastern Aurignacian. Unfortunately, there are no adult cranial remains from the early Aurignacian in western Europe; the well-known skeletons from Cro-Magnon are either later in the Aurignacian or possibly even more recent (Bouchud 1966), while the Grotte des Enfants crania 4, 5, and 6 (Mussi 1984) and Les Cottés (Pradel, personal communcation) are both cases of Gravettian burials intrusive into Aurignacian layers. As Stringer, Hublin, and Vandermeersch put it (1984:107): "apart from the Saint-Césaire skeleton of the Châtelperronian, we know nothing of the population of the beginning of the French Upper Paleolithic, particularly those of the early Aurignacian."

The resulting very conservatively defined osteological sample of the earliest post-Neandertal Europeans are all from central Europe. The specimens in this sample are: Cioclovina, Mladeč (*contra* Howell [1984], both the association of the hominids with an Aurignacian industry [Bayer 1922; Szombathy 1925] and its commensurate early date [Jelínek 1983; Svoboda 1984] seem well established), Stetten 1, Svitavka, Velika Pećina, Vindija (levels g1 and f), and Zlatý Kůň. The dental sample includes additional specimens from Dzeravá Skála, Silická Brezová, and Miesslingstal (see Frayer 1978; Smith 1984). A somewhat later cranial sample from this region includes specimens from Pavlov, Předmostí, and Dolní Věstonice.

The patterns of evolution appear to differ between central and western Europe. While it is possible that this reflects real differences in the prehistories of the regions, the absence of earlier Upper Paleolithic human remains from the west makes a resolution of this question impossible at present. The earlier central European sample *pre*dates the much better-known specimens from sites such as Cro-Magnon in western Europe. This has been an important factor in the development of hypotheses regarding the origins of the post-Neandertal Europeans. The classic comparison of the Neandertals with the Cro-Magnons has been misleading because Cro-Magnon is far from being the earliest of the post-Neandertal European sites; it is predated by morphologically more archaic samples in central and eastern Europe, and even in western Europe the skeletons are no longer regarded as being particularly early, or any longer associated with an "evolved Aurignacian" context. For this reason the post-Neandertal sample from western Europe is not used in any of the comparisons of Neandertal and post-Neandertal cranial morphology. It is felt that central Europe should indeed be *central* in considering the Neandertal problem (Radovčić 1985). Continuity in central Europe need not mean continuity in the west, but if total replacement characterized central Europe it must have characterized the west as well!

For purposes of comparison and analysis an additional sample is used, the *Skhūl/Qafzeh* sample, which is self-explanatory in composition. The importance of this sample is twofold. First, because of its morphological features, many authors feel it may represent the immediate source of the Aurignacian Europeans (i.e. as the supporters of this idea like to put it, the "proto-Cro-Magnons"), either through a direct invasion of Europe from the Levant (Vandermeersch 1981b; Stringer 1988; Delson 1988) or as a consequence of gene flow (for instance Smith, quoted in Lewin [1987]). Secondly, the age of these samples is relevant to the ancestry issue because recent thermoluminescence dating suggests that Qafzeh may be quite old (Valladas et al. 1988). Since Skhūl appears to be somewhat younger but also precedes the European Aurignacian, the Skhūl/Qafzeh sample could be an ideal *potential* ancestral population for modern Europeans. Whether it can be validly regarded as an *actual* ancestor must be determined on morphological and cultural grounds, and this issue will be addressed as well. Of course. should the early dates not stand the test of time and Qafzeh be (again) ascertained to be much younger, there would no longer be a potential question of European ancestry.

GENE FLOW AND INVASION

The potential role of gene interchange is invariably raised in discussions of a Neandertal ancestry for later Europeans. The issue is usually posed as whether or not the more recent Europeans evolved *in situ* or arrived as part of an invasion of new people into the region. Invasion, in turn, may be with or without hybridization with the indigenous Neandertals. Yet, for all the focus on whether or not there was gene exchange, the *mechanisms* of gene exchange between populations are often overlooked in discussions of the Neandertal ancestry issue (including some of those published by the author). There has developed what I like to think of as the "coffee theory" of gene flow, in which genes are said to "filter" or "percolate" into a population. It is perceived that somehow "more modern traits detectable in some Neandertals of eastern Europe and Asia could be the result . . . of genes filtering into the population from contemporaneous early modern groups" (Stringer 1984b:12).

The lack of precise definitions for the forms of gene movement has been a mistake, and it is probably important to distinguish between the movement of genes between populations due to mate exchange and the movement of genes due to the expansion or migration of the populations themselves. Weiss (1986) proposes to describe the former as "**gene flow**" and the latter as "**invasion.**" Cavalli-Sforza (Wijsman and Cavalli-Sforza 1984) uses the term "**demic diffusion**" to describe the combination of the two. I will adhere to these conventions throughout this paper.

The relation of demic diffusion to the Neandertal problem can be stated quite simply. Either the Neandertals of Europe evolved directly into the succeding populations of Europe in total isolation from the rest of the world, or some form of demic diffusion played a role in the origin of modern Europeans. It is probably too unrealistic even to discuss the possibility that the Neandertal populations evolved into modern Europeans in total isolation; for that matter, it is quite likely that local human evolution with significant periods of isolation never happened anywhere (Wolpoff et al. 1984). On the contrary, because the only evolutionary models that require the total isolation of the European Neandertals are those which attempt to explain their deviation from the main line of human evolution and their subsequent extinction without admixture or significant hybridization with the invading populations, theoretical arguments attempting to explain *in situ* evolution *rely on* the lack of isolation (Brose and Wolpoff 1971; Wolpoff et al. 1984). It follows that, unless one is willing to account totally for the origin of modern Europeans as an isolated *in situ* evolution from local Neandertals, demic diffusion played some sort of role in their appearance.

THE EXTREME: TOTAL REPLACEMENT

What role demic diffusion might have played is less than obvious, and certainly far from agreed upon. At the extreme, there could have been complete replacement of the indigenous European Neandertal populations, with little or possibly even no hybridization. As R.G. Klein is reputed to have said (quoted in Rensberger 1980:7): "I would think that the behavioral gulf between these two very different kinds of people would have been so great that there would have been no desire at all to mate." More likely, a total replacement interpretation would be forced to depend on the assumption that Neandertals and the populations who presumably replaced them were distinct biological species. A new species for modern humans (or those whom some of my colleagues refer to as "anatomically modern *Homo sapiens*," or "amhs") has more support than one might suppose (or presume from the morphological and behavioral relationships). Stringer and Andrews (1988) clearly accept the idea, and Delson (1988) supports it with reservations. Moreover, there are newly developed genetic arguments for the complete replacement of all indigenous human populations by a small group of Africans (Wainscoat et al. 1986a; Jones and Rouhani 1986a; Cann et al. 1987). These are discussed below. It seems to bother no one that this new species, presumably the result of cladogenesis, cannot be acceptably defined (Wolpoff 1986). "Replacement," as it will be used here, refers only to the model of invasion and replacement with a minimal amount or a complete lack of hybridization.

Earlier "moderns" outside of Europe

The critical question is where the invaders originated. Under the replacement hypothesis this must have been outside of Europe, and most supportive workers would place this in sub-Saharan Africa or in the Levant because of the early dates said to be associated with the first modern humans from these regions. However, problems abound with the dates provided (and reverberated through the literature) for so-called early modern humans from the Near East and (especially) southern Africa. In the Levant, the thermoluminescence and ESR dates for Skhūl and Qafzeh need to be independently confirmed (although of all the early dates discussed here, these stand the best chance of being

106

correct). There are more than adequate reasons to question the South African "dates" for an early origin of modern populations, "dates" upon which so many interpretations seem to hang. Neither Border Cave nor Klasies River Mouth Cave, the two sites thought to be especially early, has an absolute radiometric date, and in the case of Border Cave it is not even clear that most of the adult specimens have a provenience! As Rightmire in his review of the situation at Border Cave. puts it:

With the exception of a new adult mandible . . . all of the adult skeletal material was dug out of the cave by Horton and its original position in the deposits was not directly verified (1979:25) . . . The course of evolution outside of southern Africa cannot be determined from the evidence considered here. (1979:26)

As far as the Klasies River Mouth Cave specimens are concerned, the published dates are based on two faunal correlations, that of the cave fauna to coastal faunas, and that of the coastal faunas to the oxygen isotope-based sea core chronology. These widely quoted "dates" actually stand a good chance of being incorrect (Binford 1984a, 1986b) and the age of the specimens may be one half of what is generally assumed.

Moreover, since working on these remains I have wondered whether their perceived "modernity" isn't a consequence of their fragmentation and if a complete specimen composed of similar fragments wouldn't be more similar to the Ngaloba cranium than to Border Cave. Interestingly, Rightmire (1989) has come to regard Ngaloba as "modern *Homo sapiens*," but it is unclear exactly what this means. If it is meant to reflect the morphological ties between this archaic specimen and the living or recent populations of eastern Africa, I would concur with this interpretation. However, if it means that the specimen is thought to be similar in its features to these modern populations (for instance with a morphological complex that falls within the modern range, as Rightmire has said of Border Cave), I cannot agree with this characterization. The combination of facial gracilization, the lack of occipital tori, and dental reduction, makes Ngaloba an ideal intermediary between recent and living east Africans, and earlier specimens such as Broken Hill (male) and Ndutu (female) which show the beginnings of trends in these directions compared with their contemporaries from other regions of the world. However, the Ngaloba morphology is not the same as the recent and living individuals. The idea that many of the Klasies cranial fragments could conform to a Ngaloba-like morphology does not make them "modern" in my opinion.

Regardless of the dates of these specimens, there is another important aspect that should be considered, their morphology. Specimens from both Border Cave and Klasies River Mouth Cave are fundamentally African in their morphological details (Rightmire 1979, 1984; Wolpoff 1980a). In fact, throughout the history of attempts to find the origin of Europeans outside of Europe, the skeletal remains considered to be the earliest modern *Homo sapiens* invariably have the characteristics common to the region from which they derive, and not the specific characteristics of Europeans. According to the total replacement hypothesis, this would have to mean that the characteristics of Europeans developed in distinctly African populations on the way to Europe since by the time the populations arrive there, presumably to replace Neandertals, *they already are distinctly European in morphology.*

Trees as models of population history

Discussions of the total replacement hypothesis are based on assessments of population relationships as determined from trees of genetic or even morphological information that are interpreted to show a common recent origin and subsequent divergences for human populations (Cavalli-Sforza et al. 1964; Cavalli-Sforza and Edwards 1965; Edwards 1971; Howells 1973; Guglielmino-Matessi et al. 1979; Jones 1981; Nei and Roychoudhury 1982). These trees, developed on the assumption of a minimum amount of branching to account for shared features, have been calibrated to indicate the time of divergence for the living populations from a common ancestor.

However, there is a fundamental question as to whether trees based on genetics or morphology are actually relevant to the issue of the relationships between human populations, let alone to the timing if not the actuality of their divergence (Morton and Lalouel 1973; Harpending 1974; Weiss and Maruyama 1976). There are reasons to question whether trees provide any insight in the reconstruction of population history (Livingstone 1973; Wolpoff et al. 1984). This is because a branching analysis necessarily assumes that population differences arose from a common ancestry through population splitting and continued isolation. Unfortunately, just as a correlation comparing apples to

108

oranges will provide a number, a branching analysis will provide branches whether or not these actually characterized the pattern of population histories. Interpretation of the branching pattern as clusters of relationships, and calibration of these associations in terms of evolutionary difference, assumes (1) that the differences are the consequence of constantly accumulating random mutations and drift, and (2) that gene flow did not occur. Commonalities in selection may cause populations to appear more similar than their actual histories might suggest (Livingstone 1980, but see Cohan 1984). Even a small amount of gene flow between two populations will greatly reduce the magnitude of population differences and consequently minimize the estimated time since population splitting. (Weiss and Maruyama 1976), causing populations to appear to have diverged more recently than might actually have been the case. Conversely, gene flow between one population in a recently diverged sister pair and an "outside" population will make the population pair less closely related genetically. However, are they less closely related phylogenetically? The pair will certainly appear to have diverged from each other earlier than was actually the case (Weiss 1986).

The obvious historic fact is that there have been numerous invasions and a marked rate of gene flow since the end of the Pleistocene. These have affected every human population on the planet. All populations, therefore, appear genetically and morphologically to be more closely related than they are, under branching analysis based on a splitting model of populational divergences. Conversely, however, under a more general evolutionary model of regional populational divergence (Wolpoff et al. 1984; Weiss 1986) the issue of populational differences as a marker of populational histories becomes less meaningful, but then again so does the interpretation of a single recent origin for human populations.

Out of Africa: the mitochondrial connection

The most dramatic (and most highly publicized) of the replacement schemes is based on an analysis of mitochondrial (mt)DNA variation (Cann et al. 1987). From the study of fewer than 300 people, some of the mitochondrial geneticists have concluded that most of the fossil hominids earlier than the late Pleistocene (certainly all of these who lived outside of Africa) have nothing to do with the evolution of modern populations. This follows from their contention that the mitochondrial evidence shows all living people to have a common African origin. Depending on which paper is referenced, this origin is in the form of a woman (hence "Eve") either approximately 200 kyr ago, perhaps 23–105 kyr ago, or 180–360 kyr ago. The exact date is unclear because it depends on which of many assumptions are considered valid. Moreover, this determination does not help much in the question of when populations of this new species left Africa. This problem stems from the fact that according to Cann et al. (1987) the mitochondrial variation "cannot tell us exactly when these migrations took place."

The basis for the "Garden of Eden" hypothesis, with its associated but somewhat later "out of Africa" migration date, is the interpretation that the existing mitochondrial lineages reflect a tree-like divergence network from a single common mitochondrial form in the cytoplasm of a woman who lived in Africa at some time in the past (i.e. the above dates). This interpretation of mitochondrial variation also requires that "Eve" be the last common nuclear DNA mother. This is because only mitochondrial DNA forms that can be traced to "Eve" are now found throughout the world. Therefore no mitochondrial DNA variants were passed down from indigenous natives of the world who were replaced by "Eve's" descendants. For this reason, it is necessary to assume that when "Eve's" descendants spread throughout the world, the indigenous populations were replaced without admixture – especially without incorporating women of the conquered natives into the populations of the invaders. As the mitochondrial geneticists Stoneking and Cann (1989) put it, "the rather staggering implication is that the dispersing African population replaced the non-African resident populations without any interbreeding." If the lack of admixture were not almost invariably the case, the mtDNA lineages of the indigenous inhabitants would have been mixed into the gene pools of the invaders. The very observational data for the mtDNA lineages that the "Garden of Eden" model attempts to explain shows that this could not have happened. These more ancient mtDNA lineages cannot be found in the modern mtDNA data, implying that the nuclear and mtDNA origins are the same, linked in a Pleistocene holocaust of population movements.

Therefore, an unavoidable implication of the "Garden of Eden" analysis is that all *Homo erectus* and many earlier *Homo sapiens* populations not ancestral to this African "Eve" were replaced without admixture. "Eve," of course, need not have been in a modern *Homo sapiens* population. Yet if the mtDNA divergence "dates" are approximately correct, even if pre-modern, the population she presumably lived in must have eventually evolved into the African version of modern humanity (such as Florisbad or Ngaloba) before expanding to replace other populations within Africa and beyond. No matter how long ago "Eve" lived, the "no admixture" requirement of the "Garden of Eden" hypothesis requires that the migration out of Africa was by a new species, of morphologically modern humans. This, necessarily, would be *Homo sapiens*. Since the replaced indigenous populations, presumably of the species *Homo erectus*, would include most of the African fossil record and surely all of the fossil hominids found outside of Africa and dated to an earlier time than whatever date is acceptable for "Eve," the classic text by the late LeGros Clark, *The Fossil Evidence for Human Evolution*, could, on revision, be shortened dramatically.

Any contention that a common divergence date can be determined rests on two assumptions: the main source of mtDNA lineage differences (i.e. variation) is mutations, and the rate of mutation accumulation is constant (linear) for a finite period of time (presumably including the population divergences in question). But what is this rate? Cann et al. (1987:33) determine the rate for modern populational divergences from what they claim are "known" dates of migration that include 30 kyr B.P. for the peopling of New Guinea, 40 kyr for Australia (a surprising difference, since these were the same continent at this time), and 12 kyr for the New World. These estimates for the colonization times are much too low by even conservative determinations, and they may represent as little as one half the earliest appearance of modern humans in these regions. Therefore for this reason alone, the rates calculated from them are overestimated.

Moreover, what direct evidence exists for rate constancy over this time? A study of mtDNA variation in Amerindians (Wallace et al. 1985) revealed marked differences between Amerind tribes, important differences between the Amerindians and Asians, and the apparent retention of rare Asian variants in some of the Amerindian mitochondrial lineages. Adhering to the assumption of a constant mutation rate, the authors account for these observations by presuming that there were numerous founder events, some of which established extremely rare Asian variants in the Amerindians, and that the living tribes studied each represent a separate migration from Asia some 20–40 kyr B.P. A much more reasonable explanation would be an inconstant and erratic mutation rate for this period.

There is some independent evidence to support the contention that populational mixing has significantly altered the interpretation of mitochondrial variation. Mixing is ubiquitous in the historic record of human population movements, regardless of how different the physical characteristics or cultural variations of the populations might be. Clearly, mixing takes place in non-human populations. In fact, it is the analysis of mtDNA itself that provided evidence of significant hybridization between white-tailed and mule deer (Carr et al. 1986). A study of two closely related mice species with ranges that overlap in southern Denmark shows that, while the nuclear DNA of each species penetrates a few kilometers into the range of the other, the mitochondrial variants of one are widespread within the other throughout Scandinavia (Ferris et al. 1983). A tree analysis based on mtDNA for these two species would · be totally misleading (Jones 1986).

Problems in determining these recent divergence rates are seemingly multiplied over a longer timespan. This is evident from a consideration of what should have been a much less ambiguous determination, the separation of human and chimpanzee lineages. Using similar techniques, Hasegawa, Kishino, and Yano (1985) derive an estimate for the chimpanzee–human split of 2.7 ± 0.6 million years ago. The authors admit there might be some problems in this estimated splitting time because of the age of *Australopithecus afarensis*. In explanation they propose that since mtDNA can pass across the species boundary in mice, frogs, and flies, it might have done so in hominids as well. This would account for the "too recent" divergence determined by their method, since one consequence of interspecies mtDNA transfer is to make the species appear less diverged than they actually were. Hasegawa et al. go on to note (p. 171):

If interspecies transfer of mtDNA between proto-human and proto-chimpanzee did indeed occur, it is tempting to speculate in which direction the transfer occurred. The lesser intraspecies polymorphism of human mtDNA compared to that of chimpanzee ... suggests that the transfer occurred from proto-chimpanzee into proto-human.

If the estimate of the chimpanzee–human split may be too recent by as much as a factor of three because of inter*species* mtDNA transfer, how

112

much more error we can expect in the mtDNA calibration of population splitting *within Homo sapiens,* because of inter*population* mtDNA transfer? According to the assumptions required by the mitochondrial analysis discussed above, the literal answer to this would have to be "none, because there could have been no admixture." But if the idea that modern *Homo sapiens* is a new species is unrealistic, there is an alternative explanation. After reviewing many of the sources of error in rate determinations for the human populational divergences, Stoneking and Cann have backed away from their original tighter estimates and now admit (1989) that "we can probably only state with certainty that the common ancestor was present at least 50,000 but less than 500,000 years ago." This "estimate" is much closer to the Early/Middle Pleistocene boundary than the earlier (widely quoted) 200 kyr suggestion. If the additional likelihood of population mixture after divergence is taken into account, a slightly older date for this common ancestor of existing cytoplasms would no longer contradict the evidence of the fossil record. The Early/Middle Pleistocene boundary is a time that an increasing number of recent estimates (reviewed by Wolpoff and Nkini 1985) suggest *Homo erectus* might have first left Africa, and it fits the evidence for other faunal migrations into Eurasia (Turner 1984). Such an estimate would be in accord with the multiregional evolution hypothesis (Wolpoff et al. 1984) that proposes human geographic variation dates to the initial emergence of *Homo erectus* from Africa.

Other factors compound the problems in the mitochondrial analysis, including the likelihood that there is significant selection against some mitochondrial variants (Hale and Singh 1986) – now confirmed by clinical data (Holt et al. 1988). Further, and perhaps most importantly, there are alternative intepretations of what the observed pattern reveals about evolutionary history. For instance, in a study of *Drosophila subobscura* (Latorre et al. 1986), a species whose colonization of the New World involves known times and places of origin, an analysis of the mitochondrial variation "provides no clue to the precise geographic origin of the colonizers." Nor, in fact, does it provide a realistic estimate for the age of the "Eve" of the flies. This is because there probably was none!

Today's world population of *D. subobscura* consists of many millions of individuals. It might well be the case that, a few hundred thousand years hence, all *D. subobscura* flies have mtDNAs derived from morph I. That would not mean that the mtDNA of the descendants derives only from one *D. subobscura* currently living – morph I is found in 44% of the living population. More importantly, the individuals living in that remote generation would count among their ancestors not only those females from which they inherited their mitochondria, but also innumerable other females and males from which they inherited their nuclear hereditary material. (Latorre, Moya, and Ayala 1986:8652–3)

How could this be? Differential lineage survivorship, rather than singular recent common ancestry for maternal lineages, is almost certainly the cause of the mitochondrial pattern of limited variation in *Drosophila*, and may well also be in *Homo* (Avise et al. 1984), especially if human populations were linked by interconnected lines of gene flow throughout their evolutionary histories (as Weidenreich [1946] suggested so long ago).

Probability models with stochastic survivorship assumptions show that virtually all existing mitochondrial lineages will become extinct, even in a stable population. With selection or population size fluctuations, the process would be considerably more rapid. According to one set of calculations, a stable population founded by 15,000 *unrelated* females would have a 50 percent chance of appearing to descend from a single female within 18K generations, perhaps as little as 300 kyr years for humans given the current estimates of a short lifespan for premodern humans (Trinkaus and Thompson 1987), under the assumption of stochastic lineage extinctions. This time frame is suspiciously similar to the Cann et al. (1987) estimate under a branching and replacement model. However, it is an overestimate if the likelihood of selection (Hale and Singh 1986; Whittam et al. 1986) and the virtual certainty that prehistoric human populations were much smaller in number (Weiss 1984) are taken into account.

The explanation that, as all-male generations are encountered, stochastic losses of mtDNA lineages account for the limited mtDNA variation is quite different from the "Garden of Eden" hypothesis, which posits only accumulating mutations as the explanation for variation. The "Eden" view posits an "Eve" who is ancestral to both the cytoplasms and the nuclear DNA of living people because of the link between these forged by population movements in the complete replacement process. In the stochastic loss model, however, there is no such link. As Cann recently speculated (1987:37):

there is no evidence to suggest that people today have retained any of Eve's particular physical features. We know only that we have inherited her mitochondrial DNA; she might have contributed very little to the surviving pool of human nuclear DNA.

This lack of a linkage between the cytoplasmic and the nuclear DNA requires neither a series of replacements without admixture, nor any speciation events, to account for a common origin for cytoplasms *because there was no common origin for nuclear DNA.*

Gene flow between indigenous populations of pre-modern humans, combined with a constant rate of stochastic lineage extinctions, may well have resulted in a homogeneous distribution of only a few mtDNA lineages in the past. The pattern found today may simply show descent from one of only a few previously widespread lines vastly muliplied by the Holocene population explosions. The late Pleistocene provides more than sufficient time to allow for the possibility that selection and stochastic lineage extinctions could account for the limited mtDNA variation reported by Cann et al. (1987) and others. If so, the dates estimated for population divergences from this variation, the discussions about a place of origin for "Eve," and the evidence for bottlenecks in human evolution (see below), are all without meaning.

Bottlenecking: a different foundation for replacement

The second source of a genetic argument for replacement comes from recent discussions of bottlenecking. The idea that a bottleneck occurred during the formation of *Homo sapiens* developed as a consequence of mtDNA studies (Brown 1980; Wilson et al. 1985). The bottleneck involved a period of small population size, and is presumably marked in living populations by reduced genetic variability. The data supporting this interpretation derives in part from the low level of mtDNA variability reported within several human populations.

Another bottleneck argument comes from a nuclear DNA analysis for the beta-globin gene cluster (Wainscoat et al. 1986a). These data were interpreted to show a basic split between all African and non-African populations through a genetic distance analysis based on the 14 haplogypes observed for this cluster. Moreover, the loss of what the authors regard as the "common" African haplogype for this cluster in all non-African populations is regarded as evidence for bottlenecking (1986a:493) that presumably took place at the time that the populations split and *Homo sapiens* left Africa.

115

In a review article, Jones and Rouhani (1986a) bring together the mtDNA and beta-globin gene cluster data to attempt an estimate of how small the bottleneck was. The size of the bottleneck is determined from the opportunity for drift and therefore is related to the length of time between leaving Africa and dispersing through the rest of the world. Jones and Rouhani provide us with an "informed guess" of 20 kyr. For the bottlenecked population, the ancestral group for all living non-African peoples, the estimated mean population size for a bottleneck of 20 kyr length is given at 600, or alternatively six individuals for 200 years, or in the most blatantly stated "Garden of Eden" hypothesis a single couple for 60 years.

However, evidence now suggests that bottlenecks clearly tend to reduce genetic fitness (Bryant et al. 1986). This is hardly what one would expect in the population history of a group that soon after the bottlenecking event was able to expand rapidly and to outcompete indigenous populations in Europe, and elsewhere.

The beta-globin analysis also has its set of problems (Van Valen 1986). For instance, the divergence tree (and its calibration) is based on a genetic distance analysis for ten populations, in which three European populations (British, Cypriot, and Italian) are analyzed separately while two African populations (one a mix of east and west Africans, and the other Nigerians from three tribes) are lumped together. This lumping makes the African data seem more distinct from the rest of the world than might actually be the case. The African distinction is even more confused by Wainscoat et al.'s treatment of the discovery of what they regard as the unique African haplogype for the beta-globin gene cluster outside of Africa. Both African haplogypes also appear in the Melanesian sample, where, it is asserted, they are homoplasies. But there are no data presented to show that these have the "independent non-African origin" claimed for them, and evidence in this case is absolutely critical because, with both of the so-called "unique" African haplogypes found *outside* of Africa (and, suspiciously, in the same population), there is no longer evidence for a bottleneck, let alone a date estimate for when it might have occurred. Further problems arise because the beta-globin studies use the 100 kyr B.P. date published for Klasies River Mouth Cave to date the emergence of modern *Homo sapiens* (the African/non-African divergence), but as discussed above this date is hardly a solid one and may be as much as twice the actual age of the human remains. Perhaps Jones and Rouhani were premature in

116

claiming (1986a:449): "the main lesson to be learned from paleontology is that evolution always takes place somewhere else."

Total replacement and (or of?) the fossil record

Finally, it must be pointed out that if, in spite of all these considerations, the genetic data and their interpretation actually are correct and there was a fairly recent single origin for modern human populations, this explanation must apply to *all* populations. There can be no continuity between archaic and modern populations except in sub-Saharan Africa, where ironically the morphological evidence for continuity between archaic and more modern populations is poorest (Thorne 1981; Thorne and Wolpoff 1981; Rightmire 1984, 1989). This interpretation of the genetic evidence requires the conclusion that archaeological and morphological evidence for continuity in Australasia (Weidenreich 1946; Thorne and Wolpoff 1981; Jelínek 1981), north Asia (Weidenreich 1943a; Wolpoff et al. 1984; Wolpoff 1985), north Africa (Ferembach 1979; Jelínek 1980, 1985), and central Europe (Jelínek 1969, 1976, 1978, 1985; Smith 1982, 1984, 1985; Wolpoff 1982a) are incorrect. And indeed, some authors have dismissed all these fossils (Stringer 1987, 1989, this volume; Stringer and Andrews 1988; Cann et al. 1987), although never with a discussion of the detailed morphological data that has been published in support of the regional evolution hypothesis. Conversely, to accept any evidence for continuity in *any* of these places is to dismiss the mitochondria-based genetic argument for a recent origin for modern populations discussed above. In all, there can be a large Early and Middle Pleistocene fossil record of specimens ancestral to living populations, or a "Garden of Eden" hypothesis, but not both. I believe it can be clearly stated that the fossil record does not support the "Garden of Eden" hypothesis as it has been rendered by some geneticists.

Replacement of the replacement hypothesis

In sum, there is no convincing genetic argument for a complete replacement of the indigenous Neandertals by populations from another region. There is also no convincing morphological argument for complete replacement because: (1) early Europeans have never been found outside of Europe (*especially not* at Border Cave, Klasies River

Mouth Cave, Niah Cave, Fish Hoek, or Lake Mungo – the places where "modern" *Homo sapiens* has been found with dates claimed to be earlier than in Europe); (2) no African morphology is to be found among the early post-Neandertal populations of Europe (the Grotte des Enfants child is widely recognized only to appear "African" because of an inaccurate reconstruction and in any event, as mentioned above, this specimen is from the Gravettian), nor, as is detailed below, do any unique shared features link these early Aurignacian samples with the Levant hominids; and (3), especially in central Europe the morphological evidence for continuity between the local Neandertals and their post-Neandertal successors, the early Aurignacian populations of central Europe, is compelling (Weidenreich 1943b, 1945, 1947a; Howell 1951, 1952, 1957, 1958; Brace 1964, 1967, 1979; Jelínek 1969, 1976, 1978, 1983; Brose and Wolpoff 1971; Frayer 1978, 1984, 1986; Rensberger 1980; Smith and Ranyard 1980; Wolpoff 1980a, 1982a; Wolpoff et al. 1981; Smith 1982, 1983a, 1983b, 1984, 1985, this volume; Trinkaus 1982a, 1983a, 1983b, 1984a, 1986; Radovčić 1985; Smith et al. 1985; Frayer et al. 1988).

Finally, in this context it is important to re-emphasize that evidence *for* admixture is evidence *against* complete replacement of one population by another (cf. Bräuer 1980, 1981, 1982). Historically, complete replacement is an accomplishment that has not even been possible for invading populations as technologically "advanced" as the Europeans in Tasmania. A large number of individuals showing dramatic admixture persist on that island. Whatever the case for the extreme west of Europe, the fact is that only a few workers (Protsch 1975; Stringer 1984a, this volume; Stringer and Andrews 1988) contend there was complete replacement everywhere on the continent. Among the paleoanthropologists who have studied the original material, even the most ardent believers of the replacement hypothesis do not contend that the replacement in central Europe was without significant admixture. Thus, for instance, while Bräuer argues that modern populations arose first in south Africa, and over the past 50 kyr spread through the rest of the world (1984a, 1984b), he also interprets the morphology of the remains of early "modern" Europeans such as the Hahnöfersand frontal as the consequence of "hybridization" between the local Neandertals and the invaders; and one might add that the persistence of this morphology even into the Holocene (see Schwalbe 1904; Weinert 1951) could lend additional confirmation to this interpretation. He is led to this interpretation by the obvious transitional characteristics of this specimen. Such characteristics are logically either the result of *in situ* change (an unacceptable hypothesis for Bräuer [1982]) or of hybridization with invading populations. Indeed, Shackley (1980, 1983) believes that some of the Neandertals and their hybrids survived the invasion and persist to the present (but see Wolpoff 1980b; Trinkaus 1983c).

Invasion with hybridization, however, is no longer the classic replacement hypothesis. Instead, it is one of the less extreme forms of demic diffusion. Once it is realized that it is among the less extreme forms of demic diffusion that the most likely model of evolutionary change in Europe during the Würm almost certainly lies, a productive discussion focusing on the exact details of the demic diffusion can emerge.

THE DEMIC DIFFUSION MODELS

Discounting complete replacement, there are two models of demic diffusion that could apply to the appearance of the post-Neandertal Europeans: a simple model of invasion without selection, resulting in swamping with fairly uniform admixture; or a more complex model of demic diffusion, with specific genomes either promoted or opposed by local selection.

Demic diffusion in the absence of opposing selection is also the simpler hypothesis to attempt to refute, since the process would depend on an actual invasion; but, unlike the complete replacement model, an invasion with hybridization. In the absence of significant selection, populations moving into Europe and mixing with the local inhabitants would be expected to create a uniform pattern of clinal variation across Europe for most characteristics. If gene flow alone had been the only driving force of evolutionary change at this time, one would *not* expect different gradients for different features, or discontinuities in the geographic distributions of some features but not in others. Thus, a consideration of variation within specific post-Neandertal populations, subject to the limitations of variability due to the small sizes of the samples, should show that independent features display about the same degree of mixture between the ancestral indigenous Neandertal gene pools, the earlier local post-Neandertal populations and presumably the populations from the place of origin for the invading populations.

119

The more complex model, the one which would remain if the model of gene flow alone can be refuted convincingly, is that of gene flow acting with selection – the model of multiregional evolution (Wolpoff et al. 1984). If gene flow is either promoted or opposed by selection, the evolutionary modelling suggests that the different distributions of the changing morphological features would be expected to vary more or less independently.

According to Charlesworth et al. (1982:476): "The extent of genetic differentiation between two or more local populations is determined by the balance between the strength of gene flow and natural selection or random genetic drift." It is widely accepted that clines maintained by gene flow and selection characterize the geographic distribution of features in *Homo sapiens* (Livingstone 1962, 1964; Brace and Montague 1965; Birdsell 1972; Brues 1972). Indeed, this is the generally accepted explanation for differing polytypisms in any species that is widely dispersed geographically (Mayr 1963, 1969; Morris and Nute 1978; Stanley 1979; Charlesworth et al. 1982). Thus, it is reasonable to propose the hypothesis that regional distinctions in the Middle and Late Pleistocene of Europe were sustained because of selection and/or drift balanced against gene flow to produce long-lasting although not necessarily static clines for morphological features, a general model discussed in detail by a number of authors (Mayr 1954; Karlin and McGregor 1972; Lande 1980, 1982; Wright 1980; Wolpoff et al. 1984).

And where is the source of the genes being introduced into Europe? Attention has been focused for at least a decade on the Levant sample from Skhūl and Qafzeh as the direct ancestors of the post-Neandertal Europeans. Some authors derive the Europeans from these populations, following Howell's arguments that the Levant populations in turn evolved from Neandertals locally. Others suggest that the Levant folk themselves evolved elsewhere, with southern Africa currently favored as the "Garden of Eden." Either interpretation, however, makes the Skhūl/Qafzeh sample the alleged source of genes that influenced evolution in Europe. Thus, as a potential source of genetic material often thought of as "stimulating" the transformations further to the west, the Skhūl/Qafzeh sample can provide the data to examine the demic diffusion models through the comparison of specific features in the Skhūl/Qafzeh sample with the European Neandertals, and with the early Aurignacian folk. This follows from the fact that Upper Paleolithic

120

populations of Europe must somehow combine the Levant and Neandertal genomes in their inheritance if there was demic diffusion.

> *Neandertals: snatching evolutionary defeat from the jaws of adaptive victory*

Changing morphology is often regarded as a consequence of changing adaptation, and because of the dramatic adaptive changes associated with the Middle to Upper Paleolithic transition the possibility of a causal relation may be examined. Archaeological studies provide evidence for a pattern of evolutionary change that is available to be used to distinguish between these models. The ability to ascertain the evolutionary consequences of this pattern rests on an understanding of the initial and final morphological complexes, and therein lies the first problem. There is a reasonable understanding of a Neandertal adaptive pattern. However, it is not clear that this has promoted an understanding of what happened to the Neandertals. This is because a change in the Neandertal adaptive pattern has come to be regarded by some as evidence for their replacement. Thus, a contradiction has developed, since the very evidence used to show Neandertals as a well-adapted consequence of the evolutionary process has also come to be used by some to show that they were insufficiently well adapted to continue.

It seems to be assumed that many of the Neandertal adaptations somehow contributed to their extinction, since they were replaced by populations that lacked these distinctions and were adapted differently, thereby presumably leading to their advantage. Potentially maladapted morphology has been "identified" in the browridges, brain, posture, grip, and elsewhere (see excellent reviews in Trinkaus 1983a, 1985b; Laitman 1984; Russell 1985; Holloway 1985), and long after Virchow it is still regularly reported that Neandertals were unusually diseased (Ivanhoe 1970, 1985).

An example of this "catch 22" for Neandertals comes in the interpretation of their limb length. Neandertals have short distal limb segments (Tables 5.1, and 5.2 data from Trinkaus [1981]), a fact that has been classically regarded as a consequence of their adaptation to cold conditions, insofar as short distal segments are predicted by the Bergman-Allen rule (Coon 1962, 1982; Wolpoff 1980a; Trinkaus 1981, 1983b; Stringer 1984a). Moreover Neandertal limbs are characterized

Table 5.1. *Brachial indexes*

	Colder (European)	Warmer (Near Eastern)
Neandertal	73	76
Post-Neandertal	79[1]	76[2]
Modern	75[3]	79[4]

[1] Předmostí
[2] Skhūl/Qafzeh
[3] Lapps
[4] Egyptians

Table 5.2. *Crural indexes*

	Colder (European)	Warmer (Near Eastern)
Neandertal	79	79
Post-Neandertal	86[1]	85[2]
Modern	79[3]	85[4]

[1] Předmostí
[2] Skhūl/Qafzeh
[3] Lapps
[4] Egyptians

by thick cortical bone, and expanded shaft and articular head sizes relative to length. These characteristics have been considered the consequences of the daily application of dramatic strength (Brace 1968; Trinkaus 1978b, 1982a; Wolpoff 1980a). The interesting observation is how these two have been combined to explain the adaptation of Neandertals in a way that can account for their extinction.

It was argued (Trinkaus 1981, 1983a; Stringer 1984a, 1984b) that the post-Neandertal populations of Europe show longer distal limb segments because they were descended from warm-adapted populations replacing the cold-adapted indigenous Europeans. But why, then, didn't the succeeding European populations also eventually develop short distal limb segments, adapted as they were to the coldest portion of the Würm? Instead, the brachial index in the Předmostí sample (hardly the earliest Upper Paleolithic humans in central Europe – see Svoboda 1984) *increases* relative to the Skhūl/Qafzeh hominids. It is hard to explain why these earlier Europeans, who maintained an ongoing adaptation to the frigid conditions of the later Würm, have much higher brachial and crural indices than living Lapps (Table 5.1) or Eskimos (Trinkaus 1981). The post-Neandertal populations are not the only ones who don't fit the pattern. The Levant Neandertals have only slightly longer arms, and show no difference in leg proportions, compared with their European counterparts.

In all, there is something suspicious in the "warm-adapted ancestry" interpretation of the distal limb proportions of the post-Neandertal Europeans, especially since the crural index for the mammoth hunters found in the glacial conditions at Předmostí is about the same as that for south African Bantu. And if climatic adaptation is a poor alternative under the hypothesis of an invasion origin for the post-Neandertal Europeans, it is an even poorer explanation if gene flow were responsible for the changes in Europe. This is because, as argued above, the gene flow was differential and therefore represented a balance of gene flow against selection, which presumably should have worked to cause those very adaptive changes which in reality did not occur. The problem here, of course, is that climatic selection plays no obvious selection role in the limb proportion changes observed within the immediate post-Neandertal sample, although *contra* Stringer (1986a) the modern northern European populations show numerous physiological and morphological adaptations to the cold (Iampietro et al. 1959; Meehan 1955), including shortened distal limb segments.

In an alternative explanation Neandertals are characterized by dramatic body strength required by their everyday activities (Geist 1981; Trinkaus 1986), resulting from their severe limitations in advanced planning, curation of technology, and strategic use of dispersed resources (Binford 1983a, 1984a, 1986b; Trinkaus 1986). These restrictions supposedly led to a pattern of behavior in which "They spent a sufficient portion of their waking hours moving across the landscape to require an exaggerated level of endurance" (Trinkaus 1986:205). Yet another explanation relates Neandertal limb size and form to the requirements of surviving each winter "primarily on stored body fat" (Krantz 1982:96).

There have been other attempts to explain Neandertal limb proportions, and the causes of their change. Brues (1959) and Frayer (1981) have each argued for marked biomechanical changes in the proportions of the upper limbs, responding to the requirements of different weapons. Binford (1968b) proposed a model of changing locomotor activities during the Late Pleistocene, responding to the shift from large prey to smaller migratory herd animals. This would alter the advantageous proportions for the lower limbs. In fact, it is here that in my opinion the correct explanation is most likely to lie, although evidence now implicates a different source of behavioral changes requiring the evolution of efficient long-distance walking of sufficient importance to outweigh climatic selection for short distal limbs. This change is associated with the importance of trade networks across wide expanses of Europe. First significantly established in the Châtelperronian (White 1982), an industry associated with the latest Neandertals of the region, these networks expanded to include extraordinarily broad areas that came to be characterized by singular cultural norms (Soffer 1987).

Limb length is only one example. The literature is full of adaptive hypotheses available for understanding many, perhaps most, distinctive aspects of Neandertal morphology (Coon 1962, 1964; Brace 1962b, 1968; Wolpoff 1968, 1980a; Brose and Wolpoff 1971; Trinkaus 1975, 1977, 1978a, 1983a, 1984a; Heim 1978; Smith 1983a, 1985; Russell 1985; Trinkaus and Smith 1985; Rak 1986; Rosenberg 1986). The fact is that there are numerous explanations of Neandertal postcranial morphology which strongly suggest that the Neandertal populations were well adapted to their environment. Perhaps it is not totally unreasonable to begin with the precept that these adaptations *may not have been the cause of Neandertal extinction.*

Intermediates: specimens and features

One approach to the problem of modeling post-Neandertal populational origins is to examine the hominids associated with the latest Mousterian, and/or the later part of the Neandertal sample (to the extent that it can be identified) for transitional features or specimens. This search is particularly important, since the presence or absence of transitional specimens is taken as a test between the multiregional and "Garden of Eden" hypotheses by Stringer and Andrews (1988), who inexplicably proclaim (p. 239) "there is an absence of Neandertal–*Homo sapiens* transitional fossils." The question of transition raises anew the culture/biology relation which, in all its complexity, must surely involve critical evidence relevant to the Neandertal problem. The complexity of this relation is reflected in the fact that in Europe, there

124

are Neandertals associated with the early Upper Paleolithic (Saint-Césaire), and "more modern" individuals (Krapina level 8 specimens such as cranium 1 and occiput 11) associated with the latest Mousterian. Stringer (1982) seems to believe that the lack of linkage between hominids and industries argues against a hypothesis of changing selection, when in fact it would be the *linkage* of archaeology and morphology that would argue against this evolutionary model, by presenting evidence for invasion by new people with new behaviors as the causal link.

Leroi-Gourhan (1958) first proposed that there was a retention of archaic morphology in the hominids of the Châtelperronian at Arcy-sur-Cure, describing the teeth as having "preserved in part paleoanthropine characteristics" (see also Brose and Wolpoff 1971). Subsequent discoveries have shown these comments to have been very insightful, given the characteristics of the human remains associated with the Châtelperronian at Saint-Césaire (Vandermeersch 1984; Stringer et al. 1984). The cranium, mandible, and elements of post-cranial skeleton indicate that the specimen is a Neandertal. Nevertheless, several cranial features are transitional. One of these is the flattening of the posterior surface of the mastoid, which reflects an expansion of the nuchal musculature onto this surface that is unknown in other Neandertals but common throughout the early Aurignacian sample (Frayer et al. 1990) because of the combination of expanded nuchal plane breadth (muscular expansion) and stability of occipital (biasterionic) breadth. Other important transitional characters include the combination of greater medial and lesser central supraorbital torus height, compared with the earlier Neandertals (see Figure 5.3). While the specimen has been described as a "typical" Neandertal (Stringer et al. 1984), Saint-Césaire is no more a "typical" Neandertal than any other specimen could be; typical, after all, is a concept of typology and not of modern evolutionary biology. With regard to its morphological features, what can be said of it is that if a *population* with similar features were found dated to an equivalent time period, that population would be considered transitional.

At Vindija (Wolpoff et al. 1981; Smith and Ranyard 1980; Smith et al. 1985) the latest Neandertals are characterized by relatively vertical mandibular symphyses with incipient to moderately pronounced mental eminence development, reduced facial size and midfacial prognathism possibly coupled with some expression of the canine fossa, somewhat smaller (especially narrower) anterior teeth, narrower nasal apertures, thinner and less projecting supraorbital tori (on the average), with a few specimens showing only very weak torus expression, higher foreheads, vault thinning, and the absence of occipital bunning. The Kůlna specimen (Jelínek 1967) also shows some expression of the canine fossa, while the anterior teeth of the Šipka mandible (Vlček 1969) and all of the Hortus anterior teeth (de Lumley 1973) are markedly reduced, especially in breadth. At Krapina, in the uppermost portion of the rockshelter's Mousterian deposits, which were at the shelter's roof, occipital 11 has an occipital plane that is somewhat more curved in lateral view than the other Krapina occiputs, circumlambdoidal flattening is clearly absent, and although not preserved to the midline the specimen probably lacked a suprainiac fossa.

In sum, when taken as a whole the latest Neandertals in both central and western Europe are transitional between the earlier Neandertal sample and the Aurignacian-associated populations that followed them in time. Of course, this does not, and indeed cannot, mean that every specimen was transitional, or that each of the specimens was transitional in the same way. A transition is a concept that can only apply to a population.

Are the Skhūl/Qafzeh hominids ancestors of the earliest Aurignacian folk?

The continued focus on what happened to the Neandertals has almost come to be a case of tunnel vision with regard to any understanding of the morphological details and adaptations of the Aurignacians, and their changes in later Upper Paleolithic Europeans, in spite of numerous publications by Frayer (1977, 1978, 1980, 1984, 1986) emphasizing the course and magnitude of evolutionary changes within the Upper Paleolithic European sample. Indeed, more is known of Neandertal adaptations than is known of the adaptive pattern found in early Aurignacian populations. This is a consequence of the precept that, when the post-Neandertal populations appear, human evolution effectively ended so that there is no need to study the morphology or adaptations of the Aurignacians in detail. No doubt, as long as this aspect of the problem is generally overlooked, a realistic understanding of what happened in Europe during this time will always escape paleoanthropology.

Moreover, in considerations of where these Aurignacian peoples might have come from, the *earliest* specimens are virtually never isolated from the rest of the sample and systematically compared with potential source populations. While it is said that they are descended from Africans, from Levant folk such as represented at Skhūl and Qafzeh, or from their Neandertal predecessors in Europe, a detailed comparison of characteristics with the presumed ancestors from these regions has never been attempted. Such a comparison should be attempted with the Skhūl/Qafzeh sample at this time, because of the early dates reported for Qafzeh and therefore the potential for European ancestry in this sample.

These early Qafzeh dates were intitially heralded as an unexpected victory for the "Garden of Eden" hypothesis (Stringer and Andrews 1988; Delson 1988). But on reflection is there such a victory? These early Qafzeh dates certainly raise some interesting problems. Not the least of these is the designation of these people as "Proto-Cro-Magnons" (Valladas et al. 1988). This is unfortunate, not only because Cro-Magnon is very far from being the earliest of the post-Neandertal Europeans, but also from the point of view that especially the male specimens from Cro-Magnon are very much *unlike* the earliest of these post-Neandertal folk. Moreover, even if a firm link could be made between the Levantine Mousterians from Qafzeh and the Aurignacian populations of central Europe, there still would remain the question of what they were doing between their early appearance in western Asia and their late entrance onto the European stage. Perhaps they were off somewhere else developing what Delson (1988:206) describes as "Late Paleolithic technology," which he believes then "spread throughout modern *H. sapiens* populations" (evidently these populations do not include the people of the earliest European Upper Paleolithic, since a Neandertal is associated with this industry). On the other hand, Stringer (1988:566) has come to deny this Qafzeh–Cro-Magnon link and states "it now seems less likely that the Qafzeh sample bears the special relationship to the much younger Cro-Magnons of Europe implied by the name 'Proto-Cro-Magnons'." However, it does raise a different problem. Mainly, how could the question of a special relation between populations from Qafzeh and the Aurignacian sites of Europe be decided by whether Qafzeh was only somewhat older or much older than the Europeans? One would have thought this was a morphological question, and therefore it is the morphological relationship that will be examined here.

127

Dental evolution provides an example of the insight gained by isolating an early Upper Paleolithic sample, and then comparing this sample with its potential ancestors. Frayer (1978, 1984) has shown that the latest Neandertals have tooth sizes that are virtually identical to the earliest Upper Paleolithic Europeans. It has been claimed that Frayer's earlier analysis is invalid because he placed the Předmostí sample in his earliest Upper Paleolithic set and it was asserted that taking Předmostí out of the sample would "modify, and in some cases, nullify the claimed evolutionary trends" (Stringer 1982:432). Therefore, in Frayer's more recent dealings with this problem (1984) the Předmostí teeth are excluded from this earliest sample and instead used as a later sample for comparison with the earliest Upper Paleolithic Europeans. Clearly, the later Předmostí teeth are much smaller, continuing the earlier trend of reduction in size and strongly supporting his earlier conclusions. Frayer (1984) also demonstrates that the maxillary teeth show the same trends as do the mandibular ones (again *contra* Stringer 1982:433, and in this volume as well).

Earlier, the Neandertal teeth also decrease in size. This can be seen when comparing pre-Würm with the Würm samples. Decrease in size can be shown within the Würm Neandertals if the late Neandertal sample is isolated and compared with the earlier material. European populations of the Upper Paleolithic continue this reduction, and perhaps surprisingly the greatest reductions in tooth size come between the earlier post-Neandertal sample and the Předmostí population. The fact that there is virtually no difference in tooth size between the latest Neandertals and the populations that followed them in time modifies somewhat the idea that this period is characterized by changes that necessarily "represent a *major* acceleration in the rate of Late Pleistocene human morphological evolution" (Trinkaus and Smith 1985:326). That some anatomical systems undergo major rapid changes at this time while others, which change significantly both earlier and later, do not change at all, suggests that selection rather than gene flow alone (i.e. invasion) is the operative mechanism orienting the magnitudes and directions of changes. On the contrary, if invasion (especially replacement without admixture) was the explanation of this change, all features would be expected to change together, in concert, as one group of people took the place of another.

And what of the question of source for the genetic input into the earliest central European Upper Paleolithic sample? Figure 5.1 shows

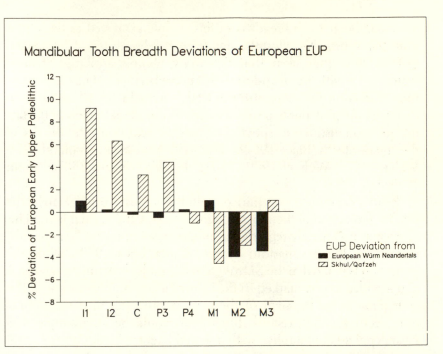

Figure 5.1. Mean breadths of the mandibular teeth in the earliest central European Upper Paleolithic sample expressed as percentage differences from the European Würm Neandertals (entire Würm associated sample) and from the Skhūl/Qafzeh sample. For instance, if the mean Neandertal I1 breadth were 10.0 mm and the mean breadth for the earliest central European Upper Paleolithic sample were 9.5 mm, the deviation would be −5 percent. By expressing the mean breadths as percentage deviations from each of these potentially ancestral populations, it is possible to depict graphically the amount and pattern of changes required by the two extreme hypotheses of ancestry for these central Europeans. In the dentition anterior to the molars the deviation from the Levant sample is very much greater, and indeed only in the third molar is the deviation from the Neandertals signficantly greater. This is particularly significant in view of the uniqueness of the anterior size of Neandertal teeth; the more anterior teeth of the post-Neandertal populations of central Europe are equivalent to the Neandertals, and both European samples contrast with the Levant hominids. If reduced anterior tooth size (for instance as in the Předmostí sample) came to central Europe as a consequence of migration, it came long after the more modern-appearing hominids arrived!

the mandibular tooth breadths of this sample expressed as deviations from the Würm Neandertals, and from the hominids of Skhūl and Qafzeh. It is quite clear that the overwhelming similarity of these Europeans is with the Neandertals that preceded them. The similarity is most marked in the more anterior teeth – actually for all of the teeth except for the posterior two molars. This is important in view of the fact that the most distinctive aspect of Neandertal dentitions is in the size of the anterior teeth (Brace 1962b, 1968, 1979; Brose and Wolpoff 1971; Wallace 1975; Wolpoff 1979, 1980a, 1982b; Trinkaus 1983a; Smith 1985; Rak 1986).

Another example of comparison with the earliest Aurignacians is the inferior projection of the mastoid process below the cranial base. This projection is generally regarded as uniquely small in the Neandertals, dwarfed by the paramastoid process (Santa Luca 1978), while the projection is marked in the Skhūl/Qafzeh sample (9.0 mm, $n=6$) and is also regarded as very marked in the Upper Paleolithic Europeans. If this contention about the sizes of the mastoid processes in these samples were accurate, the mastoid dimensions would be an example of a Neandertal autapomorphy, with a shared likeness between the Levant and later European hominids. In fact, however, the mastoid process in the early Aurignacian sample is even *less* projecting (6.0 mm, $n=5$) than in the Neandertals (6.8 mm, $n=22$). In the later Upper Paleolithic Europeans, the average projection is almost twice as great (11 mm, $n=7$). Thus, expansion of mastoid projection is *not* a characteristic of the transition, as is commonly supposed, and if these data are relevant to the question of a Skhūl/Qafzeh ancestry for post-Neandertal Europeans, the Levant folk would only be ancestral to the later Upper Paleolithic Europeans, and not to the earlier ones.

Figure 5.2 summarizes some other cranial differences. Male Neandertal, Skhūl/Qafzeh, and early Aurignacian crania are close to the same size (Frayer et al. 1990). Therefore, their metrics can be directly compared. Figure 5.2 shows the percentage deviation of the earliest Upper Paleolithic male sample from these two potential ancestors for measures taken from the auricular point, projected into the sagittal plane. Only males are considered because there are no Skhūl/Qafzeh females complete enough to allow the auricular point observations. Compared with the Neandertals, the earliest Upper Paleolithic sample shows by far the smaller magnitude of deviations, with the single exception of the auricular–bregma distance (cranial height) which

130

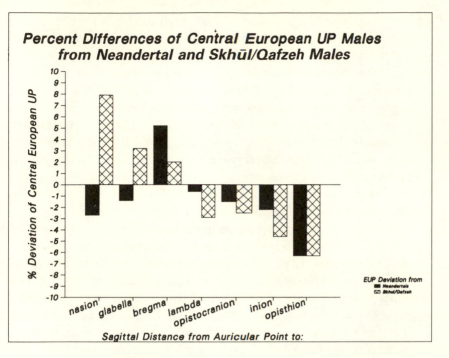

Figure 5.2. Mean sagittal distances from the auricular point to various positions on the cranium for the males of the earlier central European Upper Paleolithic sample (including the Gravettian = Pavlovian burials), expressed as percentage differences from the Würm Neandertal males, and from the Skhūl/Qafzeh male sample. Expression of the differences as percentage deviations from each of these potential ancestors allows discussion of the pattern of evolutionary changes each hypothesis of ancestry requires. Males only are reported because there are no females allowing this determination in the Skhūl/Qafzeh sample, and sexual dimorphism is significant in these cranial dimensions. The points measured to are standard anthropometric positions. The projected distance to nasion is a measure of the total facial prognathism. I have chosen to use a direct measure rather than a relative one such as proposed by Trinkaus (1983a) because of the similarities in cranial size (for instance as reflected in the cranial capacities) seen in comparing the means for all of the samples, and since a relative measure relating a facial to a limb dimension would significantly reduce the already small sample sizes.

131

differs more from the Neandertal males than the Levant males. Compared with the Levant specimens, the most significant differences are in the projection of the middle and upper face, a morphological complex in which the Neandertals are singularly unique and in which the earlier central European post-Neandertals are most like them.

An increase in cranial height, required by a Neandertal ancestry for the central European early Upper Paleolithic humans, is a common evolutionary change during the late Pleistocene. In contrast, an expansion of middle and upper facial projection, required by a Skhūl/Qafzeh ancestry, goes against evolutionary trends elsewhere and requires the incoming populations, if there were any, to take on the unique characteristics of the populations they were replacing.

The region of the upper face is quite important in sorting out the genetics of ancestry because of the unique combination of Neandertal facial features (Rak 1986). The upper facial region of the European Neandertals is markedly projecting as seen in the coronal plane. For instance, the projection of nasion anterior to the bi-fmt line is quite high, 29 mm. This is a characteristic shared with the earliest Upper Paleolithic sample, showing an only slightly smaller projection of 21 mm. In contrast, the Skhūl/Qafzeh sample (and also Zuttiyeh, which I consider as representing a population ancestral to it), have very flat upper faces. Thus for the Levant sample the projection of nasion is only 8 mm. The nasal profile also differs markedly between regions, with the Neandertals and the earliest Upper Paleolithic sample sharing a very marked angulation of the nasal bones at the nasal root, and an elevation of the nasal bones above the superior (i.e. nasal) borders of the maxillae, which forms a nasal pillar with sides that face laterally relative to the parasagittal plane. This morphology contrasts with the flattened and much less projecting nasal bones (and nasal borders of the maxillae) in Skhūl/Qafzeh specimens. However, the projection of the nasal bones is more variable. For instance in Skhūl 5 the preserved superior portion of the nasals is quite flat across the superior maxillary borders while in Qafzeh 6 the superior portion of the nasals projects above these borders.

The form of the supraorbitals also differs for some of the specimens. For instance, no late Pleistocene Europeans have supraorbitals resembling those of Qafzeh 7. The dimensions of the supraorbitals (Figure 5.3), on the other hand, are mainly distinctive in the central European Upper Paleolithic sample. In projection anterior to the frontal's internal surface, the Skhūl/Qafzeh sample is most like these later Europeans,

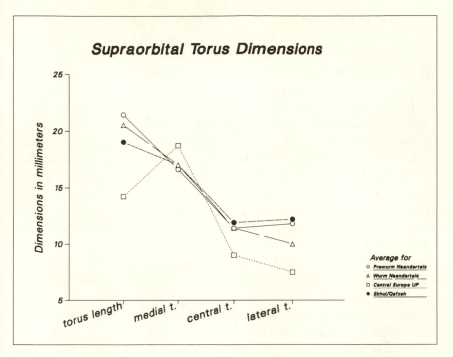

Figure 5.3. Supraorbital torus dimensions for Neandertals (divided into pre-Würm and Würm samples), central European earlier Upper Paleolithic specimens (same site composition as in figure 5.2), and the Skhūl/Qafzeh hominids. Both sexes are combined in this analysis, because the majority of the supraorbitals are unsexable fragments. Measurements shown are the torus length, as defined by Smith and Ranyard (1980) as the minimum distance from the internal surface of the frontal to the anterior surface of the supraorbital at the midorbital position, and the torus thicknesses as defined by Weidenreich (1943a) at the medial, central, and lateral positions. In general the earlier hominid samples are most similar while the post-Neandertal Europeans are distinct. This, perhaps, is surprising for those who regard the Skhūl/Qafzeh sample as "essentially modern." In the length (i.e. anterior projection) of the torus, these Levant hominids are intermediate between the Neandertals and the post-Neandertal populations of central Europe. However, in the thickness measures of the supraorbitals the Levant transitional sample is actually like the earlier of the Neandertal samples, and it is the later Würm Neandertals who have the transitional position that links the earlier Neandertals and the post-Neandertals of Europe.

but in the lateral thickness of the torus it is the Levant folk who have the closest resemblance to the Würm Neandertals. In the other thicknesses all the archaic samples closely resemble each other. Thus, in this case the resemblances of the central European Upper Paleolithic specimens are mixed.

Finally, in my opinion it is important to examine the pattern of variation in the postcranial remains from the earliest Upper Paleolithic, because it has been argued that too many models of Neandertal evolution are faulted because they rely uniquely on craniodental data (Trinkaus 1982b). The search for intermediate characteristics in the sample of postcrania is hampered by the virtual absence of postcranial remains for the really early Aurignacian folk. Thus, Trinkaus's publications (Trinkaus 1981, 1982a, 1983b, 1984a, 1986; Trinkaus and Smith 1985) on changes in postcranial morphology "at the transition" (as he likes to put it) almost uniquely describe specimens that are later in time; in those few cases when early Aurignacian materials are known, they are included in samples that comprise mostly later specimens. This comment is not meant to be a criticism of Trinkaus's work; the quality and thoughtfulness of these papers is undisputable, and we all are constrained to work with the specimens at hand. Nevertheless, because of the temporal distribution of the postcranial sample, little is known of the specific details of the postcranial transition.

For this reason, although few in number, it is worthwhile focusing on the postcranial remains of the earliest Aurignacians. For instance, there is a single vertebra from Mladeč, an isolated C3. McCown and Keith (1939) pointed to the unusually squat vertebral centra of the Neandertals, showing that relative to their surface dimensions (length and width) the vertical craniocaudal thickness of the Neandertal vertebral bodies is small. I regard this as an indication of a high weight/ height ratio for the Neandertals. The high vertebral centrum height/ breadth ratio is the result of both a short cervical segment of the spine, as Trinkaus puts it (1983a:186) within but at the low end of the human range, and the expanded weights of the muscular Neandertal bodies discussed above that create the need for large centrum surface areas. With regard to the relative C3 height (table 5.3), for the later Předmostí sample ($n=3$) the ratio of the dorsal centrum thickness compared with the transverse width of the cranial surface averages 0.59. The value for Skhūl 5, the only Levant specimen with this information, is almost the same at 0.56. As McCown and Keith (1939) recognized in their

Table 5.3. *Cervical 3 centrum height to width ratio*

	Ratio
La Ferassie 1	0.46
Krapina 111.1	0.46
Mladeč 11	0.46
Skhūl 5	0.56
Předmostí mean	0.59
Předmostí min	0.53
Předmostí max	0.63

discussion, the Neandertal values (only known for La Ferrassie 1 and a Krapina female) are indeed markedly lower, 0.46 for both specimens. This is exactly the same value that is obtained for Mladeč 11.

A further aspect of the earliest Aurignacian postcranial sample is the relative sizes of many of the limb joints. For instance, considering the acetabula and holding sex constant, virtually every Neandertal acetabulum is larger than later Upper Paleolithic specimens. Because Neandertals are the shorter people, this is a reflection of the relatively and absolutely large joint surfaces in the Neandertals. There are two acetabula in the earlier Upper Paleolithic sample from Mladeč. Unfortunately, there is not enough left of the innominates to allow the *relative* dimensions of the acetabula to be determined. In terms of absolute size, the maximum diameter in the male (60 mm) exceeds every other Upper Paleolithic male (56.0–58.6 mm), and the female maximum diameter (54.0 mm) exceeds every Upper Paleolithic female (49.5–53.3 mm). Conversely, both of these are fully within the ranges and close to the means of the Neandertal male and female samples. Therefore, unless the Mladeč folk were even larger than the Cro-Magnons, it is quite likely that the absolute sizes of the acetabula reflect a relatively large joint surface in the earliest post-Neandertals.

More evidence for a relatively large joint surface in some of the Mladeč hominids can be gleaned from an isolated complete talus. The tali of the European hominids change considerably over the transition. For instance, in the Neandertal sample a measure of the relative size of the articular surface can be calculated from the width of the tibial articular surface expressed as a percentage of the total talus length. This relative articular surface width, 64.6 percent ($n = 10$), is significantly larger than the relative joint size for the later hominids of the early Upper Paleolithic sample (54.2 percent, $n = 5$). The value for the Mladeč talus is 67.2 percent, a very large relative joint size indeed.

While according to virtually everybody who has written on the subject, the reduction of relative joint size was expected to occur *at* the transition (Trinkaus and Smith 1985, among the most recent), it would appear that this reduction actually took place later, and that many of the early post-Neandertals resemble the Neandertals in this postcranial feature.

So what of the question of ancestry? The morphological comparisons strongly suggest that an unmodified ancestry of the Aurignacian folk of Europe in the possibly much earlier Skhūl/Qafzeh sample is very unlikely. There are simply too many morphological connections to the European Neandertals that involve fairly unique combinations of characteristics. And there are other problems as well. It is difficult to understand how the presumably earlier Qafzeh folk of the Levant were able to coexist with the possibly intrusive Neandertals (Valladas et al. 1987), given that they lived at the same time in the same places, manufactured the same tool industries, utilized the same technology, and adapted with the same subsistence patterns *unless they became the same people* (just as McCown and Keith [1939] suggested might have been the case). Hardly a pillar of support for the complete replacement hypothesis, this would firmly establish the genetic relations of (what we would have to regard as) these two races, and suggest the possibility of a mixed ancestry for the source of gene flow into Europe that contributed to the post-Neandertal populations of the region.

I believe it must be concluded that a pattern of gene flow *without selection* cannot account for the evolutionary changes in Europe. Simply put, the morphology of the early Aurignacians is neither obviously directly descendant from the Levant populations, nor is it simply the result of a uniform mixture of the Levant populations and the Neandertals. Some of the features of the early Aurignacian folk could be traced to the Levant populations (see Stringer et al. 1984) and might reflect the effects of gene flow from this region to the European periphery. However, other features are unique within Europe and closely align the post-Neandertal Europeans with the Neandertals themselves. The point is that the early Aurignacian folk are not simply gracilized Neandertals, nor are they little changed descendants of the Levant folk, nor are they in some intermediate position between the

136

Neandertals and the Levant samples. These Europeans have some elements of inheritance from the Levant (or perhaps elsewhere) and others from their Neandertal predecessors, but varying proportions in different anatomical systems, and moreover they differ from both in some respects. Therefore, no simple model of genetic swamping can account for their variation and it is reasonable to conclude that selection played a critical role.

The multiregional model: gene flow and selection

The multiregional evolution hypothesis proposes that a balance between gene flow and selection oriented the direction of evolutionary change in human populations of the middle and late Pleistocene (Thorne and Wolpoff 1981; Wolpoff et al. 1984; Wolpoff 1985). Based largely on data from eastern Asia (van Valen 1986), it is reasonable to ask whether or how this model might validly account for the pattern of evolutionary change in the late Pleistocene of Europe. One can only hope that the recent widely publicized mischaracterization of this hypothesis, its predictions, and the data said to relate to it (Stringer and Andrews 1988) does not obscure attempts to answer this question.

The key to interpreting late Pleistocene events at the European periphery lies in the relation between gene flow and selection, and the effect this would be expected to have on observations of change in a limited and somewhat unrepresentative fossil record. In computer modeling of evolutionary events in Europe, it is the spread of alleles with specific fitness values that is generally the object of simulation, *and this is an unrealistic evolutionary model*. The extraordinary genetic similarity of humans and chimpanzees has been recognized for more than a decade (King and Wilson 1975; Brown et al. 1982; Templeton 1983; Wilson et al. 1985). The contrast between the number of shared alleles and the divergent morphology for these two living species has been interpreted in almost every possible way, but the most obvious is that the notable morphological differences between these two species are mainly a result of differing allele frequencies (Lewontin 1974). The genetic data from different living human populations are also interpreted in numerous ways. Here, too, it was the genetic similarity that proved to be surprising (Lewontin 1974, 1984; Jones 1981; Nei and Roychoudhury 1982). This similarity was also found in the mtDNA studies, and once again given a variety of interpretations (Cann et al.

137

1982, 1984; Brown et al. 1982). But if these data mainly indicate that virtually all of the genetic differences between populations that have evolved over the course of human history are the result of frequency differences, *it follows that gene flow must also be regarded as almost always changing frequencies of existing alleles, and not as introducing new ones.*

Gene flow, especially over short periods, therefore cannot usually be expected to have a "stimulating" effect on human evolution by introducing new alleles for selection to act on. Instead, the usual, perhaps invariable, effect of gene flow is change in frequencies of existing alleles effected by the balance between gene flow and local selection. Gene flow may help establish new allelic combinations but it is unlikely to introduce, let alone establish by itself, new alleles. However, this implies that changes in local selection are absolutely critical in understanding the pattern of *in situ* evolution, just as changes in the rate and sources of gene flow are. Yet, if new alleles are but rarely introduced, when there is a balance between gene flow and selection the role of gene flow in any locale could be envisioned as mainly providing an unending source of recombinatorial possibilities for selection to act on. The emphasis is on the balance between gene flow and selection, as discussed above. The details of this balance at any one time are complex, but once it has been recognized that this is the relevant evolutionary model it is possible at least to attempt to use the existing data to gain insight about how this balance changes in specific cases of evolution.

The post-Neandertal populations of Europe might well be one of the best examples of this shifting balance model, as applied to the fossil record. It is quite clear that dual ancestry best explains the pattern of relationships of these early Europeans with the Neandertal and the Skhūl/Qafzeh samples. Moreover, the uncoupling, although hardly the independence, of changes in human morphology from changes in lithic industry, strongly implicates demic diffusion and the diffusion of new ideas into this peripheral region. These finally come together to combine as the "modern" European populations with their Upper Paleolithic industries. But it is the period of change that is of most interest and importance for an understanding of the evolutionary process. We are far from fully understanding the details of what happened in Europe during this period of adaptive, cultural, and morphological changes. However, recognizing that there was a *process* and not a *parade*, is surely the best way to begin.

CONCLUSIONS

More than four decades after Weidenreich's specific discussion of European descent from the Neandertals, and more than three decades after Howell presented this contention in an evolutionary context, it remains clear that these essential insights were correct: some Neandertals were ancestral to the post-Neandertal populations of Europe. The evolution of these Neandertals into the more modern populations that followed them involved the same mechanisms as evolution everywhere; selection, mutation, gene exchange, and drift. In particular, because total replacement can be ruled out as the source of the post-Neandertal populations of Europe, it is the shifting balance of gene flow and selection that provides the basis for understanding the morphological changes characterizing the period of transition from recognizably Neandertal to recognizably "modern" European morphology. Comparisons of the post-Neandertal Europeans with the Skhūl/Qafzeh hominids and with the earlier Neandertal populations, reveal a large set of unique shared features linking each of these with the post-Neandertals of Europe. Within each set, features are not present in equal proportion, showing that gene flow (whether with or without invasion as the vehicle for distributing genes) without selection cannot account for the origins of the post-Neandertal Europeans. Therefore, with a clinical balance between gene flow and promoting or opposing selection as the mechanism of evolutionary change, focus is brought to the changes in adaptation which must have occurred in Europe, just before, during, and just after the Middle to Upper Paleolithic transition.

Elucidation of the details of this transition has been hampered by both a lack of agreement on the appropriate evolutionary model, and a lack of appreciation of the significance of changing adaptation and morphology within the populations of the European Upper Paleolithic. Other factors that have not helped include the lack of precise working definitions of gene flow, invasion, and replacement, a continued misunderstanding of the role of isolation in modeling evolutionary instances of regional continuity, disagreement as to whether data from other regions are irrelevant or absolutely critical, a mixture of phenetic and cladistic clustering criteria, and the lack of focus on testable predictions that could be derived from the explanatory models that are proposed.

Western Europe has been an area of misplaced focus by most of the commentators on the Neandertal problem (the main exceptions to this are in publications by the central and eastern European workers). Whether central and eastern European Neandertals alone, or western European Neandertals as well, had a significant if not a predominant genetic input in the ancestry of the post-Neandertal Europeans makes no difference whatsoever in the evolutionary models that account for this genetic input. **Simply put, if** *some* **Neandertals are ancestral to post-Neandertal Europeans, then** *Neandertals* **are ancestral to post-Neandertal Europeans**.

Acknowledgments

I deeply appreciate the opportunity to attend the School of American Research advanced seminar, and I thank Erik Trinkaus for inviting me, and the SAR for its sponsorship and wonderful hospitality. I am very grateful to Rachel Caspari, Con Childress, Karen Rosenberg, Chris Stringer, and Erik Trinkaus for their indispensable help in editing this paper, and for aiding me in rethinking some of the precepts in it. I thank Fred H. Smith for incessantly asking me the questions I have attempted to answer here, and Alan Mann for quoting this paper before it was written (Weiss and Mann 1985:378–9). I deeply appreciate conversations with Olga Soffer, who made me think about habitation densities, culture areas, and the long limbs of the Upper Paleolithic natives of central and eastern Europe. The research upon which this paper is based was supported by NSF grants BNS 75–21756 and BNS 76–82729, and grants from the National Academy of Sciences Eastern European Program. For permission to examine the specimens in their care, I thank A. Acanfora, K.D. Adam, E. Aguirre, V.P. Alexeev, H. Bach, G. Bräuer, V. Correnti, the late I. Crnolatac, H. Delporte, R. Feustel, C. Girard, J.L. Heim, W.W. Howells, J. Hublin, J. Jelínek, A. Leguebe, M.-A. de Lumley, M. Malez, E. Serge Naldini, J. Piveteau, J. Radovčić, R. Singer, P. Smith, C.B. Stringer, J. Szilvassy, I. Tattersall, M. Thurzo, A.-M. Tillier, P.V. Tobias, T. Toth, E. Trinkaus, B. Vandermeersch, and J. Zias.

The work reported here reflects the results of joint research efforts with two scholars, Dr. David W. Frayer of the University of Kansas and Dr. Alan G. Thorne of the Australian National University. Many of the ideas presented at the advanced seminar and in this paper are theirs (if either had been present they would have said that the good ones were theirs and the bad ones mine, perhaps with an element of truth), and although Frayer and Thorne were not there to present their concepts, their significant contributions to this work should be remembered throughout.

6

From the Middle to the Upper Paleolithic: transition or convergence?

JEAN-PHILIPPE RIGAUD

The study of the "transition" from the Middle to the Upper Paleolithic, especially in Europe, has emphasized the changes in the archaeological record at that time in human prehistory, producing, in effect, the image of a pronounced change in human adaptation. Recent critical analysis of the available data from Paleolithic archaeology has shown, however, that there was no necessary synchronism between the various factors at this time, such as climatic fluctuations, change in human biology, shifts in artifactual typology, the appearance of technological innovations, general behavioral modifications and different stages in the expression of symbolic behavior. Yet one can predict that there would have been certain cause-and-effect interrelationships between various of these factors, without there having been any necessary chronological correlation between them. Could there have been differing amounts of inertia in certain adaptive processes such that there was a significant lag between the cause and the effect? Furthermore, even though there are many prehistoric markers of the Middle to Upper Paleolithic transition, whether they are perceived in the artifactual typology, in aspects of technology or in human biology, do they necessarily have the intrinsic significance that has been frequently attributed to them?

With these considerations in mind, let us examine the nature of this

142

Middle to Upper Paleolithic "transition" in western Europe in the light of recent data and approaches. Currently, there are a number of general paradigms, none of them mutually exclusive, employed by archaeologists to understand this period, four of which follow.

1. The lithic and osteological artifactual assemblages are seen as the material evidence of prehistoric cultures. Their qualitative and quantitative variations are taken to represent successive chronological stages and/or distinct cultural (= ethnic) entities. Certain objects are given a precise cultural or chronological significance, which permits their use as "type fossils," in much the same fashion that certain species of ammonites characterize specific stages in the Jurassic for geologists. Following the same parallel with geology, certain lithic or osteological assemblages deriving from "classic" sites have been considered as "type assemblages" in the same framework as the stratotypes of geologists.

2. Assimilation or confusion, intentional or not, between the concepts of "material cultures" (as perceived by archaeologists) and human morphotypes (as perceived by human paleontologists). A reciprocity between these two concepts (each a product in part of the typological thinking shared with paradigm 1), once established, leads to the interpretation that different material cultures were made by different human morphotypes and that the similar material cultures are the products of similar, if not identical, human biological groups.

In this, typological similarities are seen frequently to imply affiliations and/or influences between human groups. It should also be kept in mind that, frequently, the term "material culture" is mistakenly made synonymous with an identified "typological assemblage" of lithic or osteological artifacts, such as is implied by the terms "industry" or "tool kit." Therefore, in this approach, there are major unjustified extrapolations between the elements that comprise the archaeological record (objects, features, etc.) and culturally or biologically defined human groups.

3. The term "evolution" is frequently used to describe the succession of archaeological industries. In this, those industries, being defined on the basis of numerous technological and typological criteria, are perceived as autonomous units, rather than as the products of past human behaviors. It is obvious that objects themselves do not evolve, being deprived of reproductive capabilities. One can refer to the improvement or perfecting of techniques, but not to the evolution of objects themselves. In this regard, technological improvements can

appear to reverse through time, sometimes rapidly and spectacularly, as in the typological poverty of the denticulate Mousterian assemblages compared to the richness of the typical Mousterian, or as in the technological poverty of the Badegoulian (early Magdalenian) compared to the preceding Solutrean and the succeeding late Magdalenian. However, with respect to the latter example, the technologically and typologically poor lithic assemblages of the Badegoulian were made by people capable of producing a bone industry both rich and varied and of painting caves such as Lascaux. This provides, in particular, a good example of the possible separation between the techno-typological level of a particular human group and its archaeologically defined "material culture." Furthermore, it shows the potential for a lack of reflection of major changes in human cultural behavior in certain aspects of the archaeological record, especially the ubiquitous lithic remains which, unfortunately, are all too often our primary indication of past human behavioral patterns.

4. The history of past "cultures" (or material remains) is seen as a continuum, of which we see only brief moments with respect to the climatic history of the same region. The preservation of these cultural histories took place at different rates at different times and places, with resultant large periods of silence in the record. Under these conditions, it is often difficult to make correlations between technological changes, human biological evolution, and the evolving associated biosphere.

Despite these problems and the limitations of these paradigms, new archaeological data allow us to reconsider the nature of this branching "evolution" of the Paleolithic in western Europe.

THE MOUSTERIAN PERIOD

The lithic industries and chronology of the Mousterian have been defined and described in large part by F. Bordes for western Europe. However, following on new research, especially in southwestern France (e.g., La Chaise [excavations by Debenath], Les Tares [excavations by Texier], La Micoque [excavations by Debenath and Rigaud], and La Grotte Vaufrey [excavations by Rigaud]), several new perspectives on it have emerged.

The contemporaneity of the Acheulian *sensu stricto* with true Mousterian industries has now been established (Debenath 1976; Rigaud and Texier 1981; Rigaud 1982). In the Grotte Vaufrey, for

144

example, there is a fully Mousterian industry in level VIII. This level is attributed to oxygen isotope stage 7 by F. Delpech and to the beginning of stage 6 by H. Laville (Rigaud 1982; Delpech and Laville 1987), and absolute dates for the same level provide an age of approximately 200 kyr B.P. (Blackwell and Schwarcz 1987; Huxtable and Aitken 1987). Therefore, from this late Middle Pleistocene ("Rissian") time period, there are fully Middle Paleolithic industries in western Europe. Furthermore, from the beginning they exhibit a degree and pattern of variability that is seen in the Mousterian industries of the early Würm. This variability is in contrast to the remarkable stasis seen in certain facies, such as the "typical Mousterian," whose typological and technological characteristics changed very little from 200 kyr B.P. to 40 kyr B.P. (Rigaud 1982).

In effect, as stated by Bordes (1977), the Mousterian is, before anything else, a techno-typological level in human cultural evolution, a level that was not reached synchronously through the Old World. Furthermore, the associated human remains show clearly that the Mousterian industries were not necessarily directly associated with the Neandertals, since the human fossils associated with these early phases of the Mousterian were not full, "classic" Neandertals.

In contrast, about 38 kyr B.P., a technological and typological change appeared and spread, suddenly and rapidly. It consisted primarily of a thinning of the tools (leptolithization) in the industries, and the flaking became increasingly dominated by blades. Yet, the lithic reduction techniques that can produce blades were known in the Acheulian and were even used a little more frequently in the Mousterian along with the Levallois technique. There are no fundamental conceptual differences between the blade core reduction techniques of the Upper Paleolithic (e.g., of the Gravettian) and those that produced Levallois blades. Nonetheless, with the Castelperronian, a systematization of blade production appears which is unknown for earlier periods. On the other hand, at the same time there was a typological shift that resulted in the production of "Upper Paleolithic" typological forms, such as burins and end-scrapers, on a substrate of Mousterian technology, typological forms that were known since the Acheulian but remained extremely rare then and were only slightly more common in the Mousterian. The blending of a different range of forms and a leptolithization of the lithic blanks gives the Castelperronian an overall appearance that is strikingly different from that of the preceding Mousterian industries (a difference reinforced by the tendency of archaeologists to use an equally different typology to characterize the Castelperronian).

Despite these contrasts, there was a continuity between Mousterian industries (primarily the Mousterian of Acheulian Tradition [M.T.A.]) and those of the Castelperronian, which went through a period of rapid change between 40 and 35 kyr B.P., leading eventually to the industries of the Upper Paleolithic. Unfortunately, the processes involved in the lithic technological and typological shift cannot be followed completely within the confines of southwestern France.

THE EARLY UPPER PALEOLITHIC OF SOUTHWESTERN FRANCE

While the makers of the Castelperronian industry were occupying shelters in the Périgord and Charente, other shelters were being utilized by the makers of early Aurignacian assemblages. This contemporaneity of the Aurignacian and Castelperronian industries is even demonstrated by the interstratification of Aurignacian and Castelperronian assemblages, such as at the sites of Roc-de-Combe and Le Piage (Bordes and Labrot 1967; Champagne and Espitalier 1981).

The lithic assemblages of the Aurignacian and Castelperronian are typologically very distinct from each other, and so-called mixed assemblages (those that exhibit typological characteristics of both industries) are usually the products of mixed levels, as a result of either geological processes or poor excavations. Thus, the Aurignaco-Perigordian of G. Laplace (1957), based on certain mixed assemblages, has not been confirmed through subsequent, careful excavations. Furthermore, the common origin for the Castelperronian and the Aurignacian as proposed by Laplace also runs counter to the current human paleontological evidence (Vandermeersch 1984). Nothing, therefore, reinforces the Aurignaco-Perigordian of Laplace, which was born and should be buried in the drawers of old museums.

There is thus a distinct typological discontinuity between the Castelperronian and the Aurignacian. Yet, this archaeological discontinuity (indicating a populational change) is neither supported nor contradicted by a similar discontinuity in the currently known human paleontological record. Whereas Neandertals are associated with the Castelperronian at Saint-Césaire, we lack diagnostic human remains associated with the early Aurignacian industries. The *Homo sapiens*

146

sapiens discovered at Cro-Magnon are probably not associated with the earliest Aurignacian of the Périgord. The morphology of the people responsible for the earliest Perigordian Aurignacian is therefore unknown. In the apparent absence of evidence for a local origin, this early Aurignacian population, which co-existed for some time with those responsible for the Castelperronian, probably had a more distant origin. Such an origin may be indicated by industries such as the one from level 11 of Bacho Kiro (Kozłowski 1982), which one can see as a "proto-Aurignacian". More recently, Onoratini (1982) has suggested a Mediterranean origin for the Aurignacian of southern France, but the lack of precise data makes it difficult to maintain at this time.

The hypothesis of a typological and cultural continuity between the Castelperronian and the later Gravettian ("Upper Perigordian") was proposed by D. Peyrony and supported by F. Bordes (1968b), but this interpretation has not been universally accepted. A. Leroi-Gourhan and H. Delporte have seen them as two distinct cultural entities, and the discovery at Saint-Césaire has served to reinforce this latter point of view, such that the idea of a Castelperronian-Gravettian cultural continuity has now been largely abandoned. It appears that the Gravettian population, which had largely succeeded those responsible for the Aurignacian in the Périgord by 26 kyr B.P., came from elsewhere. It is unlikely that this place of origin was in the Iberian peninsula, where there is no likely precursor for the Gravettian. For similar reasons, an origin from the north also appears unlikely. Most likely, it was derived, as suggested by Kozłowski, from central Europe, where industries with backed knives, as essential element of the Gravettian, are known as early as 30 kyr B.P. (Rigaud 1987).

To conclude on this point, the Upper Paleolithic in the Périgord does not appear to have had a local origin, and its early phases appear to have been the products of two successive waves of human populations, Aurignacian and Gravettian, deriving from the east and adapting successfully in the cul-de-sac of western Europe. These human populations, deriving probably from central Europe, apparently were already familiar with technological, typological, and artistic developments, for which there are no precursors in the late Middle Paleolithic of Atlantic Europe. This only accentuates the impression of a discontinuity between the Middle and Upper Paleolithic in this region. This apparent discontinuity should not, however, obscure certain continuities that could have existed between the Middle and Upper Paleolithic in this region. Certain authors (e.g., White 1982) have perceived a reduction in assemblage variability between the Middle and Upper Paleolithic. However, this interpretation is based on typological analyses of old collections of variable quality. Using recent data and taking into account the inequality of the Middle and Upper Paleolithic typologies, it is now evident that interassemblage variability was similar in the early Upper Paleolithic to that in the Middle Paleolithic of the early last glacial.

If the lithic technology and typology is inadequate to establish the nature of the transition between the Middle and the Upper Paleolithic, what other indicators exist to provide insights into this period? I will discuss, with respect to this, the evidence for bone and antler technology, exploitation of resources, spatial organization, burials, and symbolic expression.

BONE AND ANTLER TECHNOLOGY

The working of bone is not completely unknown in the Acheulian or the early Mousterian, since notched objects in bone have been noted by A. Debenath in the Rissian levels at La Chaise (Debenath and Duport 1971), and several worked bones from the Rissian Mousterian of the Grotte Vaufrey have been described (Rigaud 1982; Vincent 1988). Furthermore, in the Mousterian from the Würm and in the Castelperronian, worked bone has been noted (e.g., Leroi-Gourhan 1961). However, at no point during the Acheulian, the Mousterian or even the Castelperronian can bone be considered to have been a common form of raw material. It is only with the Aurignacian that one sees the development of a technology using bone and antler for making a significant part of the tool kit, in particular for manufacturing projectile points (*sagaies*). This tendency in the Aurignacian to make projectile points from bone in turn contrasts with that in the Gravettian, in which projectile points were made almost exclusively from flint (e.g., Gravette points and Font-Robert points) and rarely in bone.

The appearance of this new technology using bone and antler seems to correspond with the arrival of the Aurignacian in Atlantic Europe. Furthermore, this technology was already quite developed by the time it appeared in western Europe, suggesting that it emerged elsewhere and then was introduced into that region. Yet the appearance of this technological innovation only with the Aurignacian does not necess-

148

arily imply that projectile points did not exist previously; they were perhaps in wood, for which we have but little evidence during the Lower and Middle Paleolithic (e.g., Clacton and Lehringen). At the same time, it should be kept in mind that the appearance of a technological innovation does not necessarily imply the emergence of a completely new activity; more likely it indicates a new and different means of performing the same activity and/or accomplishing the same goals.

Whether they were in bone or in flint, the projectile points of the Upper Paleolithic are easily distinguished from those of the Lower and Middle Paleolithic by their weight and dimensions, both of which were more appropriate for a weapon that was thrown or projected (e.g., *sagaies*, spears or javelins). The unresolved question as to whether Mousterian "points" were indeed points or merely convergent scrapers highlights the fact that, if points, they were unlikely to have been projectile points for more than hand-held thrusting spears. The importance of this innovation, in the overall context of human technological acquisitions, is perhaps that it permitted more effective hunting. This in turn could have had profound socioeconomic consequences.

STRATEGIES OF RESOURCE EXPLOITATION

One important aspect of human behavior in the Paleolithic can be analyzed through the archaeological record, namely the apparent strategies of lithic raw material exploitation. Recent work in Périgord (e.g., Chadelle 1983; Geneste 1985; Rigaud 1982) has shown that the territories of lithic material acquisition for Paleolithic sites in the middle Dordogne valley were identical from the middle Riss (200 kyr B.P.) to the beginning of the later Würm (25 kyr B.P.). They consist, in the study area, of zones of 60 km in radius around a site, and the use of local versus distant raw materials *vis-à-vis* the technology and the general economy does not seem to have undergone any major changes with the arrival of *Homo sapiens sapiens*. It appears that the first major shift in raw material exploitation occurred near the maximum of the late last glacial, that is considerably later, around 18 kyr B.P. (Larick 1983). It is therefore difficult to use the data from lithic exploitation to maintain an argument that there were profound changes in social relationships at the time of the Middle to Upper Paleolithic transition.

The data from faunal remains similarly suggest stable patterns of behavior from the end of the early Würm to the beginning of the late Würm. Faunal assemblages from late Mousterian levels are very close, in their species diversity and body part representation, to those of the early Aurignacian. In contrast, by the time of the middle Magdalenian, there is a significant shift in faunal exploitation patterns, with the appearance of real specialized hunting (Delpech 1983).

THE ORGANIZATION OF SPACE

In the last two decades there has been an increasing rate of discovery of habitation structures, corresponding in part to the improvement of excavation techniques but also due to the reputation of the excellent work of A. Leroi-Gourhan and colleagues at Pincevent. However, this "syndrome de Pincevent" has led, unfortunately, to the frequent description of barely believable *structures d'habitat*.

Truly constructed hearths are relatively rare before the early Würm, and my personal experience suggests that during the Riss such constructed hearths did not exist (Rigaud and Geneste 1987). Such hearths as can be seen resulted solely from the opportunistic use of natural and/or advantageous areas within the living space on the prehistoric land surface. It should be kept in mind that a concentration of burnt material does not constitute a true hearth, even if heat-discolored rocks are also included. The identification of a true hearth implies that there was some construction and utilization of it for this purpose. Choosing a few heat-altered rocks in the middle of a layer of cobbles does not constitute an objective analysis of a hearth structure.

In the Aurignacian levels of Le Flageolet I, the hearths remain extremely modest, although other Aurignacian sites (e.g., Abri Pataud [Movius 1966] and the Abri du Facteur [Delporte 1968]) have more discrete constructed hearths. In contrast, in the Gravettian levels of Le Flageolet the hearths are much more highly structured and associated with other satellite structures (e.g., piles of heated rocks).

It is primarily during the course of the Upper Paleolithic that one sees the increasing organization of space and the appearance of truly differentiated activity areas, as much in open air sites (e.g., Pincevent, Etiolles, Verberie, Villerest) as in rockshelters (e.g., Le Flageolet) (Leroi-Gourhan and Brezillon 1972; Rigaud 1978; Audouze et al. 1981; Taborin 1983). Yet, if such an organization of living space is common to Magdalenian sites, as with Aurignacian and Gravettian sites after 28

150

kyr B.P., it has yet to be fully established for the initial stages of the Upper Paleolithic.

BURIALS AND SYMBOLIC EXPRESSION

Intentional burials appear relatively late in the early Würm, in Mousterian contexts (the La Ferrassie burials are Mousterian, and not Castelperronian). The ultilization of ochre, which is often given symbolic significance, is known to have begun at least as early as the Mousterian at Pech-de-l'Azé (Bordes 1972). Cannibalism (ritual or otherwise) has not yet been solidly established for these time periods. The mere presence of human remains showing signs of breakage and gnawing in faunal assemblages is insufficient to demonstrate that humans ate each other, whether for dietary or ritual purposes. Recent taphonomic studies suggest that these human remains were most likely consumed by scavengers.

Bodily ornamentation appeared in the Castelperronian, but it became considerably more elaborate in the Aurignacian and the Gravettian. Recent excavations, using more refined techniques, have demonstrated the level of variation of bodily ornamentation that was present in these later archaeological periods, even more so than can collections from old excavations. They have shown that, with the Aurignacian, there was considerable variation in both the form of the bodily ornaments and in the raw materials used (e.g., bone, antler, ivory, teeth, and shell). There was a similar level of variation in the Gravettian, with the possibility that there was a preference at this time for the use of shell.

The earliest art of the Aurignacian, whether bodily ornamentation or portable objects, remained heavy and poorly made. It is only with the Gravettian, and a later stage of this period, that we see the refinement of portable art and the appearance of parietal art. The first faltering attempts at symbolic expression did not become true artistic expression until about 25 kyr B.P., that is about 10 kyr after the appearance in the Périgord of *Homo sapiens sapiens*.

CONCLUSIONS

The process of hominization which led, eventually, to modern humans has long been seen as following an exponential acceleration, very slow at the beginning, increasing slightly in the Middle Paleolithic, and experiencing an abrupt acceleration with the Upper Paleolithic. Furthermore, each important technological change was seen as corresponding to a shift in human morphology, each one closer and closer to modern humans.

In light of recent research, this simple and naive scenario needs to be replaced by a more realistic and complex view of hominization, one in which the various elements that made up the process of human evolution did not appear synchronously, not only across western Europe, central Europe, the Near East, Africa, etc., but also within a geographical area as limited as Atlantic Europe. For example, the Mousterian, long considered as more "evolved" than the Acheulian, appeared contemporaneously with it as early as oxygen isotope stage 7 at several European sites. Certain lithic technological innovations, such as blade reduction strategies, are not linked to the appearance of *Homo sapiens sapiens*, and lithic thinning appeared considerably earlier in the Near East (Bar-Yosef this volume). Intentional burials were performed by late Neandertals, as were a few tentative attempts at individual decoration, but significant changes in subsistence strategies, in bone technology, and in portable and parietal art probably appeared in the Périgord only with the Gravettian, that is around 28 to 25 kyr B.P., well after the arrival of the first Aurignacian inhabitants of the region.

Therefore, in place of the model of exponential acceleration as frequently proposed, one could provide a more progressive model to explain the processes that led to the developments that are known as the cultures of the Upper Paleolithic. Yet such a model needs to be synthetic and global, since the various elements that make up these "cultures of the Upper Paleolithic" were variably distributed geographically and chronologically. Thus, each regional sequence is necessarily incomplete, as is that of Atlantic Europe and especially that of southwestern France, despite its time-honored role as a reference sequence. Recent research in archaeology in this region has shown conclusively that there was, around the time of this Middle to Upper Paleolithic transition, little or no continuity in human biology, technology, and probably culture between successive populations in this European "cul-de-sac."

Technological innovations, stylistic and/or "cultural" continuities, shifts in human biology, the development of various manifestations of spirituality, all are elements which converged to produce the transition

152

from a "Middle Paleolithic" human condition to an "Upper Paleolithic" one. Yet, this shift in human condition, far from being a simple linear process, appears increasingly to have been the product of an accumulation of relatively independent, multiple but convergent factors. This accumulation took place over a period of time considerably longer than that of the last (Riss/Würm) interglacial (oxygen isotope stage 5e). In effect, the so-called "Middle to Upper Paleolithic transition" was a long process which started early within the Mousterian sequence and continued somewhat after the appearance of the first *Homo sapiens sapiens* in the Aurignacian. This process, from the Middle to the Upper Paleolithic, was completed in western Europe when people, bearing a technology with a remarkable potential for creativity, organizing its activities in space in a complex manner, possessing diversified means of subsistence, practising systematic hunting, and possessing a mature artistic sense, were established in western Europe.

7
Upper Pleistocene cultural stratigraphy in southwest Asia

The aim of this paper is to provide an updated summary of the palaeoenvironmental and archaeological records pertinent to the discussion of the emergence of modern humans in western Asia. I will also cover topics such as chronostratigraphy, faunal spectra, sites and their contents, and the techno-typological traits of lithic assemblages. If the temporal and spatial organization of the data sets as presented here is accepted, then the origins and dating of the western Asian Neanderthals are resolved. However, we are still far from understanding the relatively sudden appearance of what are generally referred to as Upper Palaeolithic cultures.

Chronological control over the period under discussion (late Middle Pleistocene and Upper Pleistocene) is reached by a variety of methods. Conventional radiocarbon dates cover the entire span of the Upper Palaeolithic. The dating of the preceding Middle Palaeolithic period is minimal, consisting of only a few uranium series and thermoluminescence dates. Available dates, by both methods, are as yet so few that we should await further verifications. Therefore, relative chronologies, especially those based on the sequence of palaeoclimate fluctuations as interpreted from palynological, sedimentological, and faunal records, are still needed.

Many years of systematic efforts in western and central Europe have

154

revealed archaeological sequences that are better controlled chronologically than those of any other part of the Old World. Land-to-sea correlations have enabled us to replace the alpine glacial time-scale with the sequence of the Emiliani oxygen-isotope stages. When the old alpine terminology is used today it bears different connotations, and pre-Würm stadials and interstadials are recognized as having the status of glacials and interglacials. Moreover, progress in the study of climatic events, as reflected in deep-sea and ice cores, improves the resolution of detailed correlations. This might enable us in the future to test the validity of anthropological models in which abrupt climatic changes may have played a major role in cultural evolution.

Little beyond general environmental reconstructions and interpretations of the effects of human activities in the formation of bone accumulations can be drawn from the available mammalian faunal lists in southwest Asia (e.g. Garrod and Bate 1937; Hooijer 1961; Tchernov 1981, 1984a, in press; Davis 1982; Garrard 1982; Payne 1983; Gilead and Grigson 1984). In most studies, body parts are not listed, and research on cut marks and breakage patterns has just begun. Evidence for faunal accumulations created by recent scavengers exists, but only one study has been published (Skinner et al. 1980).

The most abundant finds which form the archaeological sequence discussed here are the lithic assemblages, known for their durability. The Bordian descriptive method is commonly used in order to obtain a set of observations about Middle Palaeolithic industries (Bordes 1961b). However, current interpretations of the quantitative and qualitative observations are debatable. One such debate is the by-now-famous "functional" versus "cultural" argument between Binford and Bordes (Bordes and de Sonneville-Bordes 1970; Bordes 1973; Binford 1973), although the Bordian approach recently received some support from lithic microwear studies (Beyries 1984). Additional interpretations can be formed by examining the influence of raw material on techno-typological properties or by searching for the various optional ways of obtaining Levallois products. Typological frequencies can be interpreted as reflecting activities such as the expedient use of lithics, curation, resharpening, retooling, etc. (Binford 1973; Crew 1975; Munday 1976, 1979; Bordes 1980; Boëda 1986a; Geneste 1985). Little is yet known about the effects of these activities on the discard patterns of Middle Palaeolithic assemblages, but new studies are beginning to provide interesting insights (e.g. Munday 1984; Dibble 1987).

In this paper, I will use the term "Middle Palaeolithic" in its broadest sense, which in western Asia incorporates the Acheulo-Yabrudian and Mousterian complexes under one label. Names of entities within the Upper Palaeolithic sequence will be mentioned and references will be given in the text. It is my contention that only for the late Upper Palaeolithic, or Epi-Palaeolithic, do we have sufficient evidence in the Levant to define entities as "archaeological cultures" (Bar-Yosef 1980).

Overall comparisons between the Middle and Upper Palaeolithic often serve as departing statements for further explanations (e.g. Mellars 1973; White 1982; Gilman 1984). A similar Levantine comparison will be reserved for a later part of this paper.

PALAEOENVIRONMENTAL CHANGES

The current status of Upper Pleistocene research in western Asia is still far behind that of western Europe, with its detailed level of available information. In this respect it is compatible with other areas of the Old World such as Egypt or south Africa (Ya'alon and Ganor 1975; Horowitz 1979; Farrand 1979; Sanlaville 1981; Besançon 1981; Roberts 1982; Bintliff 1982; Goldberg 1984; Issar and Bruins 1985).

The major palaeoclimatic events of the late Middle Pleistocene and the Upper Pleistocene are henceforth briefly summarized. Needless to say, this version is mine, and none of my colleagues, whose works are referred to, are responsible for the following presentation. The available radiometric dates are given in Table 7.1. The dates for the oxygen-isotope stages are drawn from various sources.

Several guidelines were used in building this sequence. First, there is a general correlation in time between glacials and interglacials in both the Atlantic and the Indian Oceans (e.g. Duplessy 1982). Secondly, time correlations between the cooling and warming events in the seas and on land are treated with caution, although a few works have already demonstrated their overall contemporaniety (e.g. Heusser and Shackleton 1979; Woillard and Mook 1982; Kukla and Briskin 1983). Finally, I have assumed that most of the characteristics of stage 2 cold phase as studied by CLIMAP (1981) could be relevant for stage 4 with a slightly subdued intensity.

Stage 6 (190 kyr–127 kyr B.P.)

Pluvial conditions prevailed over most of the Levant including the desert margins. These are indicated by the fluviatile terrace accumulations in Nahr el Kebir, the Orontes River, etc. (Besançon 1981), as well as by the sedimentation of lacustrine or palustrine layers in interior basins such as El-Kowm and the Jordan Valley (Horowitz 1979). Upper Acheulian sites and spot finds occur in numerous localities, and Acheulo-Yabrudian sites are within a specific geographical distribution (Copeland and Hours 1983).

Stage 5e (127 kyr–118/115 kyr B.P.)

Sea-level rise resulted in the Enfean II formation (Gvirtzman et al. 1983/4) which contains *Strombus bubonius* shells. Dunal accumulations from the previous sea retreat along the Israeli coast were stabilized and formed the westernmost sandstone (*kurkar*) ridge. The sandy deposits in the lower part of the Tabun cave sequence (layers F and E) were originally related to this stage or to the time of a following sea regression (Farrand 1979; Jelinek 1982a), stage 5d or 5b. An alternative interpretation relates this important accumulation to an earlier age, namely that of stage 6 (Bar-Yosef and Goren 1981).

Stage 5d–5a (118/115 kyr–73 kyr B.P.)

This was a period with fluctuations of wetter and drier conditions. High sea levels reached heights similar to Enfean I, originally named Enfean II and Naamean by Sanlaville. The damper period caused the deposition of fine-grain sediments upstream and gravels downstream in various wadis. This climate made the early Levantine Mousterian occupation in the Negev possible (Horowitz 1979; Marks 1981; Goldberg 1984). Inland lakes, such as Lisan Lake (2,500 km^2), El Jafr (1,000–1,800 km^2), Azraq and Sirhan (1,000–1,500 km^2), and Palmyra (510 km^2), were formed and expanded (Roberts 1982), thus elevating the carrying capacity of the semiarid and arid regions.

Stage 4 (73 kyr–61 kyr B.P.)

Major sea-level retreat caused the expansion of the coastal plain, mainly between Mt. Carmel and the Nile delta. Intensive dunal accumulations

Table 7.1. *Radiometric dates for the Middle and early Upper Palaeolithic sequence*

Note: *Mousterian dates later than 38 kyr* B.P. *are considered invalid and were not included in this list.*

Sample no.	Level	Material	Date
Th^{230}/U^{234}			
El Kowm			
Humm 2	Yabrudian		156±16 kyr
Oumm 3	Yabrudian		139±16 kyr
Oumm 5	pre-Yabrudian		245±16 kyr
Oumm 4	inter Yab-Mousterian		76±16 kyr
Tell 6	Yabrudian		99±16 kyr
Zuttiyeh			
76ZU 1a	pre-Yabrudian		164±21 kr
76ZU 4	pre-Yabrudian		148±6 kyr
76ZU 1	inter Yab-Mousterian		95±10 kyr
76ZU 6	inter Yab-Mousterian		97±13 kyr
Naame			
	Strombus level, Enfean II		90±20 kyr
	Strombus level		93±kyr
	Vermet level (Naamian)		90±10 kyr
Mousterian cave sites			
(radiocarbon dates unless otherwise mentioned)			
Douara			
TK-165	top IVB	ash	38.9±1.7 kyr
TK-166	mid IVB	ash	>43.2 kyr
TK-167	mid IVB	ash	>43.0 kyr
TK-168	lower IVB	ash	>43.2 kyr
GrN-7599	lower IVB	ash	>52.0 kyr
GrN-8058	IIIB	ost	>53.8 kyr
(fission track)	IIIB	travertine	70.0 kyr
(fission track)	IVB	barite	75.0 kyr
Shanidar			
GrN-2527	layer D	ch	46,900±1,500
GrN-1495	layer D	ch	50,600±3,000
Kunji			
SI-247	135 cm	ch	>40 kyr
SI-248	145 cm	ch	>40 kyr
Ksar 'Akil			
GrN-2579		b(?)	43,740±1,500
GrN-2574/5	layer 26		43,300±1,200
Ras el Kelb			
GrN-2556		b	>52,000
Jerf Ajla			
NZ-76		ch	43,000±2,000

Geula			
GrN-4121		ch	42,000±1,700
Rosh Ein Mor			
Tx-1119		ost	<37 kyr
Pta-543		ost	<44 kyr
Pta-546		ost	<50 kyr
Tabun			
GrN-2534	upper B	ch	39,700±800
GrN-2729	mid C	ch	40,900±1,000
Early Upper Palaeolithic			
Boker Tachtit			
SMU-580	level 1	ch	47,280±9,050
SMU-259	level 1	ch	46,930±2,420
SMU-184	level 1	ch	>45,570
GY-3642	level 4	ch	>35,000
Boker A			
SMU-578		ch	37,920±2,810
SMU-260		ch	>33,420
SMU-187		ch	>33,600
Shanidar			
GrN-2501	lower C		34,540±500
GrN-2016	lower C		35,440±600
W-650	lower C		33,300±1,000
L-3351	base C		32,300±3,000
GrN-1830	mid C		33,900±900
GrN-1494	mid C		34,000±420

ch=charcoal; ost=ostrich eggshell; b=bone
Sources: Schwarcz et al. 1980; Leroi-Gourhan 1980; Hennig & Hours 1982.

along the shoreline are evidenced in the now submerged *kurkar* ridges. Fluviatile terrace accumulations were interrupted by an event or events of major down-cutting in wadis and rivers (Besançon 1981; Goldberg 1984). Lakes decreased in size, and deposition turned to a dominance of marls in cases like Lisan Lake.

Stage 3 early part (61 kyr–40 kyr B.P.)

There was a return to moderate climatic fluctuations between wetter and colder and somewhat drier and colder conditions. Red soil (*hamra*) was formed under thick vegetation on the *kurkar* ridges. Redeposition of loessial (siltic) accumulations occurred in the northern Negev.

Stage 3 later part (40 kyr–22 kyr B.P.)

There were continued fluctuations of wetter and slightly drier periods. A damper phase is evidenced in caves where Mousterian layers were eroded (e.g. Shukbah), and the deposition of early Upper Palaeolithic industries was interrupted (e.g. El Wad, Kebara, Rakefet). A somewhat later wetter period is radiocarbon-dated mainly in the Negev and Sinai to 34–30 kyr B.P. The following millennia became cooler and finally drier, culminating in the maximum of the late glacial (isotope stage 2). Abundant geomorphic evidence for this period demonstrates continuous siltic/loessic accumulations, increased dune activities, and the retraction of inland lakes, followed by a phase of increased erosion and lake shrinkage (Goldberg 1981, 1984, 1986; Roberts 1982; Bintliff 1982).

Owing to the schematic nature of the terrestrial sequence described above, two aspects essential to dating the relationship between cultural and environmental changes are as yet uncertain. The first concerns the emergence of the Mousterian and sequential changes within it, and the second involves possible correlations between a particular climatic fluctuation and the emergence of the Upper Palaeolithic. Both are discussed in the following sections.

THE ARCHAEOLOGICAL SEQUENCE

The relevant archaeological sequence commences in the late Middle Pleistocene. The earliest industry pertinent to this survey is the upper or late Acheulian which, based on two sites – Tabun cave and Yabrud I rockshelter – predates the Acheulo-Yabrudian complex (Garrod and Bate 1937; Rust 1950; Hours 1975, 1981; Jelinek 1982a; Copeland and Hours 1983). The Levantine upper Acheulian dates as far back as 0.5 myr, or even earlier, in sites such as Gesher Benot Ya'acov (Bar-Yosef and Goren 1981).

The entire sequence of the upper Acheulian is built up from surface and rare *in situ* occurrences uncovered in fluviatile, limnic, and hilly environments and a few cave sites. A quantitative and qualitative picture emerges from the descriptions of lithic assemblages, especially concerning the biface artifact group. The early intentional use of the Levallois technique is scarcely documented (Goren-Inbar 1985a). Products of this technique were reported from several upper Acheulian

160

sites. However, over 50 kyr separates these sites from the Levantine Mousterian, which is commonly characterized by the use of the Levallois technique.

The subsequent entity, the Acheulo-Yabrudian, recently renamed by Jelinek (1981) as the "Mugharan Tradition," also contains bifaces. Thus, as in the European sequence, these core-tools continued to be made during the first part of the Middle Palaeolithic.

The Acheulo-Yabrudian is currently known only from the northern and central Levant (Fig. 7.1). Despite intensive surveys it has not been found in the Negev and Sinai or the desert region of southern Jordan. Uranium series dates place it between 150 and 100 kyr B.P. (Table 7.1) and in several sites it is overlain by Mousterian assemblages (Hummal I, Yabrud I, Bezez, Tabun, Zuttiyeh). Three facies (which some researchers considered as independent industries) were defined on the basis of quantitative studies. The "Yabrudian facies" contains numerous side-scrapers, often made on thick flakes (resulting in relatively high frequencies of Quina and demi-Quina retouch), a few Upper Palaeolithic tools, rare blades, and a few, or a total absence of, Levallois products (Skinner 1965; Jelinek 1982a; Copeland and Hours 1983). Jelinek (1982a) defined the "Acheulian facies" (within the Mugharan Tradition) as having up to 15 percent bifaces with numerous scrapers fashioned in the same way as the Yabrudian ones. The "Amudian facies" (end-scrapers, burins, backed knives, and rare bifaces) seems, following the Tabun excavations, to be closer to the Acheulian than the Yabrudian and contains evidence for limited practice of the Levallois technique (Jelinek 1982a). The use of this technique increased rapidly during the time of the Transitional Unit (X) in Tabun, thus evolving into the fully fledged Mousterian complex. Jelinek (1982a,b) has suggested a possible correlation between the various facies of the Mugharan Tradition and environmental conditions. The Yabrudian lasted when the interpluvial/interglacial conditions prevailed, while the Acheulian and Amudian (as well as the early Mousterian) were associated with pluvial/glacial conditions.

The southwest Asian Mousterian does not differ markedly from certain Mousterian facies of other major geographic regions. Except for most of the Zagros area and a few additional Levantine sites, the Mousterian industry is characterized by the use of the Levallois technique. However, the classical radial core preparation is a relatively rare phenomenon in most sites. Considerable proportions of almost every

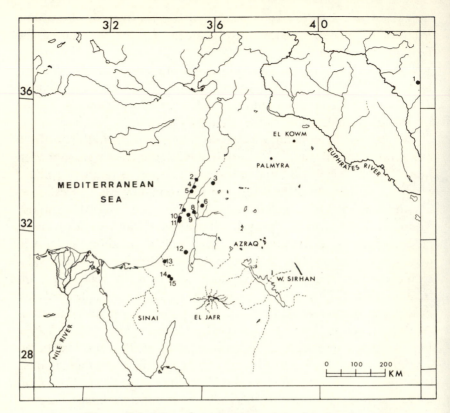

Figure 7.1. Map of southwestern Asia showing the main
Mousterian and early Upper Palaeolithic sites
Legend: 1 Shanidar; 2 Masloukh; 3 Yabrud; 4 Ksar 'Akil, Abri
Antelias; 5 Adlun caves – Bezez and Abri Zumoffen; 6 Biqat
Kuneitra; 7 Hayonim cave; 8 Nahal Amud Caves – Amud,
Zuttiyeh, Emireh; 9 Qafzeh cave; 10 Skhūl, El-Wad and
Tabun caves; 11 Kebara cave; 12 Judean Desert sites: Oumm
Qatafa, Abu Zif, Sahba, Erq el-Ahmar; 13 Fara II; 14 Nahal
Zin sites: Rosh Ein Mor, Boker and Boker Tachtit; 15 Ain
Aqev.

assemblage were produced by the bipolar, unipolar Levallois blade/flake
or point technique.

The Levantine Mousterian sequence was traditionally subdivided on
the basis of stratified sites. The type-locality, although an outdated
concept, was Tabun cave. Based on its sequence, the Levantine
Mousterian was subdivided into three phases termed "Tabun D,"

162

"Tabun C," and "Tabun B" (Copeland 1975). The basic technological and morphological characteristics of each phase were described as follows: (1) "Tabun D" blanks were predominantly removed from Levallois unipolar cores (for blades and points) with minimal preparations of the striking platforms. Elongated points, numerous blades, scrapers, and burins are among the common tool types. Rare bifaces occur. (2) "Tabun C" blanks are often struck from Levallois cores, with radial preparation ("Levallois classique") resulting in broad oval flakes. Triangular points decrease considerably in number. (3) "Tabun B" blanks were removed from either unipolar or bipolar Levallois cores. Radially prepared cores were also used. Points are often short and broad; flakes are thin, narrow, and often laminar.

Copeland's scheme was further substantiated by Jelinek's meticulous analysis of Tabun's material, in which the systematic collection of metrical attributes was accompanied by the use of Bordes' type-list (Jelinek 1977, 1981, 1982a,b). The variance (as well as the mean) of the width/thickness ratio of unretouched flakes was found to be time progressive (Jelinek 1982a, Fig. 8; 1982b, Fig. 4). The Mousterian "phase 1" includes sites such as Tabun unit IX (approximately Tabun D), Rosh Ein Mor, Nahal Aqev 3, and Abu Sif layers C and B. Mousterian "phase 2–3" encompasses Tabun unit I ("Tabun C"), Kebara, Shukbah D, Skhūl B, Qafzeh layers I, L and other assemblages (see Jelinek 1982a for additional details). Jelinek further concluded that the chronological ordering of the various sites as based on the Tabun sequence suggests that the "Neanderthals" of Tabun and Amud are earlier than the more modern hominids of Skhūl and Qafzeh (Jelinek 1982a: 99, 1982b: 1374). However, acceptance of the Tabun chronological sequence as a developmental one requires additional support from well-dated stratified sites.

The Upper Palaeolithic commenced with two versions of a "Transitional Industry," one in the central Levant (Ksar 'Akil) and the other in the southern Levant (Boker Tachtit). The Ksar 'Akil collections enabled Copeland (1975) to describe the transition from Mousterian to Upper Palaeolithic as characterized by the continuation of the unipolar Levallois core reduction strategy. The blanks, which were originally shaped into scrapers and points, were later formed into end-scrapers, chamfered blades (a different type of end-scraper in which the working edge was obtained by a transverse blow), and burins. However, a reanalysis of the collections by Marks and Volkman (1987) demonstrated that the topmost assemblages are dominated by more radial preparation and thus cast doubts on a direct technological continuation. Boker Tachtit in the southern Levant was shown by Marks (1983a, b) to demonstrate a gradual shift within four levels from bipolar blade and Levallois core reduction to the dominance of a unipolar blade core reduction stategy. The earlier tool types include Emireh points, Levallois points, end-scrapers, and burins. The uppermost layer contains Levallois points, classified by the excavators as "non-Levallois," which were removed from unipolar cores, as well as burins, scrapers, etc. (Marks and Kaufman 1983). Thus in both sites the major visible shift is first typological and later technological, an observation which supports the claim for autochthonous change.

The Upper Palaeolithic sequence that follows the initial transitional phase is characterized by blade/bladelet industries. It has recently been named the Ahmarian Tradition (Gilead 1981; Marks 1981) and is dated to about 35 through 22 kyr B.P. What seems to be a continuous sequence is interrupted by a different industry commonly referred to as "Levantine Aurignacian." The typical Aurignacian assemblages are characterized by the dominance of flake production, nosed and carinated scrapers, El-Wad points, and a bone and antler industry, and it occurs in cave sites. It was subsequently followed by other flake industries (Bar-Yosef 1980; Gilead 1981; Marks 1981).

The Ahmarian blade/bladelet assemblages dominate the later Upper Palaeolithic sequence, especially from 22 kyr B.P. onwards. Their Terminal Pleistocene expressions are the various Epi-Palaeolithic cultures. It is quite difficult to define "archaeological cultures" for most of the Upper Palaeolithic sequences. The situation changes with the Epi-Palaeolithic. We assume that the loose, open, flexible social networks which characterized the earlier millennia constantly became more restricted and territorially oriented (e.g. Isaac 1972; Gamble 1984) as the result of steadily growing populations of modern humans.

DATING THE SOUTHWESTERN ASIAN HOMINIDS

Dating human fossils is one of the primary tasks of prehistoric research but, unfortunately, there is little agreement about the chronological interpretation of the available geomorphological, sedimentological, and faunal data gathered in the Levant. The scarcity of radiometric dates simply contributes to the overall confusion (e.g. Farrand 1979; Jelinek 1981, 1982a,b; Bar-Yosef and Vandermeersch 1981; Vandermeersch 1982; Trinkaus 1984a).

The hominids were found in sites such as Zuttiyeh, Tabun, Skhūl, Kebara, Qafzeh, and Amud, all in the Levantine region, and Shanidar in the Zagros (about 1,000 km eastward from the Mediterranean coast).

Current controversies among palaeoanthropologists include the ages of western Asian Mousterian hominids and their phylogenetic relationships to European Neanderthals, and to north African and east Asian populations. Thus the treatment of chronological issues becomes inseparable from the efforts to describe the emergence of modern humans.

Most researchers agree that the fragmentary skull from Zuttiyeh (Turville-Petre 1927) is an archaic *Homo sapiens* (e.g. Vandermeersch 1982) found under the Acheulo-Yabrudian layers of this cave site (Gisis and Bar-Yosef 1974). Therefore this hominid is dated to either oxygen isotope stage 6 or 5e (145–97 kyr B.P.), depending on the interpretation of the Th/U dates (Table 7.1).

It is commonly accepted that the end of the Mousterian sequence is bracketed between the latest ^{14}C dates obtained in Mousterian sites and the earliest Upper Palaeolithic occupations (Table 7.1). Forty kyr B.P. represents a cautious averaged date, although the actual cultural transition may have occurred slightly earlier, around 44/43 kyr B.P. A major debate concerns the date of the onset of the Mousterian. Those who rely on Sanlaville's coastal stratigraphy correlate the sea-level rises in Lebanon with those of New Guinea (Farrand 1982). This would place the earliest Mousterian around 90/80 kyr B.P. A different correlation, recently suggested by Gvirtzman (1983), places the Enfean II (the *Strombus* beach) in oxygen isotope stage 5e (127–115 kyr B.P.). This contention is supported by other circum-Mediterranean dates for the *Strombus* fauna (Hearty 1986).

Problematic too is the relationship between the fossil shorelines and the overlying industries. Accepting the Tabun cave sequence as a standard scale for the southern Levant means that major sea regression (either stage 5d, 5b or 4) was followed by Tabun D-type industries. But the Mousterian assemblage which overlies the Enfean II beach at Naame, north of Sidon (100 km north of Tabun), is similar to Tabun C or B, i.e. "phase 2–3" of the Mousterian (Kirkbride et al. 1983). Therefore the question of whether there is a unilinear evolutionary sequence of the Levantine Mousterian is of prime importance. Those who regard the Tabun sequence as a standard reference scale can find support for the early part of the sequence in the preliminary results of the new excavations in El-Kowm (northeast Syria, about 500 km from Tabun). The Hummalian, which overlies the Acheulo-Yabrudian, is an early blade non-Levallois industry with Mousterian tool forms resembling the industry of Abu Sif C or Tabun D type (Copeland 1985). It is followed by a regular Mousterian of Levallois facies (sometimes still referred to as Levalloiso-Mousterian).

Jelinek has offered the width/thickness ratio, mentioned above, as a reliable scale for the relative dating of assemblages. Without having measured the Lebanese–Syrian collections in the same way it is impossible to evaluate the degree of their correspondence to the Israeli data sets. Thus, for the time being, we should rely only on techno-typological considerations such as those used in previous studies (e.g. Skinner 1965; Schroeder 1969; Copeland 1975).

A different approach to Mousterian chronology draws relative ages from faunal sequences. Although the accumulations of large and medium-sized mammals in Mousterian sites were attributed to human activities, micro-mammal remains in the sites resulted from the activities of birds of prey. The main agent in Israel is the barn owl (*Tyto alba*), the habits of which are well known (Bunn et al. 1982).

The Mousterian micro-mammals were studied by G. Haas and E. Tchernov (Tchernov 1968, 1981, 1984a, in press; Haas 1972) and have served as a yardstick to point out the problems of correlating the Tabun sequence with that of Qafzeh cave (Bar-Yosef and Vandermeersch 1981).

Table 7.2 exhibits the presence, extinction, temporary disappearance, and appearance of most indicative micro-mammal species. Those which lasted through most of the Pleistocene were omitted from this figure (for the full lists see Tchernov 1981, 1984a, in press). The criteria used for building up the sequence (in which Tabun is the only stratified one), were as follows: (1) the presence and absence of primitive archaic forms (long disappeared from the global record); (2) species extinct in the Levant but present elsewhere; (3) arrival of new species; (4) temporal penetration and regression of species; (5) evolution of endemic forms; (6) range of variability within the same species; and (7) the influence of human occupation on the quantitative presence of certain species. Finally, we must emphasize that the poor recovery techniques,

Table 7.2. *Chronostatigraphic distribution of selected species*

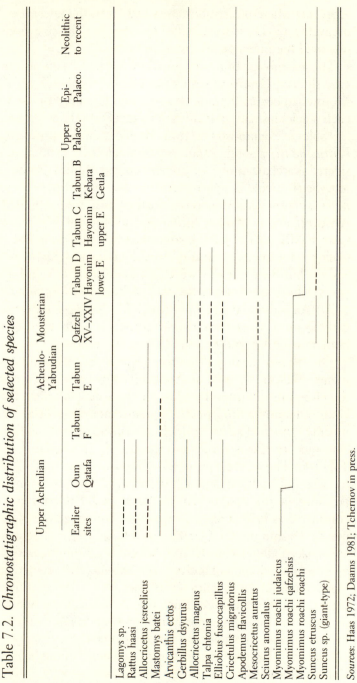

	Upper Acheulian			Acheulo-Yabrudian	Mousterian						
	Earlier sites	Oum Qatafa	Tabun F	Tabun E	Qafzeh XV–XXIV	Tabun D Hayonim lower E	Tabun C Hayonim upper E	Tabun B Kebara Geula	Upper Palaeo.	Epi-Palaeo.	Neolithic to recent
Lagomys sp.											
Rattus haasi											
Allocricetus jesreelicus											
Mastomys batei											
Arvicanthis ectos											
Gerbillus dsyurus											
Allocricetus magnus											
Talpa chtonia											
Elliobius fuscocapillus											
Cricetulus migratorius											
Apodemus flavicollis											
Mesocricetus auratus											
Sciurus anomalus											
Myomimus roachi judaicus											
Myomimus roachi qafzehsis											
Myomimus roachi roachi											
Suncus etruscus											
Suncus sp. (giant-type)											

Sources: Haas 1972; Daams 1981; Tchernov in press.

167

especially where preservation was bad, as in the lower levels at Tabun excavated by D. Garrod, affected the sample size and may have obscured the presence of rare species.

The assemblage from the upper Acheulian layers at Oumm Qatafa cave (Judean Desert) serves as the baseline (Table 7.2). There are no Mousterian occupations in this site, and the range of variations within each species is small, indicating a relatively short time of accumulation.

Table 7.2 demonstrates that *Lagomys* sp., a primitive hare, and *Rattus haasi*, a south Asian rat, now globally extinct and thus considered as archaic forms, are present only in Oumm Qatafa. *Allocricetus jesreelicus*, a cold-steppe hamster is also an extinct form. *Mastomys batei*, a commensal African rat like the house-mouse in the Levant, and *Arvicanthis ectos*, another African rat, are present in Tabun F and E and Qafzeh XIX–XXIV. Jelinek suggested that they were late stragglers in Qafzeh, due to its proximity to the ecological niche of the Jordan Valley, but their remains were not found in the Amud and Shovakh caves, which are closer to the valley (Binford 1966; Suzuki and Takai 1970). An additional argument for Qafzeh's old age is the presence of an early form of *Myomimus roachi qafzensis*, a Eurasian dormouse still present in Turkey and Russia (Tchernov, in press).

The species missing from the Qafzeh records require some comments. Field mice, such as *Apodemus flavicollis*, live in trees and are therefore missing from the Qafzeh open-steppe fauna. However, two kinds of hamsters, *Allocricetus magnus* and *Mesocricetus auratus*, are missing from the Qafzeh collections without a reasonable explanation. The modern grey hamster occurred only in Hayonim lower E and Tabun C. The sporadic presence of the European mole (*Talpa chtonia*) has also not been explained satisfactorily. The appearance and disappearance of the desertic rough-tailed gerbil (*Gerbillus dasyurus*) is considered as indicating the expansion and retraction of arid environments. To sum up, the Qafzeh assemblage seems to be most appropriately placed after Tabun E (the Acheulo-Yabrudian) and either before or in partial contemporaneity with Tabun D. Recently, validated by thermoluminescence dates (Valladas et al. 1988), this chronology suggests that there is more than one facies of "early Mousterian" and perhaps even more than one transition from the Acheulo-Yabrudian to the Mousterian. It would also give credence to the cited presence of the "Tabun C" industry in northern Lebanon immediately above the Enfean II beach.

The acceptance of Qafzeh's early date has important implications in evolutionary terms. Since the human remains from this cave were defined as *Homo sapiens sapiens* (or "Proto-Cromagnoids"), it means that the Levantine Neanderthals (Tabun, Amud, Kebara) may have been latecomers into the region, as claimed by one school (e.g. Vandermeersch 1981a, 1982).

This conclusion can be reached from interregional comparisons. It is agreed by most researchers that Neanderthals, as a special adaptive form, were a pan-European population, locally developed, absent from Africa or east Asia (e.g. Trinkaus and Howells 1979; see also Wolpoff this volume). Even a cursory survey indicates that the European Neanderthals evolved from isotope stage 6 (Riss III) populations into the fully classic type during stage 4 and a large part of stage 3. They survived as the bearers of what is considered the first stage of the Upper Palaeolithic, namely the Castelperronian (Stringer et al. 1984). What is currently debated is the origin of the southwest Asian Neanderthals, who could have derived from part of the original European Neanderthal population and experienced a spatial expansion in later times.

The Levantine sequence, although poor in fossils in its early part, demonstrates that most known southwest Asian Neanderthal or Neanderthaloid remains are relatively late in the Mousterian sequence (e.g. Tabun C, Kebara, the earlier group in Shanidar). A cautious age estimate, now supported by thermoluminescence dates from Kebara cave (Valladas et al. 1987), will be around 70–50 kyr B.P. Thus the arrival of the Neanderthals in western Asia could be explained as resulting from migration or gene flow into Mediterranean coastal ranges or along inland steppic routes leading eastward.

This population expansion could have happened with the onset of the cold and dry conditions of stage 4 in western Europe, which evidently caused drastic changes in the availability, reliability and accessibility of basic food resources. The southward and eastward expansion of continental glaciers, as well as the advent of mountain glaciers, enlarged the surface of periglacial lands and shifted the boundaries of vegetational belts. Regions like Belgium turned into polar deserts (Cordy 1984). Environmental changes such as occurred in southwestern France led to the replacement of red deer, wild horse, and roe deer mainly by reindeer herds in the area of Combe Grenal (Delpech and Prat 1980; Chase 1986), challenging the abilities of Mousterian people to adapt to a more precarious meat resource (Burch 1972). A somewhat similar faunal change is evident also in central Europe (Gábori 1976). In sum, the new environmental configuration in Europe challenged the foraging technologies, the social structure, and the spatial organization of Mousterian populations, forcing them to move into Mediterranean lands. However, discussing in detail all the possible environmental effects on the Eurasian Mousterian adaptations is beyond the scope of this chapter.

If this reconstruction is verified, then the arrival of Neandertals or Neanderthaloid morphological features in southwest Asia occurred around 70 kyr B.P. It also supports the contention that the Neanderthals are not necessarily the direct ancestors of modern *Homo sapiens sapiens* (Howells 1976).

Many researchers have expressed their scepticism about the possibility of coexistence of two hominid types, side by side, for a long period of time. In the above scenario the expansion of west European populations is seen as a necessity enhanced by the attraction of the Levantine lusher pluvial conditions. While the newcomers took over the more forested and colder mountainous parts of southwestern Asia, the local Mousterian population could exploit the previously semi-desertic region. Whether interbreeding was the mechanism through which Neanderthal morphological forms had disappeared is unknown.

The lithic industries as described by the Bordian techno-typological analysis do not reflect the differences or changes in hominid morphology. The only proposition to detect such a change in the lithics was made by Jelinek (1982a), who regards the rapid decrease in the relative thickness of the flakes in the Tabun sequence as indicating the emergence of modern humans. However, given the techno-typological similarities among Mousterian industries in several remote regions of the Old World, the selective role of raw material in dictating knapping techniques, and the various optional core reduction strategies within the Levallois technique (Boëda 1986a,b), we should be cautious in adopting this interpretation.

VARIOUS ASPECTS OF THE ARCHAEOLOGICAL RECORDS

Cave site formation processes

Most Palaeolithic geologists have been busy during the last four decades deciphering the climatic implications of rockshelters and cave sedi-

170

ments and the natural agencies responsible for their accumulations (e.g. Farrand 1979; Laville et al. 1980). Little attention has been given to the contribution and effects of animals and humans (Goldberg 1980; Butzer 1982). Therefore we still know very little about biogenic interventions in the processes which govern the sedimentation in caves and rockshelters. The natural agencies include local rock deterioration, karstic activities, eolian effects, and lowering of the water table and subsidence of deposits. These affected the continuity of accumulation in southwest Asian caves and caused in some instances stratigraphic gaps of unknown duration, such as those noted in Tabun, Bezez, Kebara, Hayonim, and Shukbah (Bar-Yosef and Vandermeersch 1972, 1981; Farrand 1979; Goldberg 1980; Kirkbride et al. 1983; Goldberg and Laville in press). These local conditions inside caves and rockshelters, as well as their locations in relation to resources, influenced their potential use by animals and humans.

In the Levantine caves, those rich in archaeological assemblages, it is not an easy task to sort out human occupation debris from the residues of lairs or dens. Observations made recently in Kebara cave in Unit XIII (Bar-Yosef et al. 1986) can be interpreted as intermittent occupations. Human activities left a series of hearths (either rounded or irregular in shape) with a few artifacts, while animal occupations are evidenced by concentrations of coprolites.

Given the available archaeological evidence, it is not clear to what extent Middle Palaeolithic humans modified their natural shelters. There is scanty evidence for intrasite variability but none for surface modification or the erection of supplementary partition walls. Anthropogenic contributions to the depositional processes reflect shifting activities. One example is the Qafzeh terrace (which is effectively the entrance zone). There the lower layers, in which the hominid burials were uncovered, are relatively poor in artifacts and large or medium-sized mammalian bones, but they preserved discrete hearths (Vandermeersch 1981a). These layers contain extremely rich micro-mammal bone collections, testifying to periods of abandonment when birds of prey nested in the cave. On the other hand, the proliferation of the African rat (*Mastomys batei*) is interpreted by Tchernov (1984b) as indicating abundant refuse typical of human habitation. Whether the main occupation took place inside the cave or somewhere near the cave is unclear. The upper layers on the terrace demonstrate a major change. They are rich in broken animal bones, have abundant lithics, but contain no microfauna, no burials, and no distinct features such as hearths. It seems that the nature of the occupation changed and thus the character of the deposits. Unfortunately the brecciation of these layers makes their detailed study by traditional methods a difficult task.

The Mousterian hearths and the ashy lenses in Kebara cave (not to be confused with possibly natural brushfires in Tabun C) are other examples of human activities. While ashy lenses extend over one to two square meters and have no regular shape, the hearths are often rounded or oval and in a few cases were lit inside a shallow cavity dug in the cave's earth floor. The fires could result from the need for warmth, light, roasting meat, and perhaps even parching wild pulses, for which some evidence was uncovered in Kebara. No Levantine Mousterian site has provided evidence for warmth banking (Binford 1982b) in the form of fire-cracked rocks or heated pebbles.

When Middle Palaeolithic sites are compared to Upper Palaeolithic ones we should keep in mind that most of the Upper Palaeolithic cave occupations were excavated in the 1930s, and the recent investigations in the Negev, northern Sinai and Trans-Jordan were on open-air sites. Beyond this limitation, Upper Palaeolithic occupations are seemingly better organized. Built-up fireplaces with stones, various types of simple hearths, discrete garbage zones, etc., have been uncovered (Belfer-Cohen and Bar-Yosef 1982; Marks 1983a). But even in such instances, our knowledge about the processes involved in the formation of these various layers is still very limited.

Site size and settlement pattern

Measuring site size is problematic even in terminal Pleistocene occurrences, let alone in earlier ones. The delineation of a utilized or occupied area is often hardly detectable in archaeological contexts. Excavations are commonly limited in surface and do not necessarily correspond to the presumably original occupations. Erosion and deflation have removed portions of large sites and in many instances have destroyed entirely the flimsy residues left in ephemeral campsites. However, a few brief comments based on the available literature are worth while.

The observable dichotomy in occupation intensity between the sites on the Levantine western hilly flanks and those on the eastern flanks (often the drier side) has already been noted by S. Binford (Binford 1968b). But there is more to it. Corridor-like caves were less habitable

172

because of space configuration, difficulties of illumination, and relatively higher dampness in the rear areas. Thus high- and low-occupation intensities occur within the same vegetational belt, namely the Mediterranean. At the same time, intensive occupations took place in oasis situations, such as in the Negev highlands (Rosh Ein Mor, Nahal Aqev).

The impression that there are more open-air Upper Palaeolithic sites is probably false. Most Mousterian land surfaces were already removed in antiquity or are buried under later accumulations (Marks and Friedel 1977; Goldberg 1984).

A similar pattern emerges from the scanty data from Iran and Iraq. Large and rich cave sites are not known except for Shanidar, but those of the Zagros can be subdivided into intensively and sparsely occupied shelters (Smith 1986).

A reconstructed Mousterian settlement pattern based on the distribution of sites in the Negev has been presented by Marks (1981). He identified a base camp surrounded by ephemeral hunting stations and quarry workshops dispersed over the territory. A similar pattern can be recognized for the Mousterian in the Carmel–Galilee area or the El-Kowm basin. The recognition that the interpretation of intrasite variability affects our understanding of regional patterning led Munday (1984) to examine again the available quantitative data sets for 21 Mousterian sites in the Negev highlands. He concluded that intrasite variation, as exhibited in techno-typological traits, indicates a relationship between site type, core reduction techniques, and intrasite patterning, which all together directly affected the intersite patterning. Unfortunately, the absence of bones prevents a more extensive examination of the proposed interpretation.

The Mousterian site Fara II in the northern Negev sheds some light on this problem (Gilead and Grigson 1984). The animal bones, predominantly of equids, wild oxen, and hartebeest were recovered with a rich lithic assemblage, showing typical features of a quarry workshop, with only 5.0 percent retouched pieces. It lends the impression that knapping was possibly an activity for which more time was allocated in certain places but was hardly the main task.

Upper Palaeolithic cave sites with higher occupational intensity, such as Ksar 'Akil, El Wad, and Kebara, differ from those where special activities (possibly seasonal) were recognizable in the excavated area (Belfer-Cohen and Bar-Yosef 1982). While rockshelters, such as

173

Yabrud II and Erq el Ahmar, indicate ephemeral occupations, only the semiarid region provides sufficient evidence indicating that a higher degree of mobility characterizes the Upper Palaeolithic settlement pattern (Marks and Friedel 1977; Marks 1983b).

When the geographic distributions of Mousterian and Upper Palaeolithic sites are compared, the former indicate higher dependence on wetter conditions. The situation changes with the Late Mousterian, a time unit to which sites like Douara Cave (Palmyra) are assigned. Exploitation of the Irano-Turanian vegetational belt became a viable option, perhaps due to the development of hunting techniques. During both periods caves higher than 1,400 m above sea level in Iran and the Caucasus could have been only summer occupations, thus demonstrating an early vertical seasonal movement.

Temporal movements are also expressed in the lithic assemblages, and quite a few examples can be cited for sites where only retouched and used pieces were found (Kunji) or where the number of recovered pieces indicates an ephemeral occupation (Erq el Ahmar, Sefunim). Intrasite variability is recorded from caves such as Kebara, where garbage zones are rich in debitage, cores, and bones and central areas have hearths, higher frequencies of retouched pieces, utilized pieces, complete flakes, blades, and points (Schick and Stekelis 1977).

Given the scanty evidence from many Upper Palaeolithic sites, only those recovered in the Negev and Sinai demonstrate a clear pattern of lithic distribution (Bar-Yosef and Belfer 1977; Marks 1983a). In most instances the higher tool and debitage densities are around the hearths. In cave sites the picture tends to be blurred because of more active biogenic and natural post-depositional processes.

The faunal records

Bone collections from Middle Palaeolithic sites were often considered as sources for reconstructing environmental changes (e.g. Hooijer 1966; Tchernov 1968, 1981; Davis 1977, 1982; Garrard 1982; Payne 1983). The only palaeoanthropological debate was about their capacity to serve this purpose or whether they merely reflect the "hunter's choice." Recently Garrard (1982) and Davis (1982) concluded that the faunal spectrum in each site records the surrounding environments not only in Mousterian times, but also until the onset of animal domestication, about 9 kyr B.P.

174

The contention that Lower and Middle Palaeolithic people were hunters was not challenged until recently (Binford 1981, 1984a). Testing this hypothesis in a way similar to the one proposed by Binford cannot be done on the basis of the available Near Eastern faunal reports where, in most cases, counts of body parts are not given. The available bone counts are presented in Tables 7.3 and 7.4, which are organized in a generalized chronological order. They exhibit four phenomena:

a. One third of the mammalian bones in several Acheulo-Yabrudian sites are of large animals (*Bos primigenius*, rhino, equids).

b. Large mammals are predominant in the two open-air Mousterian sites – Fara II (Gilead and Grigson 1984) and Biqat Kuneitra (Hovers 1986).

c. The tendency to consume medium- and small-sized mammals continued without apparent change from the Mousterian through the Upper and Epi-Palaeolithic.

d. Relatively high frequencies of red deer in Qafzeh cave, exceptional among both Middle and Upper Palaeolithic assemblages, call for a reexamination of the collections.

We may tentatively conclude that the overall trend demonstrates that hunting techniques developed during Mousterian times. In prime situations where scavenging was a time- and energy-saving strategy, Mousterian people took advantage of the available carcasses. This would explain the spectrum of Fara II, a site located in the gallery forest along Nahal Besor, which flows through the flat steppic environment of the northern Negev.

A somewhat similar situation is provided by Biqat Kuneitra, which lies in a basin surrounded by dead volcanoes on the Golan Heights. Even today the lower part of the basin is flooded during the winter. In prehistoric times a fresh pond occupied this area in the summer. The site, located on the edge of the pond, contained a rich Mousterian industry with numerous cores and many retouched and reutilized pieces (Goren-Inbar 1985b). The bone collection is dominated by large mammals such as *Bos primigenius* and equids (about 80 percent), with rare rhino, some deer and gazelle (about 20 percent). Numerous fragments bear gnawing and cut marks (Hovers 1986). The high frequencies of large mammals possibly indicate a mixed strategy of

Table 7.3. Frequencies of large, medium, and small sized mammals from Mousterian sites in southwest Asia (excluding carnivores)

	Bos sp.	Alcelaphus	Gazelle	Capra sp.	Red deer	Fallow deer	Roe deer	Wild boar	Hippo.	Equid	Rhino	Camelus sp.	Hyrax	Hare	Hedgehog Porcupine	n=
Masloukh	64.8	–	–	0.8	3.7	8.0	0.8	0.4	+	4.0	17.3	–	+	+	–	1273
Abri Zumoffen	22.4	0.2	–	–	–	61.8	0.5	2.0	–	9.7	3.6	–	–	–	–	196
Tabun Eb	22.0	–	8.8	1.2	7.4	46.2	0.2	1.9	–	6.0	3.1	–	0.7	–	–	411
Tabun Ea	9.1	–	26.5	3.8	8.8	43.0	0.3	1.2	+	3.3	2.3	–	0.3	–	0.5	336
Qafzeh XVII–XXII	20.0	–	21.8	8.2	16.4	12.7	–	1.8	–	17.3	1.8	–	–	–	–	110
Qafzeh XV–XII	16.8	–	3.8	13.6	36.4	5.0	–	5.0	–	2.9	1.2	–	–	–	–	338
Qafzeh V–XI	21.3	2.7	14.8	9.2	23.2	10.2	0.7	14.8	–	3.7	–	0.3	–	–	–	108
Tabun D	11.5	–	38.7	1.8	9.3	25.1	–	2.1	1.4	0.7	3.2	–	2.5	–	2.2	277
Tabun C	24.3	–	32.8	3.8	4.2	9.0	–	5.5	3.8	3.2	4.7	+	1.3	0.5	1.0	376
Tabun B	2.3	–	12.6	1.6	1.0	77.2	0.1	0.2	–	2.4	–	–	0.2	–	–	1723
Tabun Chim.	–	–	0.4	–	0.4	98.5	–	–	–	–	–	–	–	–	–	1461
Ras El-Kelb	11.8	0.5	4.2	3.6	0.7	64.3	1.0	8.0	–	+	2.4	–	+	–	–	994
Bezez B	2.8	–	22.5	0.7	0.7	46.6	–	1.4	–	–	–	–	–	–	–	142
Ksar Akil 29–26	19.8	–	0.5	4.7	0.3	73.1	1.5	+	–	–	+	–	+	–	–	2719
Ksar Akil 36–30	2.7	–	2.9	20.6	–	70.7	3.1	+	–	–	–	–	–	–	–	451
Kebara Moust.	2.0	+	62.0	1.0	4.0	28.0	+	2.0	–	1.0	+	–	–	–	–	2098
Hayonim Moust.	+	–	86.0	2.0	2.0	6.0	3.0	1.0	–	+	–	–	–	–	–	186
Shukbah Moust.	15.4	–	48.4	+	–	38.0	–	+	0.8	1.2	–	–	+	+	–	?
Farah II	24.0	31.3	0.8	0.8	–	–	–	–	–	38.0	–	4.0	–	–	–	147
Douara	–	0.4	24.0	29.8	–	–	–	–	–	4.1	–	7.2	1.0	25.0	8.1	650
Shanidar 10–8	+	–	+	98.0	+	–	1.0	–	–	–	–	–	–	–	–	319
Shanidar 8–7	–	–	–	99.0	0.5	–	–	0.5	–	–	–	–	–	–	–	602
Shanidar 7–	–	–	–	98.0	1.0	–	–	1.0	–	–	–	–	–	–	–	169
Skhul	89.5	+	+	+	+	–	0.2	+	0.5	9.7	+	–	+	+	+	(668)

After Hooijer 1961; Bouchud 1974; Davis 1977, 1982; Evins 1982; Garrard 1982, 1983; Payne 1983

Table 7.4. Frequencies of large, medium, and small sized mammals from Upper Palaeolithic sites in southwest Asia (excluding carnivores)

	Bos sp.	Alcelaphus	Gazelle	Capra sp.	Red deer	Fallow deer	Roe deer	Wild boar	Hippo.	Equid	Rhino	Camelus sp.	Hyrax	Hare	Hedgehog Porcupine	n=
Ksar 'Akil 25–19	5.0	–	2.0	29.0	–	56.0	4.0	+	–	–	–	–				1049
Ksar 'Akil 18–10	2.0	+	4.0	22.0	–	49.0	23.0	+	–	–	–	–				1393
Ksar 'Akil 9–6	–	+	2.0	25.0	–	43.0	30.0	+	–	–	–	–				3268
Ksar 'Akil 5–1	1.0	–	1.0	30.0	1.0	53.0	15.0	+	–	–	–	–				1856
Kebara* UP	1.0		62.0	1.0	2.0	28.0	1.0	+	–	+	–	–				2098
Hayonim D	+	1.0	89.0	2.0	1.0	5.0	1.0		–	+	–	–				1730
El-Wad E	10.7	1.6	13.5	0.9	6.6	63.0	0.2	1.2	–	0.2	–	–	0.2	1.1	0.2	964
El-Wad D	6.9	1.7	56.3	1.8	4.2	24.1	0.2	2.2	–	0.7	–	–	–	1.3	0.7	597
Kebara E	11.4	5.4	21.1	–	4.9	48.8	3.0	0.6	–	4.8	–	–				166
Kebara D	11.2	3.3	20.9	–	3.3	58.5	1.4	–	–	1.4	–					215
Rakefet Aur.	5.2		64.4	–	7.8	18.4	0.3	3.9	–	–	–	–				309
Fazael IX	2.0	–	72.0	5.0	1.0	19.0	1.0	1.0	–	–	–	–				82
Fazael X	–	–	89.0	–	–	11.0	–	1.0	–	–	–	–				124
Fazael IIIA	1.0	–	73.0	5.0	–	18.0	2.0	2.0	–	–	–	–				85
Ein Gev I	3.0	–	44.0	15.0	7.0	28.0	1.0	1.0	–	–	–	–				397

After Hooijer 1961; Saxon 1974; Davis 1977, 1982; Garrard 1982, 1983.

scavenging with some hunting by the Mousterian people. Repeated occupations of the same locale resulted in the reutilization of many artifacts. To sum up, the possibility that hunting developed during the Levantine Middle Palaeolithic is a viable option. Whether it resulted from environmental stress (fluctuations within isotope stage 5 or stage 4), accompanied by the intensification of human social networks, is unknown.

The lithic industries

Lithic studies led to the definition of the main Palaeolithic entities and their temporal or spatial subdivisions. Bordes' type-list enabled a common descriptive language to be used for the Middle Palaeolithic. Additional attribute analyses used by various researchers, both metric and technological, furnished complementary data. Thus we have today the means for making observations but not necessarily the means for interpreting them.

Much of the emphasis in recent research is given to the study of technology. The description of core reduction strategies is expected to give us some insights into the knapper's succession of decisions. We try to find out whether such decisions were influenced by the type, kind, and accessibility of raw material; the daily needs, the pattern of the annual cycle, the manual capacities, and possibly the presence or absence of well-delineated "cultural areas." Often, replicative experiments, as well as the tedious refitting efforts, are very revealing.

Technological analysis was the basis for Copeland's linear subdivision of the Mousterian (Copeland 1975). Jelinek's metrical studies demonstrated a similar trend, which he interpreted in terms of evolutionary sequence (Jelinek 1982a,b). The decrease in relative thickness of flakes/blades/points is related by him to the emergence of anatomically modern humans.

Munday's analysis of the Negev Mousterian suggested a direct relationship between intensity of occupation and the predominant core reduction technique, which he interpreted as resulting from the nature of the subsistence strategy (Munday 1977a, 1979). Thus the earlier predominance of points over blades (with meticulous platform preparation) in sites with high densities of artifacts (numerous repeated occupations?) is contrasted with the later dominance of simply detached blades and ephemeral occupations. It is assumed that the difference between

176

the two patterns reflects the shifts in the degree of mobility, which became higher because of increasing aridity. It is suggested that the augmentation in unipolar and bipolar blade/flake cores heralded the later Transitional Industry of Boker Tachtit.

Increasing reliance on the results of debitage studies has raised the problem of defining the Levallois technique (Copeland 1983). Without repeating the wealth of arguments, it seems that the southwest Asian Levallois technique exhibits a variety of possible core reduction strategies, all of which can be included under this category.

No relationship between debitage forms and morphological types of retouched pieces was found. The detailed typology of Mousterian side-scrapers (*racloirs*) can be interpreted in terms of resharpening (Dibble 1987) and can thus indicate the relationship between occupation intensity and accessibility of raw material. Long curation periods are possibly exhibited in Acheulo-Yabrudian assemblages in which resharpening resulted in steep and Quina retouch. High frequencies of retouched pieces (Copeland and Hours 1983) in most sites indicate intense occupations and fewer trips to the sources of raw materials. When the Levallois technique was practiced on the same raw materials, the results were different, especially in the decreasing relative thickness of the pieces, indicating the greater efficiency of this technique over the preceding one.

The lack of a direct relationship between forms of retouched pieces and types of blanks is exemplified in the Transitional Industries mentioned above. Typical blanks of Middle Palaeolithic techniques were shaped into the common Upper Palaeolithic tool types (Copeland 1975; Marks 1983b).

Upper Palaeolithic core reduction strategies, except for the Aurignacian and its related flake assemblages, were basically versions of blade knapping (the Ahmarian Tradition). Unipolar blade cores are often the dominant type among the discarded cores of the Ahmarian. The augmentation of bipolar (including 90°) cores in certain assemblages possibly resulted from temporary scarcities of raw material.

Symbolic activities

Mortuary practices are one source of information about human symbolic activities. The Mousterian burials are no exception. Intentional, well-organized inhumations were uncovered in Skhūl, Qafzeh, Amud,

177

Shanidar, and Kebara caves (Garrod and Bate 1937; Suzuki and Takai 1970; Solecki 1971; Vandermeersch 1981a; Bar-Yosef et al. 1986).

The evidence for grave offerings is rare and includes a wild boar skull with Skhūl V, deer antlers with a child burial in Qafzeh, and possible flowers in Shanidar. Although the entire sample is small, it seems that most buried people were laid in shallow pits in a semiflexed position. The minimal disturbance caused to some of these burials indicates that the caves were not occupied systematically every year.

In Qafzeh a few Mediterranean *Glycymeris* sp. shells were collected in the lower Mousterian layers but their relationship to the inhumations is unclear. Red ochre is occasionally found in the form of small lumps. A large one, with signs of scraping, from Qafzeh is an exception (Vandermeersch 1966).

The Upper Palaeolithic sequence is poor in human remains. Except for a rare burial in Nahal Ein Gev I (Arensburg 1977) only a few isolated human bones were found in various sites, but this might indicate shallow burials that were later disturbed. If graves were dug outside the occupational horizons, the chances of recovery will be only accidental. Epi-Palaeolithic sites do provide some evidence. Two isolated semiflexed burials occur in Ein Gev I and Neve David, and charred human remains are known from Kebara cave and two burials in Kharaneh (Jordan).

The changes in mortuary practices during the southwest Asian Upper Pleistocene do not as yet indicate a major cultural shift from Middle to Upper Palaeolithic. The use of red ochre, if the qualitative observations can be translated into quantitative aspects, indicates an increase during the Upper Palaeolithic times. The same is true for marine shells, which are found in almost every site and assemblage from around 25,000 B.P.

In contrast to the European sequence, mobile art objects are extremely rare in the Near East. Rock engravings or paintings are not known and relating this poverty only to deterioration of organic matter or bad preservation of cave walls does not seem a plausible explanation.

SUMMARY

The recent spurt of interest in the problematic issue of the origins of modern humans comes after about two decades during which other topics were the highlights of palaeoanthropology. This time interval has seen the development of new dating techniques such as thermoluminescence and uranium series, the opening of new research fields in biology, and the reexamination of fossil collections, as well as the discovery of new ones. Thus it is not surprising that we feel the need to revise our earlier paradigms and test current hypotheses with the available evidence. However, it does not seem that we can currently reach satisfying resolutions concerning major issues, such as the dating of several important fossils, the processes responsible for site formation during the Middle Palaeolithic, or the validity of the recent biological evidence (e.g. mtDNA). In this state of uncertainty even the following summary should be regarded as a tentative overview:

1. The schematic Upper Pleistocene chronological scale of southwestern Asia points to the possibility that "Neanderthals" reached the region during the middle or later phases of the Middle Palaeolithic period, perhaps around 70/65 kyr B.P.

2. The degree of resolution of palaeoclimatic fluctuations during the last 150 kyr does not allow us to establish a direct correlation between environmental change and shifts in core reduction strategies. Moreover, major cultural transitions were not necessarily linked with major climatic changes, although the latter could have triggered a process which reached its archaeological expression only several millennia later. The Middle/Upper Palaeolithic transition occurred when environmental conditions similar to those of the late Mousterian prevailed.

3. Shifts within the faunal spectra possibly demonstrate the development of hunting during the Middle Palaeolithic, thus enabling the temporary exploitation of the semiarid region in the late Mousterian and afterwards.

4. The gradual transition from Middle Palaeolithic to Upper Palaeolithic lithic manufacturing techniques, coupled with the palaeontological evidence, can be taken to indicate that the study of Levantine prehistory may provide some new insights concerning the emergence of modern humans. Serving as the continental corridor between Eurasia and Africa and the boundary zone for two populations, the excavations of Levantine sites are crucial for testing rival hypotheses.

179

Acknowledgments:

I am very grateful to my colleagues A. Belfer-Cohen, I. Gilead, P. Goldberg, N. Goren-Inbar, L. Meignen, D. Pilbeam, E. Tchernov, and E. Trinkaus, who read an earlier version of this paper and made many helpful comments. All omissions and errors are only mine.

8

The adaptive basis of Neandertal facial form, with some thoughts on the nature of modern human origins

FRED H. SMITH and STEVEN P. PAQUETTE

Historically, European Neandertals have almost always been considered unlikely ancestors for modern humans. It is true that the idea of a "Neandertal phase" in human evolution gained an uneasy acceptance at the turn of the century (Spencer and Smith 1981; Spencer 1984), but general recognition of such a "phase" was brought to a swift end primarily due to the powerful, detailed arguments of Marcellin Boule (e.g. 1911–13, 1914, 1921). Boule took the position that Neandertals were too primitive in some features and too specialized in others to have given rise to modern humans in the available time. He believed that the morphology of Neandertals was sufficiently distinctive to warrant their placement in a separate species from *Homo sapiens*. Furthermore, Boule asserted that Neandertals had become "extinct without posterity" and that "no modern human type can be considered a direct descendant, even with modifications, of the Neanderthal type" (1923:244, 245).

Though scientific perspectives on Neandertals and on modern human origins in general have altered significantly since Boule's day, his assessment that Neandertals did not play a significant role in modern European origins is still, with certain alterations, the majority opinion today. The recent suggestion that modern humans are the result of a biological speciation event between 76 and 200 kyr ago in southern Africa and that they then radiated to colonize the world (Cann et al. 1987; Gould 1987; Stringer and Andrews 1988; Stringer 1988; Delson 1988; Lewin 1987) is an excellent example of the inclination to disavow any biological contribution of Neandertals to modern Europeans. A number of other researchers, however, have consistently recognized that at least some degree of morphological continuity connects Neandertals to early modern Europeans, and consequently some contribution of Neandertals to modern European gene pools has been acknowledged in recent years (e.g. Wolpoff 1980a, this volume; Smith 1985; Trinkaus and Smith 1985; Trinkaus 1986; Smith et al. in press). But given the relatively short time seemingly available for Neandertals to have evolved into modern Europeans, the still substantial morphological changes necessary to derive the latter from the former, and the apparently greater antiquity of the modern human form outside than within Europe, most paleoanthropologists would emphasize that the prime mover in the emergence of modern Europeans was probably an influx of modern humans (or at least the genetic basis of modern human form) from a source outside Europe (e.g. Howell 1958; Trinkaus and Howells 1979; Howells 1976; Hublin 1983; Stringer et al. 1984; Trinkaus 1986).

In our opinion, an important aspect in assessing the possibility of a Neandertal component to modern European origins is an understanding of the functional significance of Neandertal morphology and the functional/adaptive basis of the differences that characterize Neandertals and modern Europeans. If functional/adaptive explanations can be established for key Neandertal anatomical complexes, we can then evaluate such issues as the types of changes in adaptation underlying the emergence of a modern human anatomical pattern in those complexes, the intensity of selection that should operate on such complexes, and the amount of time such a process might involve. Indeed, it could be argued that, without such knowledge, dogmatic interpretations regarding overall tempo and mode of Late Pleistocene human evolution or the role of European Neandertals in this process are unjustified.

In this chapter, we present a partial test for one functional explanation for a specific Neandertal anatomical complex: the face. We also discuss some possible phylogenetic implications of changes in this complex and some of the factors possibly responsible for such changes. Finally, we

182

comment on what we see as a re-emergence of a strict Boulian replacement model for the emergence of all modern human populations outside Africa.

NEANDERTAL FACIAL MORPHOLOGY

The diagnostic features of the Neandertal face are reviewed in a number of recent contributions (Heim 1976, 1978; F. Smith 1976, 1982, 1984; Wolpoff 1980a; Trinkaus 1983a, 1986, 1987a; Stringer et al. 1984). Basically these include markedly elongated vertical facial dimensions, a very large nasal skeletal aperture, and a more anteriorly placed dentition and midsagittal facial segment than in modern humans. The more forward placement of the face's midline is apparent in the higher values for such dimensions as basion–nasion length, basion–prosthion length, and prosthion radius in Neandertals compared to moderns (see Table 8.1). Facial prognathism is also indicated by several mandibular features reflecting a forward shift of the mandibular dentition relative to the ramus and corpus base. These include presence of retromolar spaces, receding mandibular symphyses, and rather posteriorly placed mental foramina relative to the tooth row. Other anatomical features of Neandertals – such as wide interorbital areas, paranasal and inferior orbital buttresses, column-like lateral orbital pillars, and thick supraorbital tori – suggest very robust upper faces. Also, the infraorbital plate is rotated at an angle to the coronal plane and provides an essentially vertical bony connection between the alveolar process and the inferior orbital margin, lateral orbital pillars, and interorbital area. Furthermore, the structural integrity of the infraorbital region is not compromised by the presence of an inframalar notch or canine fossa.

In most discussions of Neandertal faces since Coon's (1962), midsagittal facial projection is generally presented as a specialized, derived (autapomorphic) feature of these hominids. The implication is that Neandertal midfaces have migrated anteriorly to a significant extent compared with earlier humans (e.g. see Rak 1986). The data in Table 8.1, however, suggest that this phenomenon may be more complex. Unscaled midsagittal measurements (basion–prosthion, basion–nasion, prosthion radius) clearly *do* indicate that Neandertal faces exhibit more midsagittal projection than *Homo erectus* (ER 3733),[1] European early moderns (EEM), or recent Europeans. However, use of such unscaled measurements can be misleading since they do not consider the effects

183

Table 8.1. Comparative metric data and indices for selected fossil hominids and a recent human sample. All measurements are in mm and are defined by Howells (1973). Values in brackets indicate estimation. Unless otherwise noted, all measurements were taken by F. Smith. To be utilized in this analysis, a specimen must preserve basion, and measurements from the transmeatal axis must be possible.

Measurement/Index	KNM-ER 3733[1]	Petralona[2]	Broken Hill[3]	Neandertals	Early modern Europeans[4]	Norse[5]	Zalvar[5]	Berg[5]	Modern European average[6]
Basion–prosthion (BPL)	112	117	117	115.4 (n=7, SD=7.8)	109.5 (n=4, SD=2.1)	95.4	94.6	91.9	94
Basion–nasion (BNL)	103	111	111	112.7 (7, 8.4)	104.8 (4, 3.4)	99.6	98.9	95.8	98.1
Maximum cranial length (NOL)	175	209	206	198.1 (7, 13.3)	194.3 (4, 7.4)	182.5	178.4	173	178
Zygomaxillary radius (ZMR)	[84]	[77]	[75]	75.8 (4, 4.1)	81.3 (4, 3.8)	71.3	70.4	69.6	70.4
Prosthion radius (PRR)	116	120	121	120 (4, 4.7)	111.5 (4, 5.3)	98.4	98	96	97.5
BPL/NOL×100	64	56	56.8	58.4 (7, 2.7)	56.3 (4, 1.4)	52.3	53	53.1	53.8
BNL/NOL×100	58.9	53.1	53.9	57.4 (7, 1.6)	54.1 (4, 3.0)	54.6	55.4	55.4	55.1
ZMR/NOL×100	48	36.8	36.4	35.6 (3, 1.6)	41.9 (4, 2.1)	39	39.5	40.2	39.6
PRR/NOL×100	66.3	57.4	58.7	58 (3, 2.1)	57.4 (4, 1.6)	53.9	54.9	55.6	54.8

Notes: [1] KNM-ER 3733 values were taken on a cast, but comparable values are virtually identical to selected measurements published by Leakey and Walker (1985:147–9). Also, while contacts between the face and neurocranial vault appear sound, there could be a slight play in the positioning of the face relative to the neurocranium. Thus measures taken from the transmeatal axis or basion might vary slightly from biological reality.
[2] Petralona measurements are from Stringer et al. (1979) and Stringer (1983).
[3] Broken Hill's right temporal is missing. Thus all radii are technically estimates, but care was taken to keep the transverse bar of the radiometer parallel to the coronal plane of the specimen.
[4] Early modern Europeans date to >25 kyr B.P.
[5] The Norse, Zalvar, and Berg samples are recent European crania series. The data were extracted from Howells (1973), where detailed

of overall size. When these values are scaled against a measure of overall cranial size, in this case nasion–opistocranion length, their relative contributions to the longitudinal structure of the cranium can perhaps be more properly evaluated, and some interesting patterns emerge.[2] Both measures of relative prosthion projection (BPL/NOL and PRR/NOL) are lower for Neandertals than for ER 3733 and both show a consistent decrease from Neandertals, through the EEM sample, to recent Europeans. Broken Hill and Petralona, used here to exemplify intermediates between *H. erectus* and Neandertals, exhibit values similar to the Neandertals, although their BPL/NOL indices suggest slightly less prosthion projection than in the Neandertals. Overall, when the data are viewed in this manner, Neandertals make reasonable intermediates between pre-Upper Pleistocene and more recent hominids in relative projection of the lower face.

Relative nasion projection (BNL/NOL) exhibits a somewhat different pattern. Neandertals are more projecting in the upper midsagittal face than the EEM and recent human samples. For *H. erectus*, the BNL/NOL index can be calculated for three specimens (ER 3733, ER 3883, OH9), and the average of these values is 57.4 – identical to the Neandertal mean. This would seemingly suggest that upper midsagittal facial prognathism in Neandertals is no more pronounced than in earlier hominids. However, the values for Broken Hill/Petralona complicate the picture in that they are lower (relatively less projecting) than any other sample, including recent *H. sapiens*. The meaning of this is unclear, but we would point out that, while Neandertals might be considered specialized in regard to this feature compared to Broken Hill/Petralona and modern Europeans, the latter also undergo relative upper facial midsagittal elongation compared to Broken Hill/Petralona. Whichever phylogenetic interpretation of this sequence one prefers, some reversal in pattern occurs. Certainly an explanation for this increased upper midsagittal facial projection in Neandertals *vis-à-vis* later and certain earlier hominids is required.

Midsagittal projection in Neandertals is even more accentuated by the posterior placement of the lateral face in these hominids. Relative lateral facial projection (ZMR/NOL) exhibits a pattern of decrease from ER 3733, through Broken Hill/Petralona, to the Neandertals; but then it increases with the EEM sample. Recent European lateral faces are positioned more posteriorly than in the EEM sample but are still quite anteriorly placed compared to Neandertals.

FRED H. SMITH and STEVEN P. PAQUETTE

These patterns support Trinkaus's (1983a, 1987a) observation in the Shanidar crania that midfacial prognathism in Neandertals results more from posterior migration of the lateral face relative to the midline than from appreciable increase in forward projection of the facial midline itself. While the latter certainly occurred to some extent, particularly at nasion, we believe midfacial prognathism in Neandertals can be explained in functional/adaptive terms and that derivation of the modern European cranial form from that of Neandertals can at least theoretically be explained through changes in functional demands. In this regard, it is important to note that the so-called flat "generalized" faces noted to exist prior to Neandertals (e.g. *H. erectus*, Zuttiyeh, Petralona, Arago) actually exhibit total facial prognathism. The midface (at least the lower part) is just as anterior as in Neandertals, but unlike Neandertals the lateral face is also positioned anteriorly. Thus, only modern *H. sapiens* faces are truly orthognathic in the strict sense of the word, because in these hominids both the midface and lateral face are positioned in a more posterior position compared to earlier humans. While uncritical application of cladistic analysis could label the Neandertal condition as uniquely derived (an autapomorphy), to do so clearly oversimplifies and ultimately obscures biological reality. Modern orthognathism is not a retained ancestral condition (a plesiomorphy) but is itself a derived feature. Therefore, faces like those of Petralona, Zuttiyeh, and Arago are certainly reasonable structural antecedents of both Neandertal and modern facial forms; but we feel they are not more similar to the moderns, as has often been suggested (e.g. Howells 1975; Vandermeersch 1981b; Rak 1986).

A prognathic face and tooth row is not an optimal situation in terms of general masticatory efficiency, especially once the zygomatic arches and axis of masseter and temporalis action migrate posteriorly (Trinkaus 1983a; Smith 1983a). When this occurs, more muscular exertion becomes necessary for both masticatory and paramasticatory (non-dietary) purposes and can be achieved only at high energetic costs. Furthermore, certain structural modifications may be necessary to deal with the expanded forces generated by the increased muscular exertion (Smith 1983a). Since Neandertals remain prognathic despite these drawbacks, it is important to understand why. It is difficult to believe, given the obvious adaptive significance of maximizing masticatory efficiency, that a complex which significantly reduces this efficiency

186

would be maintained unless it performs an even more critical adaptive function.

Three specific mechanisms have been suggested to account for Neandertal prognathism. Coon (1962) attributed it and other aspects of Neandertal facial form to cold adaptation. While not theoretically impossible, this model has been criticized (see summaries in Hylander [1977] and Smith [1983a]) and remains untested. Heim (1976, 1978) has suggested that prognathism results from sinus expansion. However, it is difficult to understand why sinuses would be the prime mover in such a structural modification, because no primary functional or adaptive rationale for increasing sinus size has ever been demonstrated. Sinuses appear to develop as secondary consequences of structural change (Enlow 1975). Finally, Hrdlička postulated many years ago (1911) that certain aspects of cranial evolution in humans could be related to differences in how the dentition was utilized for mastication and other purposes. Brace has modified and greatly expanded this hypothesis (Brace 1962a, 1964, 1979), particularly with regard to anterior tooth use in Neandertals. Over the years, other evidence has been marshalled in support of this anterior dental loading hypothesis (e.g. F. Smith 1976, 1983a; Ryan 1980; Wolpoff 1980a; Brace et al. 1981), so that today it is generally considered the best available explanation for this complex in Neandertals (Trinkaus 1983a, 1986, 1987a; Smith 1983a, 1985; Trinkaus and Smith 1985; Rak 1986; but see Oleksiak 1987, 1988 for a recent criticism of this model). Apart from pointing out its logical consistency and explanatory power, however, no aspect of the model has ever been tested. It has been suggested that the structural demands of large anterior teeth and requirements for efficient dissipation of the forces generated would require large, prognathic faces. But does a relationship truly exist between anterior tooth size, root size, and facial dimensions? Are there studies that specifically *demonstrate* what structural modifications would be useful in dealing with massive anterior dental loading? Is there specific evidence that anterior teeth were subjected to such use in Neandertals?

The function of Neandertal anterior teeth

It is obvious that during the evolution of *Homo* in the Pleistocene, the anterior and posterior dentitions followed different patterns of evolutionary change. The posterior dentition, which functions almost totally for mastication, exhibits a relatively consistent pattern of reduction over time. Neandertal and other archaic *H. sapiens* posterior teeth are reduced to the extent that they generally fall well within modern *H. sapiens* ranges of variation (Wolpoff 1971; Twiesselmann 1973; F. Smith 1976; Frayer 1978; Trinkaus 1983a). The anterior teeth, however, remain large even in archaic *H. sapiens*. In Neandertals the anterior teeth are significantly larger than in the vast majority of modern human populations (Brace 1962a, 1979; F. Smith 1976; Wolpoff 1980a; Trinkaus 1983a). Furthermore, there are numerous features which strongly indicate that Neandertal anterior teeth were utilized for more than just normal masticatory purposes. These include patterns of differential wear, enamel chipping and microfractures, and a high incidence of shovel-shaping. Detailed discussions of this evidence are presented elsewhere (F. Smith 1976, 1983a; P. Smith 1977; Ryan 1980; Brace et al. 1981; Wolpoff et al. 1981; Trinkaus 1983a) and will not be repeated here. Finally, several aspects of Neandertal occipitomastoid morphology are consistent with heavy anterior dental loading, as is the morphology of their cervical vertebral spines (F. Smith 1976, 1983a; Trinkaus 1983a, 1986, this volume).

Taken together, these observations and analyses strongly suggest that the anterior dentition functioned somewhat differently and, therefore, responded to different patterns of selection from those of the posterior dentition during the Pleistocene. All available information is consistent with the interpretation that these differences relate to the paramasticatory and nonmasticatory use of the anterior teeth by Neandertals and thus support the anterior dental loading hypothesis.[3]

In modern humans, there is considerable evidence that tooth crown size and morphology are under relatively strong genetic control (Lundstrom 1948; Horowitz et al. 1958; Osborne et al. 1958; Garn et al. 1965, 1967, 1968; Goose 1967; Lewis and Grainger 1967; Kraus et al. 1969; Alvesalo and Tigerstedt 1974; Potter et al. 1976), although environmental influences on crown size also exist (particularly in the effects of stress on the organism during the period of crown formation). In Neandertals, it is reasonable to assume that genetic control of anterior tooth size and morphology was at least as stringent as in modern humans and perhaps more so, due to the apparent adaptive importance of maintaining large anterior dentitions in these early hominids.

188

Anterior tooth root–crown size relationships

The first step in testing the anterior dental loading hypothesis is to determine whether Neandertal anterior tooth roots are indeed systematically larger than those of modern humans and to establish what relationship exists, if any, between root and crown dimensions for individual teeth. Intuitively, one would expect large-crowned teeth to exhibit large roots, since the roots function basically as support and anchoring structures for the functional portion of the tooth: the crown. However, little systematic study of human dental root size has been carried out.

In order to test this relationship, anterior maxillary tooth roots were measured in a series of Neandertals from central Europe and compared to a larger series of Amerindians from South Dakota. Results of these comparisons (Paquette 1985) demonstrate that Neandertal anterior tooth roots are significantly larger in root length, maximum mesiodistal diameter, and maximum buccolingual diameter (P > .0001).

There are indications in modern humans that root dimensions are closely related to crown dimensions. Garn and his coworkers (1978a, 1978b, 1979) have identified positive pooled-sex correlations between root lengths and both mesiodistal and buccolingual crown diameters in the mandibular dentition (C-M2) of a modern white sample. They relate these positive correlations to the presence of a dimensional field affecting all dimensions of each tooth (crown and root alike) as a single structure. Except for these studies, there has been little interest in investigating the interrelationships of crown and root dimensions in *H. sapiens*. In fact, no study of such relationships in anterior maxillary teeth could be located.

Relationships between root and crown size were investigated in the Neandertal and Amerindian samples used here through a series of simple linear and multiple regressions (Table 8.2). Results indicate that, while not all correlations of crown/root size in Neandertals reach statistical significance, there is a clear pattern of strong correspondence between root length and other root dimensions and between root diameters (especially labiolingual) and corresponding crown diameter.[4] Thus, the data demonstrate that large-crowned anterior teeth are indeed accompanied by large roots.

Although little work has been done on determining what factors contribute to root size in humans, there are indications of significant

189

Table 8.2. *Degrees of freedom, R^2 values, and F statistics for each of the regression models fitted to the values of the dental dimensions*

Model	Neandertal			Amerinidian		
	Error DF	R^2	F	Error DF	R^2	F
Root Length = bo + b1 (Root M–D) + b2 (Root B–L)						
I^1	6	0.054	0.17	102	0.018	0.96
I^2	11	0.482	5.14*	102	0.350	27.50***
C^-	10	0.360	2.83	102	0.182	11.29***
Root Length = bo + b1 (Crown M–D) + b2 (Crown B–L)						
I^1	6	0.229	0.90	47	0.007	0.19
I^2	11	0.176	1.18*	49	0.119	3.32*
C^-	10	0.205	1.29	58	0.072	2.27
Root M–D= bo + b1 (Crown M–D)						
I^1	7	0.673	14.46**	48	0.404	32.58***
I^2	12	0.183	2.69	50	0.203	12.80**
C^-	11	0.002	.03	61	0.438	47.58***
Root B–L = bo + b1 (Crown B–L)						
I^1	7	0.779	24.73**	57	0.535	65.73***
I^2	12	0.624	19.99**	60	0.669	121.30***
C^-	11	0.829	53.62***	63	0.676	131.98***

*$P<0.05$
**$P<0.01$
***$P<0.0001$

genetic influence in this process (e.g. Kovacs 1967; Lind 1972; Jakobsen and Lind 1973). As noted above, the analyses of Garn and his associates (1978a, 1978b, 1979) suggest that a dimensional field exists for each tooth which affects all dimensions of both root and crown as single integrated structures. Thus, since crown dimensions are genetically controlled, it would be illogical to postulate that root size lacked an equally strong genetic component.

On the other hand, there is evidence of an environmental factor in tooth root size development as well. Kovacs recognizes that "the apical third of the tooth root that develops during the penetrative phase is influenced by normal and physiologic anatomical circumstances and by pathologic circumstances; i.e., by the paratype that, combined with the genotype, gives it its phenotypical character" (1967:873). In Eskimos, rather high incidences of anterior tooth root resorption have been noted and attributed to the effects of extreme loading of these teeth (Hylander 1977). Furthermore, Taylor (1969) attributes variation in maxillary incisor root lengths to space limitations in the subnasal alveolar region, which impinge on their development, and Riesenfeld (1970a, 1970b) has demonstrated that root sizes in rats can be affected by various types of artificially induced stress.

Based on the studies cited above, it is clear that some degree of environmental influence on tooth root size, particularly root length, exists. However, the cervical two-thirds of the root appear to develop with only minimal environmental influence (Kovacs 1967, 1971). Thus the maximum mesiodistal and bucco (labio-) lingual dimensions of the root would not appear to be significantly affected by environmental determinants to any greater extent than are crown dimensions; and the genetic component to development of root length would appear to be at least as influential as environmental factors since the latter apparently affect only the apical third of the root.

The specific selective advantage of large roots in a hominid charac-terized by marked anterior dental loading is not difficult to demonstrate. Larger roots increase the surface contact between the root and alveolus and thus would function to increase efficiency of force dissipation from the tooth to the supporting bony structures. Longer roots are also desirable, because they allow for greater surface area for the attachment of the periodontal ligament (Selmer-Olsen 1949b; Merbs 1968). Hylander (1977) points particularly to the role of the periodontal ligament in this regard and notes that enlargement of root diameters, especially the lingual surface, permits the attachment of more fibers connecting the tooth and alveolus. Thus, mesiodistally broader and absolutely longer roots would function to provide a highly efficient and effective structural mechanism operating to accommodate and dissipate the high levels of vertical and transverse force generated by anterior dental loading (Smith 1983a).[5]

Based on this evidence, we believe there was positive selection for maintaining both large root and crown size in Neandertal anterior dentitions. The best alternative explanation would be that large teeth were maintained as secondary effects of an enlarged, projecting face in Neandertals (Coon 1962; Heim 1976, 1978; Oleksiak 1987, 1988).

Although this is not impossible, it does not explain the presence of differential attrition patterns nor the fact that it is only the anterior teeth that remain large. If the teeth are large only as a secondary response to "filling in space," it would seem that both anterior and posterior teeth should have been involved.

Root size – facial size relationships in a modern human test sample

In the explanatory model of Neandertal craniofacial morphology proposed by Smith (1976, 1983a), the expanded vertical facial dimensions and facial prognathism characteristic of these archaic *H. sapiens* are suggested to result from the structural requirements of larger anterior tooth roots and functional demands involving the resistance to and dissipation of forces resulting from anterior dental loading. Structurally, longer roots require vertically elongated alveoli (tooth sockets), and expanded transverse root diameters in incisors and canines necessitate broader and at least slightly more anteriorly projecting alveolar processes. Furthermore, roughly vertical sockets would facilitate the ability of the anterior roots to dissipate effectively the vertical occlusal forces generated by anterior dental loading (see also Hylander 1977). This could be accomplished only by more forward positioning of the alveolar process, particularly the superior portions.

Elongation of other vertical facial dimensions (upper facial height, cheek height, nasal height) would serve to resist bending moments acting on the face during anterior biting (Hylander 1977), especially in a prognathic face (Smith 1983a:150). Even if this elongation did not have biomechanical consequences, it would probably occur anyway (at least in part) as a secondary result of the structurally required alveolar elongation discussed above. This would result from the coordinated manner in which primate, and specifically human, faces grow (Enlow 1975; Lavelle et al. 1977; Sullivan 1978). In order to bring about alveolar elongation (i.e. from the inferior nasal rim to the alveolar margin), it would be necessary to continue growth trajectories which would unavoidably influence most vertical dimensions of the face. Furthermore, vertical facial elongation cannot occur to any significant extent without increasing forward projection (prognathism) of the face. Craniofacial growth data clearly establish that human faces do not just grow down, but down and *forward* (Enlow and Moyers 1971; Enlow

192

1975; Bjork and Skieller 1976). This means that the prognathism of Neandertals is to some extent a secondary structural result of vertical facial elongation as well as a primary structural response to increased root diameters. Finally, though not a subject of this analysis, the Neandertal supraorbital torus can be viewed as both a structural response to a prognathic face and a functional response to the massive occlusal forces generated by Neandertal anterior dental loading (Smith and Raynard 1980; Russell 1985; Smith et al. 1989).

The next stage in the present analysis is to test aspects of this portion of the anterior dental loading model by determining the extent of interrelationships between anterior dental root size and selected facial dimensions. Although several studies have established significant relationships between anterior maxillary root size and facial size and protrusion in non-human mammals (Riesenfield and Siegel 1970; Riesenfield 1970a, 1970b; Siegel 1972), little such analysis has been undertaken for humans. In a study of Norwegian Lapps, Selmer-Olsen (1949a) identified a significant correlation between maxillary anterior root length and upper facial height, a relationship one would certainly expect to find, given the discussion above. Unfortunately, relationships with other facial variables were not examined. Perhaps even more unfortunately, Selmer-Olsen's is the only study reported in the literature in which dental root–facial relationships are examined in humans.

Since there are too few Neandertals with full anterior dentitions and complete faces to meet statistical requirements, we utilized a large ($N=90$) series of modern Amerindians from South Dakota for analysis of root/facial size associations. Root dimesions and selected facial measurements (Table 8.3) were taken on each individual. A canonical correlation analysis was employed to test the strength of association between the root and face variables (see Table 8.4). Only the first canonical correlation demonstrated statistical significance (canonical correlation = 0.781), but the relationships indicated in this correlation are of considerable interest.

The first canonical variable (Table 8.5) for the facial measurements emphasizes the canine and prosthion radii with a moderate weight for alveolar height, subspinale and the M^1 radii. The mesiodistal root diameter of the central incisor and canine, and the root length of the lateral maxillary incisor, exhibit substantial loadings on the first canonical variable for the root dimensions. Judging from the distribution of weights on the first canonical correlation, individuals characterized by

Table 8.3. *Variable names, codes, and definitions*

Variable name	Code	Definition
Facial dimensions		
1. Upper facial height	UFH	nasion to alveolare
2. Alveolar height	ALVH	nasospinale to alveolare
3. Bicanine breadth	BICBR	maximum diameter between the canines at the midpoint of the alveolus
4. Palatal breadth	PB	maximum diameter of the palate of M^1–M^2 (interproximal)
5. Palatal length	PL	orale to staphylion
6. Palatal depth	PD	maximum depth of the palate at M^1–M^2 (interproximal)
7. Nasal breadth	NB	alare to alare
Radii		
1. Subspinale	SSR	the perpendicular to the transmeatal axis from subspinale
2. Prosthion	PRR	the perpendicular to the transmeatal axis from prosthion
3. M^1 Alveolar	M^1R	the perpendicular to the transmeatal axis from the midpoint of left M^1
4. Nasion	NAR	the perpendicular to the transmeatal axis from nasion
5. Infraorbitale	IOR	the perpendicular to the transmeatal axis from a point inferior to the infraorbital foramen
6. Canine	CAR	the perpendicular to the transmeatal axis from the midpoint of the left canine alveolus
Root dimensions		
1. Root length	RTI1–RTLC	cemento–enamel junction to apex
2. Mesiodistal	RMDI1–RDMC	maximum diameter mesiodistally
3. Buccolingual	RBLI1–RBLC	maximum diameter buccolingually
Crown dimensions		
1. Mesiodistal	CMDI1–CMDC	maximum diameter between contact points
2. Buccolingual	CBLI1–CBLC	maximum breadth perpendicular to mesiodistal diameter

high values for the sub-nasal radii and alveolar height demonstrate similarly elevated values for the mesiodistal dimensions of the canine and central incisor roots and for root length of the lateral incisor. Anterior mesiodistal root expansion displays the strongest relationship with those radii representing forward projection along the anterior alveolar process from the canine to prosthion. Evidence is thus offered substantiating the hypothesis of structural integration between the size of the anterior tooth roots and alveolar protrusion/elongation.

Table 8.4. *Results of the canonical correlation analysis for the combined set of 22 dento-facial variables*

Canonical correlation	Variance ratio	Canonical R²	F statistic
1. 0.78091	1.5629	0.60981	1.7190*
2. 0.71547	1.0488	0.51190	1.2205
3. 0.45579	0.2622	0.20775	0.7486
4. 0.36778	0.1564	0.13526	0.6597
5. 0.36232	0.1511	0.13127	0.6332
6. 0.32935	0.1217	0.10847	0.5524
7. 0.25114	0.0673	0.06307	0.4213
8. 0.20338	0.0431	0.04136	0.3218
9. 0.08888	0.0080	0.00789	0.1226
Trace = 3.421536			

*P<.001.

Table 8.5. *Standardized canonical coefficients for the root and facial dimensions on the first canonical variables*

Variable	Facial 1	Variable	Root 1
UFH	−0.3636	RTLI1	−0.1886
ALVH	0.5073	RBLI1	−0.1538
BICBR	0.1806	RMDI1	0.4133
NB	−0.1016	RTLI2	0.4203
PB	0.2432	RBLI2	−0.1640
PD	0.2252	RMDI2	−0.2813
PL	−0.1172	RTLC−	−0.1774
NAR	0.3528	RBLC−	−0.2486
SSR	0.4948	RMDC−	−0.4541
PRR	−1.0624		
M¹R	−0.5643		
IOR	−0.3826		
CAR	1.7643		

An examination of the canonical structure for the first pair of canonical variables further illustrates the nature of the associations identified between the anterior root and facial measurements (Table 8.6). The correlations between the facial dimensions and their first canonical variable also reveal the contribution from the sub-nasal and canine radii, as well as from two measurements representing vertical

195

Table 8.6. *Canonical structure: correlations between the original dimensions and their first canonical variable*

Variable	Facial I	Variable	Root I
UFH	0.5785	RTLI1	0.6846
ALVH	0.5858	RBLI1	0.3940
BICBR	0.5364	RMDI1	0.5007
NB	0.2899	RTLI2	0.6502
PB	0.4224	RBLI2	0.3501
PD	0.4596	RMDI2	0.4081
PL	0.5503	RTLC	0.7326
NAR	0.6345	RBLC	0.7281
SSR	0.7125	RMDC	0.6279
PRR	0.7449		
M^{1}R	0.5405		
IOR	0.5036		
CAR	0.8029		

displacement of the upper face (alveolar height and upper facial height). Except for the canine, the breadth diameters of the anterior tooth roots display the weakest association with their first canonical variable, and this is similar to the pattern seen in the distribution of the standardized canonical coefficients. However, the contributions of the central incisor and canine root lengths are observed to parallel root length of the lateral incisor. The mesiodistal dimensions of the roots maintain their strong correlation with the first canonical variable. Thus, the effect measured on the first canonical correlation relates primarily to the integration between alveolar prognathism and mesiodistal expansion of the anterior tooth roots, with a notable relationship also apparent between root elongation and vertical facial heights.

The pattern of canonical weights, together with review of canonical structure for the facial dimensions, pinpoints the key variables involved in this correlation. These are radii measuring protrusion of the anterior alveolar process. The effect is strongest from the canine forward, but it is also apparent at the point of the first molar radius. The corresponding canonical variable for the dental dimensions emphasizes the mesiodistal diameters of the anterior tooth roots in conjunction with the root length of the lateral incisor. Moreover, correlations between root measurements and their first canonical variable indicate an additional contribution from the root lengths of the canine and central incisor. Thus, there is a clear tendency for individuals in the modern sample who have large anterior dental roots to exhibit more prognathic faces and vertically expanded alveoli and upper faces. Correlations, of course, do not necessarily imply causal relationships, but the existence of a significant correlation between the facial and dental dimensions in this comparative population of modern *Homo sapiens* suggests that anterior tooth size, as reflected by selected dimensions of the root, is structurally integrated with both vertical facial displacement and the degree of subnasal prognathism. It also demonstrates a structural integration between facial elongation and prognathism which conforms to expectations generated from what is known about the pattern of human facial growth (Enlow 1975).

Genetic vs. developmental basis of Neandertal facial form

It has been suggested from time to time that some of the extreme aspects of Neandertal facial morphology might be mechanistic responses to certain circumstances, rather than a primarily genetically controlled complex which endured because of its selective advantage. Some possible support for this is to be found in Guagliardo's (1982) study of the effects of dental utilization and age on selected cranial features in a series of modern populations. Basically, it was shown that such features as facial height, frontal flatness, facial forwardness, and supraorbital torus projection increased with age and the cumulative effects of heavy biting and chewing. However, while such factors undoubtedly affected Neandertal cranial form as well, they are not of demonstrable magnitude in modern populations to suggest seriously that Neandertal cranial form could be produced from a more "generalized" cranial form due entirely (or even mainly) to their effects.

On the other hand, there is considerable evidence that the size and distinctive morphology of the Neandertal face are not mechanistic responses to functional demands. This evidence comes in part from juvenile Neandertals, who already exhibit characteristic Neandertal facial features at very young ages (Vlček 1970; Smith 1976; Wolpoff 1980a; Smith and Ranyard 1980; Heim 1982b; Tillier 1982). Even a feature like the supraorbital torus, which does not undergo its greatest development until adolescence (Smith and Ranyard 1980), is clearly visible in an incipient stage of development in very young Neandertals (Vlček 1970; Smith and Ranyard 1980). Thus, these features begin to develop seemingly before mechanical stress or some other catalyst would be extensive enough to stimulate a mechanistic response in craniofacial form.

In a recent study, Leigh (1985a, 1985b) examined patterns of ontogenetic allometry of Neandertal and modern human palates. Results of his regression analysis show that allometric growth in the palate of the two groups is similar. This is demonstrated by the maintenance of very similar slopes in regression lines for the two groups. However, the modern human regression line exhibits a downward shift compared to Neandertals, which is reflected in a lower intercept value for the modern regression. This transpositional relationship between the two groups suggests that Neandertal palates are larger at the outset of postnatal growth but then follow growth trajectories similar to those of modern humans. Leigh's study further supports the argument that Neandertal and modern faces are already quite different at birth and that the morphology of the former does not reflect a developmental or mechanistic response during growth.

ANTERIOR DENTAL LOADING AND THE SHIFT TO MODERN HUMANS: A MODEL FOR "INDEPENDENT" MULTIPLE DEVELOPMENT OF MODERN FACIAL FORM

The data and other information present in the previous sections support the interpretation that the functional and structural basis of Neandertal facial form is related to anterior dental loading, as outlined by Smith (1983a; see also Trinkaus 1983a, 1986, 1987a; Trinkaus and Smith 1985; Rak 1986; Demes 1987). Neandertal faces were well adapted to the dissipation of extensive, vertical-occlusally derived forces. Although to some extent this is probably a holdover from earlier hominids, Neandertals do sophisticate the system and thus can be considered to exhibit some specialized features. For example, the structure of the infraorbital plate, with its essentially vertical and structurally "uninterrupted" surface, must be considered a Neandertal specialization. It clearly would facilitate effective transferral of forces from the dentition to the upper face. Also, the medial rotation of this plate and other features noted for the architecture of the Neandertal midface by Rak (1986) and Demes (1987) suggest that Neandertals perfected the structural adaptation to anterior dental loading to a greater extent than earlier

198

forms. However, this modification was not brought about primarily by anterior movement of the dentition but rather through posterior migration of the lateral face (see Table 8.1). It is the posterior migration of the lateral face which is the most derived (apomorphic) feature of the Neandertals. In the same vein, we would argue that the relatively anterior position of nasion in Neandertals and *H. erectus* relates structurally to the development of more vertical anterior tooth roots and associated alveoli, which facilitate efficient dissipation of vertical occlusal forces from the anterior teeth. These specializations of the Neandertal face should be viewed as components of a functionally based morphological complex rather than independent uniquely derived features (autapomorphies).

The most difficult issues remaining to be considered are the behavioral basis for retention of anterior dental loading in Neandertals and, perhaps more importantly, the specific factors responsible for the absence (or at least marked reduction in emphasis) of this behavioral propensity in modern humans. Actually, postulating general ways in which anterior dental loading could have been adaptively significant in earlier humans is not difficult (see Brose and Wolpoff 1971; Hylander 1977; Smith 1983a). However, available evidence gives no indication what precise non-dietary functions Neandertal anterior teeth were performing, although behaviors that generated high *vertical* occlusal forces would appear most commensurate with their general facial morphology. These would encompass various types of behavior in which the anterior teeth were used in the manner of a vise.

Whatever these specific behaviors were, two points need to be made. First, the factors which influenced change in the behaviors involving anterior dental loading certainly involved technology. The need for utilizing the teeth to perform certain tasks was replaced or markedly reduced by more efficient non-somatic methods of accomplishing those tasks. This same argument can be applied to the changes in postcranial robusticity which also herald the emergence of modern humans (Trinkaus 1983b, 1986, this volume). Secondly, even though biology certainly places limits on behavior, behavioral changes generally precede morphological adaptations related to such changes (often by a rather long time) once large-scale adaptive trends are established (Mayr 1963). Thus the technological changes underlying the shift away from habitual anterior dental loading were probably made long before behavioral adjustments to this new technology would result in a morphological response. Thus, we should not expect to find evidence of such behavioral changes at the same time as presumably related morphological change. This point was made quite clearly in respect to the emergence of modern humans some years ago (Brose and Wolpoff 1971), but it has generally been ignored.

In our opinion, the technological/behavioral changes that ultimately resulted in reduction of the anterior dental loading complex were probably well underway while portions of this morphological complex were still being sophisticated. Specifically, we believe such features as the refinement and habitual use of prepared core technology, the trend toward more diversity in lithic tool types, and the increased efficiency of pyrotechnology which generally characterize the Middle compared to the Lower Paleolithic (see papers in Ronen 1982) fostered the beginnings of behavioral changes which put more emphasis on technology rather than muscle in dealing with certain aspects of the environment. We would expect, however, that this would not be reflected in hominid morphology until thousands of years later. Demonstrated patterns of dental and facial reduction between early and late Neandertals, particularly in central Europe (Smith and Ranyard 1980; Wolpoff 1980a; Wolpoff et al. 1981; Smith 1982, 1984; Smith et al. in press), may reflect the beginnings of such a morphological response.

While the arguments presented here are centered around the Neandertals, evidence would suggest that no matter when or where modern *H. sapiens* appeared, they passed through a stage with a craniofacial complex very similar to that of European Neandertals. Thus the anterior dental loading hypothesis is not an issue pertinent only to the phylogenetic position of Eurasian Neandertals, but it is relevant to the question of the origin of modern human facial form even if Neandertals are considered irrelevant to the process. For example, some researchers consider southern Africa to be the point of origin for modern humans (e.g. Beaumont et al. 1978; Bräuer 1984a). It is true that certain archaic *H. sapiens* there (e.g. Florisbad, Ngaloba) exhibit aspects of facial reduction before they occur in western Eurasia, but logic dictates that these forms must have evolved from the earlier Broken Hill/Bodo group (though not identical in all aspects). The Broken Hill/Bodo group exhibits facial morphology basically similar to Neandertals (Smith 1985), so ultimately facial reduction from earlier and later African archaic *H. sapiens* must also be explained. Alterations in the utilization of the anterior dentition may also be a reasonable explanation here, since Broken Hill (the only adult African archaic *H. sapiens* preserving anterior teeth) exhibits Neandertal-sized incisors and canines. Also, the establishment of modern human form in Africa and western Asia in Middle Paleolithic contexts (Smith 1985) demonstrates that the technological/behavioral prerequisites for establishment of modern human form are to be found in the Middle Paleolithic. Upper Paleolithic levels of cultural development are not required.

As previously noted, increasing human facial size involves both downward and forward components (Enlow and Moyers 1971; Enlow 1975; Bjork and Skieller 1976; Sullivan 1978). Therefore, reducing a large prognathic human face must essentially follow the reverse course; the face should decrease in vertical length and anterior projection. Acting within the constraints of primate facial growth patterns, basic modern human facial form is the *only* pattern obtainable through reduction of earlier hominid faces. Variation in degree of reduction and in certain details of facial form would certainly occur in different regions, and this may be one factor explaining patterns of cranial variation documented (e.g. Howells 1973) in recent human samples. However, no matter how many different times relatively independent reduction of facial size might have taken place during the late Pleistocene, we believe the structural result would have been very similar in all cases. With this in mind, the argument that all modern humans are so similar to each other in cranial form that they must all result from a single, recent evolutionary event may not necessarily be valid.

Just how feasible is an essentially independent development of modern human facial form in several regions? If the process of facial growth and the basis of archaic *H. sapiens* facial form was environmentally determined, this would be no problem. Once the mechanical stimulus for large faces was removed, reduction would occur and the resulting modern form could emerge independently as often as the appropriate situation arose. But, as was noted previously, craniofacial form is not a mechanistic response in archaic *H. sapiens*. It appears to be under rather stringent genetic control. Thus the emergence of modern human facial form certainly involved genetic change, and a claim that identical genetic change occurred independently several times in Late Pleistocene humans would be virtually impossible to accept. It is for this reason that Weidenreich, who was convinced that moderns had evolved independently in different regions, was forced to view orthogenesis as a significant factor in human evolution (1947a, b).

Although a genetic basis for patterns of human facial growth is a demonstrable fact, the details of the system are very poorly understood. While it is clear that the mechanism is polygenic in nature, it is not possible to isolate how many loci are involved or what their specific effects are (Nakata et al. 1974; McNamara 1976; Carlson 1979). It is probable that the effects of these loci are additive, and it is possible that change at *any* locus would function to bring about reduction, once selection favoring reduction began. In other words, it is possible that reduction of the face did not result from *identical* genetic change in all regions where modern humans might have evolved from archaic forerunners. This would make basically independent derivation of modern facial form theoretically feasible without recourse to orthogenesis.

GENE FLOW, REPLACEMENT, AND REALITY

Even though the relatively independent development of modern cranial form might have been theoretically possible, this does not mean that it occurred. Based on currently available information, it does appear that modern human form emerges earlier outside than within Europe (Bräuer 1984a; Stringer 1988, this volume; Valladas et al. 1988). If it is true that modern human anatomical form appears relatively late in Europe, it would be much more likely that it did not emerge independently there. In our opinion a more reasonable interpretation, under these circumstances, would be that a substantial portion of the genetic basis of modern human anatomical form did enter Europe from areas where this form had a greater antiquity. Thus it is obvious that gene flow in some form was central to the process of modern European origins.

There is, however, a tendency re-surfacing to view the appearance of modern humans in Europe and most other regions of the Old World as the result of total replacement in the Boulian sense. According to this perspective, the emergence of modern humans was a true biological speciation event probably occurring in southern Africa (Stringer and Andrews 1988). Once moderns emerged, it is claimed, they were either genetically incompatible with Neandertals and other archaic humans (Eldredge and Tattersall 1982:152) or so behaviorally different that matings would be highly unlikely (Lieberman 1984). If this is true, then

202

the origin of modern humans in all areas of the Old World, except their initial point of origin, must have resulted from actual influx of modern populations. No genetic input from indigenous archaic humans would be possible in regions other than the point of origin since moderns would have been reproductively isolated from indigenous archaic forms. The biological evidence responsible for this new total replacement perspective derives mainly from a series of genetic and molecular studies which suggest a recent African origin for all modern humans (see below). This perspective has also been supported by the assertion that fundamental behavioral differences existed between Neandertals and modern humans (Klein 1983a; Binford 1984a, 1985a, this volume; Cartmill et al. 1986; Pilbeam 1986).

Studies of 85 protein and blood group systems (Nei and Roychoudhury 1982), nuclear DNA polymorphisms in the B-globin gene cluster (Wainscoat et al. 1986a), and mitochondrial DNA (mtDNA) variation in human populations (Cann et al. 1982, 1987; Wilson et al. 1985) agree in asserting that modern humans arose in Africa and subsequently spread to the rest of the world. The split between African and non-African modern human populations is calculated to have occurred between 76 kyr and 200 kyr B.P., depending upon the system examined and how rates of changes are calibrated. Estimates of splitting times are based on the assumption that the rate of change in the pertinent DNA sequences is constant, which implies that such changes are random and neutral.

There are various reasons to question the assumptions on which all these estimates of splitting times are based (Weiss and Maruyama 1976; Giles and Ambrose 1986; Latorre et al. 1986; Van Valen 1986; Weiss 1986; Wolpoff this volume), but even if modern human populations did share a *recent* common origin in Africa, does this mean that localized populations of archaic *H. sapiens* in other regions are excluded from any genetic role in modern *H. sapiens* in the appropriate region? Basically, if one accepts certain aspects of the genetic evidence as support of this scenario, the answer must be yes. For example, the mitochondrial DNA data are interpreted as suggesting a recent origin for modern humans, in part because interpopulational variability in mtDNA is much less on a world-wide scale in humans than for our closest primate relatives (Cann et al. 1982, 1987; Wilson et al. 1985). Thus, if archaic *H. sapiens* had *any* genetic effect on modern humans, it would be difficult to explain why the variability of mtDNA in modern humans remained so low, since the various regional archaic *H. sapiens* populations presumably were differentiated long enough to accumulate considerable interpopulational variability in mtDNA. If modern populations in Asia and Europe assimilated genetic material from localized archaic *H. sapiens*, then this greater variability, which should be present in the archaic forms, should also be reflected in the modern gene pools. Since interpopulational variability appears to be quite low in modern humans, either biological hindrance to genetic exchange between archaic and modern *H. sapiens* must be evoked, or it must be admitted that variation in human mtDNA might not be random and neutral. Thus the importance of the mtDNA data to the re-emergence of a total replacement model for modern human origins (and vice versa) is obvious.

Our problem with accepting both the total replacement model and the mtDNA argument centers on the fossil record. While there are certainly disagreements regarding its relative importance *vis-à-vis* possible external factors, local morphological continuity has been demonstrated between archaic and modern *H. sapiens* in several regions of the Old World. The best cases are central Europe (Smith 1982, 1984; Frayer 1986) and east Asia (Wolpoff et al. 1984). Reasonable cases can also be made for north Africa and the Near East (Wolpoff 1980a; Trinkaus 1984a; Smith 1985), although recent thermoluminescence dating of Kebara (Valladas et al. 1987) and Qafzeh (Valladas et al. 1988) has made a continuity argument for the Near East less tenable than previously was the case. Because morphological continuity (when it exists) certainly denotes at least *some degree* of genetic continuity, total replacement does not seem reasonable as an explanation for the emergence of modern humans. Since we agree with Jones (1986:317) that the genetic data "can only supplement, and never replace, that which comes from paleontology," we are compelled to regard some aspects of the present interpretation of this genetic data with suspicion.

We do not necessarily question the interpretation that modern human genetic structure ultimately had its origin in Africa. It is the timing of this origin that troubles us. Indeed Wainscoat (1987) has recently pointed out that factors other than so recent an origin for all modern humans might explain the mtDNA data. Specifically, he notes that genetic drift might be responsible for the fixation of one ancestral mtDNA type at a time when human population sizes were markedly constricted. He states further:

. . . it is tempting to relate the occurrence of the ancestral mitochondrial DNA type back to a constriction in population size (bottleneck). If this assumption is correct, the timing of such bottlenecks may correlate with major evolutionary events. It would be interesting to see where a more precise dating puts the ancestral mitochondrial DNA type in relation to our own evolution. (Wainscoat 1987:13)

It may well be that the mtDNA data reflect the initial spread of humans out of Africa during the *Homo erectus* period, rather than a spread of modern humans after 200 kyr B.P. Certainly the radiation of *H. erectus* was an important event in human evolution and one in which bottlenecking and genetic drift undoubtedly had significant effects. Furthermore, if one uses a slower rate for mtDNA evolution, like that calculated by Nei (1985), the initial branching point of mtDNA variability moves back to a time very close to the period when *Homo erectus* began the original radiation of humans out of Africa. We view this possibility as more supportable in light of the human fossil record.

BRAINS AND BEHAVIOR

Few would doubt that the Upper Paleolithic in Europe exhibits some important changes compared to the Middle Paleolithic in such factors as technology, site complexity, preserved artistic expression and body ornamentation, mortuary practices, and perhaps even hunting and general organizational abilities (Laville et al. 1980; White 1982; Dennell 1983; Binford 1985a; Gamble 1986; and the archaeology contributions to this volume). It is increasingly suggested that these changes heralded a fundamental restructuring of human behavior, resulting in patterns that are qualitatively different in most respects from the preceding Middle Paleolithic. While all this *may* be true, it is not clear exactly how these changes relate to the origin of modern humans in Europe or elsewhere.

For example, it is generally assumed that both art and body ornamentation reflect a well-developed sense of self-awareness, presence of sophisticated cognitive ability, and evidence of symbolically based culture (White this volume). Implicit in this assumption is that both art and body ornamentation also reflect a modern human level of neurological organization. Again, while this is probably true, absence of art and body ornamentation in media and methods that preserve in the archaeological record for thousands of years do not preclude modern human status in brain or behavior. To date, evidence for elaborate body ornamentation and art of the magnitude found even in the earliest European Upper Paleolithic are lacking in the earliest representations of modern humans in other regions.[6] The burials from Skhūl and Qafzeh contain no indications of body ornamentation (S.R. Binford 1968a), and there is no evidence of other forms of artistic expression associated with these hominids. Yet their anatomical status as early modern *H. sapiens* is convincing (Wolpoff 1980a; Trinkaus 1984a; Smith 1985). The same is true for the presumably very modern human remains associated with the African Middle Stone Age in southern and eastern Africa (Bräuer 1984a; Smith 1985). And there are clearly groups of modern humans in the ethnographic present who lacked extensive, elaborate art that would preserve for thousands of years in archaeological contexts but who otherwise possessed symbolically based culture. Thus, to imply that absence of such behaviors in Neandertals is an indirect indicator of fundamental neural primitiveness or less efficient communication compared to modern humans seems unsupportable unless one is willing to deny modern human status to Skhūl/Qafzeh or the anatomically modern *H. sapiens* specimens associated with the African MSA.

The development of elaborate art and body ornamentation in the Upper Paleolithic of Europe may have been a significant event in human prehistory; but it is important to note that, while some manifestations are associated with the earliest Upper Paleolithic (Châtelperronian and Aurignacian I), the veritable explosion in artistic expressions generally associated with the Upper Paleolithic takes place after 30–27 kyr B.P. (Conkey 1983; Dennell 1986). Dennell (1986) implies that this and other changes at *c.* 27 kyr B.P. were perhaps just as fundamental as those marking the Middle/Upper Paleolithic boundary, but no one has yet suggested that this results from fundamental neurological change or reflects a speciation event.

If neural reorganization did take place between Neandertals and modern Europeans (or within the latter), could we recognize it anatomically? Differences in language ability between Neandertals and moderns are often cited as resulting from such reorganization. But even Lieberman (1984), who argues strongly that Neandertal speech ability was inferior to that of modern humans, is careful to point out that difference in speech abilities between these two hominids (which is reflected in supposed anatomical differences on the cranial base and upper respiratory system) does not imply significant differences in cognitive ability. Thus, we are left only with evidence from studies of endocasts to judge whether neural differences do exist between Neandertals and moderns. The difficulties of telling anything topographically from endocasts are well known (Weidenreich 1947b). Still, Holloway (1985) has stated that he can identify nothing primitive on Neandertal endocasts compared to those of modern humans. It is true that internal circuitry of Neandertal (or early modern human) brains cannot be investigated, and one could speculate that differences exist there. But based on the *positive evidence* of similarity in endocranial volume and general topography between Neandertals and early modern humans, we feel there is no anatomical basis at the present time for the view that the two are fundamentally different neurologically.

Though space limitations prevent discussions of each of the other archaeological factors in detail, it is instructive to examine evidence for the association of modern humans in other regions of the Old World with the type of behavioral reorganization characteristic of the European Upper Paleolithic. Modern humans are associated with Middle Paleolithic industries in western Asia, north and east Africa, and probably south Africa (Smith 1985; but see Binford 1984a, for doubts about south Africa). Admittedly our understanding of behavior, as opposed to technology, is less adequate in the Paleolithic of these regions than in Europe, but there is no significant positive evidence (see note 6) that the appearance of the earliest modern humans in these non-European regions was associated with periods of fundamental restructuring of behavior.

A SUMMARY STATEMENT

The evidence presented in this paper supporting the anterior dental loading model as a functional explanation of Neandertal (and other archaic *H. sapiens*) craniofacial form also speaks to habitual behavioral differences between archaic and modern *H. sapiens*. No modern human population exhibits this pattern of morphological adaptation, which suggests that Neandertals probably habitually loaded their anterior teeth in a manner and with an intensity not practiced in any modern groups. Thus, we obviously do not believe that archaic and modern *H. sapiens* were behaviorally or anatomically identical. However, based on the discussion presented above we do doubt that behavioral differences, or inferences made from them (e.g. different patterns of neural organization), are definitive enough to be used to argue for a species-level distinction between archaic and modern forms of *H. sapiens* or as evidence for a total replacement model to explain modern *H. sapiens* origins. In our opinion, the population dynamics of the archaic-to-modern *H. sapiens* transition were exceedingly complex; and genetically simple models, like total replacement by speciation, are unlikely to reflect biological reality. Much more reasonable in this case is a model of geographically extended phyletic change which involves interaction between gene flow, local genetic continuity, changes in adaptive demands placed on the hominids, and the extent to which technology and other aspects of behavior are able to compensate for those demands (Wolpoff et al. 1984; Smith 1985; Wolpoff this volume).

According to this model as we see it, the genetic changes underlying modern human cranial form probably occurred only once and developed gradually over an extended period of time. Multiple centers of partial or complete origins of such changes, as suggested for modern cranial form earlier in this chapter, are theoretically possible but not a requirement of the model. As the genetic basis for this complex spreads (through small-scale population movement and localized genetic exchange), it could potentially be introduced into a given archaic *H. sapiens* population (even a peripheral one) any number of times. However, such genes would not have been integrated into a particular gene pool until the changes resulting from them would satisfy the adaptive requirements of that particular population. Thus, emergence of modern cranial form and other changes, such as the modification and reduction of postcranial robusticity (Trinkaus 1983a, 1983b, 1986, and this volume), would occur in a region only when the adaptive necessity of maintaining the archaic *H. sapiens* conditions was supplanted in that region. Once that occurred, we feel that the genetic basis of the less hypertrophied and relatively more energetically (and in some cases biomechanically) efficient modern anatomical form would be quickly incorporated into regional archaic human gene pools. The result could be a very rapid (in a geologic sense) replacement of archaic human anatomical form by modern human anatomical form in a particular region without extensive influx of modern human beings from outside that region.

The obvious question, then, is what supplants the need for archaic *H. sapiens* robusticity? In our opinion, the key is technology and how that technology is used. In Europe, Africa and the Near East, changes in archaic *H. sapiens* morphology occur within the Middle Paleolithic. In Africa and the Near East, these changes lead to the emergence of modern human cranial form *before* the end of the Middle Paleolithic.[7] In Europe, although changes are clearly taking place in the direction of the modern condition (at least in central Europe), modern cranial form is not found until the Upper Paleolithic;[8] but this is clearly the exception to the pattern rather than the rule. Thus, too much emphasis has been placed on the Upper Paleolithic and equivalent cultural expressions in the quest for understanding modern human origins. We need instead to concentrate our efforts more on understanding why the Middle Paleolithic in Africa and the Near East permits the replacement of archaic human form by modern human form while the Middle Paleolithic of Europe seemingly does not. In our opinion such a shift in research emphasis is more likely to be productive in terms of explaining modern human origins than stressing possibly fundamental behavioral shifts that seem to be generally uncorrelated with modern human origins on a world-wide scale.

Notes

1 Sample sizes for the *H. erectus* comparisons are also small. Often ER 3733 is the only specimen that can be compared by the method employed here. We recognize that basing arguments on such small sample sizes is extremely unwise, but lack of other useable specimens makes it a necessity in this case.
2 Using nasion–opistocranion length as a scaling measurement is not ideal, since patterns of encephalization in *Homo* influence this measurement. Thus increases in brain size and changes in chondocranial shape, in addition to facial projection, will have an effect on the indices. Despite this drawback, we continue to view these indices as useful indicators of relative facial projection and believe they are worthy of discussion.
3 A number of objections to this interpretation have been raised and are dealt with elsewhere (Smith 1983a:146–8).
4 In fact, the correspondence is stronger than a cursory assessment of Table 8.2. indicates. In many cases, the R^2 values of Neandertals are *higher* than those of the Larson Amerindians, even though the correlations are statistically significant for the latter and not the former sample. This demonstrates that the failure of these Neandertal correlations to reach statistical significance is an artifact of sample size.

5 Interestingly, root length increase is much more strongly correlated with increase of mesiodistal root diameter in Neandertals than in the Amerindian sample and is negatively correlated with labiolingual root diameter increase (Paquette 1985). Thus Neandertal roots are not just enlarged versions of modern roots. The longer roots of Neandertals are also proportionately broader mesiodistally. Thus, they are enlarged in a manner that specifically counters vertically directed biting force in the anterior teeth.

6 Evidence of egg-shell beads and pigments are found in the Howieson's Poort of south Africa, but the very early dates for these horizons at the Klasies River Mouth Cave sites has been called into question (Binford 1984a), and the hominid remains are not from these levels (Singer and Wymer 1982). Furthermore there is no evidence for the spread of such practices through the intervening region between south Africa and Europe.

7 We have omitted discussion of the postcranial skeleton because the postcranial anatomy of the earliest African modern humans is essentially unknown (see Smith 1985).

8 A possible exception is the Krapina A juvenile cranium, which *may* represent a modern specimen in association with the Mousterian (Wolpoff 1980a). This specimen is at the top of the long Mousterian sequence at Krapina and is much more recent than the clearly Neandertal remains from the site.

Acknowledgments

We wish to express our thanks to the School of American Research for sponsoring the advanced seminar "The Origin of Modern Human Adaptations" and to Jean Auel and the L.S.B. Leakey Foundation for support of the seminar and interest in paleoanthropology. Permission to study the fossil and recent hominid samples used in this analysis was kindly granted by W.M. Bass, (the late) I. Crnolatac, R. Feustel, J.-L. Heim, J. Jelínek, M. Malez, K. Sakač, M. Sakka, and J. Szilvássy. Certain aspects of the work reported here have been supported by the U.S. National Science Foundation (BSN 8606674), the Alexander von Humboldt Foundation, and the University of Tennessee at Knoxville's Faculty Research, Development, and Leave Program. We are most grateful to these individuals and programs for their cooperation and support. Finally, we thank D.C. Boyd, R.L. Jantz, J. Radovčić, J. Simek, M.O. Smith, E. Trinkaus, and M.H. Wolpoff for various forms of assistance in the preparation of this manuscript.

9

Toward a contextual understanding
of the earliest body ornaments

RANDALL WHITE

The important discoveries in southwestern France in the 1860s made it clear that the material record of the *Age du Renne* was the work of behaviorally modern humans (Lartet and Christy 1875). Portable art and body ornaments were among the first objects to be retrieved from stratigraphically controlled excavations. Even the great debate of the late 1800s concerning the authenticity of parietal art had little or nothing to do with whether humans of the time were capable of such art. Rather, it was the degree of preservation, or other physical attributes (Harlé 1881), that were difficult for scholars such as Cartailhac (1902) to accept. In essence, from the beginning of scientific research on the Upper Paleolithic, there has been a consensus that neurological and biological capacities for symbolically based human culture had been achieved by the onset of the Upper Paleolithic. Clearly implicit in this consensus is the assumption that a more or less modern grade of language (cf. White 1985) formed part of the behavioral repertoire of *Homo sapiens sapiens*.[1]

The assumption of behavioral uniformity between late Pleistocene members of our species and ourselves seemed to justify the use of ethnographic examples to understand the Upper Paleolithic record (Sollas 1911). Unfortunately, Broca's impact on French anthropology,

characterized by an inherent racialism, suppressed a broad and sophisticated use of ethnographic generalizations to articulate fully the cultural
implications of the archaeological record then being recovered. Broca's
influence is evident in the racial interpretations of D. Peyrony (1933),
which were influential as late as the 1950s. While the impact of
ethnographic science is evident in early cave art research (Reinach 1903;
Breuil 1952), the analysis of excavated materials made little use of
ethnographic insight.

This state of affairs, combined with the fact that ethnological science
in the early part of the twentieth century remained highly particular-
istic, meant that certain classes of artifacts were never incorporated into
a general "cultural" framwork. One such class of artifacts was that
related to bodily adornment. A second was that of burials. With the
ferment of the 1960s, however, new questions and frameworks for
recombining various aspects of the archaeological record stimulated
Sally Binford (1968a and see Harrold 1980 for a critical review) to
combine these two classes of data in a seminal comparison of treatment
of the dead in the Mousterian and Upper Paleolithic. Since the
discoveries at Grimaldi, Cro-Magnon, Aurignac and elsewhere, it had
been recognized that the dead had been elaborately decorated with a
variety of ornamental constructions. Like most previous investigators, it
was in the context of burials that Binford concerned herself with body
ornamentation. Although she was among the first to seek regularities
and trends in the record of Paleolithic burials and their decorative
treatment, the everyday use of ornamentation remained a subject of
interest only to popular writers and artists.

Binford's (1968a:147) survey of evidence concerning Middle and
Upper Paleolithic burial practices led to some important conclusions on
changing social organization across the Middle/Upper Paleolithic transition. These are crucial to the present article:

1. "Some of the most striking differences between the
   Mousterian and Upper Paleolithic burials are reflected in
   grave furnishings."
2. "Personal adornments – beads, pendants, necklaces of
   ivory or of fish vertebrae – occur in great number in the
   Upper Paleolithic and are totally absent in the
   Mousterian."
3. "In Western Europe shell beads occurred in the hundreds

212

and thousands with individuals. These are not the kind of goods that can be collected and donated to a burial by a single family, while the furnishings with Mousterian burials are. This, then, is one of the major differences between the Mousterian of Europe and the Upper Paleolithic – the degree of corporate involvement in mortuary ritual."

4. "The elaboration of personal adornment in the Upper Paleolithic also reflects increased means of symbolizing the status of individuals."

My purpose here is to address the issue of the explosion of items of bodily adornment at the beginning of the Upper Paleolithic and to understand more about the cultural contexts in which they were operating and about which they can inform us. Specifically, I wish to push us away from the prevalent phrasing of analyses of body ornaments solely in terms of mortuary practices and nudge us in the direction of a concern with self-definition and social display and their evolutionary causes and consequences. I also wish to examine the relationship between body decoration and exotic raw materials, from both an ethnographic and a Paleolithic perspective. With respect to raw materials, I want to examine the ways in which nature was being culturally appropriated for social purposes. Finally, I seek to examine the technology of bead and ornament production to achieve a greater understanding of the labor and expertise committed to bodily ornamentation. Most importantly, I seek to accomplish the above with reference to a sample from the basal Upper Paleolithic, thus avoiding the tendency to compare the Mousterian to much later developments, rather than to focus on the transition itself (Gamble 1982; Straus 1983). The focus of this paper is on objects no more recent than the Aurignacian (roughly 34–28,000 B.P.).

An important issue that must be addressed is the basis for the interpretation that the objects considered here were indeed bodily adornments. The possibility certainly exists that some perforated objects were used for other purposes. However, later burials that have been recovered seem to leave no doubt. Bader's (1964, 1970) description of the 25,000-year-old Sungir' burials, for example, indicates that the beads were sewn or strung on clothing. He has even gone so far as to reconstruct the nature of the garments on the basis of the bead

213

distributions. Since this is not an isolated occurrence, it seems probable that most of the perforated objects that concern us here were worn.

BODY ORNAMENTATION: SOME SOCIAL CONSIDERATIONS

Turner (1980:112) raises a provocative point in observing that

the surface of the body seems everywhere to be treated, not only as the boundary of the individual as a biological and psychological entity but as the frontier of the social self as well.

The surface of the body ... becomes the symbolic stage upon which the drama of socialisation is enacted, and bodily adornment (in all its culturally multifarious forms, from body painting to clothing and from feather head-dresses to cosmetics) becomes the language through which it is expressed.

If indeed body ornamentation is a language through which the socially defined self is expressed, then it should be fertile ground for archaeology. After all, most body decoration is done with material objects, many of them archaeologically preservable. Clearly, however, there are limits to our ability to find meaningful patterns. These limits are due primarily to difficulties in determining the behavioral context of use. For example, it is clear from our own cultural experience and the ethnographic record that the same individual will dress more or less elaborately, depending upon the social context. Death and burial are only one such context.

Perhaps because this latter context is so easily identifiable archaeologically, and can therefore be held constant, mortuary studies of variation in body decoration have come to dominate our attention (see Tainter 1978; O'Shea 1984). However, this should not be taken to indicate that burials provide exhaustive insight into the social personae of extinct cultures. Indeed, a focus on ornaments as they were used in treatment of the dead denies the dynamic, situational, even negotiable nature of body decoration in life. Social personae are not carved in stone, but are contextually variable.

In addition to reflecting a limited range of social contexts, mortuary studies of body ornamentation make use of a number of tenuous interpretive conventions when addressing social questions. For example, the discovery of a juvenile burial with very elaborate adornment, such as at La Madeleine (Capitan and Peyrony 1928) or Sungir' (Bader

214

1970) is likely to lead to the inference that some form of ascribed status was in operation. Weiner's work (1987) on body decoration in the Trobriands illustrates just how naive our interpretive conventions may be, and the degree to which they ignore the sociopolitics of bodily adornment:

Men not only must provide food for their children, but they are also responsible for enhancing their children's beauty. When an infant is only a few months old, is still naked and only beginning to eat a bit of yam, the baby is decorated with shells by its father to make it "beautiful."
When an infant is born ... shell decorations add a fundamental degree of power to the baby's potential social beauty. A few shell decorations may seem insignificant, yet the shells symbolize the first important political step in a child's life. During a baby's first year its father tries to obtain a necklace of red chama shells which, ornamented with a few black and white dried seeds in the center, is fastened around the infant's neck. These necklaces are very valuable if the tiny shell discs are thin and uniformly polished. Color is also a distinguishing feature of a fine necklace as the shells that are a pale reddish-pink are more prized than red ones. Access to these shells is difficult for there are only a few islands in the southern Massim where men still grind and polish them.
When a child wears a necklace, its value is attached to the child as a representation not only of the child's father's political worth, but as a statement of the political potentiality of the child as well.

While the European Upper Paleolithic was certainly not the Trobriands, Weiner's detailed analysis of ornament use provides insight into the complex range of often indirect social contexts in which body decoration may well have been embedded.

Margaret Conkey (1978, 1980, 1984), in a pioneering study, attempted to place abstract images in Cantabrian Magdalenian portable art within the context of stylistic expression of group identity. Indeed, the results are thought-provoking, but it is worth asking why, if one is interested in the question of the expression of self and social identity, one would not focus on decorative objects worn directly by the individuals concerned. Within obvious limits, this kind of analysis would be in the realm of that carried out by Wobst (1977) on Yugoslavian folk dress. Moreover, it would deal with objects that were much more socially visible than small bits of engraved bone.

It is important to point out that, for the most part, *early Aurignacian beads and pendants do not occur in burial contexts.* In the small number of very prolific French and German sites of this period, they seem simply to be part of the debris scattered on living surfaces. At Geissenklosterle Cave in Germany, Hahn (1986) shows ornamental objects to be associated with an area thought to have been the focus of clothing manufacture. This may also have been true of the ornament-rich sites of Abri Blanchard (Didon 1912), Abri Castanet (Peyrony 1935), and La Souquette (Delage 1938) in the Vallon de Castelmerle (Dordogne), where immense quantities of beadwork were recovered in the absence of any burials (see also White 1986a and 1986b).

It should also be emphasized that there is great variation among early Aurignacian sites in the frequency of ornamental objects. As Taborin (1985) has also noted with regard to exotic shells, there are points of concentration which she alludes to as "markets" (marchés). Many of these same locales have also yielded impressive quantities of ornaments. Such is certainly true of the contiguous Vallon de Castelmerle sites mentioned above. In contrast, the culture-stratigraphically contemporaneous site of Abri Cellier (c. 5 km distant) has produced less than ten such objects. Likewise, Rigaud's (1982) painstaking excavations of the Aurignacian levels at Flageolet I in the Dordogne Valley yielded but two perforated red deer canines, ten pierced shells, and a small ivory pendant. Hahn's (1972) inventory of engraved objects and pendants indicates that precisely the same kind of differential distribution is true for the central and eastern European Aurignacian. There appear to be four possible explanations for this pattern of variation.

First, it is possible that there are chronological differences in the frequency of ornament production (see Winters 1968). Since the chronology for the early Upper Paleolithic is very loose, typologically similar sites may well be hundreds of years apart. If the production of ornaments was stochastic, quantitative differences between sites may be a function of time. If this is so, it is necessary to understand the significance of these chronological differences.

Secondly, there may have been geographic and social contexts, represented by sites with abundant ornaments and exotic shells, in which bodily ornaments were more important. These may, for example, have been major centers for the procurement/exchange of exotic shells, ivory, or other raw materials. It is also possible that these sites of abundance reflect social situations in which the need for and use of body ornamentation was more marked.

Thirdly, since my own examination of fabricated ornaments reveals an overwhelming preference for ivory, it is possible that the richest ornament sites are associated with woolly mammoth procurement

216

localities. However, the ornament-rich sites of the Vallon de Castelmerle do not contain a single woolly mammoth bone!

Fourthly, the surprisingly small size of most early Aurignacian ivory beads (mean = less than 0.6 cm in diameter), makes differences in excavation techniques a potentially important factor in inter-site variation. Indeed, the excavations at Abri Cellier (Collie 1927; Nesbitt 1928; A. Pond personal communication) were much less rigorous with regard to small objects, fauna and débitage than excavations in the Vallon de Castelmerle, where careful sieving and washing of sediments was standard practice (Pond 1924; Peyrony 1935). Recent, very careful excavations (Rigaud 1982) have revealed early Aurignacian levels with little or no body ornamentation. Excavation quality, then, is a factor that must be assessed on a site-by-site basis.

While much emphasis has been placed on the social implications of body ornaments, it is clear ethnographically that a thorough analysis of body ornamentation extends far beyond an understanding of social personae within a cultural system. There are important linkages with technology, subsistence, procurement, and cosmology that must be part of any research design.

IDEATIONAL CONSIDERATIONS

It is surprising that few Paleolithic archaeologists have seen the linkage between body ornamentation and the ideational realm. Since at least 1903 (Reinach 1903), it has been advisable to assume a relationship between cave and portable art, and cosmology, religious beliefs, and rituals. There are probably no legitimate prehistorians today who would deny outright the demonstration that *parietal art* is highly patterned (Laming-Emperaire 1962; Leroi-Gourhan 1965; Vialou 1982), although there would be much disagreement on the specific interpretation of this patterning. Quantitative relationships have been proposed between certain species of animals, geometric signs and locations within caves. Therefore, it is surprising that we have neglected to examine *objects of adornment* for similar forms of patterning. We do not even have a reliable quantification of which animal species most frequently have their teeth transformed into social objects, surely a matter of more than just personal esthetics.

In a recent analysis of animal wall art in the Périgord, Rice and Paterson (1985) observe a correlation between the size and relative

217

danger of an herbivore species and the frequency with which it was represented on cave walls. It is puzzling that, if danger is one of the attributes of animals that made them symbolically more interesting, carnivores were represented in such low frequencies. However, the mirror image can be seen in body ornaments. Excluding shells and purposely fabricated beads for the moment, carnivore teeth, notably those of felids and canids, were the most frequently employed raw material for jewelry.[2] It is easy to imagine that this has something to do with the differential social and ideational value of various animal species. It is surely more than just coincidence that animals that hunt other animals were singled out for use in social display by the most dangerous predator of all.

The earliest forms of body ornamentation do not include, except in rare instances, objects of representational art. This pattern has been recognized ethnographically as well, and this ethnographic context provides us with one possible framework for understanding the system of meaning reflected by early ornamental constructs. In a provocative note in their work on body decoration in the Mount Hagen area of Highland New Guinea, Strathern and Strathern (1971:177) observe the following:

If we turn to self-decoration itself, there also we fine a lack of representational art. The process of decoration in Hagen is not representational but metonymical: that is, when Hageners wish to associate themselves with magically powerful things, such as birds, they do not construct masks, carvings, or paintings of these. Instead they actually take *parts* of the birds, their feathers, and attach these to themselves as decorations.

It may be asked at least, whether teeth of carnivores (especially canids) and to a lesser extent those of red deer, were chosen for body ornamentation with a view to the perceived powers of these animals.

If we shift our discussion for a moment to fossil and extant shells, a very important component of the earliest body decoration, complex patterns of disproportionate species representation are evident. In a sophisticated study of shell procurement in the Upper Paleolithic of France, Taborin (1985) notes a markedly restricted choice of species. She concludes that not all had the same "value" (the term is used here in the anthropological, not the economic, sense). She notes a very strong representation of small, round species, easily sewn onto leather, and of tubular forms such as *Dentalium*, which are easily strung. These she considers the more pedestrian species ("fonds habituel"). She contrasts these with symbolically important species (espèces à valeur symbolique) that have more complex morphology. Their openings are most often in the form of slits and they have asymmetrical profiles not unlike the perforated red deer incisors and artificially manufactured beads and pendants found in early Upper Paleolithic contexts.

Moreover, it is my impression from a careful examination of decorated ivory objects (many of them pendants) from Abri Blanchard and La Souquette, that at least one shell species was the inspiration for a linear, punctuated pattern of decoration (Fig. 9.1). In my opinion, Marshack's (1964, 1972a) hyper-functionalist assumptions led him to mistake this artistic appropriation of a natural pattern for a form of calendric notation. This same punctuated pattern, often on very small objects, is frequent at La Souquette and Abri Blanchard (Fig. 9.2), and has recently been demonstrated for the early Aurignacian of Germany (Hahn 1982) at the site of Geissenklosterle. Another example of this artistic appropriation of a natural form is evident in the reproduction, in bone and ivory, of the asymmetrical outline of red deer restigial canines.

Finally, abstract markings are a frequent characteristic of early Upper Paleolithic pendants. This has been demonstrated for central and eastern Europe by Hahn (1972), and is equally apparent in the abundant materials that I have examined from the southwestern French Aurignacian. Although the sample is small, there is room to examine species/symbol relationships and other patterns of association, an avenue that I intend to explore in upcoming research.

Thus, it is only prudent to exercise considerable caution before concluding that similarity and variation in body decoration, particularly in mortuary contexts, reflects social distinctions. Clearly, variation between regions may be related to differences in belief systems and systems of symbolic expression. Likewise, given the impossibility, for the early Upper Paleolithic, of establishing contemporaneity within even a millennium, the possibility of changing belief systems and symbolic frameworks must be considered. Moreover as Leroi-Gourhan (1965) has nicely demonstrated, such changes need not have been linked to alterations in stone and bone technology, the usual means by which we gauge change through time. One provocative indicator of changing decorative and symbolic systems (not to mention economic ones) is provided by Taborin (1985), whose data clearly indicate that shell procurement was far more prevalent in the Aurignacian than in

Figure 9.1. *Pirenella plicata* shell from the early Aurignacian at La Souquette. The meandering rows of punctuations on this type of shell seem to have been transferred to numerous ivory objects at this and other Aurignacian sites.

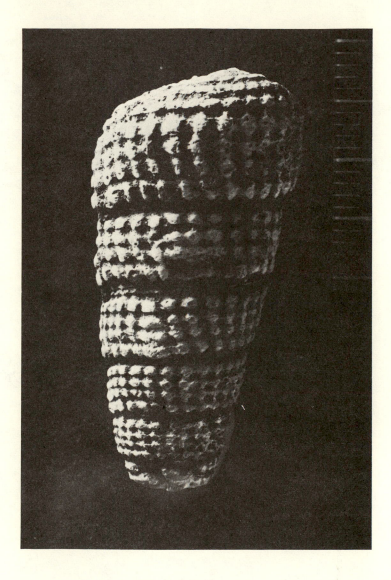

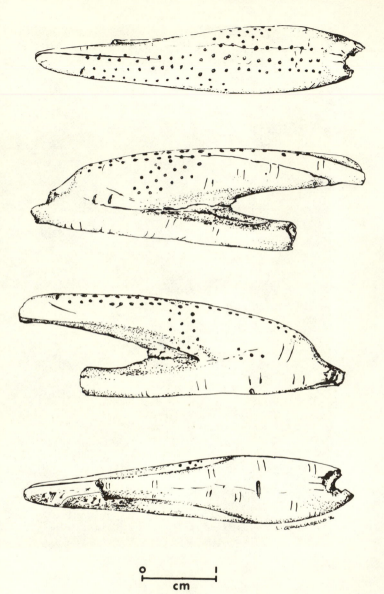

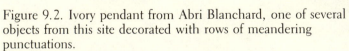

Figure 9.2. Ivory pendant from Abri Blanchard, one of several objects from this site decorated with rows of meandering punctuations.

either the Châtelperronian or Gravettian, and that linkages between southwestern France and the Mediterranean were much stronger in the Aurignacian.

TECHNOLOGICAL CONSIDERATIONS

The links between technology, subsistence, and exchange on one hand, and body ornamentation on the other, seem clear. Certain techniques of production can be reliably reconstructed from the preserved record for the early Aurignacian (see Peyrony 1935 for an early, but incomplete attempt). The technology of production is surprisingly complex and diverse, as evidenced by production debris and stigmata on the objects themselves. At least ten different types of pendants, representing at least five different production techniques, are recognizable in collections I have examined from the Aurignacian levels at Abri Blanchard, Abri Cellier, and La Souquette: (1) animal teeth, usually carnivore canines, perforated through the root; (2) circular or oval perforated beads made from bone, antler, and ivory; (3) elongated perforated beads made from ivory; (4) basket-shaped perforated beads made from stone and ivory; (5) engraved and perforated pendants made from bone and ivory; (6) tubular or disk-like perforated beads made from stone; (7) intact, but altered animal bones (phalanges, patellae) perforated for suspension or attachment; (8) fossils and worked bone, antler, and ivory objects circumincised at one end for suspension; (9) intact marine shells (both fossil and actual) perforated for suspension, and (10) ivory and stone "plugs."

The production sequence for basket-shaped beads alone comprises at least five discrete stages. These include extensive grinding and fine polishing, processes not usually recognized as significant components of Upper Paleolithic technologies. Moreover, the final products of this labor-intensive process (Fig. 9.3) are remarkably uniform in size and proportions (Fig. 9.4), within and even between sites, hinting at incipient craft specialization among early *Homo sapiens sapiens*.

This raises a different but important point. Focusing on western Europe, it is impossible to avoid observing that there are no prototypes for Châtelperronian and early Aurignacian ornamental objects and the complex and various techniques used to produce them. From the distance of 35,000 years, body ornamentation appears as intrusive as the figurative art, complex bone and antler technology, and considerable biological changes with which it co-occurs. An isolated fragment of

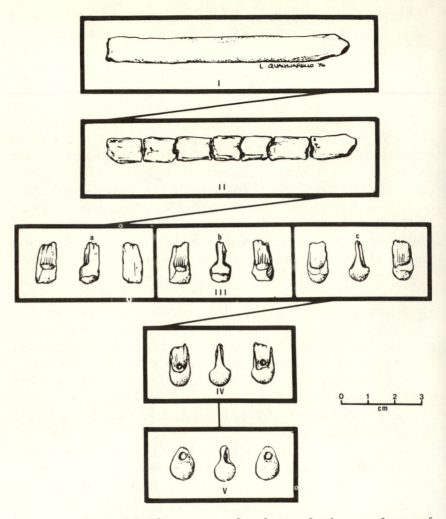

Figure 9.3. The sequence of production for the manufacture of early Aurignacian ivory beads, as reconstructed from collections from Abri Blanchard, Abri Castanet, and La Souquette. I: Pencil-like ivory baton. II: Bead-blanks created by circumincision and snapping of baton. III: Bilateral thinning of one end of blank by splitting along natural laminae of ivory. Preliminary polishing (Optional). IV: Perforation of thinned blank near "bulb." V: Polishing and grinding to remove most of thinned portion, to render more delicate the margins of the perforation, and to round the bulbar end.

224

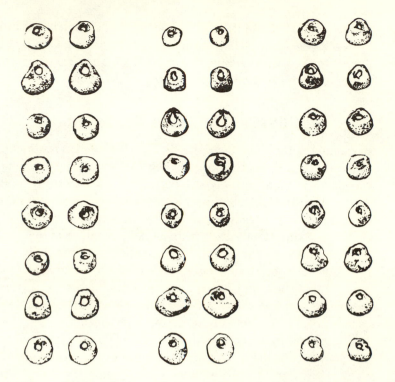

Figure 9.4. A selection of stone and ivory basket-shaped beads from the Aurignacian at Abri Blanchard. Shown actual size.

pierced bone from Pech de l'Azé (Bordes 1969), a fox tooth with a gouged depression supposedly from the Mousterian at La Quinn[3] (Martin 1907–10), and a fossil shell incised with a "cross" (Vértes 1964) as well as a "smoothed" plate of mammoth tooth from Tata, Hungary (Vértes 1959) stand out amidst thousands of years of symbolic silence. Without conclusive evidence for patterning and repetition, it is fruitless to maintain that these objects were operative in a symbolic context, let alone one of body ornamentation.

It is significant, for the purposes of this volume, that the abruptness of the *cultural* transition is more easily measured, and the material more abundant, than is the *biological* transition. A decorated pendant is a decorated pendant. It is not a transitional form. It is not a quantitative construct as is skeletal morphology.[4] Given the record now available, the emergence of technology for the manufacture of body ornaments in

Europe is sudden and the technology itself is complex and full-blown from the beginning. The implications are interesting to ponder with respect to the long-standing and unresolved question of *in situ* versus intrusive origins of the European Upper Paleolithic.

SUBSISTENCE IMPLICATIONS

In examining the ivory, bone, tooth, and shell used as raw material, one might expect a direct relationship between what was hunted and what was worn. In fact, precisely the opposite it true. In studying the early Aurignacian and Châtelperronian beads and pendants from France, it is clear that carnivore teeth, especially fox, make up less than 10 percent of the present sample; and apart from an occasional bovid or cervid tooth, the remainder of our sample is dominated by artificially produced, labor-intensive beads and pendants made from ivory (the majority), bone, antler, shell, and stone. Two animal pendants, one from the Abri Blanchard and one from La Souquette, appear to represent seals, not exactly an everyday item of diet in the Vézère Valley.

The relative frequencies of animals killed for food can be determined and compared with the frequencies of their teeth and tusks in ornamental constructions. Unlike parietal art, in which there is at least some relationship between an animal's food value and the frequency with which it was represented (Rice and Paterson 1985), no relationship exists in body ornaments between the abundance of an animal species's bones in the food debris of a living site and the frequency with which its body parts were used for decoration. In general, we tend to expect least-effort simplicity and we find labor-intensive complexity. Of course, the very fact that people decorate themselves goes against any assumption of least effort in later hominid evolution. Nevertheless, it is clear that the world of body ornamentation and presentation of self was subject, from the very beginning, to complex systems of meaning and modes of exchange.

PROCUREMENT CONSIDERATIONS

Sources of raw material, given a solid research program, can be accurately identified, providing vectors between original source and ultimate place of discard or loss (Demars 1982; Geneste 1985). In examining objects of body ornamentation for which geographic sources can be determined, most notably fossil and actual shells, we are struck by the distances that objects or raw materials traveled; in some cases several hundred kilometers, even though non-marine shells were locally available. The two conventions most often used to explain these exotica are long-distance movement of people (Bahn 1977) and participation in extensive networks of exchange (White 1985, 1987). I prefer the latter on what I believe to be solid grounds. If regular movements of people over hundreds of kilometers were the cause, one would expect substantial quantities of exotic flints, something that we do not generally observe (Larick 1983). On the other hand, reciprocal exchange networks are highly selective and usually involve greatly *valued* objects.

For example, it is important to consider the possibility that the ivory used for bead manufacture was itself exotic to the vicinity of the sites concerned. None of the ornamentally rich Vallon de Castelmerle sites has yielded woolly mammoth bones as part of its food debris. While it is possible that mammoth bones were not transported back to the living site with the meat, it is equally plausible that mammoth tusk was procured from distant sources by the same mechanisms which brought Atlantic and Mediterranean shells into the sites.

Bahn (1977) suggested that Mediterranean shells in southwestern French Upper Paleolithic sites indicate nothing more than that people were moving great distances and, in the process, collecting "trinkets." This unduly trivializes the tendency for cultural systems to impose value on what to us seems insignificant. It also ignores a great body of ethnographic literature pertaining to the process of reciprocal exchange of valued objects as a means of moving them across the cultural and natural landscape (Sharp 1952; Winters 1968; Wiessner 1982).

This issue of *value* is an important one with regard to ornaments conveying one's social identity. Ethnograpically, where we have information, it appears that body ornaments circulate more than any other component of material culture (Weiner 1987). These objects, which are frequently shells, take on increased *value* not because of their scarcity alone, but because of their social importance. Where we have good ethnographic evidence, we find that material objects, and especially ornaments, are one of the means by which political discourse takes place. Objects are "less dangerous" politically (Weiner 1983) than verbal encounters because of the nature of reciprocal obligations and because objects refer to social, not individual, categories. At the same time, they contain the force of authority and they may outlast a human

227

life and take on histories that are known and recounted (Weiner 1985). This authority is often called into play in disputes over land tenure, territory, and political authority, even in the "simplest" of societies.

While this seems a long way from the Middle/Upper Paleolithic transition, I wish to emphasize that one of the most striking differences between 35,000 and 30,000 years ago is that there was an explosion of ornamentation, much of it made on exotic raw material. We must consider whether complex conceptions of social value and material definition of self had something to do with this explosion.

BIOCULTURE LINKAGES

A conjunction of several factors would have been necessary for ornamentation to have emerged. Foremost among these must have been a modern grade of neurological complexity and organization (Coppens 1981; White 1985), providing the neural capacity for language and culture as we know it. Hunting technology and organization, as well as food-gathering techniques, had to have reached a level of sophistication that allowed the expenditure of considerable amounts of energy on non-subsistence pursuits, in a situation of sufficient environment richness and diversity. I do not wish to resurrect the old "leisure-time" explanation for esthetic and symbolic endeavor. Rather, I wish to suggest that bead-making, and other "artistic" pursuits (apparently having been highly valued), successfully competed for time and labor with subsistence pursuits. That this was so seems to be implied by the life-expectancy data presented by Trinkaus (this volume). Upper Paleolithic societies supported members long after they had passed reproductive age. That this must have been seen by Upper Paleolithic people as desirable and adaptive is perhaps indicated by the fact that they were doing this even while the society as a whole was suffering certain nutritional deficits (M.U. Brennan pers. comm.). It is clearly worth asking whether knowledge of hunting and gathering techniques, healing practices, ceremonies, social relations and kinship, distant territories – and complex systems of meaning, demanding the use of body decoration – might have been the qualities for which these older people were valued. This would have been a radical step in the evolution of hominid behavior.

The implications for the inter-generational transfer of knowledge would have been immense. The much shorter adult life of Neanderthals may well have prevented the recognition of long-term environmental patterns and recurrences of the "I remember when ..." variety. This means that pre-Upper Paleolithic societies would not have had access to the store of knowledge of thousands of square miles of landscape documented, for example, by Binford (1982b) for old Eskimo men and by Myers (1986) for the Pintupi of Australia. The adaptive consequences are self-evident.

Clearly, the ethnographic data base of anthropology demonstrates that, while old people contribute relatively little to actual food procurement, they exert a major influence on social and ideational domains. One wonders whether longevity and the development of a specialized body of ideational and social expertise went hand in hand. Fully language-competent humans organized into units capable of maintaining a complex body of technological, social, and ideational knowledge were clearly prerequisite for the highly patterned and redundant nature of early Upper Paleolithic technology, art, and ornamentation. However, the manipulation and transmission of a complex body of knowledge has within it the seeds of innovation and change. The more component parts of a system of knowledge, the greater the possibilities for their recombination and reintegration, the process we call invention. This latter is one of the most prominent characteristics of the Upper Paleolithic, which saw more innovation in its first 5,000 years than had occurred in the preceding 100,000 years. Moreover, the more complex a system of knowledge, the more likely that regional differences will arise, in part due to historical accident and in part to the specifics of local adaptation.

CONCLUSIONS

I have articulated a number of methodological, empirical, and evolutionary questions surrounding the sudden emergence of body ornamentation in western Europe around 35,000 years ago. Careful consideration of the western and central European record leads to the examination of certain, more general issues such as

(1) The degree to which the patterns identified here occur in regions other than western and central Europe. For example, while Mediterranean shells are ubiquitous in Near Eastern Upper Paleolithic sites, labor-intensive

beadwork is virtually absent (Bar-Yosef pers. comm.), except for pierced teeth, which are clearly present in the Aurignacian (Belfer-Cohen and Bar-Yosef 1982). Moreover, beads and pendants seem rare in eastern Europe until the Gravettian (Pavlovian), at which time many of the same techniques, earlier employed farther west by the Aurignacians, are evident in quantity at sites such as Sungir', Předmostí and Dolní Věstonice (Otte 1981; Klima 1976).

(2) The selective advantages conferred by bodies of knowledge and activity unrelated directly to subsistence pursuits,

(3) The relationship beween language, neurological evolution, developmental changes, and the numerous changes across the transition to culturally modern humans,

(4) The complex social geography of western Europe at 32,000 years ago and the degree to which art and body ornamentation might have played a role in the contemporaneity and interaction of two different morphological types (Lévèque and Vandermeersch 1980, 1981), seemingly associated with very different sets of material culture. While the Middle/Upper Paleolithic transition may be earlier in eastern Europe and the Near East (Kozłowski 1982), body ornaments manifest themselves only during the later version of this transition in western and central Europe, and

(5) The degree to which there is justification for the recent tendency to see the early Upper Paleolithic as somehow transitional to the supposedly more complex Solutrean and Magdalenian societies, since, in my opinion, ornamentation is just as complex in the early Aurignacian as it is in later periods.

In sum, the thrust of future research on early body ornamentation must be to move away from the prevalent emphasis on mortuary aspects of body ornamentation and the undue emphasis on the Magdalenian in discussions of the Middle to Upper Paleolithic transition. Future investigations must seek to understand more about the cultural, environmental, and evolutionary contexts impinging on the conception, manufacture, and display of some of the earliest objects ever used

230

to adorn the human body. This chapter has been an attempt to point out some potentially fruitful avenues for future research.

Notes

1. This assumption in turn raises the issue of the phylogenetic relationship between modern humans and Neanderthals. In this regard, I wish merely to echo the largely ignored query of Eldredge and Tattersall (1982) and Tattersall (1986) as to whether biological, neurological, and behavioral differences across the Middle to Upper Paleolithic transition might not reflect a speciation event. As Stringer (personal communication) has pointed out, this proposition should be testable by monitoring the extent of hybridization between these two morphological types.
2. The seeming predominance of beaver incisors at the Aurignacian site of Mladeč in Czechoslovakia (Szombathy 1925) may indicate regional differences in animal species chosen for ornamentation.
3. While it may be late Mousterian, this object seems suspiciously Aurignacian, both in the species of the tooth and in the indelicate technique used to prepare the root and to perforate it.
4. Although one could clearly argue for degrees of elaborateness of construction and decoration.

Acknowledgements

I wish to express my gratitude to Erik Trinkaus for the invitation to participate in the Sante Fe conference and to Doug Schwartz and Jonathan Haas of the School of American Research, and Jean Auel and the L.S.B. Leakey Foundation for making that conference possible. The work described here was funded by research grants from the Wenner-Gren Foundation for Anthropological Research, the National Endowment for the Humanities and the National Science Foundation. This paper owes much to the aid of the curators of the Logan Museum of Anthropology at Beloit College (Ed Way, Jane Troszak) and the Field Museum of Natural History, Chicago (Glen Cole). Others whose comments were invaluable include Ann-Marie Cantwell, David Frayer, Anne Hendrickson, Heidi Knecht, Laurie Matthews, Fred Myers, Bambi Schieffelin, Ann Pike Tay, and Annette Weiner. The paper is dedicated to the remarkable Alonzo W. Pond whose rigor and meticulous record-keeping in the 1920s contribute to knowledge in the 1980s.

References

Adam, K. 1951. Der Waldelefant von Lehringen, eine Jagdbeute des Diluvialen Menschen. *Quartär* 5:75–92.

Alexeyev, V.P. 1976. Position of the Staroselye find in the hominid system. *Journal of Human Evolution* 5:413–21.

Alvesalo, L., and P.M.A. Tigerstedt 1974. Heritabilities of human tooth dimensions. *Heriditas* 77:311–18.

Arensburg, B. 1977. New Upper Palaeolithic remains from Israel. *Paléorient* 13:208–15.

Ashton, N., and J. Cook 1986. Dating and correlating the French Mousterian. *Nature* 324:113.

Audouze, F., D. Cahen, L.H. Keeley, and B. Schmider 1981. Le site magdalénien du Buisson Campin à Verberie (Oise). *Gallia Préhistoire* 24:99–143.

Avise, J.C., J.E. Neigel, and J. Arnold 1984. Demographic influences on mitochrondial DNA lineage survivorship in animal populations. *Journal of Molecular Evolution* 20:99–105.

Bader, O. 1964. The oldest burial? The Illustrated London News, Sept. 9:731.

1970. The boys of Sungir'. *The Illustrated London News*, March 7:24–6.

Badoux, D.M. 1965. Probabilité d'une différentiation due au climat chez les Néandertaliens d'Europe. *L'Anthropologie* 69:75–82.

Bae, K.T. 1980. Chon'gong-ni Palaeolithic site excavation report. In

References

Archaeology in Korea, 1979, vol. 7, ed. by Kim Won-Yong, pp. 27–39. Seoul: University Museum, Seoul National University.

Bahn, P. 1977. Seasonal migration in South-west France during the Late Glacial period. *Journal of Archaeological Science* 4:245–57.

Bailey, G. 1983. *Pleistocene hunters and gatherers in Europe*. New York: Cambridge University Press.

Bailey, H.P. 1960. A method of determining the warmth and temperateness of climate. *Geografiska Annaler* 43:1–16.

Bánesz, L. 1968. *Barca bei Košice*. Bratislava: Vydavateľstvo Slovenskej Akadémie Vied.

Bar-Yosef, O. 1980. The prehistory of the Levant. *Annual Review of Anthropology* 9:101–33.

1988. The date of south-west Asian Neandertals. In *L'Homme de Néandertal 3: L'Anatomie*, ed. by E. Trinkaus, pp. 31–8. Etudes et Recherches Archéologiques de l'Université de Liège 30.

Bar-Yosef, O., and A. Belfer 1977. The Lagaman industry. In *Prehistoric investigations in Gebel Maghara, northern Sinai*, ed. by O. Bar-Yosef and J.L. Phillips, pp. 42–84. Jerusalem: Institute of Archaeology, Hebrew University.

Bar-Yosef, O., and N. Goren 1981. Notes on the chronology of the Lower Palaeolithic in the southern Levant. In *Las industrias mas antiquas Pre-Acheulense y Acheulense* (preprint), ed. by J.D. Clark and G.L. Isaac, pp. 28–42. Mexico City: UISSP Congress.

Bar-Yosef, O., and B. Vandermeersch 1972. The stratigraphical and cultural problems of the passage from Middle to Upper Palaeolithic in Palestinian caves. In *Origine de l'Homme Moderne*, vol.1, ed. by F. Bordes, pp. 221–5. Paris: UNESCO.

1981. Notes concerning the possible age of the Mousterian layers in Qafzeh Cave. In *Préhistoire du Levant*, ed. by P. Sanlaville and J. Cauvin, pp. 281–5. Paris: Editions du C.N.R.S.

Bar-Yosef, O., B. Vandermeersch, B. Arensburg, P. Goldberg, H. Laville, L. Meignan, Y. Rak, E. Tchernov, and A.M. Tillier 1986. New data on the origin of modern man in the Levant. *Current Anthropology* 27:63–4.

Bayer, J. 1922. Das Aurignac-Alter der Artefakte und menschlichen Skelettreste aus der "Fürst Johanns-Höhle" bei Lautsch in Mähren. *Mitteilungen der Anthropologische Gesellschaft in Wien* 52:173–85.

Beals, K.L., C.L. Smith, and S.M. Dodd 1984. Brain size, cranial morphology, climate, and time machines. *Current Anthropology* 25:301–30.

Beaumont, P.B. 1980. On the age of the Border Cave hominids 1–5. *Palaeontologia Africana* 23:21–33.

Beaumont, P.B., H. de Villiers, and J.C. Vogel 1978. Modern man in sub-Saharan Africa prior to 49,000 years BP: A review and evaluation with particular reference to Border Cave. *South African Journal of Science* 74:409–19.

Belfer-Cohen, A., and O. Bar-Yosef 1982. The Aurignacian at Hayonim Cave. *Paléorient* 7(2):19–42.

Besançon, J. 1981. Stratigraphie et chronologie du Quaternaire continental du Proche Orient. In *Préhistoire du Levant,* ed. by J. Cauvin and P. Sanlaville, pp. 33–54. Paris: C.N.R.S.

Beyries, S. 1984. Approche fonctionelle de la variabilité des facies du Moustérien. Thèse de Doctorat, Université de Paris X.

Binford, L.R. 1971. Mortuary practices: Their study and their potential. In *Approaches to the social dimensions of mortuary practices,* ed. by J.A. Brown, pp. 6–29. Memoirs of the Society for American Archaeology 25.

1972. Contemporary model building: Paradigms and the current state of Paleolithic research. In *Models in archaeology,* ed. by D.L. Clarke, pp. 106–66. London: Methuen.

1973. Interassemblage variability – the Mousterian problem and the "functional" argument. In *Explanation of culture change,* ed. by C. Renfrew, pp. 227–54. London: Duckworth.

1975. Historical archaeology: Is it historical or archaeological? *Popular Archaeology* 4(3–4):11–30.

1976. Forty-seven trips: A case study in the character of some formation processes of the archaeological record. In *Contributions to anthropology: The interior peoples of northern Alaska,* ed. by E.S. Hall, Jr., pp. 299–351. Archaeological Survey of Canada Paper 49. Ottawa: National Museum of Man, Mercury Series.

1978a. Dimensional analysis of behavior and site structure: Learning from an Eskimo hunting stand. *American Antiquity* 43:330–61.

1978b. *Nunamiut ethnoarchaeology.* New York: Academic Press.

1979. Organization and formation processes: Looking at curated technologies. *Journal of Anthropological Research* 35:255–73.

1980. Willow smoke and dogs' tails: Hunter-gatherer settlement systems and archaeological site formation. *American Antiquity* 45:1–17.

1981. *Bones: Ancient men and modern myths.* New York: Academic Press.

1982a. Comment on R. White: Rethinking the Middle/Upper Paleolithic transition. *Current Anthropology* 23:177–81.

1982b. The archaeology of place. *Journal of Anthropological Archaeology* 1:5–31.

1983a. *In pursuit of the past.* London: Thames and Hudson.

1983b. Reply to L. Freeman: More on the Mousterian: Flaked bone from Cueva Morin. *Current Anthropology* 24:372–7.

1983c. *Working at archaeology.* New York: Academic Press.

1983d. Long term land use patterns: Some implications for archaeology. In *Lulu Linear Punctuated: Essays in honor of George Irving Quimby,* ed. by R.C. Dunnell and D.K. Grayson, pp. 27–54. University of Michigan, Museum of Anthropology, Anthropological Papers No. 72.

References

1984a. *Faunal remains from Klasies River Mouth.* New York: Academic Press.

1984b. An Alyawara day: Flour, spinifex gum, and shifting perspectives. *Journal of Anthropological Research* 40:157–82.

1985a. Human ancestors: Changing views of their behavior. *Journal of Anthropological Archaeology* 4:292–327.

1985b. Hominid evolution: The problem of behavior and niche. Proposal submitted to the National Science Foundation. On file, Department of Anthropology, University of New Mexico, Albuquerque.

1986a. Researching ambiguity: Frames of reference and site structure. In *Method and theory for activity area research*, ed. by S. Kent, pp. 449–512. New York: Columbia University Press.

1986b. Reply to R. Singer and J. Wymer: On Binford on Klasies River Mouth: Response of the excavators. *Current Anthropology* 27(1):57–62.

1986c. Reply to Bunn and Kroll: Systematic butchery by Plio/Pleistocene hominids at Olduvai Gorge, Tanzania. *Current Anthropology* 27:444–6.

1986d. An Alyawara day: Making men's knives and beyond. *American Antiquity* 51:547–62.

1987a. Searching for camps and missing the evidence: Another look at the Lower Paleolithic. In *The Pleistocene Old World: Regional perspectives*, ed. by O. Soffer, pp. 19–31. New York: Plenum.

1987b. A taphonomic study of the fauna from the Abri Vaufrey. In *La grotte Vaufrey à Cenac-et-Saint-Julien (Dordogne): Paléoenvironnements, chronologie et activitiés humaines*, ed. by J.P. Rigaud. Mémoire de la Société Préhistorique Française 19.

1987c. Were there elephant hunters at Torralba? In *The evolution of human hunting*, ed. by M.H. Nitecki and D.V. Nitecki, pp. 47–105. New York: Plenum Press.

Binford, L.R., and S.R. Binford 1966. A preliminary analysis of functional variability in the Mousterian of Levallois Facies. In *Recent studies in paleoanthropology*, ed. by J.D Clark and F.C. Howell. *American Anthropologist* 68: 283–95.

Binford, L.R., and C.K. Ho 1985. Taphonomy at a distance: Zhoukoudian, "The cave home of Beijing Man"? *Current Anthropology* 26:413–42.

Binford, L.R., and J. O'Connell 1984. An Alyawara day: The stone quarry. *Journal of Anthropological Research* 40:406–32.

Binford, L.R., and N.M. Stone 1986. Zhoukoudian: A closer look. *Current Anthropology* 27:453–75.

Binford, L.R., M.G.L. Mills, and N.M. Stone 1988. Hyena scavenging behavior and its implications for the interpretation of faunal assemblages from FLK 22 (the Zinj floor) at Olduvai Gorge. *Journal of Anthropological Archaeology* 7:99–135.

235

Binford, S.R. 1966. Me'arat Shovakh (Mughareth esh-Shubbabiq). *Israel Exploration Journal* 16:18–32, 96–103.

1968a. A structural comparison of disposal of the dead in the Mousterian and Upper Paleolithic. *Southwestern Journal of Anthropology* 24:139–54.

1968b. Early Upper Pleistocene adaptations in the Levant. *American Anthropologist* 70:707–17.

Bintliff, J.L. 1982. Palaeolithic modelling of environmental changes in the East Mediterranean region since the last glaciation. In *Palaeoclimates, palaeoenvironments and human communities in the Eastern Mediterranean region in later prehistory*, ed. by J.L. Bintliff and W. Van Zeist, pp. 485–527. Oxford: British Archaeological Reports S133.

Birdsell, J.B. 1972. The problem of the evolution of human races: Classification or clines? *Social Biology* 19:136–62.

Bjork, A., and V. Skieller 1976. Postnatal growth and development of the maxillary complex. In *Factors affecting the growth of midface*, ed. by J.A. McNamara, pp. 61–99. Center for Human Growth and Development, Craniofacial Growth Series 6.

Blackwell, B., and H. Schwarcz 1987. La datation des spéléothems de la grotte Vaufrey par la famille de l'uranium. In *La grotte Vaufrey à Cenac-et-Saint-Julien (Dordogne): Paléoenvironnements, chronologie et activités humaines*, ed. by J.P. Rigaud. Mémoire de la Société Préhistorique Française 19.

Boaz, N.T. 1982. Comment on F.H. Smith: Upper Pleistocene hominid evolution in south-central Europe. *Current Anthropology* 23:687.

Bodmer, W.F., and L.L. Cavalli-Sforza 1976. *Genetics, evolution, and man*. San Francisco: W.H. Freeman.

Boëda, E. 1986a. Approche technologique de la concept Levallois et evaluation de son champ d'application. Thèse de Doctorat, Université de Paris X.

1986b. Etude experimentale de la technologie des pointes Levallois. In *Tailleur! Pour Quoi Faire: Préhistoire et Technologie Lithique II*, ed. by D. Cahen, pp. 23–56. Studia Praehistorica Belgica (Tervuren) 2.

Bordes, F. 1953. Essai de classification des industries "Moustériennes." *Bulletin de la Société Préhistorique Française* 50(7–8):457–66.

1961a. Mousterian cultures in France. *Science* 134:803–10.

1961b. *Typologie de Paléolithique Ancien et Moyen*. Bordeaux: F. Delmas.

1967. La stratigraphie du gisement du Roc de Combe (Lot) et ses implications, by François Bordes with J. Labrot. *Bulletin de la Société Préhistorique Française* 64(1):15–28.

1968a. *The old stone age*. New York: McGraw-Hill.

1968b. La question périgordienne. In *La Préhistoire, problèmes et tendances*, ed. by F. Bordes and D. de Sonneville-Bordes, pp. 59–70. Paris: C.N.R.S.

1969. Os percé moustérien et os gravé acheuléen du Pech de l'Azé II. *Quaternaria* 11:1–6.

References

1971. Observations sur l'Acheuléen des grottes en Dordogne. *Munibe* 23:5–23.

1972. *A tale of two caves.* New York: Harper and Row.

1973. On the chronology and the contemporaneity of different Palaeolithic cultures in France. In *The explanation of culture change*, ed. by C. Renfrew, pp. 217–26. London: Duckworth.

1977. Time and space limits of the Mousterian. In *Stone tools as cultural markers*, pp. 37–9. Canberra: Australian Institute of Aboriginal Studies.

1980. Les débitages Levallois et ses variantes. *Bulletin de la Société Préhistorique Française* 77:45–9.

1981. Vingt-cinq ans après: Le complexe moustérien revisité. *Bulletin de la Société Préhistorique Française* 78:77–87.

1984a. *Leçons sur le Paléolithique II: Le Paléolithique d'Europe.* Paris: C.N.R.S.

1984b. *Leçons sur le Paléolithique III: Le Paléolithique hors d'Europe.* Paris: C.N.R.S.

Bordes, F., and J. Labrot 1967. La stratigraphie du gisement de Roc-de-Combe (Lot), et ses implications. *Bulletin de la Société Préhistorique Française* 64:15–28.

Bordes, F., and D. de Sonneville-Bordes 1970. The significance of variability of Palaeolithic assemblages. *World Archaeology* 2:61–73.

Bosinski, G. 1982. The transition Lower/Middle Palaeolithic in northwestern Germany. In *The transition from Lower to Middle Palaeolithic and the origin of modern man*, ed. by A. Ronen, pp. 165–75. Oxford: British Archaeological Reports S151.

Bouchud, J. 1966. Remarques sur les fouilles de L. Lartet a l'abri de Cro-Magnon. *Bulletin de la Société de Recherche Préhistorique Les Eyzies* 15.

1974. Etude préliminaire de la faune provenant de la grotte Djebel Qafzeh, près de Nazareth, Israël. *Paléorient* 2:87–102.

Boule, M. 1911–13. L'homme fossile de La Chapelle-aux-Saints. *Annales de Paléontologie* 6:111–72; 7:21–58, 85–192; 8:1–70.

1914. L'Homo néanderthalensis et sa place dans la nature. *Congrès International de l'Anthropologie et Archéologie Préhistorique 1912* II:392–5.

1921. *Les hommes fossiles.* Paris: Masson et Cie.

1923. *Fossil men.* Edinburgh: Oliver and Boyd.

Brace, C.L. 1962a. Refocusing on the Neanderthal problem. *American Anthropologist* 65:729–41.

1962b. Cultural factors in the evolution of the human dentition. In *Culture and the evolution of man*, ed. by M.F.A. Montagu, pp. 343–54. New York: Oxford.

1964. The fate of the "Classic" Neanderthals: A consideration of hominid catastrophism. *Current Anthropology* 5:3–43.

1966. More on the fate of the "Classic" Neanderthals: Reply. *Current Anthropology* 7:210–14.

237

1967. *The stages of human evolution.* Englewood Cliffs: Prentice Hall.

1968. Neandertal. *Natural History* 77(5):38–45.

1979. Krapina, "Classic" Neanderthals, and the evolution of the European face. *Journal of Human Evolution* 8:527–50.

Brace, C.L., and M.F.A. Montagu 1965. *Man's evolution.* New York: MacMillan.

Brace, C.L., A.S. Ryan, and B.H. Smith 1981. Comment on tooth wear in La Ferrassie man. *Current Anthropology* 22:426–30.

Bräuer, G. 1980. Die morphologischen Affinitäten des jungpleistozänen Stirnbeines aus dem Elbmündungsgebiet bei Hahnöfersand. *Zeitschrift für Morphologie und Anthropologie* 71:1–42.

1981. New evidence on the transitional period between Neandertal and modern man. *Journal of Human Evolution* 10:467–74.

1982. A comment on the controversy "Allez Neanderthal." *Journal of Human Evolution* 11:439–40.

1984a. A craniological approach to the origin of anatomically modern *Homo sapiens* in Africa and implications for the appearance of modern Europeans. In *The origins of modern humans: A world survey of the fossil evidence,* ed. by F.H. Smith and F. Spencer, pp. 327–410. New York: Alan R. Liss.

1984b. The "Afro-European *sapiens* hypothesis" and hominid evolution in East Asia during the late middle and upper Pleistocene. In *The early evolution of man, with special emphasis on southeast Asia and Africa,* ed. by P. Andrews and J.L. Franzen, pp. 145–65. Courier Forschungsinstitut Senckenberg 69.

Bräuer, G., and R.E. Leakey 1986. The ES-11693 cranium from Eliye Springs, west Turkana, Kenya. *Journal of Human Evolution* 15:289–312.

Breuil, H. 1912. Les subdivisions du Paléolithique supérieur et leur signification. *Congrès International d'Anthropologie et d'Archéologie Préhistoriques* 14:1–238.

1952. *Quatre cents siècles d'art pariétal.* Montignac: Centre d'études et de documentation préhistoriques.

Bromage, T.G., and M.C. Dean 1985. Re-evaluation of the age of death of immature fossil hominids. *Nature* 317:525–7.

Brose, D.S., and M.H. Wolpoff 1971. Early upper Paleolithic man and late middle Paleolithic tools. *American Anthropologist* 73:1156–94.

Brown, W.M. 1980. Polymorphism in mitochondrial DNA of humans as revealed by restriction endonuclease analysis. *Proceedings of the National Academy of Sciences of the United States* 77(6):3605–9.

Brown, W.M., E.M. Prager, A. Wang, and A.C. Wilson 1982. Mitochondrial DNA sequences of primates: Tempo and mode of evolution. *Journal of Molecular Evolution* 18:225–39.

Brues, A. 1959. The spearman and the archer: An essay on selection in body build. *American Anthropologist* 61:457–69.

References

1972. Models of clines and races. *American Journal of Physical Anthropology* 37:389–99.

Bryant, E.H., S.A. McCommas, and L.M. Combs 1986. The effect of an experimental bottleneck on quantitative genetic variation in the housefly. *Genetics* 14:1191–211.

Bunn, D.S., A.B. Warburton, and R.D.S. Wilson 1982. *The barn owl.* Poyster (England): Calton.

Bunn, H.T. III 1982. Meat-eating and human evolution; Studies on the diet and subsistence patterns of Plio-Pleistocene hominids in East Africa. Ph.D. Dissertation, University of California, Berkeley.

Bunn, H.T. III and E. Kroll 1986. Systematic butchery by Plio-Pleistocene hominids at Olduvai Gorge, Tanzania. *Current Anthropology* 27:431–52.

Bunn, H.T. III, J.W.K. Harris, G. Isaac, Z. Kaufulu, E. Kroll, K. Schick, N. Toth, and A.K. Behrensmeyer 1980. FxJj50: An Early Pleistocene site in northern Kenya. *World Archaeology* 12:109–36.

Bunney, S. 1986. Did Neanderthal babies have bigger brains than ours? *New Scientist* 110:28–30.

Burch, E.S. Jr. 1972. The caribou/wild reindeer as a human resource. *American Antiquity* 37:339–68.

Butzer, K.W. 1980. The Holocene lake plain of North Rudolph, East Africa. *Physical Geography* 1(1):42–58.

1982. *Archaeology as human ecology.* Cambridge: Cambridge University Press.

Butzer, K.W., F.H. Brown, and D.L. Thurber 1969. Horizontal sediments of the lower Omo valley: Kibish formation. *Quaternaria* 11:15–29.

Cann, R.L. 1987. In search of Eve. *The Sciences* (September/October): 30–7.

Cann, R.L., W.M. Brown, and A.C. Wilson 1982. Evolution of human mitochondrial DNA: A preliminary report. In *Human genetics, part A: The unfolding genome,* ed. by B. Bonné-Tamir, T. Cohen, and R.M. Goodman, pp. 157–65. New York: Alan R. Liss.

1984. Polymorphic sites and mechanisms of evolution in human mitochondrial DNA. *Genetics* 106:479–99.

Cann, R.L., M. Stoneking, and A.C. Wilson 1987. Mitochondrial DNA and human evolution. *Nature* 325:31–6.

Capitan, L., and D. Peyrony 1928. *La Madeleine: Son gisement, son industrie, ses oeuvres d'art.* Paris: Nourry.

Carey, J.W., and A.T. Steegman, Jr. 1981. Human nasal protrusion, latitude, and climate. *American Journal of Physical Anthropology* 56:313–19.

Carlson, D.S., ed. 1979. *Craniofacial Biology I.* Center for Human Growth and Development, Craniofacial Growth Series 10.

Carr, S.M., S.W. Ballinger, J.N. Derr, L.H. Blankenship, and J.W.

Bickham 1986. Mitochondrial DNA analysis of hybridization between sympatric white-tailed deer and mule deer in west Texas. *Proceedings of the National Academy of Sciences USA* 83:9576–80.

Carrier, D.R. 1984. The energetic paradox of human running and hominid evolution. *Current Anthropology* 25:483–95.

Cartailhac, E. 1902. Mea culpa d'un sceptique. *L'Anthropologie* 13.

Carter, D.R., and D.M. Spengler 1982. Biomechanics of fracture. In *Bone in clinical orthopaedics*, ed. by G. Sumner-Smith, pp. 305–34. Philadelphia: Saunders.

Cartmill, M., D. Pilbeam, and G. Isaac 1986. One hundred years of paleoanthropology. *American Scientist* 74:410–20.

Cavalli-Sforza, L.L., I. Barrai, and A.W.F. Edwards 1964. Analysis of human evolution under random genetic drift. *Cold Spring Harbor Symposium on Quantitative Biology* 29:9–20.

Cavalli-Sforza, L.L., and A.W.F. Edwards 1965. Analysis of human evolution. In *Genetics today*, ed. by S.J. Geerts, pp. 923–33. Proceedings of XIth International Congress of Genetics, 1963, vol. 3.

Chadelle, J.P. 1983. *Technologie et utilisation du silex au Périgordien supérieur: L'exemple de la couche VII du Flageolet I*. Toulouse: Ecole des Hautes Etudes en Sciences Sociales.

Champagne, F., and R. Espitalier 1981. Le Piage, site préhistorique du Lot. *Mémoire de la Société Préhistorique Française* 15:1–205.

Chang J.-H. 1968. *Climate and agriculture: An ecological survey*. Aldine: Chicago.

Chang, K.C. 1963. *The archeology of ancient China*. New Haven: Yale University Press.

Charlesworth, B., R. Lande, and M. Slatkin 1982. A Neo-Darwinian commentary on macroevolution. *Evolution* 36:474–98.

Chase, P.G. 1986. Relationships between Mousterian lithic and faunal assemblages at Combe Grenal. *Current Anthropology* 27:69–71.

Chierici, G., E.P. Harrold, and K. Vargervik 1973. Morphogenetic experiments in facial asymmetry; The nasal cavity. *American Journal of Physical Anthropology* 38:291–300.

Churchill, S.E., and E. Trinkaus 1988. Neandertal scapular glenoid fossa morphology (abstract). *American Journal of Physical Anthropology* 75:196.

Clark, J.D. 1982. The transition from Lower to Middle Palaeolithic in the African continent. In *The transition from Lower to Middle Palaeolithic and the origin of modern man*, ed. by A. Ronen, pp. 235–55. Oxford: British Archaeological Reports S151.

1983. The significance of culture change in the early later Pleistocene in northern and southern Africa. In *The Mousterian legacy*, ed. by E. Trinkaus, pp. 1–12. Oxford: British Archaeological Reports S164.

1985. Leaving no stone unturned: Archaeological advances and behavioral adaptation. In *Hominid evolution: Past, present, and future*, ed. by P.V. Tobias, pp. 65–8. New York: Alan R. Liss.

References

Clark, J.D., and C.V. Haynes 1970. An elephant butchery site at
    Mwanganda's Village, Karonga, Malawi, and its relevance for
    Palaeolithic archaeology. *World Archaeology* 1:390–411.
Clark, J.D., and H. Kurashina 1976. New Plio-Pleistocene archaeological
    occurrences from the Plain of Gadeb, Upper Webi Shebib Basin,
    Ethiopia, and a statistical comparison on the Gadeb sites with other
    Early Stone Age assemblages. Paper presented at the Union
    Internationale des Sciences Préhistoriques et Protohistoriques, IX
    Congrès, Nice.
Clarke, R.J. 1985. A new reconstruction of the Florisbad cranium, with
    notes on the site. In *Ancestors: The hard evidence*, ed. by E. Delson,
    pp. 301–5. New York: Alan R. Liss.
Clastres, P. 1972. The Guayaki. In *Hunters and gatherers today*, ed. by
    M.G. Bicchieri, pp. 138–74. New York: Holt, Rinehart and
    Winston.
CLIMAP 1981. *Seasonal resonstructions of the earth's surface at the last
    glacial maximum*. Geological Society of America Map and Chart
    Series MC-36.
    1984. The last interglacial ocean. *Quaternary Research* 21:123–224.
Cohan, F.M. 1984. Can uniform selection retard random genetic
    divergence between isolated conspecific populations? *Evolution*
    38(3):495–504.
Collie, G. 1927. *The Aurignacians and their culture*. Logan Museum
    Bulletin 1. Beloit, Wisconsin: The Logan Museum, Beloit College.
Collins, D. 1969. Cultural traditions and environment of early man.
    Current Anthropology 10:267–316.
Conkey, M.W. 1978. Style and information in cultural evolution. Toward
    a predictive model for the Paleolithic. In *Social archaeology*, ed. by
    C.L. Redman, M.J. Berman, W.T. Longhorne, Jr., N.M. Versagg,
    and J.C. Wanser, pp. 61–85. New York: Academic Press.
    1980. The identification of prehistoric hunter-gatherer aggregation sites:
    The case of Altamira. *Current Anthropology* 21:609–30.
    1983. On the origins of Paleolithic art: A review and some critical
    thoughts. In *The Mousterian legacy: Human biolcultural change in
    the Upper Pleistocene*, ed. by E. Trinkaus, pp. 201–27. Oxford:
    British Archaeological Reports S164.
    1984. To find ourselves: Art and social geography of prehistoric hunter
    gatherers. In *Past and present in hunter-gatherer studies*, ed. by C.
    Schrire, pp. 253–76. New York: Academic Press.
Cook, J., C.B. Stringer, A.P. Currant, H.P. Schwarcz, and A.G. Wintle
    1982. A review of the chronology of the European Middle Pleistocene
    record. *Yearbook of Physical Anthropology* 25:19–65.
Coon, C.S. 1962. *The origin of races*. New York: Knopf.
    1964. Comment on C.L. Brace: The fate of the "Classic" Neanderthals:
    A consideration of hominid catastrophism. *Current Anthropology*
    5(1):21–2.

1982. *Racial adaptations. A study of the origins, nature, and significance of racial variations in humans.* Chicago: Nelson-Hall.

Copeland, L. 1975. The Middle and Upper Palaeolithic of Lebanon and Syria in light of recent research. In *Problems in prehistory: North Africa and the Levant,* ed. by F. Wendorf and A.E. Marks, pp. 317–50. Dallas: Southern Methodist University Press.

1983. Levallois/Non-Levallois determinations in the early Levant Mousterian: Problems and questions for 1983. *Paléorient* 9:15–28.

1985. The pointed tools of Hummal Ia (El Kowm, Syria). *Cahiers de l'Euphrate* 4:177–90.

Copeland, L., and F. Hours 1983. Le Yabroudian d'El Kowm (Syrie) et sa place dans le Paléolithique de Levant. *Paléorient* 9:21–38.

Coppens, Y. 1981. Exposé sur le cerveau: Le cerveau des hommes fossiles. Institute de France, Académie des Sciences, January 12 meeting, pp. 3–24.

Cordy, J.M. 1984. Evolution des faunes Quaternaires en Belgique. In *Peuples chasseurs de la Belgique préhistorique dans leur cadre naturel,* ed. by D. Cahen and P. Haesaerts, pp. 67–78. Brussels: Institute Royal des Sciences Naturelles de Belgique.

Crew, H. 1975. An evaluation of the relationship between the Mousterian complexes of the eastern Mediterranean. In *Problems in prehistory: North Africa and the Levant,* ed. by F. Wendorf and A.E. Marks, pp. 427–38. Dallas: Southern Methodist University Press.

Daams, R. 1981. The dental pattern of the dormice *Dryomys, Myomimus, Microdryomys* and *Peridryomys. Utrecht Micropaleontology Bulletin Special Publications* 3:1–115.

Davis, S.J.H. 1974. Incised bones from the Mousterian of Kebara Cave (Mount Carmel) and the Aurignacian of Ha-yonim Cave (western Galilee), Israel. *Paléorient* 2:181–2.

1977. The ungulate remains from Kebara Cave. *Eretz Israel* 13:150–63.

1982. Climate change and the advent of domestication: The succession of ruminant artiodactyls in the late Pleistocene–Holocene period in the Israel region. *Paléorient* 8:5–16.

Day, M.H. 1971. Postcranial remains of *Homo erectus* from Bed IV, Olduvai Gorge, Tanzania. *Nature* 232:383–7.

1982. The *Homo erectus* pelvis: Punctuation or gradualism? In *L'Homo erectus et la place de l'Homme de Tautavel parmi les hominidés fossiles* (prétirage), ed. by H. de Lumley, pp. 411–21. Paris: C.N.R.S.

Day, M.H., and C.B. Stringer 1982. A reconsideration of the Omo Kibish remains and the *erectus–sapiens* transition. 1er Congrès International de Paléontologie Humaine, Nice: Colloque International C.N.R.S. 2:814–46.

de Lumley, M.-A. 1973. Anténéandertaliens et Néandertaliens du bassin Méditerranéen Occidental Européen. *Etudes Quaternaires* (Université de Province) 2:1–626.

de Sonneville-Bordes, D., and J. Perrot 1954–6. Lexique typologique du

Paléolithique supérieur. *Bulletin de la Société Préhistorique Française* 51:327–35; 52:76–9; 53:408–12, 547–59.

Deacon, H.J. 1985. Review of L.R Binford: *Faunal remains from Klasies River Mouth. South African Archaeological Bulletin* 40:59–60.

Deacon, H.J., V.B. Geleijnse, A.I. Thackeray, J.F. Thackeray, M.L. Tusenius, and J.C. Vogel 1986. Late Pleistocene cave deposits in the southern Cape: Current research at Klasies River. *Palaeoecology of Africa and the Surrounding Islands* 17:31–7.

Dean, M.C., C.B. Stringer, and T.G. Bromage 1986. Age at death of the Neanderthal child from Devil's Tower, Gibraltar and the implications for studies of general growth and development in Neanderthals. *American Journal of Physical Anthropology* 70:301–9.

Debenath, A. 1973. Un foyer aménagé dans le Moustérien de Hauteroche à Chateauneuf-sur-Charente (Charente). *L'Anthropologie* 77:329–38.

    1976. Les civilisations du Paléolithique inférieur en Charente. In *La Préhistoire Française*, ed. by H. de Lumley, pp. 1070–6. Paris: C.R.N.S. 1(2).

Debenath, A., and L. Duport 1971. Os travaillés et os utilisés de quelques gisements préhistoriques Charentais. *Bulletins et Mémoires de la Société Archéologique et Historique de la Charente* 1971:189–202.

Debenath, A., J.P. Raynal, and J.P. Texier 1982. Position stratigraphique des restes humains paléolithiques marocains sur la base des travaux récents. *Compte Rendu Hebdomadaire des Séances de l'Académie des Sciences, Paris* 294:1247–50.

Delage, F. 1938. L'abri de la Souquette. *Bulletin de la Société Historique et Archéologique du Périgord* 65:3–25.

Delpech, F. 1983. *Les Faunes de Paléolithique supérieur dans le sud-ouest de la France.* Paris: C.N.R.S.

Delpech, F., and H. Laville 1987. Climatologie et chronologie de la grotte Vaufrey. Confrontation des hypothèses et implications. In *La Grotte Vaufrey à Cenac-et-Saint-Julien (Dordogne): Paléoenvironnements, chronologie et activités humaines*, ed. by J.P. Rigaud. Mémoire de la Société Préhistorique Française 19.

Delpech, F., and F. Prat 1980. Les grands mammifères Pleistocènes de Sud Ouest de la France. In *Problèmes de stratigraphies quaternaires en France et dans les pays limitrophes*, ed. by J. Chaline, pp. 268–97. Supplément au Bulletin de l'Association Française des Etudes Quaternaires 1.

Delporte, H. 1968. L'Abri du Facteur à Tursac (Dordogne). *Gallia Préhistoire* 11:1–112.

    1984. L'Aurignacien de La Ferrassie. In *Le Grande Abri de La Ferrassie*, ed. by H. Delporte. *Etudes Quaternaires* 7:145–234.

Delson, E. 1985. Late Pleistocene human fossils and evolutionary relationships. In *Ancestors: The hard evidence*, ed. by E. Delson, pp. 296–300. New York: Alan R. Liss.

    1988. One source not many. *Nature* 332:206.

Demars, P.-Y. 1982. *L'Utilisation du silex au Paléolithique supérieur: Choix, approvisionnement, circulation*. Cahiers du Quaternaire 5.

Demes, B. 1987. Another look at an old face: Biomechanics of the neandertal facial skeleton reconsidered. *Journal of Human Evolution* 16:297–303.

Denaro, M., H. Blanc, M.J. Johnson, K.H. Chen, E. Wilmsen, and L.L. Cavalli-Sforza 1981. Ethnic variation in Hpa 1 endonuclease cleavage patterns of human mitochondrial DNA. *Proceedings of the Nationl Academy of Sciences* USA 78:5768–72.

Dennell, R. 1983. *European economic prehistory: A new approach*. London: Academic Press.

1986. Needles and spear-throwers. *Natural History* 95:70–9.

Dibble, H.L. 1987. The interpretation of Middle Palaeolithic scrapers. *American Antiquity* 52:109–17.

Didon, L. 1912. Faits nouveaux constatés dans une station aurignacienne des environs de Sergeac. *Congrès International d'Anthropologie et Archéologie Préhistorique* 6:337–50.

Duplessy, J.C. 1982. Glacial to interglacial contrasts in the northern Indian Ocean. *Nature* 295:494–8.

Edwards, A.W.F. 1971. Mathematical approaches to the study of human evolution. In *Mathematics in the archaeological and historical sciences*, ed. by D.G. Hodson, R. Kendall, and P. Tautu, pp. 347–55. Edinburgh: Edinburgh University Press.

Eldredge, N., and I. Tattersall 1982. *The myths of human evolution*. New York: Columbia University Press.

Endo, B., and T. Kimura 1970. Postcranial skeleton of the Amud man. In *The Amud man and his cave site*, ed. by H. Suzuki and F. Takai, pp. 231–406. Tokyo: Academic Press of Japan.

Enlow, D.H. 1975. *Handbook of facial growth*. Philadelphia: Saunders.

Enlow, D.H., and R.E. Moyers 1971. Growth and architecture of the face. *Journal of the American Dental Association* 82:764–74.

Ennouchi, E. 1962. Un Néandertalien: L'homme du Jebel Irhoud (Maroc). *L'Anthropologie* 66:279–99.

Evins, M.A. 1982. The fauna from Shanidar Cave: Mousterian wild goat exploitation in northern Iraq. *Paléorient* 8:37–58.

Farrand, W.R. 1979. Chronology and palaeoenvironment of Levantine prehistoric sites as seen from sediment studies. *Journal of Archaeological Science* 6:369–92.

1982. Environmental conditions during the Lower/Middle Palaeolithic transition in the Near East and the Balkans. In *The transition from the Lower to the Middle Palaeolithic and the origins of modern man*, ed. by A. Ronen, pp. 105–8. Oxford: British Archaeological Reports S151.

Ferembach, D. 1976. Les restes humains de la Grotte de Dar-es-Soltane 2 (Maroc) Campagne 1975. *Bulletins et Mémoires de la Société d'Anthropologie de Paris, Série XIII* 3:183–93.

1979. L'émergence du genre *Homo* et de l'espèce *Homo sapiens*. Les faits. Les incertitudes. *Biométrie Humaine* 14:11–18.

Ferring, C.R. 1975. The Aterian in north African prehistory. In *Problems in prehistory: North Africa and the Levant*. ed. by F. Wendorf and A.E. Marks, pp. 113–26. Dallas: SMU Press.

Ferris, S.D., W.M. Brown, W.S. Davidson, and A.C. Wilson 1981. Extensive polymorphism in the mitochondrial DNA of apes. *Proceedings of the National Academy of Sciences USA* 78:6319–23.

Ferris, S.D., R.D. Sage, C.M. Huang, J.T. Nielsen, U. Ritte, and A.C. Wilson 1983. Flow of mitochondrial DNA across a species boundary. *Proceedings of the National Academy of Sciences USA* 80:2290–4.

Foley, R. 1982. A reconsideration of the role of predation on large mammals in tropical hunter-gatherer adaptation. *Man* 17:393–402.

Franciscus, R.G., and E. Trinkaus 1988a. Nasal morphology and the emergence of *Homo erectus*. *American Journal of Physical Anthropology* 75:517–27.

1988b. The Neandertal nose (abstract). *American Journal of Physical Anthropology* 75:209–10.

Frayer, D.W. 1977. Dental sexual dimorphism in the European Upper Paleolithic and Mesolithic. *Journal of Dental Research* 58:871.

1978. Evolution of the dentition in Upper Paleolithic and Mesolithic Europe. *University of Kansas Publications in Anthropology* 10:1–201.

1980. Sexual dimorphism and cultural evolution in the Late Pleistocene and Holocene of Europe. *Journal of Human Evolution* 9:399–415.

1981. Body size, weapon use, and natural selection in the European Upper Paleolithic and Mesolithic. *American Anthropologist* 83:57–73.

1984. Biological and cultural change in the European late Pleistocene and early Holocene. In *The origins of modern humans: A world survey of the fossil evidence*, ed. by F.H. Smith and F. Spencer, pp. 211–50. New York: Alan R. Liss.

1986. Cranial variation at Mladeč and the relationship between Mousterian and Upper Paleolithic hominids. *Anthropos* 23:243–56.

Frayer, D.W., J. Jelínek, N. Minugh, M. Oliva, L. Seitl, F.H. Smith, and M.H. Wolpoff 1990. Upper Pleistocene human remains from the Mladeč Cave, Moravia. In prep.

Freeman, L.G., Jr. 1978. The analysis of some occupation floor distributions from Earlier and Middle Paleolithic sites in Spain. In *Views of the past: Essays in Old World prehistory and paleoanthropology*, ed. L.G. Freeman, Jr., pp. 57–115. The Hague: Mouton.

Freund, G. 1982. Der Ubergang von alt-zum Mittelpaläolithikum in Sud-Deutschland. In *The transition from Lower to Middle Palaeolithic and the origin of modern man*, ed. by A. Ronen, pp. 151–63. Oxford: British Archaeological Reports S151.

Gábori, M. 1976. *Les Civilisations du Paléolithique Moyen entre les Alpes et l'Oural*. Budapest: Akadémiai Kiadó.

Gábori-Csánk, V. 1968. *La Station du Paléolithique Moyen d'Erd, Hongrie.* Budapest: Akadémiai Kiadó.

Gamble, C. 1982. Comment on R. White: Rethinking the Middle/Upper Paleolithic transition. *Current Anthropology* 23:169–92.

1984. Culture and society in the Upper Palaeolithic of Europe. In *Hunter-gatherer economy in prehistory,* ed. by G. Bailey, pp. 201–11. Cambridge: Cambridge University Press.

1986. *The Palaeolithic settlement of Europe.* Cambridge: Cambridge University Press.

Garn, S.M., P.E. Cole, and W.L. Van Alstine 1979. Sex discriminatory effectiveness using combinations of root lengths and crown diameters. *American Journal of Physical Anthropology* 50:115–18.

Garn, S.M., A.B. Lewis, and R.S. Kerewsky 1965. Genetic, nutritional, and maturational correlates of dental development. *Journal of Dental Research* 44:228–42.

Garn, S.M., A.B. Lewis, D.R. Swindler, and R.S. Kerewsky 1967. Genetic control of sexual dimorphism in tooth size. *Journal of Dental Research* 46:963–72.

Garn, S.M., A.B. Lewis, and A.J. Walenga 1968. Genetic basis of the crown-size profile pattern. *Journal of Dental Research* 47:1190.

Garn, S.M., W.L. Van Alstine, and P.E. Cole 1978a. Intraindividual root length correlations. *Journal of Dental Research* 56:270.

1978b. Relationship between root lengths and crown diameters of corresponding teeth. *Journal of Dental Research* 56:636.

Garrard, A.N. 1982. The environmental implications of a reanalysis of the large mammal fauna from the Wadi el-Mughara caves, Palestine. In *Palaeoclimates, palaeoenvironments and human communities in the eastern Mediterranean region in later prehistory,* ed. by J.L. Bintliff and W. Van Zeist, pp. 165–87. Oxford: British Archaeological Reports S133.

1983. The Palaeolithic faunal remains from Adlun and their ecological context. In *Adlun in the Stone Age: The excavations of D.A.E. Garrod in the Lebanon 1958–1963,* ed. by D.A. Roe, pp. 397–410. Oxford: British Archaeological Reports S159.

Garrod, D.A.E., and D. Bate 1937. *The Stone Age of Mount Carmel I.* Oxford: Clarendon Press.

Geist, V. 1981. Neanderthal the hunter. *Natural History* 90(1):26–36.

Geneste, J.-M. 1985. Analyse lithique d'industries moustériennes du Périgord: Une approche technologique du comportement des groupes humains au Paléolithique moyen. Thèse de Doctorat d'Etat, Université de Bordeaux I.

Geraads, D., and E. Tchernov 1983. Fémurs humains du Pléistocène moyen de Gesher Benot Ya'acov (Israël). *L'Anthropologie* 87:138–41.

Ghosh, K. 1982. Pebble-core and flake elements: Process of transmutation and the factors thereof. A case study of the transition from Lower to Middle Palaeolithic in India. In *The transition from Lower to Middle*

Palaeolithic and the origin of modern man, ed. by A. Ronen, pp. 265–82. Oxford: British Archaeological Reports S151.

Gilead, I. 1981. Upper Palaeolithic tool assemblages from the Negev and Sinai. In *Préhistoire du Levant*, ed. by J. Cauvin and P. Sanlaville, pp. 331–42. Paris: C.N.R.S.

Gilead, I., and C. Grigson 1984. Far'ah II: A Middle Palaeolithic open air site in the Northern Negev, Israel. *Proceedings of the Prehistoric Society* 50:71–97.

Giles, E., and S.H. Ambrose 1986. Are we all out of Africa? *Nature* 322:21–2.

Gilman, A. 1984. Explaining the Upper Palaeolithic revolution. In *Marxist perspectives in archaeology*, ed. by M. Spriggs, pp. 115–26. Cambridge: Cambridge University Press.

Gisis, I., and O. Bar-Yosef 1974. New excavations in Zuttiyeh Cave, Wadi Amud, Israel. *Paléorient* 2:175–80.

Goldberg, P. 1980. Micromorphology in archaeology and prehistory. *Paléorient* 6:159–64.

1981. Late Quaternary stratigraphy of Israel: An eclectic view. In *Préhistoire du Levant*, ed. by J. Cauvin and P. Sanlaville, pp. 55–66. Paris: C.N.R.S.

1984. Late Quaternary history of Qadesh Barnea, northeastern Sinai. *Zeitschrift für Geomorphologie N.F.* 28:193–217.

1986. Late Quaternary environmental history of the southern Levant. *Geoarchaeology* 1:225–44.

Goldberg, P., and H. Laville in press. The collapse of the Mousterian sedimentary regime and the beginning of the Upper Palaeolithic at Kebara Cave, Mount Carmel. In *Prehistoric investigations in the southern Levant*, ed. O. Bar-Yosef and B. Vandermeersch. Oxford: British Archaeological Reports.

Goose, D.H. 1967. Preliminary study of tooth size in families. *Journal of Dental Research* 56:959–62.

Goren-Inbar, N. 1985a. The lithic assemblage of the Berekhat Ram Acheulian site, Golan Heights. *Paléorient* 11:7–28.

1985b. Un site moustérien de plein air à Biqat Quneitra. *L'Anthropologie* 89:251–4.

Gorjanović-Kramberger, D. 1904. Potijče li moderni čovjek ravnó od dilúvijalonga *Homo* primigeniusa? *I Kongress srpskih lekara i Prirodnjaka*, pp. 1–8.

1918. Pračovjek iz Krapine. *Priroda* 8:162–5.

Gould, R.A. 1980. *Living archaeology*. Cambridge: Cambridge University Press.

Gould, S.J. 1987. Bushes all the way down. *Natural History* 96(5):12–19

Gould, S.J., and E.S. Vrba 1982. Exaptation – a missing term in the science of form. *Paleobiology* 81:4–15.

Gribbin, J., and J. Cherfas 1982. *The monkey puzzle: Reshaping the evolutionary tree*. London: Bodley Head.

Griffin, P.B. 1984. Forager resource and land use in the humid tropics: The Agta of northeastern Luzon, the Philippines. In *Past and present in hunter-gatherer studies*, ed. by C. Schrire, pp. 95–121. New York: Academic Press.

Guagliardo, M.F. 1982. Craniofacial structure, aging and dental function: Their relationship in adult human skeletal series. Ph.D. Thesis, University of Tennessee, Knoxville.

Guglielmino-Matessi, C.R., P. Gluckman, and L.L. Cavalli-Sforza 1979. Climate and the evolution of skull metrics in man. *American Journal of Physical Anthropology* 50:549–64.

Gvirtzman, G. 1983. Coastal terraces and prehistoric sites in Lebanon – correlation with Quaternary sedimentary cycles in Israel and a chronological interpretation (abstract). Abstracts of the Annual Meeting of the Israel Society for Quaternary Research, pp. 14–20.

Haas, G. 1972. The microfauna of the Djebel Qafzeh cave. *Palaeovertebrata* 5:261–70.

Habgood, P.J. 1986. The origin of the Australians: A multivariate approach. *Archaeology and Physical Anthropology in Oceania* 21:130–7.

Hahn, J. 1972. Aurignacian signs, pendants and art objects in Central and Eastern Europe. *World Archaeology* 3:252–6.

1982. Demi-relief aurignacien en ivoire de la grotte Geissenklosterle, près d'Ulm (Allemagne fédérale). *Bulletin de la Société Préhistorique Française* 79:73–7.

1986. *Kraft und Aggression. Die Botschaft der Eiszeitkunst im Aurignacien Suddeutschlands?* Tubingen: Verlag Archaeologica Venatoria 7.

Hahn, J., and L.R. Owen 1985. Blade technology in the Aurignacian and Gravettian of Geissenklosterle Cave, southwest Germany. *World Archaeology* 17:61–75.

Hale, L.R., and R.S. Singh 1986. Extensive variation and heteroplasmy in size of mitochondrial DNA among geographic populations of *Drosophila melanogaster*. *Proceedings of the National Academy of Sciences USA* 83:8813–17.

Harlé, E. 1881. La grotte d'Altamira, près de Santander (Espagne). *Materiaux pour l'Histoire de l'Homme* 17:275–83.

Harpending, H. 1974. Genetic structure of small populations. *Annual Review of Anthropology* 3:229–43.

Harris, J.W.K. 1978. Karari industry: Its place in African prehistory. Ph.D. Dissertation, University of California, Berkeley.

Harrold, F.B. 1980. A comparative analysis of Eurasian Palaeolithic burials. *World Archaeology* 12:195–211.

1983. The Châtelperronian and the Middle Upper Paleolithic transition. In *The Mousterian legacy*, ed. by E. Trinkaus, pp. 123–40. Oxford: British Archaeological Reports S164.

Hasegawa, M., H. Kishino, and T. Yano 1985. Dating of the human–ape splitting by a molecular clock of mitochondrial DNA. *Journal of Molecular Evolution* 22:160–74.

Hayden, B. 1979. *Paleolithic reflections: Lithic technology and ethnographic excavations among Australian Aborigines.* Canberra: Australian Institute of Aboriginal Studies.

Hearty, P.J. 1986. An inventory of Last Glacial (*sensu lato*) Age deposits from the Mediterranean basin. *Zeitschrift für Geomorphologie,* N.F. Suppl. Bd. 62:51–69.

Heim, J.L. 1976. Les hommes fossiles de La Ferrassie I. *Archives de l'Institut de Paléontologie Humaine* 35:1–331.
  1978. Contribution du massif facial à la morphogenèse du crâne Néanderthalien. In *Les origines humaines et les époques de l'intelligence,* ed. by J. Piveteau, pp. 183–215. Paris: Masson et Cie.
  1982a. Les hommes fossiles de La Ferrassie II. *Archives de l'Institut de Paléontologie Humaine* 38:1–272.
  1982b. *Les Enfants Néandertaliens de La Ferrassie.* Paris: Masson.

Hendey, Q.B., and T.P. Volman 1986. Last interglacial sea levels and coastal caves in the Cape Province, South Africa. *Quaternary Research* 25:189–98.

Henke, W., and N. Xirotiris 1982. New human Upper Paleolithic fossils of middle Europe. In *Man and his origins,* ed. by J. Jelínek, pp. 263–80. Brno: Moravian Museum.

Hennig, G.J., and F. Hours 1982. Dates pour le passage entre l'acheuléen et le Paléolithique moyen à El Kowm (Syrie). *Paléorient* 8:81–4.

Henry, J. 1964. *Jungle people.* New York: Vintage Books, Random House.

Heusser, L.E., and N.J. Shackleton 1979. Direct marine–continental correlation: 150,000 year oxygen-isotope pollen record from the north Pacific. *Science* 204:837–8.

Hietala, H.J. 1983. Boker Tachtit: Intralevel and interlevel spatial analysis. In *Prehistory and paleoenvironments in the Central Negev, Israel III,* ed. by A.E. Marks, pp. 217–81. Dallas: Southern Methodist University Press.

Hietala, H.J., and A.E. Marks 1981. Changes in spatial organization at the Middle to Upper Paleolithic transitional site of Boker Tachtit, Central Negev, Israel. In *Préhistoire du Levant,* ed. by P. Sanlaville and J. Cauvin, pp. 307–18. Paris: C.N.R.S.

Hietala, H.J., and D. Stevens 1977. Spatial analysis: Multiple procedures in pattern recognition studies. *American Antiquity* 42:539–59.

Hodder, I. 1982. Theoretical archaeology: A reactionary view. In *Symbolic and structural archaeology,* ed. by I. Hodder, pp. 1–16. Cambridge: Cambridge University Press.

Hogan, J.P. 1977. *Inherit the stars.* New York: Ballantine.

Holloway, R.L. 1985. The poor brain of *Homo sapiens neanderthalensis*: See what you please. In *Ancestors: The hard evidence,* ed. by E. Delson. pp. 319–24. New York: Alan R. Liss.

Holmberg, A.R. 1969. *Nomads of the long bow*. Garden City, New York: Natural History Press.

Holt, I.J., A.E. Harding, and J.A. Morgan-Hughes 1988. Deletions of muscle mitochondrial DNA in patients with mitochondrial myopathies. *Nature* 331:717–19.

Hooijer, D. 1961. The fossil vertebrates of Ksar Akil, a Palaeolithic rockshelter in Lebanon. *Zoologische Verhandelingen* 49:4–65.

Horowitz, A. 1979. *The Quaternary of Israel*. New York: Academic Press.

Horowitz, S.L., R.H. Osborne, and F.V. De George 1958. Hereditary factors in tooth dimensions: A study of the anterior teeth of twins. *Angle Orthodontist* 28:87–93.

Hours, F. 1975. The Lower Palaeolithic of Lebanon and Syria. In *Problems of prehistory: North Africa and the Levant*, ed. by F. Wendorf and A.E. Marks, pp. 249–72. Dallas: Southern Methodist University Press.

———. 1981. Le Paléolithique inférieure de la Syrie et du Liban. Le point de la question en 1980. In *Préhistoire du Levant*, ed. by J. Cauvin and P. Sanlaville, pp. 165–84. Paris: C.N.R.S.

Hovers, E. 1986. The application of geographical models in prehistoric research: A case study from Biqat Quneitra. *Mitequfat Haeven* 19:30–42.

Howell, F.C. 1951. The place of Neanderthal man in human evolution. *American Journal of Physical Anthropology* 9:379–416.

———. 1952. Pleistocene glacial ecology and the evolution of "classic Neandertal" man. *Southwest Journal of Anthropology* 8:377–410.

———. 1957. The evolutionary significance of variation and varieties of "Neanderthal" man. *The Quarterly Review of Biology* 32:330–47.

———. 1958. Upper Pleistocene men of the southwest Asian Mousterian. In *Hundert Jahre Neanderthaler*, ed. by G.H.R. von Koenigswald, pp. 185–98. Utrecht: Kemink en zoon.

———. 1965. *Early man*. New York: Time-Life Books.

———. 1984. Introduction. In *The origins of modern humans: A world survey of the fossil evidence*, ed. by F.H. Smith and F. Spencer, pp. xiii-xxii. New York: Alan R. Liss.

Howell, N. 1982. Village composition implied by a paleodemographic life table: The Libben site. *American Journal of Physical Anthropology* 59:263–9.

Howells, W.W. 1973. Cranial variation in man. A study by multivariate analysis of patterns of difference among recent human populations. *Papers of the Peabody Museum of Archaeology and Ethnology* 67:1–259.

———. 1975. Neanderthal man: Facts and figures. In *Paleoanthropology, morphology and paleoecology*, ed. by R. Tuttle, pp. 389–407. Mouton: The Hague.

———. 1976. Explaining modern man: Evolutionists versus migrationists. *Journal of Human Evolution* 5:477–95.

References

1983. Origins of the Chinese people: Interpretations of the recent
evidence. In *The origins of Chinese civilization*, ed. by D.N.
Keightley, pp. 297–319. Berkeley: University of California Press.
Hrdlička, A. 1911. Human dentition from the evolutionary standpoint.
Dominion Dental Journal 23:403–22.
1914. The most ancient skeletal remains of man. *Annual Report of the
Smithsonian Institution* 1913:491–552.
1929. The Neanderthal phase of man. *Annual Report of the
Smithsonian Institution* 1928:593–623.
1930. The skeletal remains of early man. *Smithsonian Miscellaneous
Collections* 83.
Hublin, J.J. 1978. Le torus occipital transverse et les structures associées:
Evolution dans le genre *Homo*. Thèse de Troisième Cycle. Université
de Paris VI.
1982. Les Anténéandertaliens: Présapiens ou Prénéandertaliens. *Geobios
Mémoire Special* 6:345–57.
1983. Les origines de l'homme de type moderne en Europe. *Pour la
Science* 64:62–71.
Hublin, J.J., and A.M. Tillier 1981. The Mousterian juvenile mandible
from Irhoud (Morocco): A phylogenetic interpretation. In *Aspects of
human evolution*, ed. by C.B. Stringer, pp. 167–85. London: Taylor
and Francis.
Hublin, J.J., A.M. Tillier, and J. Tixier 1987. L'humérus d'enfant
moustérien (Homo 4) du Djebel Irhoud (Maroc) dans son contexte
archéologique. *Bulletin et Mémoires de la Société d'Anthropologie de
Paris Série XIV* 14:115–41.
Huntingford, W. 1955. The economic life of the Dorobo. *Anthropos*
50:602–31.
Hutterer, K.L. 1977a. Reinterpreting the southeast Asian Paleolithic. In
Cultural–ecological perspectives on Southeast Asia, ed. by W. Wood,
pp. 9–28. Athens, Ohio: Ohio University Center for International
Studies.
1977b. Reinterpreting the Southeast Asian Palaeolithic. In *Sundra and
Sahul: Prehistoric studies in Southeast Asia, Melanesia and Australia*,
ed. by J. Allen, J. Golson, and R. Jones, pp. 31–71. New York:
Academic Press.
Huxtable, J., and M.J. Aitken 1987. Datation par la thermoluminescence
de la grotte Vaufrey. In *La grotte Vaufrey à Cenac-et-Saint-Julien
(Dordogne): Paléoenvironnements, chronologie, et activités humaines*,
ed. by J.P. Rigaud. Mémoire de la Société Préhistorique Française 19.
Hylander, W.L. 1977. The adaptive significance of Eskimo craniofacial
morphology. In *Orofacial growth and development*, ed. by A.A.
Dahlberg and T.M. Graber, pp. 129–69. Moulton: The Hague.
Iampietro, P.F., R.F. Goldman, E.R. Buskirk, and D.E. Bass 1959.
Response of negro and white males to cold. *Journal of Applied
Physiology* 14:798–800.

Inskeep, R.R. 1978. *The peopling of southern Africa*. London: David Philip.

Isaac, G.L. 1971. The diet of early man: Aspects of archaeological evidence from Lower and Middle Pleistocene sites in Africa. *World Archaeology* 2:278–98.

1972. Chronology and tempo of cultural change during the Pleistocene. In *Calibration of hominid evolution*, ed. by W.W. Bishop and J.A. Miller, pp. 381–430. Edinburgh: Scottish Academic Press.

1977. *Olorgesailie: Archaeological studies of a Middle Pleistocene lake basin in Kenya*. Chicago: University of Chicago Press.

1981a. Archaeological tests of alternative models of early hominid behavior: Excavation and experiments. *Philosophical Transactions of the Royal Society of London* 292B:177–88.

1981b. Stone Age visiting cards: Approaches to the study of early land use patterns. In *Pattern of the past: Studies in honor of David Clarke*, ed. by I. Hodder, G.L. Isaac, and N. Hammond. pp. 131–55. Cambridge: Cambridge University Press.

1983. Aspects of the evolution of human behavior: An archaeological perspective. *Canadian Journal of Anthropology* 3:233–43.

Issar, A., and H. Bruins 1983. Special climatological conditions in the deserts of Sinai and the Negev during the latest Pleistocene. *Palaeogeography, Palaeoclimatology, Palaeoecology* 43:63–72.

Ivanhoe, F. 1970. Was Virchow right about Neandertal? *Nature* 227:577–9.

1985. On the Neandertal pubis and acromegaly. *Current Anthropology* 26(4):526–7.

Jacob-Friesen, K.H. 1956. Eiszeitliche Elefantenjäger in der Luneburger Heide. *Jahrbuch des Romisch-Germanischen Zentralmuseums Mainz* 3:1–22.

Jakobson, R., and V. Lind 1973. Variation in root length of the permanent maxillary central incisor. *Scandinavian Journal of Dental Research* 81:335–8.

Jelinek, A.J. 1977. A preliminary study of the flakes from Tabun Cave, Mount Carmel. *Eretz Israel* 13:87–96.

1981. The Middle Palaeolithic in the southern Levant from the perspective of the Tabun Cave. In *Préhistoire du Levant* ed. by J.Cauvin and P. Sanlaville, pp. 265–80. Paris: C.N.R.S.

1982a. The Tabun Cave and the Paleolithic man in the Levant *Science* 216:1369–75.

1982b. The Middle Palaeolithic in the Southern Levant, with comments on the appearance of modern *Homo sapiens*. In *The transition from the Lower to Middle Palaeolithic and the origin of modern man*, ed. by A. Ronen, pp. 57–104. Oxford: British Archaeological Reports S151.

Jelínek, J. 1959. Der fossile Mensch Brno II. *Anthropos* 9:17–22.

1967. Der Fund eines neandertales Kiefers (Kulna I) aus der Kulna-Höhle in Mähren. *Anthropologie* (Brno) 5:3–19.

References

1969. Neanderthal man and *Homo sapiens* in central and eastern Europe. *Current Anthropology* 10:475–503.

1976. The *Homo sapiens neanderthalensis* and *Homo sapiens sapiens* relationship in central Europe. *Anthropologie* (Brno) 14:79–81.

1978. Comparison of mid-Pleistocene evolutionary process in Europe and in South-East Asia. Prague: *Proceedings of the Symposium on Natural Selection, Liblice 1978*, pp. 251–67.

1980. Variability and geography. Contribution to our knowledge of European and north African Middle Pleistocene hominids. *Anthropologie* (Brno) 18:109–14.

1982. The east and southeast Asian way of regional evolution. *Anthropologie* (Brno) 21:195–212.

1983. The Mladeč finds and their evolutionary importance. *Anthropologie* (Brno) 22:57–64.

1985. The European, Near East, and North African finds after *Australopithecus* and the principal consequences for the picture of human evolution. In *Hominid evolution: Past, present, and future. Proceedings of the Taung Diamond Jubilee International Symposium*, ed. by P.V. Tobias, pp. 341–54. New York: Alan R. Liss.

Jia L.P., Gai P., and You W. 1972. Excavation report of the Paleolithic site of Shiyu, Shanxi (in Chinese). *Kaogu Xuebao* 1:39–58.

Johnson, M.J., D.C. Wallace, S.D. Ferris, M.C. Rattazzi, and L.L. Cavalli-Sforza 1983. Radiation of human mitochondria DNA types analyzed by restriction endonuclease cleavage patterns. *Journal of Molecular Evolution* 19:255–71.

Jones, J.S. 1981. How different are human races? *Nature* 293:188–90.

1986. The origin of *Homo sapiens*: The genetic evidence. In *Major topics in primate and human evolution*, ed. by B. Wood, L. Martin, and P. Andrews, p. 317–30. London: Cambridge University Press.

Jones, J.S., and S. Rouhani 1986a. How small was the bottleneck? *Nature* 319:449–50.

1986b. Mankind's genetic bottleneck. *Nature* 322:599–600.

Jorde, L.B. 1985. Human genetic distance studies: Present status and prospects. *Annual Review of Anthropology* 14:343–73.

Karlin, S., and J. McGregor 1972. Polymorphisms for genetic and ecological systems with weak coupling. *Journal of Theoretical Population Biology* 3:210–38.

Kelly, R.L. 1983. Hunter-gatherer mobility strategies. *Journal of Anthropological Research* 39:277–306.

Kennedy, G.A. 1984a. Are the Kow Swamp hominids "archaic"? *American Journal of Physical Anthropology* 65:163–8.

1984b. The emergence of *Homo sapiens*: The postcranial evidence. *Man* 19:94–110.

Kent, S., and H. Vierich in press. The myth of ethnic and economic determinism – anticipated mobility and site organization of space. In *Farmers as hunters – the implications of sedentism* ed. by S. Kent. Cambridge: Cambridge University Press.

Kim, W.Y., and Chung, Y.W. 1978. A preliminary report of Chon-Gok-Ni Acheulean biface culture (in Korean). *Jindan Kakbo* 46–7: whole nos.

King, M.C., and A.C. Wilson 1975. Evolution at two levels in humans and chimpanzees. *Science* 188:107–16.

Kirkbride, D., S. de Saint Mathurin, and L. Copeland 1983. Results, tentative interpretation and suggested chronology. In *Adlun in the Stone Age*, ed. by D. Roe, pp. 415–32. Oxford: British Archaeological Reports S159.

Klein, R.G. 1969. *Man and culture in the late Pleistocene*. Chicago: Chandler Pub.

    1973. *Ice-age hunters of the Ukraine*. Chicago: University of Chicago Press.

    1976. The mammalian fauna of the Klasies River Mouth sites, Southern Cape Province, South Africa. *South African Archaeological Bulletin* 31:75–98

    1978. Stone age predation on large African bovids. *Journal of Archaeological Science* 5:195–217.

    1983a. What do we know about Neanderthals and Cro-Magnon man? *American Scholar* 52:386–92.

    1983b. The stone age prehistory of southern Africa. *Annual Review of Anthropology* 12:25–48.

    1984. The large mammals of southern Africa: Late Pliocene to recent. In *Southern African prehistory and paleoenvironments*, ed. by R.G. Klein, pp. 107–46. Rotterdam: Balkema.

    1985. Breaking away. *Natural History* 94(1):4–7.

    1986. Review of L.R. Binford: *Faunal remains from Klasies River Mouth*. *American Anthropologist* 88:494–5.

    1987. Reconstructing how early people exploited animals: Problems and prospects. In *The evolution of human hunting*, ed. by M.H. Nitecki and D.V. Nitecki, pp. 11–45. New York: Plenum Press.

Klíma, B. 1963. Dolní Věstonice. *Monumenta Archaeologica* (Prague) 11:1–427.

    1976. Le Pavlovien. In *Périgordien et Gravettien en Europe*, ed. by B. Klíma, pp. 128–41. Nice: IXe Congrès de l'UISPP.

Kovacs, I. 1967. Contribution to the ontogenetic morphology of roots of human teeth. *Journal of Dental Research* 46:865–74.

    1971. A systematic description of dental roots. In *Dental morphology and evolution*, ed. by A.A. Dahlberg, pp. 211–56. Chicago: University of Chicago Press.

Kozłowski, J.K., ed. 1982. *Excavation in the Bacho Kiro Cave (Bulgaria): Final report*. Warsaw: Państwowe Wydawnictwo Naukowe.

Krantz, G.S. 1982. The fossil record of sex. In *Sexual dimorphism in Homo sapiens: A question of size*, ed. by R.L. Hall, pp. 85–106. New York: Praeger.

Kraus, B.S., R.E. Jordan, and L. Abrams 1969. *Dental anatomy and occlusion*. Baltimore: Williams and Wilkins.

References

Kroeber, A.L. 1923. *Anthropology.* London: George G. Harrap.
   1939. *Cultural and natural areas of native North America.* Berkeley: University of California Press.
Kuhn, S. 1984. Changing lower limb morphology and land use across the Middle to Upper Paleolithic transition. Unpublished manuscript, University of New Mexico.
Kukla, G., and M. Briskin 1983. The age of the 4/5 isotope state boundary on land and in the oceans. *Palaeogeography, Palaeoclimatology, Palaeoecology* 42:35–45.
Laitman, J.T. 1984. The anatomy of human speech. *Natural History* 93(8):20–7.
Laming-Emperaire, A. 1962. *La signification de l'art rupestre paléolithique.* Paris:
Lande, R. 1980. Genetic variation and phenotypic evolution during allopatric speciation. *American Naturalist* 116:463–79.
   1982. Rapid origin of sexual isolation and character divergence in a cline. *Evolution* 36:213–33.
Laplace, G. 1957. Typologie analytique: Application d'une nouvelle methode d'étude des formes et des structures aux industries à lames et lamelles. *Quaternaria* 4:1–32.
Larick, R.R. 1983. The circulation of Solutrean foliate point cherts: Residential mobility in the Périgord. Ph. D. Thesis, State University of New York, Binghamton.
Lartet, E., and H. Christy 1875. *Reliquiae aquitanicae.* London: Rupert Jones.
Latorre, A., A. Moya, and F.J. Ayala 1986. Evolution of mitochondrial DNA in *Drosophila subobscura. Proceedings of the National Academy of Sciences USA* 83:8649–53.
Lavelle, C.L.B., R.P. Shellis, and D.F.G. Poole 1977. *Evolutionary changes to the primate skull and dentition.* Springfield, Illinois: C.C. Thomas.
Laville, H., J.P. Rigaud, and J. Sackett 1980. *Rock shelters of the Périgord: Geological stratigraphy and archaeological succession.* New York: Academic Press.
Leakey, R.E.F., K.W. Butzer, and M.H. Day 1969. Early *Homo sapiens* remains from the Omo River region of south-west Ethiopia. *Nature* 222:1132–8.
Leakey, R.E.F., and A. Walker 1985. Further hominids from the Plio-Pleistocene of Koobi Fora, Kenya. *American Journal of Physcial Anthropology* 67:135–63.
Lee, R.B. 1979. *The !Kung San.* Cambridge: Cambridge University Press.
Leigh, S.R. 1985a. Ontogenetic and static allometry of the Neandertal and modern hominid palate (abstract). *American Journal of Physical Anthropology* 66:195.
   1985b. The allometry of the palate of archaic *Homo sapiens* and modern *Homo sapiens.* M.A. Thesis, University of Tennessee, Knoxville.

255

Leroi-Gourhan, André 1958. Etude des restes humains fossiles provenant des Grottes d'Arcy-sur-Cure. *Annales de Paléontologie* 44:87–148.

1961. Les fouilles d'Arcy-sur-Cure (Yonne). *Gallia Préhistoire* 4:3–16.

1965. *La préhistoire de l'art occidental*. Paris: Mazenod.

Leroi-Gourhan, A., and M. Brézillon 1972. Fouilles de Pincevent. Supplement à *Gallia Préhistoire* 7:1–327.

Leroi-Gourhan, Arlette 1980. Les analyses polliniques au Moyen Orient. *Paléorient* 6:79–92.

1984. La place du Néandertalien de St-Césaire dans la chronologie würmienne. *Bulletin de la Société Préhistorique Française* 81:196–8.

Leroy-Prost, C. 1974. Les pointes en matière osseuse de l'Aurignacien. *Bulletin de la Société Préhistorique Française* 71:449–58.

Leroyer, C., and A. Leroi-Gourhan 1983. Problèmes et chronologie: le castelperronien et l'aurignacien. *Bulletin de la Société Préhistorique Française* 80:41–4.

Lévêque, F., and J.C. Miskovsky 1983. Le Castelperronien dans son environment géologique. *L'Anthropologie* 87:369–91.

Lévêque, F., and B. Vandermeersch 1980. Les découvertes de restes humains dans un horizon castelperronien de Saint-Césaire (Charente-Maritime). *Bulletin de la Société Préhistorique Française* 77:35.

1981. Le néandertalien de Saint-Césaire. *Recherche* 12:242–4.

Lewin, R. 1987. Africa: Cradle of modern humans. *Science* 237:1292–5.

Lewis, D.W., and R.M. Grainger 1967. Sex-linked inheritance of tooth size, a family study. *Archives Oral Biology* 12:539–44.

Lewontin, R.C. 1974. *The genetic basis of evolutionary change*. New York: Columbia University Press.

1984. *Human diversity*. San Francisco: Freeman.

Lieberman, P. 1984. *The biology and evolution of language*. Cambridge, Mass.: Harvard University Press.

Lind, V. 1972. Short root anomaly. *Scandinavian Journal of Dental Research* 80:85–93.

Livingstone, F.B. 1962. On the non-existence of human races. *Current Anthropology* 3:279–81.

1964. On the non-existence of human races. In *The concept of race*, ed. by M.F.A. Montagu, pp. 46–60. New York: Free Press.

1973. Gene frequency differences in human populations: Some problems of analysis and interpretation. In *Methods and theories of anthropological genetics*, ed. by M.H. Crawford and P.L. Workman, pp. 39–67. Albuquerque: University of New Mexico Press.

1980. Natural selection and random variation in human evolution. In *Current developments in anthropological genetics* 1: *Theory and methods*, ed. by J.H. Mielke and M.H. Crawford, pp. 87–110. New York: Plenum.

Lovejoy, C.O. 1982. Diaphyseal biomechanics of the locomotor skeleton of Tautavel man with comments on the evolution of skeletal changes in late Pleistocene man. *In L'*Homo erectus *et la Place de l'homme de

References

Tautavel parmi les hominidés fossiles (prétirage), ed. by H. de Lumley, pp. 447–70. Paris: C.N.R.S.

Lovejoy, C.O., and E. Trinkaus 1980. Strength and robusticity of the Neandertal tibia. *American Journal of Physical Anthropology* 53:465–70.

Lundstrom, A. 1948. *Tooth size and occlusion in twins.* New York: Karger.

Lyubin, V.P. 1977. *Must'erski kultury kavkaza.* Leningrad: Academy of Sciences.

Macintosh, N.W.G., and S.L. Larnach 1976. Aboriginal affinities looked at in world context. In. *The origin of the Australians,* ed. by R.L. Kirk and A.G. Thorne, pp. 113–26. Canberra: Australian Institute of Aboriginal Studies.

Magori, C.C., and M.H. Day 1983. Laetoli hominid 18: An early *Homo sapiens* skull. *Journal of Human Evolution* 12:747–53.

Marks, A.E. 1981. The Middle Paleolithic of the Negev, Israel. In *Préhistoire du Levant,* ed. by J. Cauvin and P. Sanlaville, pp. 287–98. Paris: C.N.R.S.

  1983a(ed.). *Prehistory and paleoenvironments in the Central Negev, Israel III: The Avdat/Aqev area.* Dallas: Southern Methodist University Press.

  1983b. The Middle to Upper Paleolithic transition in the Levant. In *Advances in world archaeology,* vol. 2, ed. by F. Wendorf and A.E. Close, pp. 51–98. New York: Academic Press.

Marks, A.E., and D.A. Friedel 1977. Prehistoric settlement patterns in the Avdat/Aqev area. In *Prehistory and paleoenvironments in the Central Negev, Israel II,* ed. by A.E. Marks, pp. 131–58. Dallas: Southern Methodist University Press.

Marks, A.E., and D. Kaufman 1983. Boker Tachtit: The artifacts. In *Prehistory and paleoenvironments in the Central Negev, Israel III,* ed. by A.E. Marks, pp. 69–125. Dallas: Southern Methodist University Press.

Marks, A.E., and P. Volkman 1987. The Mousterian of Ksar Akil: Levels XXVIA through XXVIIIB. *Paléorient* 12:5–20.

Marshack, A. 1964. Lunar notation on Upper Paleolithic remains. *Science* 146:743–5.

  1972a. *The roots of civilization.* London: Weidenfeld and Nicolson.

  1972b. Cognitive aspects of Upper Paleolithic engraving. *Current Anthropology* 13:445–77.

  1976. Some implications of the Paleolithic symbolic evidence for the origin of language. *Current Anthropology* 17:274–82.

  1982. Non-utilitarian fragment of bone from the Middle Paleolithic layer. In *Excavation in the Bacho Kiro Cave (Bulgaria),* ed. by J.K. Kozłowski, p. 117. Warsaw: Państwowe Wydawnictwo Naukowe.

Martin, H. 1907–10. *Recherches sur l'évolution du Moustérien dans le gisement de La Quina I.* Paris: Librairie C. Reinwald.

257

Marzke, M.W., and M.S. Shackley 1986. Hominid hand use in the Pliocene and Pleistocene: Evidence from experimental archaeology and comparative morphology. *Journal of Human Evolution* 15:439–60.

Matiegka, J. 1924. Crâne de Podbaba (Böhmen). *Anthropologie* (Prague) 2:1–14.

1934. *Homo předmostensis: Fosilní Člověk z Předmostí na Moravě* I. Prague: Nákladem Českě Akademie Věd a Umění.

1938. *Homo předmostensis: Fosilní Člověk z Předmostí na Moravě* II. Prague: Nákladem Českě Akademie Věd a Umění.

Mayr, E. 1954. Changes of genetic environment and evolution. In *Evolution as a process*, ed. by J.S. Huxley, A.C. Hardy, and E.B. Ford, pp. 188–213. London: Unwin.

1963. *Animal species and evolution.* Cambridge: Belknap.

1969. *Principles of systemic zoology.* New York: McGraw-Hill.

McBurney, C.B.M. 1967. *The Haua Fteah (Cyrenaica) and the Stone Age of the south-east Mediterranean.* Cambridge: Cambridge University Press.

McCown, T.D., and A. Keith 1939. *The Stone Age of Mount Carmel* II: *The fossil human remains from the Levalloiso-Mousterian.* Oxford: Clarendon Press.

McNamara, J.A., ed. 1976. *Factors affecting the growth of the midface.* Center for Human Growth and Development. Craniofacial Growth Series 6.

Meehan, J.P. 1955. Individual and racial variations in a vascular response to a cold stimulus. *Military Medicine* 116:330–4.

Meggitt, M. 1962. *Desert people.* Sydney, Australia: Angus and Robertson.

Mellars, P. 1973. The character of the Middle–Upper Paleolithic transition in southwest France. In *The explanation of culture change: Models in prehistory*, ed. by C. Renfrew, pp. 255–76. London: Duckworth.

1986a. A new chronology for the French Mousterian period. *Nature* 322:410–11.

1986b. Dating and correlating the French Mousterian. *Nature* 324:113–14.

Merbs, C.F. 1968. Anterior tooth loss in Arctic populations. *Southwestern Journal of Anthropology* 24:20–32.

Misra, V.N., and P. Bellwood, eds. 1985. *Recent advances in Indo-Pacific prehistory.* Oxford IBH, New Delhi.

Morant, G.M. 1928. Studies of Palaeolithic man III: The Rhodesian skull and its relationships to Neanderthaloid and modern types. *Annals of Eugenics* 3:337–60.

Morris, L.N., and P.E. Nute 1978. Effects of isolation on genetic variability: Macaque populations as model systems. In *Evolutionary models and studies in human diversity*, ed. by R.J. Meier, C.M. Otten, and F. Abdel-Hameed, pp. 105–25. The Hague: Mouton.

References

Morton, N.E., and J. Lalouel 1973. Topology of kinship in Micronesia. *American Journal of Human Genetics* 25:422–32.

Mount, L.E. 1979. *Adaptation to thermal environment*. London: Arnold.

Movius, H.L., Jr. 1944. Early man and Pleistocene stratigraphy in southern and eastern Asia. *Papers of the Peabody Museum of American Archaeology and Ethnology* XIX(3).

1966. The hearths of the Upper Perigordian and Aurignacian horizons at the Abri Pataud, Les Eyzies (Dordogne), and their possible significance. *American Anthropologist* 68:296–325.

1969. The Châtelperronian in French archaeology: The evidence of Arcy-sur-Cure. *Antiquity* 43:111–23.

Munday, F.C. 1976. Intersite variability in the Mousterian occupation of the Avdat-Aqev Area. In *Prehistory and paleoenvironments in the Central Negev, Israel* I, ed. by A.E. Marks, pp. 113–40. Dallas: Southern Methodist University Press.

1977a. Nahal Aqev (D 35): A stratified, open-air Mousterian occupation in the Avdat-Aqev area. In *Prehistory and paleoenvironments in the Central Negev* II, ed. by A.E. Marks, pp. 35–60. Dallas: Southern Methodist University Press.

1977b. The Mousterian in the Negev: A description and explication of intersite variability. Ph.D. Dissertation, Southern Methodist University.

1979. Levantine Mousterian technological variability: A perspective from the Negev. *Paléorient* 5:87–104.

1984. Middle Paleolithic intrasite variability and its relationship to regional patterning. In *Intrasite spatial analysis in archaeology*, ed. by H. Hietala, pp. 32–43. Cambridge: Cambridge University Press.

Murdock, G.P. 1934. *Our primitive contemporaries*. New York: MacMillan.

Murdock, G.P., and D.O. Morrow 1970. Subsistence economy and supportive practices: Cross-cultural codes 1. *Ethnology* 9:302–30.

Musgrave, J.H. 1971. How dextrous was Neanderthal man? *Nature* 233:538–41.

Mussi, M. 1986. On the chronology of the burials found in the Grimaldi Caves. *Antropologia Contemporanea* 9:95–104.

Myers, F. 1986. *Pintupi country, Pintupi self: Sentiment, place and politics among Western Desert aborigines*. Washington: Smithsonian Institution Press.

Nakata, M., R. Yu, B. Davis, and W.E. Nance 1974. Genetic determinants of craniofacial morphology: A twin study. *Annals of Human Genetics* (London) 37:431–43.

Nei, M. 1982. Evolution of human races at the gene level. In *Human genetics, part A: The unfolding genome*, ed. by B. Bonne-Tamir, T. Cohen, R.M. Goodman, pp. 167–81. New York: Alan R. Liss.

1985. Human evolution at the molecular level. In *Population genetics and molecular evolution*, ed. by T. Ohta and K. Aoki, pp. 41–64. Tokyo: Japan Scientific Series Press.

Nei, M., and A.K. Roychoudhury 1982. Genetic relationship and evolution of human races. In *Evolutionary biology* 14, ed. by M.K. Hecht, B. Wallace, and G.T. Prace, pp. 1–59. New York: Plenum Press.

Nesbitt, P. 1928. Le Ruth, an Upper Paleolithic site in the Dordogne Valley. Masters thesis, University of Chicago.

Oakley, K.P., P. Andrews, L.H. Kelley, and J.D. CLark 1977. A reappraisal of the Clacton spearpoint. *Proceedings of the Prehistoric Society* 43:13–30.

Ohel, M.Y. 1979. The Clactonian: An independent complex or an integral part of the Acheulian? *Current Anthropology* 20:685–726.

O'Leary, B. 1985. Salmon and storage: Southern Tutchone use of an "abundant" resource. Ph.D. Dissertation, University of New Mexico.

Oleksiak, D.A. 1987. Body size and dental scaling of Upper Pleistocene human populations: A test of the Paramasticatory Hypothesis. Ph.D. Thesis, State University of New York, Binghamton.

1988. Dental scaling in Neandertals (abstract). *American Journal of Physical Anthropology* 75:255.

Onoratini, G. 1982. Préhistorie, sédiments, climats du Würm III à l'Holocène dans le Sud-est de la France. Thèse, Université d'Aix-Marseille III.

Orquera, L. 1984. Specialization and the Middle/Upper Paleolithic transition. *Current Anthropology* 25:73–98.

Osborne, R.H., S.L. Horowitz, and F.V. De George 1958. Genetic variation in tooth dimensions: A twin study of the permanent anterior teeth. *American Journal of Human Genetics* 10:35–56.

O'Shea, J. 1984. *Mortuary variability: An archaeological investigation.* New York: Academic Press.

Otte, M. 1979. Le Paléolithique supérieur ancien en Belgique. *Monographies d'Archéologie Nationale* 5:1–684.

1981. *Le Gravettien en Europe centrale.* Brugge: Dissertationes Archaeologicae Gandenses.

Paddayya, K. 1982. The Lower/Middle Palaeolithic transition in the Hunsgi Valley, peninsular India. In *The transition from Lower to Middle Palaeolithic and the origin of modern man*, ed. by A. Ronen, pp. 257–64. Oxford: British Archaeological Reports S151.

Paquette, S.P. 1985. Patterns of variation in the permanent maxillary anterior tooth roots: A different approach to the problem of anterior dental reduction during the transition from Archaic to Modern *Homo sapiens*. M.A. Thesis, University of Tennessee, Knoxville.

Payne, S. 1983. The animal bones from the 1974 excavations at Douara Cave. In *Palaeolithic sites of Douara Cave and palaeogeography of the Palmyra Basin in Syria*, ed. by K. Hanihara and T. Akazawa, pp. 1–108. University Museum, University of Tokyo Bulletin 21.

Pei Wen Chung, and Senshui Chang 1985. A study on the lithic artifacts of *Sinanthropus*. *Palaeontologia Sinica* 168 n.s. D(12).

Perlès, C. 1976. Le Feu. In *La Préhistoire Française*, vol. 1(1), ed. by H. de Lumley, pp. 679–83. Paris: C.N.R.S.

1977. *Préhistoire du Feu*. Paris: Masson.

Peyrony, D. 1933. Les industries "aurignaciennes" dans le bassin de la Vézère. *Bulletin de la Société Préhistorique Française* 30:543–59.

1935. Le gisement Castanet, Vallon de Castelmerle, commune de Sergeac (Dordogne). Aurignacien I et II. *Bulletin de la Société Préhistorique Française* 32:418–43.

Pfeiffer, J.E. 1982. *The creative explosion*. New York: Harper and Row.

Pilbeam, D. 1986. The origin of *Homo sapiens*: The fossil evidence. In *Major topics in primate and human evolution*, ed. by B. Wood, L. Martin, and P. Andrews, pp. 331–8, Cambridge: Cambridge University Press.

Pond, A. 1924. Letter from Alonzo Pond to Frank Logan dated August 12, 1924.

Potter, R.H., W.E. Nance, P. Yu, and W.B. Davis 1976. A twin study of dental dimensions II. Independent genetic determinants. *American Journal of Physical Anthropology* 44:397–412.

Potts, R., and P. Shipman 1981. Cutmarks made by stone tools on bones from Olduvai Gorge, Tanzania. *Nature* 291(5816):577–80.

Price, T., and J.A. Brown, eds. 1985. *Prehistoric hunter-gatherers: The emergence of cultural complexity*. New York: Academic Press.

Protsch, R. 1975. The absolute dating of Upper Pleistocene sub-Saharan fossil hominids and their place in human evolution. *Journal of Human Evolution* 4:297–322.

1978. *Catalogue of fossil hominids of North America*. New York: Fischer.

Putnam, P. 1963. The Pygmies of the Ituri Forest. In *A reader in general anthropology*, ed. by C.S. Coon, pp. 322–42. New York: Holt, Rinehart and Winston.

Pycraft, W.P. 1928. *Rhodesian Man and associated remains*. London: British Museum (Natural History).

Quechon, G. 1976. Les sépultures des hommes du Paléolithique supérieur. In *La Préhistoire Française*, vol. 1(1), ed. by H. de Lumley, pp. 728–33. Paris: C.N.R.S.

Qui, Z. 1985. The Middle Palaeolithic of China. In *Palaeoanthropology and Palaeolithic archaeology in the People's Republic of China*, ed. by Wu Rukang and J.W. Olsen, pp. 187–210. New York: Academic Press.

Radovčić, J. 1985. Neanderthals and their contemporaries. In *Ancestors: The hard evidence*, ed. by E. Delson, pp. 310–18. New York: Alan R. Liss.

Rak, Y. 1986. The Neanderthal: A new look at an old face. *Journal of Human Evolution* 15:151–64.

Rak, Y., and B. Arensburg 1987. Kebara 2 Neanderthal pelvis: First look at a complete inlet. *American Journal of Physical Anthropology* 73:227–31.

Reinach, S. 1903. L'Art et la magie. A propos des peintures et des gravures de l'âge du renne. *L'Anthropologie* 14:257–66.

Rensberger, B. 1980. The emergence of *Homo sapiens*. *Mosaic* 11(6):2–12.

Rice, P., and A. Paterson 1985. Cave art and bones: Exploring the interrelationships. *American Anthropologist* 87:94–100.

Riesenfeld, A. 1970a. The effect of environmental factors on tooth development: An experimental investigation. *Acta Anatomica* 77:188–215.

   1970b. On some "racial" features in rats, dogs, and men. *Homo* 21:163–75.

Riesenfeld, A., and M.I. Siegel 1970. The relationship between facial proportions and root length in the dentition of dogs. *American Journal of Anthropology* 33:429–32.

Rigaud, J.P. 1978. Contribution méthodologique à l'étude d'un sol d'occupation. In *Seminaire sur les structures d'habitat, Plan au sol, parois, couverture*, ed. by A. Leroi-Gourhan, pp. 39–46. Paris: Collège de France.

   1982. Le Paléolithique en Périgord: Les Données du Sud-Ouest Sarladais et leurs implications. Thèse de Doctorat d'Etat, Université de Bordeaux I.

   1987. Le peuplement gravettien du sud-ouest de la France: Problemes taxonomiques. In *Upper Pleistocene prehistory of Western Europe*, ed. by H. Dibble. Philadelphia: University Museum, University of Pennsylvania (in press).

Rigaud, J.P., and J.M. Geneste 1987. Utilisation de l'espace dans la grotte Vaufrey. In *La grotte Vaufrey à Cenac-et-Saint-Julien (Dordogne): Paléoenvironnements, chronologie et activités humaines*, ed. by J.P. Rigaud. Mémoire de la Société Préhistorique Française 19.

Rigaud, J.P., and J.P. Texier 1981. A propos des particularités technologiques et typologiques du gisement des Tares, commune de Sourzac (Dordogne). *Bulletin de la Société Préhistorique Française* 78:109–17.

Rightmire, G.P. 1979. Implications of the Border Cave skeletal remains for later Pleistocene human evolution. *Current Anthropology* 20:23–35.

   1984. *Homo sapiens* in sub-Saharan Africa. In *The origins of modern humans: A world survey of the fossil evidence*, ed. by F.H. Smith and F. Spencer, pp. 295–325. New York: Alan R. Liss.

   1989. Middle stone age humans from eastern and southern Africa. In *The origins and dispersal of modern humans: Behavioural and biological perspectives*, ed. by P. Mellars and C.B. Stringer (in press). Edinburgh: University of Edinburgh Press.

Roberts, N. 1982. Lake levels as an indicator of Near Eastern palaeoclimates: A preliminary appraisal. In *Palaeoclimates, palaeoenvironments and human communities in the Eastern Mediterranean region in later prehistory*, ed. by J.L. Bintliff and W. Van Zeist, pp. 235–67. Oxford: British Archaeological Reports S133.

Roe, D.A. 1982. The transition from Lower to Middle Palaeolithic, with particular reference to Britain. In *The transition from Lower to Middle Palaeolithic and the origin of modern man*, ed. by A. Ronen,pp. 177–91. Oxford: British Archaeological Reports S151.

Ronen, A., ed. 1982. *The transition from Lower to Middle Palaeolithic and the origin of modern man*. Oxford: British Archaeological Reports. S151.

Rosenberg, K.R. 1986. The functional significance of Neandertal pubic morphology. Ph.D. Thesis, University of Michigan.

Rosenzweig, M.L. 1974. *And replenish the earth: The evolution, consequences, and prevention of overpopulation*. Harper and Row: New York.

Ruff, C. 1987. Sexual dimorphism in human lower limb bone structure: Relationships to subsistence strategy and sexual division of labor. *Journal of Human Evolution* 16:391–416.

Russell, M.D. 1985. The supraorbital torus: "A most remarkable peculiarity." *Current Anthropology* 26:337–60.

Rust, A. 1950. *Die Höhlenfunde von Jabrud (Syrien)*. Neumunster: K. Wachholtz.

Ryan, A.S. 1980. Anterior dental microwear in hominid evolution: Comparisons with humans and nonhuman primates. Ph.D. Thesis, University of Michigan.

Sackett, J.R. 1982. Approaches to style in lithic archaeology. *Journal of Anthropological Archaeology* 1:59–112.

Saitta, D.J. 1983. The poverty of philosophy in archaeology. In *Archaeological hammers and theories*, ed. by J.A. Moore and A.S. Keene, pp. 299–304. New York: Academic Press.

Sampson, C.G. 1974. *The Stone Age archaeology of southern Africa*. New York: Academic Press.

Sankalia, H.D. 1974. *Prehistory and protohistory of India and Pakistan*. 2nd edn. Poona, India: Deccan College Press.

Sanlaville, P. 1981. Stratigraphie et chronologie du Quaternaire marin du Levant. In *Préhistoire du Levant*, ed. by J. Cauvin and P. Sanlaville, pp. 21–32. Paris: C.N.R.S.

Santa Luca, A.P. 1978. A re-examination of presumed Neandertal-like fossils. *Journal of Human Evolution* 7:619–36.

  1980. The Ngandong fossil hominids: A comparative study of a far eastern *Homo erectus* group. *Yale University Publications in Anthropology* 78:1–175.

Saxe, A.A. 1971. Social dimensions of mortuary practices in a Mesolithic population from Wadi Halfa, Sudan. In *Approaches to the social dimensions of mortuary practices*, ed. by J.A. Brown, pp. 39–57. Memoirs of the Society for American Archaeology 25.

Saxon, E.C. 1974. The mobile herding economy of Kebarah Cave, Mt. Carmel: An economic analysis of the faunal remains. *Journal of Archaeological Science* 1:27–45.

Schaefer, U. 1957. *Homo neanderthalensis* (King). 1. Das Skelet aus dem Neandertal. *Zeitschrift für Morphologie und Anthropologie* 48:268–97.

Schick, T., and M. Stekelis 1977. Mousterian assemblages in Kebara cave, Mount Carmel. *Eretz Israel* 13:97–149.

Schliz, R. 1909. Die vorgeschichtlichen Schädeltypen der deutschen Länder in ihrer Beziehung zu den einzelnen Kulturkreisen der Urgeschichte. *Archiv für Anthropologie* 7:247–55.

Schrire, C., ed. 1984. *Past and present in hunter-gatherer studies.* New York: Academic Press.

Schroeder, B. 1969. The lithic industries from Jerf Ajla and their bearing on the problem of a Middle to Upper Palaeolithic transition. Ph.D. Thesis, Columbia University.

Schwalbe, G. 1904. *Die Vorgeschichte des Menschen.* Braunschweig: Friedrich Viewug.

Schwarcz, H.P., P. Goldberg, and B. Blackwell 1980. Uranium series dating of archaeological sites in Israel. *Journal of Earth Sciences* 29:157–65.

Scott, K. 1986. Review of L.R. Binford: *Faunal remains from Klasies River Mouth. Journal of Archaeological Science* 13:89–91.

Selmer-Olsen, R. 1949a. An odontometrical study on the Norwegian Lapps. Skrifter utgitt av Det Norske Videnskaps-Akademie Oslo, I. Mat.-Nat-urw. Klasse, no. 3.

1949b. The fixation and stability of the teeth in the jaws with relation to their morphology. *The Dental Record* 69:322–34.

Shackley, M. 1980. *Neanderthal Man.* Hamden: Archon.

1983. *Wildmen: Yeti, Sasquatch and the Neanderthal enigma.* London: Thames and Hudson.

Sharp, L. 1952. Steel axes for stone age Australians. In *Human problems in technological change*, ed. by E. Spicer, pp. 69–90. New York: Wiley.

Shipman, P. 1983. Early hominid lifestyle: Hunting and gathering or foraging and scavenging? In *Animals and archaeology: Hunters and their prey*, ed. by J. Clutton-Brock and C. Grigson, pp. 31–49. Oxford: British Archaeological Reports S163.

1984a. Early hominid lifestyle: The scavenging hypothesis. *AnthroQuest* 28:9–10.

1984b. Ancestors: Scavenger hunt. *Natural History* 93:20–7.

Siegel, M.I. 1972. The relationship between facial protrusion and root length in the dentition of baboons. *Acta Anatomica* 83:17–29.

Silberbauer, G.B. 1972. The G/wi Bushmen. In *Hunters and gatherers today*, ed. by M.G. Bicchieri, pp. 271–326. New York: Holt, Rinehart and Winston.

References

Silva, A.C., C.M. Pimenta, F.S. Lemos, J. Zilhao, J. Mateus, L.
Raposo, and M.J. Coutinho 1983. A estação paleolítica de Vilas
Ruivas (Ródão) Campanha de 1979. *Arqueólogo Português* Série IV,
1:15–38.

Singer, R., and J. Wymer 1982. *The Middle Stone Age at Klasies River
Mouth in South Africa*. Chicago: University of Chicago Press.
1986. On Binford on Klasies River Mouth: Response of the excavators.
Current Anthropology 27:56–7.

Skinner, J.D., S. Davis, and G. Iliani 1980. Bone collecting by striped
hyaenas, *Hyaena hyaena*. *Paleontologica Africa* 23:99–104.

Skinner, J.H. 1965. The flake industries of South West Asia: A typological
study. Ph.D. Thesis, Columbia University.
1970. El Masloukh: A Yabroudian site in Lebanon. *Bulletin du Musée
de Beyrouth* 23:143–72.

Skinner, M. 1981. Dental attrition in immature hominids of the Late
Pleistocene: Implications for adult longevity (abstract). *American
Journal of Physical Anthropology* 54:278–9.

Smith, F.H. 1976. The Neandertal remains from Krapina: A descriptive
and comparative study. *Report of Investigations, Department of
Anthropology, University of Tennessee* 15.
1982. Upper Pleistocene hominid evolution in south-central Europe: A
review of the evidence and analysis of trends. *Current Anthropology*
23:667–703.
1983a. A behavioral interpretation of changes in craniofacial
morphology across the archaic/modern *Homo sapiens* transition. In
The Mousterian legacy, ed. by E. Trinkaus, pp, 141–63. Oxford:
British Archaeological Reports S164.
1983b. On hominid evolution in south-central Europe. *Current
Anthropology* 24:236–7.
1984. Fossil hominids from the Upper Pleistocene of central Europe
and the origins of modern Europeans. In *The origins of modern
humans: A world survey of the fossil evidence*, ed. by F.H. Smith and
F. Spencer, pp. 137–209. New York: Alan R. Liss.
1985. Continuity and change in the origin of modern *Homo sapiens*.
Zeitschrift für Morphologie und Anthropologie 75:197–222.

Smith, F.H., D.C. Boyd, and M. Malez 1985. Additional Upper
Pleistocene human remains from Vindija Cave, Croatia, Yugoslavia.
American Journal of Physical Anthropology 68:375–83.

Smith, F.H., and G.C. Ranyard 1980. Evolution of the supraorbital
region in Upper Pleistocene fossil hominids from south-central
Europe. *American Journal of Physical Anthropology* 53:589–609.

Smith, F.H., J. Simek, and M.S. Harrill 1989. Geographic variation in
supraorbital torus reduction during the European later Pleistocene. In
*The origin and dispersal of modern humans: Behavioural and
biological perspectives*, ed. by P. Mellars and C.B. Stringer,
Edinburgh: University of Edinburgh Press.

Smith, F.H., and F. Spencer, eds. 1984. *The origins of modern humans.* New York: Alan R. Liss.

Smith, P. 1977. Selective pressure and dental evolution in hominids. *American Journal of Physical Anthropology* 47:453–8.

Smith, P., R.A. Bloom, and J. Berkowitz 1983. Bone morphology and biomechanical efficiency in fossil hominids. *Current Anthropology* 24:662–3.

Smith, P.E.L. 1986. Palaeolithic Archaeology in Iran. *American Institute of Iranian Studies Monographs* 1:1–47.

Soffer. O. 1987. Upper Paleolithic Connubia and the archaeological record from eastern Europe. In *The Pleistocene Old World: Regional perspectives,* ed. by O. Soffer, pp. 333–48. New York: Plenum.

Solecki, R.S. 1971. *Shanidar – The first flower people.* New York: Knopf.

Sollas, W.J. 1911. *Ancient hunters and their modern representatives.* London: Macmillan.

Spencer, F., 1984. The Neandertals and their evolutionary significance: A brief historical survey. In *The origins of modern humans,* ed. by F.H. Smith and F. Spencer, pp. 1–49. New York: Alan R. Liss.

Spencer, F., and F.H. Smith 1981. The significance of Aleš Hrdlička's "Neanderthal phase of man": A historic and current assessment. *American Journal of Physical Anthropology* 56:435–59.

Spiess, A. 1979. *Reindeer and caribou hunters.* New York: Academic Press.

Stanley, S.M. 1979. *Macroevolution: Patterns and process.* San Francisco: Freeman.

Stewart, T.D. 1962. Neanderthal cervical vertebrae with special attention to the Shanidar Neanderthals from Iraq. *Biblioteca Primatologica* 1:130–54.

Stoneking, M., and R.L. Cann 1989. African origin of human mitochondrial DNA. In *The origins and dispersal of modern humans: Behavioural and biological perspectives,* ed. by P. Mellars and C.B. Stringer. Edinburgh: University of Edinburgh Press.

Strathern, A., and M. Strathern 1971. *Self-decoration in Mouth Hagen.* London: Duckworth.

Straus, L.G. 1977. Of deerslayers and mountain men: Paleolithic faunal exploitation in Cantabrian Spain. In *For theory building in archaeology: Essays on faunal remains, aquatic resources, and systemic modeling,* ed. by L.R. Binford, pp. 41–76. New York: Academic Press.

1982. Carnivores and cave sites in Cantabrian Spain. *Journal of Anthropological Research* 38:75–96.

1983. From Mousterian to Magdalenian: Cultural evolution viewed from Vasco-Cantabrian Spain and Pyrenean France. In *The Mousterian legacy,* ed. by E. Trinkaus, pp. 73–112. Oxford: British Archaeological Reports S164.

1987a. Hunting in late Upper Paleolithic western Europe. In *The evolution of human hunting*, ed. by M.H. Nitecki and D.V. Nitecki, pp. 147–76. New York: Plenum Press.

1987b. Upper Paleolithic ibex hunting in southwest Europe. *Journal of Archaeological Science* 14:163–78.

Stringer, C.B. 1978. Some problems in Middle and Upper Pleistocene hominid relationships. In *Recent advances in primatology*, vol. 3, ed. by D.J. Chivers and K.A. Joysey, pp. 395–418. London: Academic Press.

1982. Towards a solution to the Neanderthal problem. *Journal of Human Evolution* 11:431–8.

1983. Some further notes on the morphology and dating of the Petralona hominid. *Journal of Human Evolution* 12:731–42.

1984a. Human evolution and biological adaptation in the Pleistocene. In *Hominid evolution and community ecology*, ed. by R. Foley, pp. 55–83. New York: Academic Press.

1984b. The fate of the Neanderthal. *Natural History* 93(12):6–12.

1984c. The definition of *Homo erectus* and the existence of the species in Africa and Europe. *Courier Forschungsinstitut Senckenberg* 69:131–43.

1985. Middle Pleistocene hominid variability and the origin of Late Pleistocene humans. In *Ancestors: The hard evidence*, ed. by E. Delson, pp. 289–95. New York: Alan R. Liss.

1986a. An archaic character in the Broken Hill innominate E.719. *American Journal of Physical Anthropology* 71:115–20.

1986b. Direct dates for the fossil hominid record. In *Archaeological results from accelerator dating*, ed. by J.A.J. Gowlett and R.E.M. Hedges, pp. 45–50. Oxford Committee for Archaeology Monograph 11.

1987. Neandertals, their contemporaries, and modern human origins (abstract). 2nd International Congress of Human Paleontology (Turin). Résumés des Communications, pp. 187–8.

1988. The dates of Eden. *Nature* 331:565–6.

1989. The origins of early modern humans: A comparison of the European and non-European evidence. In *The origins and dispersal of modern humans: Behavioural and biological perspectives*, ed. by P. Mellars and C.B. Stringer (in press). Edinburgh: University of Edinburgh Press.

Stringer, C.B., and P. Andrews 1988. Genetic and fossil evidence for the origin of modern humans. *Science* 239:1263–8.

Stringer, C.B., M.C. Dean, and R.D. Martin in press. A comparative study of cranial and dental development in a recent British sample and Neanderthals. In *Primate life history and evolution*, ed. by C.J. DeRousseau. New York: Alan R. Liss.

Stringer, C.B., F.C. Howell, and J.K. Melentis 1979. The significance of the fossil hominid skull from Petralona, Greece. *Journal of Archaeological Science* 6:235–53.

Stringer, C.B., J.J. Hublin, and B. Vandermeersch 1984. The origin of anatomically modern humans in western Europe. In *The origins of modern humans*, ed. by F.H. Smith and F. Spencer, pp. 51–135. New York. Alan R. Liss.

Sullivan, P.G. 1978. Skull, jaw, and teeth growth patterns. In *Human growth II: Postnatal growth*, ed. by F. Faulkner and J.M. Tanner, pp. 381–412. London: Bailliere Tindall.

Suzuki, H., and F. Takai, eds. 1970. *The Amud Man and his cave site.* Tokyo: Academic Press.

Svoboda, J. 1984. Cadre chronologique et tendances évolutives du Paléolithique Tchécoslovaque. Essai de synthèse. *L'Anthropologie* 88:169–92.

Szombathy, J. 1925. Die diluvialen Menschenreste aus der Fürst-Johanns-Höhle bei Lautsch in Mähren. *Die Eiszeit* 2:1–34, 73–95.

Taborin, Y. 1983. La configuration des sols d'occupation à Etiolles. *Cahiers du Centre de Recherches Préhistoriques* 9:33–44.

1985. Les origines des coquillages paléolithiques en France. In *La signification culturelle des industries lithiques*, ed. by M. Otte, pp. 278–301. Oxford: British Archaeological Reports S239.

Tainter, J. 1978. Mortuary practices and the study of prehistoric social systems. In *Advances in archaeological method and theory*, vol. 3, ed. by M. Schiffer, pp. 105–41. New York: Academic Press.

Tattersall, I. 1986. Species recognition in human paleontology. *Journal of Human Evolution* 15:165–75.

Taylor, R.M.S. 1969. Variation in form of human teeth: II. An anthropologic and forensic study of maxillary canines. *Journal of Dental Research* 48:173–82.

Tchernov, E. 1968. *Succession of rodent faunas during the Upper Pleistocene of Israel.* Hamburg: Verlag Paul Parey.

1981. Biostratigraphy of the Middle East. In *Préhistoire du Levant*, ed. by J. Cauvin and P. Sanlaville, pp. 67–98. Paris: C.N.R.S.

1984a. Faunal turnover and extinction rate in the Levant. In *Quaternary extinctions*, ed. by P.S. Martin and R.G. Klein, pp. 528–52. Tucson: University of Arizona Press.

1984b. Commensal animals and human sedentism in the Middle East. In *Animals and archaeology*, ed. by J. Clutton-Brock and C. Grigson, pp. 91–116. Oxford: British Archaeological Reports S202(3).

in press. The succession of Mousterian faunas in the southern Levant. In *A Mousterian burial from Kebara Cave, Israel*, ed. by O. Bar-Yosef and B. Vandermeersch. Paris: C.N.R.S.

Templeton, A.R. 1983. Phylogenetic inference from restriction endonuclease cleavage site maps with particular reference to the evolution of humans and the apes. *Evolution* 37:221–44.

Thorne, A.G. 1981. The centre and the edge: The significance of Australian hominids to African paleoanthropology. In *Proceedings of the 8th Panafrican congress of prehistory and quaternary studies,*

References

Nairobi, ed. by R.E. Leakey and B.A. Ogot, pp. 180–1. Nairobi: TILLMIAP.

Thorne, A.G., and M.H. Wolpoff 1981. Regional continuity in Australasian Pleistocene hominid evolution. *American Journal of Physical Anthropology* 55:337–49.

Tillier, A.M. 1982. Les enfants néanderthaliens de Devil's Tower (Gibraltar). *Zeitschrift für Morphologie und Anthropologie* 73:125–48.

1984. L'enfant Homo II de Qafzeh (Israël) et son apport à la compréhension des modalités de la croissance des squelettes moustériens. *Paléorient* 10:7–48.

Tode, A. 1953. Die Untersuchung der paläolithischen Freilandstation von Salzgitter/Lebenstedt 8: Archäologische Erkenntnisse. *Eiszeitalter und Gegenwart* 3:192–215.

Tompkins, R.L., and E. Trinkaus 1987. La Ferrassie 6 and the development of Neandertal pubic morphology. *American Journal of Physical Anthropology* 73:233–40.

Torrence, R. 1983. Time budgeting and hunter-gatherer technology. In *Pleistocene hunters and gatherers in Europe*, ed. by G. Bailey, pp. 11–22. New York: Cambridge University Press.

Toth, N. 1985. The Oldowan reassessed: A close look at early stone artifacts. *Journal of Archaeological Science* 12:101–20.

Trinkaus, E. 1975. Squatting along the Neandertals: A problem in the behavioral interpretation of skeletal morphology. *Journal of Archaeological Science* 2:327–51.

1976a. The evolution of the hominid femoral diaphysis during the Upper Pleistocene in Europe and the Near East. *Zeitschrift für Morphologie und Anthropologie* 67:291–319.

1976b. The morphology of European and southwest Asian Neandertal pubic bones. *American Journal of Physical Anthropology* 44:95–104.

1977. A functional interpretation of the axillary border of the Neandertal scapula. *Journal of Human Evolution* 6:231–4.

1978a. Functional implications of the Krapina Neandertal lower limb remains. In *Krapinski Pračovjek i Evolucija Hominida*, ed. by M. Malez, pp. 155–92. Zagreb: Jugoslavenska Academija Znanosti i Umjetnosti.

1978b. Hard times among the Neanderthals. *Natural History* 87(1):58–63.

1980. Sexual differences in Neanderthal limb bones. *Journal of Human Evolution* 9:377–97.

1981. Neanderthal limb proportions and cold adaptation. In *Aspects of human evolution*, ed. by C.B. Stringer, pp. 187–224. London: Taylor and Francis.

1982a. Evolutionary continuity among archaic *Homo sapiens*. In *The transition from Lower to Middle Palaeolithic and the origin of modern man*, ed. by A. Ronen, pp. 301–14. Oxford: British Archaeological Reports S151.

269

1982b. Comment on F.H. Smith: Upper Pleistocene hominid evolution in south-central Europe. *Current Anthropology* 23:691–2.

1983a. *The Shanidar Neandertals.* New York: Academic Press.

1983b. Neandertal postcrania and the adaptive shift to modern humans. In *The Mousterian legacy,* ed. by E. Trinkaus, pp. 165–200. Oxford: British Archaeological Reports S164.

1983c. Review of M. Shackley: *Wildmen: Yeti, Sasquatch, and the Neanderthal enigma. Nature* 304:192–3.

1984a. Western Asia. In *The origins of modern humans,* ed. by F.H. Smith and F. Spencer, pp. 251–93. New York: Alan R. Liss.

1984b. Does KNM-ER 1481A establish *Homo erectus* at 2.0 myr BP? *American Journal of Physical Anthropology* 64:137–9.

1984c. Neandertal toes (abstract). *American Journal of Physical Anthropology* 63:229.

1984d. Neandertal pubic morphology and gestation length. *Current Anthropology* 25:509–14.

1985a. On the Neandertal pubis and acromegaly: Reply. *Current Anthropology* 26(4):527–9.

1985b. Pathology and the posture of the La Chapelle-aux-Saints Neandertal. *American Journal of Physical Anthropology* 67:19–41.

1986. The Neandertals and modern human origins. *Annual Review of Anthropology* 15:193–218.

1987a. The Neandertal face: Evolutionary and functional perspectives on a recent hominid face. *Journal of Human Evolution* 16:429–43.

1987b. Bodies, brawn, brains and noses: Human ancestors and human predation. In *The evolution of human hunting,* ed. by M.H. Nitecki and D.V. Nitecki, pp. 107–45. New York: Plenum Press.

1988. The evolutionary origins of the Neandertals or, Why were there Neandertals? In *L'Homme de Néandertal* 3: *L'Anatomie,* ed. by E. Trinkaus, pp. 11–29. Etudes et Recherches Archéologiques de l'Université de Liège 30.

Trinkaus, E., and S.E. Churchill 1988. Neandertal radial tuberosity orientation. *American Journal of Physical Anthropology* 75:15–21.

Trinkaus, E., and W.W. Howells 1979. The Neanderthals. *Scientific American* 241(6):118–33.

Trinkaus, E., and M. LeMay 1982. Occipital bunning among later Pleistocene hominids. *American Journal of Physical Anthropology* 57:27–35.

Trinkaus, E., and F.H. Smith 1985. The fate of the Neandertals. In *Ancestors: The hard evidence,* ed. by E. Delson, pp. 325–33. New York: Alan R. Liss.

Trinkaus, E., and D.D. Thompson 1987. Femoral diaphyseal histomorphometric age determinations for the Shanidar 3, 4, 5, and 6 Neandertals and Neandertal longevity. *American Journal of Physical Anthropology* 72:123–9.

References

Trinkaus, E., and R.L. Tompkins in press. The Neandertal life cycle: The possibility, probability and perceptibility of contrasts with recent humans. In *Primate life history and evolution*, ed. by C.J. DeRousseau. New York: Alan R. Liss.

Tuffreau, A. 1982. The transition Lower/Middle Palaeolithic in northern France. In *The transition from Lower to Middle Palaeolithic and the origin of modern man*, ed. by A. Ronen, pp. 137–49. Oxford: British Archaeological Reports S151.

Turner, A. 1984. Hominids and fellow travelers: Human migration into high latitudes as part of a large mammal community. In *Hominid evolution and community ecology*, ed. by R. Foley, pp. 193–217. New York: Academic Press.

Turner, C.G. 1984. Advances in the dental search for native American origins. *Acta Anthropogenetica* 8:23–78.

Turner, T. 1980. The social skin. In *Not work alone: A cross-cultural view of activities superfluous to survival*, ed. by J. Cherfas and R. Lewin, pp. 112–40. Beverly Hills: Sage.

Turville-Petre, F. 1927. *Researches in prehistoric Galilee (1925–1926)*. Bulletin of the British School of Archaeology in Jerusalem 14.

Twiesselmann, F. 1973. Evolution des dimensions et de la forme de la mandibule, du palais et des dents de l'homme. *Annales de Paléontologie (Vertébrés)* 59:171–277.

Urquhart, I.A.N. 1951. Some notes on jungle Punans in Kapit district. *The Sarawak Museum Journal* 5(3):495–523.

Valladas, H., J.M. Geneste, J.L. Joron, and J.P. Chadelle 1986. Thermoluminescence dating of Le Moustier (Dordogne, France). *Nature* 322:452–4.

Valladas, H., J.L. Joron, G. Valladas, B. Arensburg, O. Bar-Yosef. A. Belfer-Cohen, P. Goldberg, H. Laville, L. Meignen, Y. Rak, E. Tchernov, A-M. Tillier, and B. Vandermeersch 1987. Thermoluminescence dates for the Neanderthal burial site at Kebara in Israel. *Nature* 330:159–60.

Valladas, H., J.L. Reyes, J.L. Joron, G. Valladas, O. Bar-Yosef, and B. Vandermeersch 1988. Thermoluminescence dating of Mousterian 'Proto-Cro-Magnon' remains from Israel and the origin of modern man. *Nature* 331:614–16.

Vallois, H.V., and G. Billy 1965. Nouvelles recherches sur les hommes fossiles de l'Abri de Cro-Magnon. *L'Anthropologie* 69:47–74, 249–72.

Valoch, K. 1976. L'Aurignacian en Moravie. In *Colloque XVI, IXth Congrès, UISSP*, ed. by K. Valoch, pp. 112–23. Paris: Centre Nationale de la Recherche Scientifique.

1982. The Lower/Middle Palaeolithic transition in Czechoslovakia. In *The transition from Lower to Middle Palaeolithic and the origin of modern man*, ed. by A. Ronen, pp. 193–201. Oxford: British Archaeological Reports S151.

References

Vandermeersch, B. 1966. Découverte d'un objet en ocre avec traces d'utilisation dans le Moustérien de Qafzeh (Israël). *Bulletin de la Société Préhistorique Française* 66:157–8.

1970. Les origines de l'homme moderne. *Atomes* 25(272):5–12.

1972. Récentes découvertes de squelettes humains à Qafzeh (Israël): essai d'interprétation. In *The origin of Homo sapiens*, ed. by F. Bordes, pp. 49–54. Paris UNESCO.

1976. Les sépultures néandertaliennes. In *La Préhistoire Française*, vol. 1(1), ed. by H. de Lumley, pp. 725–7. Paris: C.N.R.S.

1981a. *Les Hommes fossiles de Qafzeh (Israël)*. Paris: C.N.R.S.

1981b. Les premiers *Homo sapiens* au Proche-Orient. In *Les Processus de l'hominisation*, ed. by D. Ferembach, pp. 97–100. Paris: C.N.R.S.

1982. The first *Homo sapiens sapiens* in the Near East. In *The transition from the Lower to the Middle Palaeolithic and the origin of modern man*, ed. by A. Ronen, pp. 297–300. Oxford: British Archaeological Reports S151.

1984. A propos de la découverte du squelette néandertalien de Saint-Césaire. *Bulletins et Mémoires de la Société d'Anthropologie de Paris Série XIV* 1:191–6.

1985. The origin of the Neanderthals. In *Ancestors: The hard evidence*, ed. by E. Delson, pp. 306–9. New York: Alan R. Liss.

Van Valen, L.M. 1986. Speciation and our own species. *Nature* 322:412.

Vértes, L. 1959. Chouringa de Tata. *Bulletin de la Société Préhistorique Française* 56:604–11.

1964. *Tata: Eine Mittelpaläolithische Travertin-Siedlung in Ungarn.* Budapest: Akademiai Kiado.

Vialou, D. 1982. Niaux, une construction symbolique magdalénienne exemplaire. *Ars Praehistorica* 1:19–45.

Villa, P.D'A. 1978. The stone artifact assemblage from Terra Amata: A contribution to the comparative study of Acheulian industries in southwestern Europe. Ph.D. Dissertation, University of California, Berkeley.

Vincent, A. 1988. L'os comme artefact au Paléolithique moyen: Principes d'étude et premiers résultats. In *L'Homme de Néandertal* 4: *La Technique*, ed. by L.R. Binford, and J.P. Rigaud. Etudes et Recherches Archéologiques de l'Université de Liège 31. In press.

Vlček, E. 1961. Pozůstatky Mladopleistocenního Člověka z Pavlova. *Památky Archeologické* 52:46–56.

1969. *Neandertaler de Tschechoslowakei.* Prague: Tschechoslowakeschen Akademie der Wissenschaften.

1970. Etude comparative onto-phylogénétique de l'enfant du Pech de l'Azé par rapport à d'autres enfants néanderthaliens. *Archives de L'Institut de Paléontologie Humaine* 33:149–80.

1973. Postcranial skeleton of a Neandertal child from Kiik-Koba, U.S.S.R. *Journal of Human Evolution* 2:536–44.

References

Volkman, P. 1983. Boker Tachtit: Core reconstructions. In *Prehistory and paleoenvironments in the Central Negev, Israel* III, ed. by A.E. Marks, pp. 127–90. Dallas: Southern Methodist University Press.

Volman, T.P. 1984. Early prehistory of southern Africa. In *Southern African prehistory and paleoenvironments*, ed. by R.G. Klein, pp. 169–220. Rotterdam: Balkema.

von Koenigswald, G.H.R. 1958. Der Solo-Mensch von Java: Ein tropischer Neanderthaler. In *Hundert Jahre Neanderthaler*, ed. by G.H.R. von Koenigswald, pp. 21–6. Utrecht: Kemink en zoon.

Wainscoat, J.S. 1987. Out of the Garden of Eden. *Nature* 365:13.

Wainscoat, J.S., A.V.S. Hill, A.L. Boyce, J. Flint, M. Hernandez, S.L. Thein, J.M. Old, J.R. Lynch, A.G. Falusi, D.J. Weatherall, and J.B. Clegg 1986a. Evolutionary relationships of human populations from an analysis of nuclear DNA polymorphisms. *Nature* 319:491–3.

Wainscoat, J.S., A.V.S. Hill, S.L. Thein, and J. B. Clegg 1986b. Reply to "Are we all out of Africa?". *Nature* 322:22.

Wallace, D.C., K. Garrison, and W.C. Knowler 1985. Dramatic founder effects in Amerindian mitrochondrial DNAs. *American Journal of Physical Anthropology* 68:149–55.

Walker, A. 1987. *Homo erectus* from Kenya (abstract). 2ème Congrès International de Paléontologie Humaine (Turin). Résumés des Communications, pp. 120–1.

Wallace, J.A. 1975. Did La Ferrassie 1 use his teeth as a tool? *Current Anthropology* 16:393–401.

Watanabi, H. 1969. Neanderthalers vs. *Homo sapiens*: Behavioral adaptability to arctic winter. *Proceedings of the 8th International Congress of Anthropological and Ethnological Sciences, Tokyo/Kyoto (1968)* 3:280–3.

1985. The chopper–chopping tool complex of eastern Asia: An ethnoarchaeological–ecological reexamination. *Journal of Anthropological Archaeology* 4:1–18.

Weckler, J.E. 1957. Neanderthal man. *Scientific American* 197(6):89–97.

Weidenreich, F. 1941. The extremity bones of *Sinanthropus pekinensis*. *Palaeontologia Sinica* 5D:1–150.

1943a. The skull of *Sinanthropus pekinensis*: A comparative study of a primitive hominid skull. *Palaeontologia Sinica*, n.s. D, no. 10 (whole series no. 127).

1943b. The "Neanderthal Man" and the ancestors of "Homo sapiens." *American Anthropologist* 45:39–48.

1945. The paleolithic child from the Teshik-Tash cave in southern Uzbekistan. *American Journal of Physical Anthropology* 3:151–64.

1946. *Apes, giants, and man.* Chicago: University of Chicago Press.

1947a. Facts and speculations concerning the origin of *Homo sapiens*. *American Anthropologist* 49:187–203.

273

1947b. The trend of human evolution. *Evolution* 1:221–36.

Weiner, A. 1983. From words to objects to magic: Hard words and the boundaries of social interaction. *Man* 18:690–709.

1985. Inalienable wealth. *American Ethnologist* 12:210–27.

1987. *The Trobrianders of Papua New Guinea*. New York: Holt, Rinehart and Winston.

Weinert, H. 1951. *Stammesentwicklung des Menschheit*. Braunschweig: Vieweg & Sohn.

Weiss, K.M. 1984. On the number of members of the genus *Homo* who have ever lived, and some evolutionary implications. *Human Biology* 56:637–49.

1986. In search of times past: The roles of gene flow and invasion in the generation of human diversity. In *Biological aspects of human migration*, ed. by N. Mascie-Taylor and G. Lasker. London: Cambridge University Press.

Weiss, K.M., and T. Maruyama 1976. Archaeology, population genetics, and studies of human racial ancestry. *American Journal of Physical Anthropology* 44:31–50.

Weiss, M.L., and A.E. Mann 1985. *Human biology and behavior: An anthropological perspective*. 4th edn. Boston: Little, Brown, and Company.

White, R. 1982. Rethinking the Middle/Upper Paleolithic transition. *Current Anthropology* 23:169–92.

1983. Changing land-use patterns across the Middle/Upper Paleolithic transition: The complex case of the Périgord. In *The Mousterian legacy*, ed. by E. Trinkaus, pp. 113–21. Oxford: British Archaeological Reports S164.

1985. Thoughts on social relationships and language in hominid evolution. *Journal of Social and Personal Relationships* 2:95–115.

1986a. Rediscovering French Ice Age art. *Nature* 320:683–4.

1986b. *Dark caves, bright visions: Life in Ice Age Europe*. New York: American Museum of Natural History.

1987. Glimpses of long-term shifts in late Paleolithic land use in the Périgord. In *The late Pleistocene Old World: Regional perspectives*, ed. by O. Soffer, pp. 263–77. New York: Plenum.

Whittam, T.S., A.G. Clark, M. Stoneking, R. Cann, and A.C. Wilson 1986. Allelic variation in human mitochondrial genes based on patterns of restriction site polymorphism. *Proceedings of the National Academy of Sciences USA* 83:9611–15.

Wiessner, P. 1982. Risk, reciprocity and social influences on !Kung San economics. In *Politics and history in band societies*, ed. by R. Lee and E. Leacock, pp. 61–84. Cambridge: Cambridge University Press.

Wijsman, E.M., and L.L. Cavalli-Sforza 1984. Migration and genetic population structure, with special reference to humans. *Annual Review of Ecology and Systematics* 15:279–301.

References

Wiley, E.O. 1981. *Phylogenetics: The theory and practice of phylogenetic systematics*. New York: John Wiley and Sons.

Wilson, A.C., R.L. Cann, S.M. Carr, M. George, U.B. Gyllensten, K.M. Helm-Bychowski, R.G. Higuchi, S.R. Palumbi, E.M. Prager, R.D. Sage, and M. Stoneking 1985. Mitochondrial DNA and two perspectives on evolutionary genetics. *Biological Journal of the Linnean Society, London* 26:375–400.

Winters, H. 1968. Value systems and trade cycles of the late Archaic in the Mid-West. In *New perspectives in archaeology*, ed. by S. and L. Binford, pp. 175–221. Chicago: Aldine.

Wissler, C. 1914. Material cultures of the North American Indians. *American Anthropologist* 16:447–505.

Wobst, M. 1977. Stylistic behavior and information exchange. In *For the director: Research essays in honor of James B. Griffin*, ed. by C. Cleland, pp. 317–42. Anthropological Papers of the Museum of Anthropology, University of Michigan 61.

Woillard, G.M., and W.G. Mook 1982. Carbon 14 dates at Grande Pile: Correlation of land and sea chronologies. *Science* 215: 159–61.

Wolpoff, M.H. 1968. Climatic influence on the skeletal nasal aperture. *American Journal of Physical Anthropology* 29:405–24.

1971. Metric trends in hominid dental evolution. *Case Western Reserve University Studies in Anthropology* 2.

1979. The Krapina dental remains. *American Journal of Physical Anthropology* 50:67–114.

1980a. *Paleoanthropology*. New York: Knopf.

1980b. Review of M. Shackley: *Neanderthal Man*. *American Anthropologist* 83:199–200.

1982a. Comment on F.H. Smith: Upper Pleistocene hominid evolution in south-central Europe. *Current Anthropology* 23:693.

1982b. The Arago dental sample in the context of hominid dental evolution. In *L'Homo erectus et la place de l'Homme de Tautavel parmi les hominidés fossiles*, pp. 389–410. Paris: C.N.R.S.

1985. Human evolution at the peripheries: The pattern at the eastern edge. In *Hominid evolution: Past, present, and future. Proceedings of the Taung Diamond Jubilee International Symposium*, ed. by P.V. Tobias, pp. 355–65. New York: Alan R. Liss.

1986. Describing anatomically modern *Homo sapiens*: A distinction without a definable difference. In *Fossil man – new facts, new ideas. Papers in honor of Jan Jelínek's life anniversary*, ed. by V.V. Novotny and A. Mizerova. *Anthropos* (Brno) 23:41–53.

Wolpoff, M.H., and A. Nkini 1985. Early and middle Pleistocene hominids from Asia and Africa. In *Ancestors: The hard evidence*, ed. by E. Delson, pp. 202–5. New York: Alan R. Liss.

Wolpoff, M.H., Wu Xinzhi, and A.G. Thorne 1984. Modern *Homo sapiens* origins: A general theory of hominid evolution involving the fossil evidence from east Asia. In *The origins of modern humans: A world survey of the fossil evidence*, ed. by F.H. Smith and F. Spencer, pp. 411–83. New York: Alan R. Liss.

Wolpoff, M.H., F.H. Smith, M. Malez, J. Radovčić, and D. Rukavina 1981. Upper Pleistocene human remains from Vindija Cave, Croatia, Yugoslavia. *American Journal of Physical Anthropology* 54:499–545.

Woo J.K., and Peng R.C. 1959. Fossil human skull of early Paleoanthropic stage found at Mapa, Shaoquan, Kwangtung Province. *Vertebrata PalAsiatica* 3:176–82.

Woodburn, J. 1968. An introduction to Hadza ecology. In *Man the hunter*, ed. by R. Lee and I. DeVore, pp. 49–55. Chicago: Aldine.

1980. Hunters and gatherers today and reconstruction of the past. In *Soviet and Western anthropology*, ed. by Ernest Gellner, pp. 95–117. London: Duckworth.

Wright, S. 1980. Genic and organismic selection. *Evolution* 34:825–43.

Wu R. 1986. A fossil skeleton from Yinkou, Liaoning Province, People's Republic of China, Archaic *Homo sapiens* or *Homo erectus*? In *The Pleistocene perspective*, ed. by M.H. Day, R. Foley, and R. Wu. London: Unwin Hyman.

Wu R., and J.W Olsen, eds. 1985. *Palaeoanthropology and Palaeolithic archaeology in the People's Republic of China*. London: Academic Press.

Ya'alon, D.H., and E. Ganor 1975. Rates of eolian dust accretion in the Mediterranean desert fringe environments of Israel. *Proceedings of the IX Congress of Sedimentology*, pp. 169–74.

Yellen, J.E. 1972. Trip V itinerary, May 24–June 9, 1968. In *Exploring human nature*, pp. 1–17. Cambridge, Mass.: Educational Development Center.

1977. *Archaeological approaches to the present*. New York: Academic Press.

Index

Abu Sif: 163, 166
Abu Zif: 162
Acheulian: 26, 28–31, 39, 40, 144, 160, 168
Acheulo-Yabrudian: 157, 160, 161, 165, 168, 175, 177
Adam, K.: 35
Adlun caves: 162
admixture: *see* gene flow
Africa: 43, 44, 77–84, 93, 109–11, 113, 115, 116, 209
Africa, northern: 46, 73, 117, 207
Africa, southern: 3, 9, 15, 207, 210
Africa, sub-Saharan: 46, 47, 65, 90, 101, 106–8, 117
Ahmarian: 164
Ain Aqev: 162
Aitken, M. J.: 145
Alexeyev, V. P.: 47
Alvesalo, L.: 188
Ambrose, S. H.: 90, 203
Amerindians: 75, 111
Amud: 162, 165, 168, 169, 177
"anatomically modern humans (*Homo sapiens*)": 4, 10, 47, 106, 107, 108
Andrews, P.: 101, 106, 117, 118, 124, 127, 137, 182, 201
Antélias, Abri: 162
Arago: 186
Arcy-sur-Cure: 102, 125

Arensburg, B.: 54, 56, 87, 178
art: 13, 35, 59, 86, 151, 178, 205, 206, 210–31
Ashton, N.: 102
Asia, central: 43, 65
Asia, eastern: 43, 74–7, 111, 204
Asia, northern: 39, 117
Asia, western: 43, 44, 46, 65, 71, 73, 97, 101, 207
Aterian: 59
Audouze, F.: 150
Aurignacian, European: 37, 70, 71, 101, 102, 118, 125, 147, 148, 150, 152, 153, 215–17, 219–21, 223, 226, 230
Aurignacian, Levantine: 164, 230
Australasia: 43, 73–7, 101, 111, 117
Australopithecus afarensis: 112
Avise, J. C.: 114

Bacho Kiro Cave: 71, 147
Badegoulian: 144
Bader, O.: 213, 214
Badoux, D. M.: 61
Bae, K. T.: 40
Bahn, P.: 227
Bailey, G.: 37
Bailey, H. P.: 24
Bánesz, L.: 60, 63

Bar-Yosef, O.: 10–16, 32, 44, 45, 73, 91, 156, 157, 160, 164–6, 171, 172, 173, 174, 178, 230
Bate, D.: 155, 160, 178
Bayer, J.: 103
Beals, K. L.: 61
Beaumont, P. B.: 36, 47, 80, 200
Belfer, A.: 174
Belfer-Cohen, A.: 172, 173, 230
Bellwood, P.: 32
Besançon, J.: 156, 157, 159
Beyries, S.: 155
Bezez: 161, 162, 171
Billy, G.: 55
Binford, L. R.: 7, 8, 11–15, 20–2, 25, 26, 28–31, 34, 36, 40, 41, 58–60, 77, 78, 85, 94, 95, 102, 107, 123, 172, 175, 203, 205–7, 210, 229
Binford, S. R.: 40, 124, 168, 172, 212
Bintliff, J. L.: 156, 160
biological determinism: 5
Biqat Kuneitra: 162, 175
Birdsell, J. B.: 120
Bjork, A.: 193, 201
Blackwell, B.: 145
Blanchard, Abri: 216, 219, 223
Boaz, N. T.: 103
Bodmer, W. F.: 101
Bodo: 200
Boëda, E.: 155, 170
Boker: 162
Boker Tachtit: 162, 163, 164, 177
Border Cave: 7, 47, 80, 83, 107, 108, 117
Bordes, F.: 31, 33, 37, 46, 50, 52, 59, 63, 103, 144, 146, 147, 151, 155
Bosinski, G.: 31, 32
Bouchud, J.: 103
Boule: M.: 181
Brace, C. L.: 90, 100, 118, 120, 122, 124, 130, 187, 188
brains: 61, 86, 87, 121, 206, 207, 211, 228, 230
Bräuer, G.: 68, 78, 80, 82, 83, 91, 101, 118, 119, 200, 201, 206
Breuil, H.: 46
Brézillon, M.: 150
Briskin, M.: 156
Broken Hill: 53, 57, 82, 83, 85, 86, 87, 185, 200, 201
Bromage, T. G.: 87
Brose, D. S.: 100, 105, 118, 124, 125, 130, 199, 200
Brown, J. A.: 37
Brown, W. M.: 89, 115, 137, 138
Brues, A.: 120, 123
Bruins, H.: 156

Bryant, E. H.: 116
Bunn, D. S.: 27, 166
Bunn, H. T. III: 27, 29
Bunney, S.: 87
Burch, E. S., Jr.: 169
burials: 14, 35, 81, 86, 151, 171, 178, 206, 212–16
Butzer, K. W.: 81, 82, 171

Cann, R. L.: 89–91, 101, 106, 109–11, 113–15, 117, 137, 182, 203
cannibalism: 151
Capitan, L.: 214
Carey, J. W.: 57
Carlson, D. S.: 201
Carr, S. M.: 112
Carrier, D. R.: 58
Cartailhac, E.: 211
Carter, D. R.: 55
Cartmill, M.: 203
Castanet, Abri: 216
Cavalli-Sforza, L. L.: 101, 105, 108
Cellier, Abri: 216, 217, 223
Chadelle, J. P.: 149
Champagne, F.: 146
Chang, J.-H.: 101
Chang, K. C.: 24
Charente: 146
Charlesworth, B.: 120
Chase, P. G.: 33, 169
Châtelperronian (Castelperronian): 37, 44, 70, 71, 102, 103, 124, 125, 145, 146, 147, 151, 169, 206, 223, 226
Cherfas, J.: 101
Chierici, G.: 56
China: 32, 39, 41, 74, 75
Christy, H.: 211
Chung, Y. W.: 40
Churchill, S. E.: 49
Cioclovina: 103
Clactonian: 39
Clark, J. D.: 26, 27, 51, 85, 95
Clarke, R. J.: 82
Clastres, P.: 24
CLIMAP: 156
Cohan, F. M.: 109
Cohuna: 74
Collie, G.: 217
Collins, D.: 39
Combe Grenal: 30, 33, 34, 169
Conkey, M. W.: 36, 59, 86, 206, 215
Cook, J.: 70, 74, 102
Coon, C. S.: 56, 61, 68, 74, 99, 121, 124, 183, 187, 191
Copeland, L.: 157, 160, 161, 163, 166, 176, 177

Index

Coppens, Y.: 228
Cordy, J. M.: 169
Crew, H.: 155
culture: 5, 7, 8, 35, 36, 38, 47, 143, 144, 209
culture areas: 22
culture history: 8, 10, 46
curation: 19, 20, 123

Daams, R.: 167
Dali: 74
Dar-es-Soltane: 47, 83, 84, 85, 91
Davis, S. J. H.: 59, 155, 174
Day, M. H.: 48, 57, 82, 83
Deacon, H. J.: 41, 77, 78, 79, 94
Dean, M. C.: 87, 94
Debenath, A.: 51, 63, 83, 144, 148
Delage, F.: 216
Delpech, F.: 58, 145, 150, 169
Delporte, H.: 50, 60, 63, 147, 150
Delson, E.: 76, 104, 106, 127, 182
de Lumley, M.-A.: 126
Demars, P.-Y.: 226
Demes, B.: 198
demic diffusion: see gene flow
Denaro, M.: 101
Dennell, R.: 205, 206
dentition: 52, 72, 85, 128–30, 187–97
de Sonneville-Bordes, D.: 59, 155
development: 13, 55, 61, 86–88, 94, 197, 198
Dibble, H. L.: 155, 177
Didon, L.: 216
Dolní Věstonice: 103, 230
Dordogne: 149
Douara Cave: 174
Duplessy, J. C.: 156
Duport, L., 51: 148
Dzeravá Skála: 103

early modern humans, Africa: 47, 51, 53, 55, 77–85, 107, 108, 117, 118
early modern humans, Australasia: 55, 74–7, 118
early modern humans, eastern Asia: 53, 74, 75
early modern humans, Europe: 44, 47, 53, 55, 57, 69–72, 92, 98, 99, 101–4, 118, 119, 120, 122, 127–36, 138, 139
early modern humans, western Asia: 44, 45, 47, 53, 55, 72, 73, 84, 85, 92, 100, 104, 106, 120, 122, 126, 127, 129–39, 165–9, 204, 210
Early Stone Age (ESA): 95
Edwards, A. W. F.: 108
Ehringsdorf: 99, 102
Eldredge, N.: 201, 231
Eliye Springs: 82, 84
El-Kowm: 166, 173

El Wad: 160, 173
Emireh: 162
Endo, B.: 54, 55
Engis: 70
Enlow, D. H.: 187, 192, 197, 201
Ennouchi, E.: 57
Epi-Pietersburg: 80
Erq el Ahmar: 162, 174
Espitalier, R.: 146
Etiolles: 150
Europe: 43, 46, 70–3, 93, 97, 207, 209
Europe, eastern: 70, 216, 219
Europe, central: 3, 32, 44, 65, 70, 100, 103, 117, 147, 204, 216, 219, 229
Europe, western: 3, 9, 12, 31, 33, 47, 65, 69, 70, 99, 100, 103, 144–53, 215, 216, 219, 229
Evins, M. A.: 175

facial skeleton: 52–3, 72, 79, 82, 83, 85, 121, 125, 132–4, 183–7, 189, 192–202
Facteur, Abri du: 150
Fara II: 162, 173, 175
Farrand, W. R.: 156, 157, 165, 171
faunal remains: 28–30, 58, 173–6, 226
Ferembach, D.: 47, 117
Ferring, C. R.: 46
Ferris, S. D.: 89, 112
fire: 63, 171, 172
Fish Hoek: 118
Florisbad: 82, 83, 85, 111, 200
Foley, R.: 23
Fontéchevade: 102
Franciscus, R. G.: 56
Frayer, D. W.: 53, 72, 103, 118, 123, 125, 126, 128, 188, 204
Freeman, L. G. Jr.: 30
Freund, G.: 32
Friedel, D. A.: 58, 60, 173, 174

Gábori, M.: 170
Gábori-Csánk, V.: 51, 63
Galley Hill: xiv
Gamble, C.: 37, 164, 205, 213
Ganor, E.: 156
Garn, S. M.: 188–90
Garrard, A. N.: 155, 174
Garrod, D. A. E.: 155, 160, 168, 178
Geissenklosterle Cave: 216
Geist, V.: 123
gene flow: 44, 62, 67–9, 72, 92, 98, 101, 104–6, 109, 112, 118–21, 137–40, 204, 208
Geneste, J.-M.: 33, 35, 149, 150, 155, 226
geographical variation: 6, 9, 24
Geraads, D.: 48

Gesher Benot Ya'acov: 45, 160
gestation: 13, 87
Ghosh, K.: 32
Gilead, I.: 155, 164, 173, 175
Giles, E.: 90, 203
Gilman, A.: 30, 36, 156
Gisis, I.: 165
Goldberg, P.: 156, 157, 159, 160, 171, 173
Goose, D. H.: 188
Goren, N.: 157, 160
Goren-Inbar, N.: 160, 175
Gorjanović-Kramberger, D.: 100
Gould, R. A.: 59
Gould, S. J., 69, 182
Grainger, R. M.: 188
Gravettian: 103, 131, 145, 147, 148, 150, 151, 223, 230
Gribbin, J.: 101
Griffin, P. B.: 24
Grigson, C.: 155, 173, 175
Grotte des Enfants: 70, 103, 118
growth: *see* development
Guagliardo, M. F.: 197
Guglielmino-Matessi, C. R.: 108
Gvirtzman, G.: 157, 165

Haas, G.: 166, 167
Habgood, P. J.: 75
Hadza: 24
Hahn, J.: 37, 216, 219
Hahnöfersand: 71, 92, 118
Hale, L. R.: 113, 114
Harle, E.: 211
Harpending, H.: 108
Harris, J. W. K.: 25
Harrold, F. B.: 36, 46, 60, 71, 86, 212
Hasegawa, M.: 112
Haua Fteah: 85
Hayden, B.: 25, 39
Haynes, C. V.: 35
Hayonim: 162, 168, 171
hearths, *see* fire
Hearty, P. J.: 165
Heim, J. L.: 50, 52, 53, 55, 124, 183, 187, 191, 197
Hendey, Q. B.: 77, 79
Henke, W.: 103
Hennig, G. J., 159
Henry, J.: 24
Heusser, L. E.: 156
Hexian: 74
Hietala, H. J.: 58, 60
Ho, C. K.: 28, 30
Hodder, I.: 39
Hogan, J. P.: 101
Holloway, R. L.: 86, 121, 207

Holmberg, A. R.: 24
Holt, I. J.: 113
Homo erectus: 10, 74, 75, 77, 87, 110, 111, 113, 183–6, 205, 209
Homo neanderthalensis: 10, 11, 39
Homo sapiens: 19, 67, 113, 115, 181
Homo sapiens sapiens: 19. 25, 36, 39, 77, 146, 149, 151–3, 169, 211
Hooijer, D.: 155, 174
Horowitz, A.: 156, 157
Horowitz, S. L.: 188
Hortus: 102, 126
Hours, F.: 157, 159–61, 177
Hovers, E.: 175
Howell, F. C.: 30, 56, 60, 61, 98, 99, 101, 103, 118, 182
Howells, W. W.: 56, 57, 67, 75, 100, 108, 169, 170, 182, 186, 201
Howieson's Poort: 78, 85
Hoxne: 30
Hrdlička, A.: 100, 187
Hublin, J. J.: 49, 53, 57, 70, 83, 103, 182
Hummal I.: 161
Hungsgai Valley: 28
hunting: 24, 29, 34, 35, 77, 78, 174, 179
Huntingford, W.: 24
Hutterer, K. L.: 22
Huxtable, J.: 145
hybridization: *see* gene flow
Hylander, W. L.: 187, 191, 192, 199

Iampietro, P. F.: 123
India: 32, 39
Indonesia: 74–7
Irano-Turanian: 174
Irhoud: 53, 57, 76, 82, 83, 84, 91
Isaac, G. L.: 25–7, 29, 36, 164
Issar, A.: 156
Ivanhoe, F.: 121

Jacob-Friesen, K. H.: 51
Jakobson, R.: 190
Jelinek, A. J.: 32, 36, 41, 52, 157, 160, 161, 163, 165, 170, 176
Jelínek, J.: 53, 103, 117, 118, 126
Jia L. P.: 41
Johnson, M. J.: 89, 90, 91
Jones, J. S.: 90, 106, 108, 112, 116, 137, 204
Jorde, L. B.: 89

Kabwe: *see* Broken Hill
Karlin, S.: 120
Kaufman, D.: 52, 164
Kebara: 2, 32, 87, 160, 162, 165, 169, 171, 172, 173, 178, 204
Keilor: 75

Index

Keith, A.: 45, 53, 55, 57, 134, 136
Kelly, R. L.: 21, 23, 25, 35
Kelsterbach: 102
Kennedy, G. A.: 55, 75, 82, 86
Kent, S.: 25
Kharaneh: 178
Kibish: see Omo-Kibish
Kim, W. Y.: 40
Kimura, T.: 54, 55
King, M. C.: 137
Kirkbride, D.: 165, 171
Kishino, M.: 112
Klasies River Mouth Cave: 29, 30, 47, 51, 77–9, 81, 85, 91, 95, 107, 108, 116, 117
Klein, R. G.: 50, 58, 60, 63, 77, 78, 81, 94, 106, 203
Klima, B.: 50, 60, 63, 230
Koobi Fora; 27, 29
Kovacs, I.: 190, 191
Kow Swamp: 74, 75
Kozłowski, J. K.: 71, 147, 230
Krantz, G. S.: 123
Krapina: 47, 102, 125, 126, 135
Kraus, B. S.: 188
Kroeber, A. L.: 18, 19, 22
Kroll, E.: 29
Ksar 'Akil: 162, 163, 173
Kuhn, S.: 56
Kukla, G.: 156
Kulna: 102, 125, 126
Kurashina, H.: 26, 27

Labrot, J.: 146
La Chaise: 144
La Chapelle-aux-Saints: 70
Laetoli: 18, 57
La Ferrassie: 70, 135, 151
Laitman, J. T.: 121
Lalouel, J.: 108
La Madeleine: 214
Laming-Emperaire, A.: 217
Lande, R.: 120
language: 14, 36, 206, 230
Laplace, G.: 146
La Quina: 225
Larick, R. R.: 149, 227
Larnach, S. L.: 75, 77, 101
Lartet, E.: 211
Lascaux: 144
La Souquette: 216, 219, 223, 226
late archaic humans, Africa: 53, 57, 62, 81–7, 106, 200, 201
late archaic humans, Australasia: 75–7, 93
late archaic humans, eastern Asia: 57, 74, 75
late archaic humans, Europe: 42–5, 47–50, 52–7, 59–62, 65, 68, 70–3, 84–7, 92–4,

97–102, 108, 118, 121–4, 126–40, 181–202
late archaic humans, western Asia: 42–5, 47–50, 52–7, 59–62, 65, 68, 73, 84–7, 92, 94, 99, 100, 121–4, 138, 165–70, 186, 204
Later Stone Age (LSA): 46
Latorre, A.: 113, 203
Lavelle, C. L. B.: 192
Laville, H.: 33, 145, 171, 205
Leakey, R. E. F.: 82, 83, 184
Lee, R. B.: 24
Le Flageolet I: 150, 216
Lehringen: 35
Leigh, S. R.: 198
Le May, M.: 61
Le Piage: 146
Leroi-Gourhan, André: 125, 147, 150, 217, 219
Leroi-Gourhan, Arlette: 70, 159
Leroy-Prost, C.: 51
Leroyer, C.: 70
Les Cottés: 103
Levallois technique: 31, 33, 145
Levant: 3, 9, 12, 44, 45, 65, 96, 99, 100, 101, 104, 106, 120, 123, 127, 132–4, 136, 137, 154–79
Lévèque, F.: 44, 70, 230
Lewin, R.: 104, 182
Lewis, D. W.: 188
Lewontin, R. C.: 137
Lieberman, P.: 202
life-cycle parameters: 13
limb-segment proportions: 48, 49, 62, 85, 86, 94, 121–4
Lind, V.: 190
Liujiang: 74, 75
living floors: 12, 25, 60, 150, 151, 171
Livingstone, F. B.: 108, 109, 120
locomotion: 47, 54–6, 85, 86, 124
longevity: 13, 60, 86, 114, 228, 229
Lovejoy, C. O.: 48, 54, 55
lower limb morphology: 54–6, 62, 85, 135, 136
Lower Paleolithic: 25–31, 38, 40
Lundstrom, A.: 188
Lyubin, V. P.: 32

Maba: see Mapa
Macintosh, N. W. G.: 75, 77, 101
Magdalenian: 215
Magori, C. C.: 57
manipulation: 15, 47, 48–50, 53, 85
Mann, A. E.: 140
Mapa: 57, 74
Marks, A. E.: 52, 58, 60, 157, 163, 164, 172–4, 177

Marshack, A.: 22, 36, 59, 71, 219
Martin, H.: 51, 225
Maruyama, T.: 108, 109
Marzke, M. W.: 50, 51
Masloukh: 162
mastoid process: 125, 130
Matiegka, J.: 53, 55, 57, 103
Mayr, E.: 120, 199
McBurney, C. B. M.: 85
McCown, T. D.: 45, 53, 55, 57, 134, 136
McGregor, J.: 120
McNamara, J. A.: 202
Meehan, J. P.: 123
Meggitt, M.: 24
Mellars, P.: 30, 36, 102, 156
Merbs, C. F.: 191
Middle Paleolithic (Mousterian): 11, 25, 31–5, 38, 40, 42, 46, 47, 50–2, 58, 59, 64, 71, 73, 85, 92, 94, 95, 97, 100, 121, 124–6, 142, 144–6, 148, 154–9, 161–3, 165, 166, 168–79, 201, 205–7, 209, 210, 212, 213, 225
Middle Stone Age (MSA): 46, 59, 65, 77–85, 92, 94, 95, 206, 210
Miesslingstal: 103
Miskovsky, J. C.: 44
Misra, V. N.: 44
mitochondrial DNA (mtDNA): 88–91, 94, 109–15, 137, 179, 203–5
Mladeč: 70, 103, 134, 135, 231
Montague, M. F. A.: 120
Mook, W. G.: 156
Morant, G. M.: 57
Morris, L. N.: 120
Morrow, D. O.: 24
Morton, N. E.: 108
Mount, L. E.: 73
Mount Carmel: 99 (*see also* Skhūl and Tabun)
Movius, H. L. Jr.: 39, 60, 63, 150
Moyers, R. E.: 192, 201
Munday, F. C.: 41, 155, 173, 176
Mungo: 75, 118
Murdock, G. P.: 24
Musgrave, J. H.: 61
Mussi, M.: 103
Mwanganda's Village: 35
Myers, F.: 229

Nahal Amud Caves: 162
Nahal Aqev 3: 163, 173
Nahal Ein Gev I: 178
Nahal Zin: 162
Nahr el Kebir: 157
Nakata, M.: 202
Ndutu: 107
Neandertals: *see* late archaic humans

Near East: 9, 32, 41, 45, 106, 154–79, 209, 229, 230
Nei, M.: 89–91, 108, 137, 203, 205
Nesbitt, P.: 217
neurocranium: 61, 72, 106, 125, 126, 130–2, 188
Neve David: 178
Ngaloba: 76, 83, 84, 85, 107, 110, 200
Ngandong: 74, 75, 76, 77
Niah: 93, 118
Nkini, A.: 113
noses: 56–7, 62, 132
nuclear DNA: 91, 110, 115, 116, 203
Nute, P. E.: 120

Oakley, K. P.: 51
O'Connell, J.: 40
Ohel, M. Y.: 39
Oldowan: 26–7, 28, 33, 40
Olduvai Gorge: 27, 29
O'Leary, B.: 19
Oleksiak, D. A.: 187, 191
Olsen, J. W.: 74
Omo: 81–3
Omo-Kibish: 81, 82, 85
Onoratini, G.: 147
Orange Free State, South Africa: 82
ornamentation: *see* art
Orquera, L.: 36
Osborne, R. H.: 188
O'Shea, J.: 214
Otte, M.: 50, 51, 230
Oumm Qatafa: 168
Owen, L. R.: 37

Paddayya, K.: 28, 32
Paderborn: 102
paleoenvironment: 13, 156, 157, 159, 160, 168, 169
Palmyra: 174
Paquette, S. P.: 7, 10–16, 43, 52, 189, 210
Pataud, Abri: 150
Paterson, A.: 217, 226
Pavlov: 70, 103
Pavlovian: 131
Payne, S.: 155, 174
Pech-de-l'Azé: 151, 225
Pei Wen Chung: 40
Peng, R. C.: 57
Périgord: 146, 147, 149, 151
Perlès, C.: 63
Perrot, J.: 59
Petralona: 185, 186
Peyrony, D.: 147, 212, 214, 216, 217, 223
Pfeiffer, J. E.: 30, 36, 59
phylogeny: 8, 10, 43–6, 67–9, 97, 108–9

Index

Pilbeam, D.: 203
Piltdown: xiv
Pincevent: 150
planning depth: 12, 19, 21, 25, 27, 34, 123
Podbaba: 102
Pond, A.: 217
Potter, R. H.: 188
Potts, R.: 29
Prat, F.: 169
Předmostí: 70, 103, 122, 128, 129, 134, 230
Price, T.: 37
"proto-Cro-Magnon": *see* early modern humans, western Asia
Protsch, R.: 101, 118
Putnam, P.: 24
Pycraft, W. P.: 48

Qafzeh: 44, 45, 55, 72, 73, 76, 79, 84, 85, 87, 91, 92, 100, 104, 106, 120, 122, 126, 127, 129, 130, 132, 133, 136, 138, 139, 162, 163, 165, 166, 168, 169, 171, 175, 177, 178, 204, 206
Quechon, G.: 60
Qui Z.: 32

Radovčić, J.: 100, 104, 118
Ranyard, G. C.: 118, 125, 133, 193, 197, 200
Rak, Y.: 52, 54, 56, 87, 124, 130, 132, 183, 186, 198
Rakefet: 160
raw material: 149, 226, 227
Reinach, S.: 212, 217
Rensberger, B.: 105, 118
respiration: 56–7
Rice, P.: 217, 226
Riesenfeld, A.: 191, 193
Rigaud, J. P.: 5–7, 9–16, 51, 59, 71, 144, 145, 147–50, 216, 217
Rightmire, G. P.: 78, 80, 82, 83, 91, 107, 108, 117
Roberts, N.: 156, 157, 160
Roc de Combe: 37, 146
Roe, D. A.: 32
Ronen, A.: 200
Rosenberg, K. R.: 87, 124
Rosenzweig, M. L.: 24
Rosh Ein Mor: 162, 163, 173
Rouhani, S.: 90, 106, 116
Roychoudhury, A. K.: 108, 137, 203
Ruff, C.: 55
Russell, M. D.: 93, 121, 124, 193
Rust, A.: 160
Ryan, A. S.: 52, 187, 188

Saccopastore: 99
Sackett, J. R.: 39

Sahba: 162
Saint-Césaire: 47, 70, 71, 92, 102, 103, 125, 146, 147
Saitta, D. J.: 39
Šala: 70, 71
Saldanha: 82
Sampson, G.: 28, 51, 59, 60
Sankalia, H. D.: 39
Sanlaville, P.: 156
Santa Luca: A. P.: 53, 74, 130
Saxe, A. A.: 60
scavenging: 23, 29, 31, 58
Schaefer, U.: 61
Schick, T.: 174
Schliz, R.: 100
Schrire, C.: 39
Schroeder, B.: 166
Schwalbe, G.: 118
Schwarcz, H. P.: 145, 159
Scott, K.: 41, 78
Sefunim: 174
Selmer-Olsen, R.: 191, 193
Senshui Chang: 40
settlement patterns: 172–4
Shackleton, N. J.: 156
Shackley, M.: 51, 119
Shanidar: 162, 169, 173, 178, 186
Sharp, L.: 227
Shipman, P.: 29
Shovakh: 168
Shukbah: 163, 171
Siegel, M. I.: 193
Silberbauer, G. B.: 24
Silická Brezová: 103
Silva, A. C.: 60
Singa: 85
Singer, R.: 36, 41, 44, 46, 47, 51, 52, 57, 59, 63, 77, 78, 85, 210
Singh, R. S.: 113, 114
Šipka: 102, 126
Skhùl: 45, 55, 73, 76, 84, 85, 87, 91, 98, 100, 104, 106, 120, 122, 126, 127, 129, 130, 132–4, 136, 138, 139, 162, 163, 165, 177, 206
Skieller, V.: 193, 201
Skinner, J. D.: 155
Skinner, J. H.: 161, 166
Skinner, M.: 60
Smith, F. H.: 7, 10–12, 14, 15, 16, 43–5, 49, 52, 67, 68, 70, 71, 84, 88, 91, 102, 117, 118, 124, 125, 128, 130, 133, 134, 136, 181–3, 186, 187, 188, 191–3, 197–201, 204, 206–10
Smith, P.: 49, 60, 188
Smith, P. E. L.: 173
Soffer, O.: 124, 140

Sohan: 39
Solecki, R. S.: 178
Sollas, W. J.: 211
Solo: 100
Spencer, F.: 5, 43, 67, 97, 181
Spengler, D. M.: 55
Spiess, A.: 58
Stanley, S. M.: 120
Starolsel'e: 47
Steegman, A. T.: 57
Stekelis, M.: 174
Stetten: 103
Stevens, D.: 60
Stewart, T. D.: 53
Stone, N. M.: 30
Stoneking, M.: 89, 110, 113
Strathern, A.: 218
Strathern, M.: 218
Straus, L. G.: 20, 30, 52, 58, 60, 213
Stringer, C. B.: 7, 9–11, 13–16, 43, 48, 53,
    56, 57, 61, 68, 70–6, 82, 83, 85–7, 90, 93,
    94, 101, 103–6, 117, 118, 123–5, 127, 128,
    136, 137, 169, 182–4, 201, 213
style: 6
subsistence: 15, 24, 28–30, 58, 79, 149, 150,
    226
Sullivan, P. G.: 192, 201
Sungir': 214, 230
Suzuki, H.: 45, 168, 178
Svitavka: 103
Svoboda, J.: 103, 122
Swanscombe: 30
symbolic behaviour: 13, 36, 205, 211, 217–19
Szeletian: 102
Szombathy, J.: 103, 231

Taborin, Y.: 150, 216, 218, 219
Tabun: 45, 99, 157, 160, 161, 162, 163, 165,
    166, 168, 169, 170, 171, 172
tactical depth: 19
Tainter, J.: 214
Takai, F.: 45, 168, 178
Talgai: 74
Tattersall, I.: 201, 231
Taylor, R. M. S.: 191
Tchernov, E.: 48, 155, 166, 167, 171, 174
technology: 15, 23–8, 50–2, 200, 208, 209
technology, antler/bone/teeth: 15, 51, 143,
    148, 149, 223, 224
technology, lithic: 15, 33, 143, 145, 148, 176,
    177, 179
technology, wood etc: 23, 58, 149
Templeton, A. R.: 137
Texier, J. P.: 144
thermal stress and adaptation: 16, 47, 57,
    61–3, 73, 86, 121–3, 187

Thompson, D. D.: 60, 114
Thorne, A. G.: 117, 138
Tigerstedt, P. M. A.: 188
Tillier, A. M.: 72, 83, 197
Tode, A.: 51
Tompkins, R. L.: 55, 87, 94
Torralba: 30, 31, 33, 34, 41
Torrence, R.: 21
Toth, N.: 39
transition: 5, 7, 8, 11, 35–9, 42, 134, 142,
    152, 225, 228, 230
trauma: 60
Trinkhaus, E.: 5–7, 9, 10, 12–16, 43–5, 47,
    48–50, 52–62, 68, 72, 73, 84–8, 92, 94,
    114, 118, 119, 121–4, 128, 130, 131, 134,
    136, 165, 169, 182, 183, 186–8, 198, 199,
    204, 206, 208
Tuffreau, A.: 32
Turner, A.: 113
Turner, C. G.: 85
Turner, T.: 214
Turville-Petre, F.: 165
Twiesselmann, F.: 188

upper limb morphology: 48–50
Upper Paleolithic: 11, 13, 18, 42, 46, 47,
    50–2, 58–60, 71, 92, 97, 121, 142, 146–54,
    159, 160, 163, 164, 172–4, 175c, 177–9,
    201, 205–7, 209, 211–31
Urquhart, I. A. N.: 24

Valladas, H.: 44, 73, 92, 101, 102, 104, 127,
    136, 168, 169, 201, 204
Vallois, H. V.: 55
Vallon de Castelmerle: 216, 217, 227
Valoch, K.: 32, 103
Vandermeersch, B.: 36, 44, 45, 47, 53, 55,
    57, 60, 70, 72, 73, 90, 101, 103, 104, 125,
    146, 165, 166, 169, 171, 178, 186, 230
Van Valan, L. M.: 90, 116, 137, 203
Vaufrey , Abri (or Grotte): 30, 144, 148
Velika Pećina: 103
Verberie: 150
vertebrae: 53, 134, 135, 188
Vértes, L.: 225
Vialou, D.: 217
Vierich, H.: 25
Villa, P. D'A: 28
Villerest: 150
Vincent, A.: 148
Vindija: 70, 71, 92, 93, 102, 103, 125
Vlček, E.: 53, 55, 126, 197
Volkman, P.: 46, 52, 85, 163
Volman, T. P.: 77, 79, 80, 94, 95
von Koenigswald, G. H. R.: 100

Index

Vrba, E. S.: 69

Wadjak: 74, 76
Wainscoat, J. S.: 90, 101, 106, 115, 203, 204
Wallace, D. C.: 111, 130
Walker, A.: 87, 184
Watanabi, H.: 22
Weckler, J. E.: 101
Weidenreich, F.: 48, 68, 74, 99, 100, 114,
    117, 118, 133, 139, 201, 207
Weiner, A.: 215, 227
Weinert, H.: 118
Weiss, K. M.: 108, 109, 114, 203
Weiss, M. L.: 140
Weissner, P.: 227
White, R.: 11–15, 30, 36, 51, 58–60, 71, 124,
    148, 156, 205, 211, 216, 227, 228
Whittam, T. S.: 114
Wijsman, E. M.: 105
Wiley, E. O.: 98
Willandra Lakes: 76, 83, 93
Wilson, A. C.: 89, 91, 115, 137, 203
Winters, H.: 216, 227
Wissler, C.: 22
Wobst, M.: 215
Woillard, G. M.: 156
Wolpoff, M. H.: 6, 7, 9–13, 16, 38, 43, 56,

57, 61, 68, 70–6, 82–4, 88, 97, 99, 100,
102, 105, 106, 108, 109, 113, 117–22, 124,
125, 130, 137, 169, 182, 183, 187, 188,
197, 199, 200, 204, 206, 208
Woo, J. K.: 57
Woodburn, J.: 21, 24
Wright, S.: 120
Wu R.: 74
Wymer, J.: 36, 41, 44, 46, 47, 51, 52, 57, 59,
    63, 77–9, 85, 210

Xirotiris, N.: 103

Ya'alon, D. H.: 156
Yabrud: 162
Yabrud I: 160, 161
Yabrud II: 174
Yabrudian: see Acheulo-Yabrudian
Yano, T.: 112
Yellen, J. E.: 25, 27

Zagros: 161, 173
Zhoukoudian: 30, 40, 74, 75
Zhoukoudian Upper Cave: 74, 75
Zlatý Kůň: 103
Zumoffen: Abri: 162
Zuttiyeh: 45, 132, 161, 162, 165, 186